DEBUGGING

DEBUGGING
Creative Techniques and Tools for Software Repair

Martin Stitt

John Wiley & Sons, Inc.
NEW YORK / CHICHESTER / BRISBANE / TORONTO / SINGAPORE

Trademark Acknowledgments

ANSI is a registered trademark of American National Standards Institute.
Periscope is a registered trademark of The Periscope Company, Inc.
TASM, TLINK, Turbo Debugger, and Sidekick are registered trademarks of
    Borland International, Inc.
MS-DOS, MASM, SYMDEB, Codeview, and DEBUG.COM are registered
    trademarks of Microsoft Corporation.
IBM, PC, XT, AT, OS/2, and Micro Channel are registered trademarks of
    International Business Machines Corporation.
Macintosh is a registered trademark of Apple Computer, Inc.
Intel is a registered trademark of Intel Corporation.
UNIX is a registered trademark of AT&T.

*In recognition of the importance of preserving what has been written,
it is a policy of John Wiley & Sons, Inc. to have books of enduring
value published in the United States printed on acid-free paper, and
we exert our best efforts to that end.*

Library of Congress Cataloging-in-Publication Data

Stitt, Martin, 1957–
    Debugging : creative techniques and tools for software repair /
Martin Stitt.
      p. cm.
    Includes bibliographical references and index.
    ISBN 0-471-55829-X (book/disk : acid-free paper). — ISBN
0-471-55831-1 (pbk. : acid-free paper)
    1. Debugging in computer science. 2. Software maintenance.
I. Title.
QA76.9D43S75 1992
005.1'4—dc20   91-46656
                                                CIP

Printed in the United States of America
10 9 8 7 6 5 4 3 2 1
Printed and bound by Malloy Lithographing, Inc.

For my wife, Carol, and son, Jason.
Their love and support made this book possible.

ABOUT THE AUTHOR

Martin Stitt began working as an Electronic Technician in 1972. His background in electronics troubleshooting has been a significant factor in his disciplined approach to debugging.

His first brush with computers came when he designed and hand-built an 8080-based system. Martin progressed from there to work as a Systems Design Engineer, developing microprocessor-based control systems for data communications, energy management, and data acquisition.

Martin now works as a Contract Software Engineer, involved in such projects as a multitasking/multiuser operating system, X.25 and NETBIOS communications drivers, database applications, CASE systems, and, of course, debugging tools.

His articles on debugging and software development have appeared in *PC Tech Journal, Dr. Dobb's Journal, Computer Language, C User's Journal,* and *Tech Specialist.*

CONTENTS
OVERVIEW

CONTENTS

FOREWORD

In the mid 1940s, Grace M. Hopper was working on one of the early computers, the Mark II, at the Computation Laboratory at Harvard. The computer was actually a very large calculator, composed of electromechanical devices, including relays. On September 9, 1945, the system stopped running. Dr. Hopper and her coworkers traced the failure to a relay into which a moth had flown. The moth had already been killed by the action of the relay. Afterward, Hopper wrote "We got a pair of tweezers. Very carefully we took the moth out of the relay, put it in the logbook, and put Scotch tape over it." Thus did the "debugging" of computers begin.

For years, there has been a surprising lack of books that thoroughly discuss software debugging at a practical level. Yes, there are the how-to books that show you how to drive a particular debugger, but these have not taken a step back and looked at the more general problem of solving program bugs. There are also some scholarly works on the topic of debugging, but these are usually targeted to a very narrow audience and have a high amount of theoretical content, with limited practical information. At long last, Marty Stitt has addressed this shortcoming. His book is a very down-to-earth, useful discussion of the causes and solutions of bugs in PC-based software. It has many tips and techniques that you can use in your day-to-day work, to help you become more productive as a programmer.

Today's PC environment is very complex, with a wide variety of hardware and software that is all supposed to work together. Unfortunately, sometimes it doesn't. When you've got a failure, you need to determine just where the problem lies. Is it the hardware? Not all machines are really fully compatible, but is that the cause of your problem? Or is it a device driver or a Terminate and Stay Resident (TSR) program that is interacting with your program and causing a failure? Or is it something as simple as a typographical error in the program's source code or something as subtle as an occasional interaction between two hardware interrupt service routines that causes a system hang once every two or three days?

Whatever the cause of the error, without the proper approach you can spend large amounts of time and money trying to solve software bugs. If you'll invest the time to read this book, I think you'll find it pays for itself very quickly, since the tools and techniques presented here give you the knowledge and direction you need to study and understand a wide variety of problems. Once you understand the problem, the solution is often straightforward.

If you are involved in the development or testing of computer software for PC-based systems, I'm sure you will find this book to be a welcome addition to your library. It explains the concepts of software debugging in an easy-to-read style and helps remove the mystery surrounding the "art" of debugging. It also give you the knowledge and tools to make debugging a science.

This book is not a theoretical analysis of the causes of bugs and their solutions. It is a real-world, practical discussion of the topic. It contains an excellent definition of the terms and concepts used in debugging, a description of the different types of tools that can be used to help solve program bugs, and a discussion of a wide variety of debugging techniques. All of us have something to learn from such a book. I've picked up some valuable techniques that I've already put to good use in my own software development.

Some would claim that you don't need to learn how to debug software, that, if you use a formal design methodology, you won't have any bugs. In a controlled, thoroughly understood environment with limited input and output, I would agree that you can achieve zero-defect software. For example, Mitsubishi has had very good success with its software development for embedded systems because of extensive use of reusable code and rigorous control of the software development process.

Toward the other end of the complexity spectrum, you have today's commercial PC-based software. In many ways, this environment is the opposite of a controlled, thoroughly understood environment. The wide variety of "clone" systems with their various BIOSes creates the need for a huge amount of special code to address the differences in machines. In at least one case, approximately 20 percent of the code in a systems software package exists just to deal with the differences among "compatible" machines! The DOS environment is well known, but we're heading into much deeper waters with Microsoft's Windows, IBM's OS/2, DOS extenders, and other 386 protected mode environments. Even the inputs and outputs are more complex, both in variety and in quantity. The plethora of peripherals in use today is simply staggering. Compared to PCs, embedded systems and mainframes have a small fraction of the variety of input/output devices to support.

In addition, we have large teams of programmers (leading to more opportunity for miscommunication) working on tight schedules. Most of these programmers use C, which is a powerful language that ironically makes it very easy for a programmer to shoot himself in the foot. One hopes that future programming languages will make it easier to describe the desired logic and let the computer do more of the work for us in the development of software, but for now it is a very time-consuming, exacting, and error-prone process. We have come a long way since the early days of the computer, but we have a very long way to go. For the moment, bugs are with us. The best approach is to design and code defensively, yet be prepared for the inevitable bugs.

Admiral Hopper recently said, "Planes started flying in 1903, and by 1943, we had a DC-2. The computer first ran in 1943. We're at the DC-2 stage. We're only at the beginning. We haven't half gotten started yet."

BRETT SALTER
President
The Periscope Company, Inc.

PREFACE

What our world needs is more programmers with strong debugging skills. When bugs do arise, as they will, such programmers would be able to locate and correct them with a minimum amount of effort, leaving more time and energy available for progressive work.

Many estimates rank debugging as the single most significant bottleneck in the production of software. The other development phases—analysis, design, coding, and testing—have much in common with more established engineering disciplines and thus are better developed. Debugging is the weakest link.

Unfortunately, the channels available to software developers to gain new knowledge and skills in debugging are few. Debugging is conspicuously absent from current-day computer science curriculums, and only a handful of books exist. Beyond an occasional article in a trade journal, programmers are left without much guidance.

I wrote this book to help fill this void. The career paths I've chosen have involved me in a great deal of debugging, and this book is my way of sharing what I've learned. Many books and journal articles refer to debugging as an "art." I approach it as a discipline, which can be learned as easily as any other technical practice.

This book brings the practice of software repair into focus for programmers by introducing the fundamentals and then following through with specific and practical information. It is packed with tips, tricks, techniques, and tactics gleaned from actual practice.

THE AIM OF THIS BOOK

The aim of this book is to make you a master debugger. When bugs arise and threaten to derail your projects, I want you to be able to exterminate them without breaking pace. As a result, you'll find your work less frustrating and more enjoyable, and your boss or clients will enjoy your increased productivity.

It is not my intent to hail any particular debugger over all others. Rather, I strive to give you a good working knowledge of a variety of debugging tools so that you can quickly choose the best tool or combination of tools for each situation and apply them with skill and grace.

To bring some reality to the treatment of software debugger features and use, Chapter 6 does include a discussion of the Periscope debugger. But please do not misunderstand—this book is not just for Periscope users. The techniques presented are just as valid when debugging without a debugger, when using the simple DEBUG.COM supplied with MS-DOS, or when using a $15,000 logic analyzer.

ORGANIZATION

This book is organized into three sections. Section One presents an overview of the debugging process, covering the following topics:

- The definition and classification of bugs
- How bugs arise
- Additional applications for debugging tools and techniques
- Basic approaches to debugging
- Basic types of debugging tools
- Clear-thinking techniques
- How to avoid time-wasting presumptions
- The basic steps involved in a debugging session
- How to manage and track details
- How to verify and track corrections
- How to design and manage program patches

Section Two explains debugging tool operation, application, and custom construction, including the following topics:

- How the 80X86-type CPU supports debugging
- The internals of a basic software debugger
- The internals of advanced software and hardware debugging tools
- The internals of the debugging tools included with this book
- The design of custom debugging tools
- The debugging application of other software tools

Section Three presents a comprehensive reference of specific debugging techniques:

- General diagnosis techniques
- Basic software debugger application
- The use of advanced debugger features
- How to set up program instrumentation
- How to analyze debugging information
- How to reverse-engineer a program
- How to deal with difficult bugs and complex environments

The primary aim of the four chapters in Section One is orientation and training. This material is best read through from beginning to end the first time, and then referred to as needed for reinforcement.

The five chapters of Section Two rank equally valuably as a training guide, as an ongoing reference, and as a tool resource. The four chapters of Section Three contain the information that can have the most direct effect on your quantity and quality of work. They are filled with real-world examples, tips, tricks, and tactical approaches ranging from simple-scale problems to complex and almost untouchable bugs.

The book also includes a glossary and sixteen Appendixes to cover related topics.

RANDOM ACCESS

Appendix A contains a "Tool and Technique Locator Chart," similar to the troubleshooting chart within many appliance manuals. You use it by scanning the problem descriptions and finding the entry or entries that most closely match the bug you are chasing. Corresponding to each of these entries will be a list of the section in the book where you can turn for pertinent information.

WHO THIS BOOK IS FOR

If your position requires you to make programs function correctly or to resolve incompatibilities between different system components, this book is for you. Therefore, in addition to software developers, it will also be of use to technical support and software testing technicians, systems integrators, and network administrators.

This book focuses on the IBM PC/AT microcomputer platform running an MS-DOS type of operating system.

Regarding languages, the basic fundamentals of debugging are universal, and I strive to shown them in that light. Most of the examples presented are in C and assembler, but use is also made of pseudocode. There are also a number of tactics involving compatibility problems between various system components, which do not involve any language at all.

Since the basic fundamentals behind the design of this book's tools are universal, the tools and techniques it presents should be adaptable to other hardware platforms and other operating systems, such as UNIX, OS/2, and the Macintosh.

THE COMPANION TOOLSET DISKETTE

A companion diskette is also available to provide a collection of powerful debugging aids as well as a program library and templates from which more tools can be built. These are not merely alternate versions of tools already on the market—they are unique. They came into existence to address needs that are not currently fulfilled by commercially available products.

These tools are not positioned as a competitive replacement for the software debugger. Rather, they can be used to supplement the software debugger by extending its capabilities. They can also complement the software debugger by addressing types of problems to which it is ill-suited.

These tools are provided in ready-made form so readers not familiar with the languages they are written in (C and assembler) will be at no disadvantage. The source code is also included, to make it possible to adapt them for specific situations. The source code files also serve as prime examples of how custom debugging tools can be constructed. The key aspects of constructing custom debugging tools are also clearly illustrated in Chapter 8.

The templates are designed to produce drivers and utilities composed of varying amounts of C and assembler code. Device drivers and TSRs can be written entirely in assembler or in a mixture of assembler and C. Stand-alone utility programs are supported as assembler only, C only, or a combination.

The program library is available to all configurations. It contains the following resources:

- Functions to manage the parsing of parameter switches
- Low-level drivers to output debugging information through direct video, serial ports, or parallel ports
- Higher-level logic to manage the routing and conversion of debugging information
- Functions to support sequence detection of debugging event markers, the detection of memory changes, and the tracing of linked lists for debugging analysis
- Functions to support the management of stack switching and interrupt intercepts
- Functions to support the management of a packetized ring bugger to record debugging events in memory
- Support functions for string manipulation, I/O, and interrupt control

Since the complete source code is also provided for the library, including the MAKE file and associated utilities required to regenerate the library, you can modify the existing functions and add new ones to suit your individual needs.

SECTION ONE

Bug-Hunting Basics

CHAPTER 1
Software Entomology

1.1 WHAT IS A BUG?

To be a successful hunter, you must be able to recognize that which you seek. This is certainly true of debugging. This chapter will introduce different classes of bugs and their characteristic behavior, take a quick look at some of the tools and techniques used in debugging, and examine what can be done to make debugging, something you spend less time doing.

It is certainly not unheard-of for a programmer or team of programmers to chase a bug for weeks. Occasionally, you even hear of a case where a bug just had to be accepted as a "new" part of the program.

The goal of this book is to enable you to cut those hour-long sessions down to five minutes, and the week-long stints down to an hour or two. All that's needed to solve any mystery is the right knowledge. While there's no magic artificial intelligence program or ultimate debugging tool that can completely automate the task, much can be done to streamline the process. Learning how to gain the right knowledge to track down software failures is what this book is all about.

1.2 HOW BUGS ARISE

Many aspects of medical diagnosis and electronic and mechanical troubleshooting are similar to debugging, but the way failures originate in these different systems is not always the same. With bodies, circuits and automobiles, components can just wear out or be damaged by extremes in environmental conditions. Corrosion can attack electrical contacts, and diseases can invade the body.

With software, if the design is logically and mathematically correct to start with, it will still be so on into infinity (excluding certain types of calendar

3

calculations, of course). Therefore, when a software failure does become apparent, we can know it to originate from within the following bounded set of possibilities:

1. A bug included in the original design or coding.
2. A bug introduced when an existing program was modified.
3. A bug introduced as a side effect of another bug fix.

Note that it is possible for a bug to remain dormant for years. Toward the more fuzzy realm, it is also possible to have a potential bug that will be actualized only when other factors in the system environment change. Some examples of this are marginal stack allocation, conflicting use of resources between system components, and timing failures, which result from a heavy system load.

Finally, there is that one type of "potential bug" from which no design is safe: corruption of the media in which a program is stored, or failure of the hardware in which it will execute.

1.3 CLASSIFYING BUGS

The debugging techniques discussed in this book are accessible through the Table of Contents, the Index, and the Tool and Technique Locator Chart in Appendix A. In many cases, the key to locating appropriate remedies for a bug is the type of failing behavior exhibited. This section will establish a standard classification method and terminology, with the aim of enabling better use of this book in finding the root cause of a bug.

First and foremost, it is important to realize that the classification of a software failure is not a static process. Seldom can you classify a bug once and let it stand unchanged. This classification is something that must be reevaluated often.

Upon your first encounter with a bug, you may, for example, classify it as a file corruption type of failure. After conducting an initial course of debugging, you may learn that when the data was written to disk from a memory buffer within the program under test, it was already in a corrupt state. With the benefit of this new knowledge, you might now reclassify this as a memory corruption type of failure. Debugging is a dynamic process.

Consistency

One of the most common classifications of a failure is whether it occurs with *consistency* or with a frustrating lack of consistency. When invoking a certain action within a program always causes the same improper result, consider yourself lucky. This is the easiest type of bug to find.

When a program's downfall occurs in an inconsistent manner, it is referred to as a variable type of failure. This is to be distinguished from an intermittent type of failure, about which more will be said shortly. As an example of a variable type of failure, consider the case of a program that sometimes fails by stalling the computer, but which at other times causes the system to reboot itself.

This can sometimes be due to the existence of multiple bugs, or it can stem from a single root cause. In either case, trying to hit a moving target is always more difficult. One of the first things to do when you encounter such a situation is to try to drive a nail into the target—to try to stabilize the system and make it behave with consistency.

If only one root cause is involved, how can different types of failures result? Let's consider the case of a program in which a certain memory location is being incorrectly overwritten due to an improper pointer manipulation. If this memory location happens to control the path of execution through a certain part of the program (e.g., a call vector), the errant behavior will be as varied as the data value that is crashed on top of that memory location.

Intermittence

Either the consistent or the variable type of failure case can also be intermittent. As you can imagine, this attribute almost always makes a bug more difficult to track down. Again, bringing a measure of stability to the situation, by some technique or other, is a primary goal

When you are confronted with a variable type of failure, an intermittent failure, or both, there can be cases where the bug will defy stabilization. Fear not—several monitoring methods will be discussed in Section Three.

Fuzzy Cases

When you cannot immediately be sure that the problem you are seeing is due to a program bug, it is referred to as a *fuzzy* bug. While this may seem like more of a preclassification state, fuzzy bugs are included here because the application of debugging tools and techniques is often required to further define their behavior and refine their classification—to prove them as either an actual failure or some other anomaly.

Usually, whether or not a bug exists is pretty clear-cut. Computers being the binary machines they are, either the results are right or they aren't. Correct operation can be difficult to ascertain, however, when working with a system that must respond to rapidly changing inputs and provide continuous processing and output. Real-time process control and artificial intelligence systems are good examples.

With data acquisition and real-time process control systems, a failure could be due to conditions beyond the control of the software. The software might be technically correct, but the events to which it must respond may be too fast. The hardware involved may be unstable due to electrical noise or temperature extremes, or it may be just plain faulty. Insufficient resolution of input data can also be a problem.

The lack of a laboratory-type control case to compare against can be a further difficulty in ascribing clear lines of demarcation with a fuzzy bug. But such is the nature of breaking new ground. In the fuzzy case, as is any other, the goal is to gain useful knowledge about a system's operation with the least possible expenditure of time and effort.

Classifying the Root Cause

Another facet of software failures that it is useful to classify is the root cause of the failure. Obviously, the purpose for considering such a classification cannot be to help in finding the root cause itself, so why expend energy in this direction?

When you go hunting for anything, be it the right job, your life-mate, a wild bull moose, or the Holy Grail, if you don't know how to recognize the object of your quest, you're likely to waste a lot of time. Knowing what is possible in the way of design errors, coding errors, hardware failures, and so forth will help you know what to expect and what to suspect in a debugging session.

Oversight errors, probably the most common source of bugs, include syntax errors, syntactically correct typos, and program statement mistakes. A syntax error is usually caught by your assembler or compiler—but not always! There are syntax-checking utilities which can check for things some compilers cannot, such as consistent use of a common variable across multiple modules (see Section 9.1, "Source Code Analyzers").

Another type of oversight error involves statements that are syntactically correct, but otherwise incorrect for the situation. For example, in the C language, working with addresses and pointer variables can be confusing. Both of the following statements will pass the compiler's syntax checking:

```
regs.x.dx = &base_ptr;
regs.x.dx = base_ptr;
```

But the effect of these two statements is entirely different. The former assigns the address of the base_ptr variable to the dx pseudoregister, whereas the latter assigns the contents of base_ptr to dx.

One kind of logic error occurs when a do . . . while loop is called for but a while . . . do loop is actually coded. Another example is not supplying the right parameters, or not supplying enough parameters, to a function; yet another example is insufficient storage to handle worst-case conditions.

This exercise can be extended through each type of coding construct. When coding a loop, proper setup conditions must be made and, to be sure, some method of exit from the loop must exist. Data fields must be wide enough to accommodate the greatest possible values that could be encountered. The order of evaluation required must match the conventions of the language, or parentheses must be used to enforce the requirement. Indexing an array past its boundaries must be prevented.

When considering the possible root causes of failure, it is important to be aware that the program exhibiting the failure is not necessarily responsible for the cause of that failure. Just because program X fails doesn't necessarily mean that program X has a bug in it. A more systemwide perspective must be used.

The actual root cause may be due to a bug in a terminate-and-stay-resident (TSR) utility or a device driver loaded in the system's memory, or even the operating system. It could also be the result of some other application program that was run an hour ago and left certain resident system code or data mangled.

Once you find a bug, it may be important to determine how the root cause came into being. Was it due to a design error or a coding error? Was the specification incorrectly supplied from the client or did imprecise language give rise to an understandable but ultimately improper interpretation?

While this can be meaningful in the overall maintenance of a software package, the scope of this book stops just before that point. This book focuses on the steps necessary for you to be able to yell "Eureka!" Making the actual repairs is so situation-specific as to elude meaningful discussion in a work of this type.

1.4   ADDITIONAL REASONS TO DEBUG

There are several uses for debugging methods besides the obvious case of mending the mistakes in a piece of logic you are developing. These include:

- The resolution of compatibility conflicts
- Exposing viruses
- Fine-tuning a program
- Proofing a program's logic

Compatibility

Given the number of different components involved in a computer system, the number of possible combinations for their interaction, and the lack of clear standards in many aspects of systems design, it's no wonder that compatibility problems are so common. Conflicting relationships can occur between the following system entities:

- The operating system
- Application programs
- Device Drivers
- TSR utilities
- Hardware

A compatibility conflict may be thrust upon you any time you must install a new product, make a change in the configuration of an existing one, or attempt to use a previously installed program in a new way. Technical support may not always be available, or when it is, they may not be able to do enough.

If you are a product developer, you are a prime candidate for compatibility problems. Regardless of whether your product is software- or hardware-based, you may have to use debugging techniques to rescue your project from certain gloom. This is especially true when your product must coexist with a wide range of other application and system components. Entities that must coexist in this way are device drivers, TSR utilities, library packages, and add-on hardware devices.

Viruses

When a virus is suspected, you must be able to make a detailed inspection of a program's code and verify the operation of that code. Since the focus of debugging tools and techniques is to expose and analyze the operation of a system, they can be of great value in dealing with viruses.

Verification of Proper Operation

There are times when a piece of software is charged with a critical responsibility and must be proven correct to the greatest degree possible. Along with thorough rounds of desk checking, static and dynamic testing, and related proving methods, the use of certain debugging tools and techniques can be very worthwhile.

While single-stepping through an entire program is only practical for relatively simple cases, the use of system call–tracing tools can easily help expose insufficient error-handling logic and pinpoint redundant operations. In addition, tools that detect uninitialized pointer use, array bounds errors, dangling memory allocation, and memory writes outside of a program's boundaries are highly beneficial.

Fine-Tuning

As with the above cases, refining a program to be highly efficient requires an intimate level of contact with its inner workings. Indeed, there are cases where inadequate performance is so severe as to be considered a bug itself. The methods and tools described in Section 13.10, "Performance Bugs," are equally applicable to super-tuning.

1.5 THE REAL COST OF BUGS

Debugging is quite often a high-pressure undertaking. Sometimes your ego or reputation is all that's on the line; sometimes it may be a large sales prospect or your job. Since most bug chasers are also programmers, debugging is often viewed as an aberration to progress. Those involved lament the time spent at it and dream of what could be.

To regard debugging as an aberration can, however, be detrimental to your overall progress. Being well-prepared, through a study of debugging practices, to deal with the bugs that will inevitably occur can be an effort that pays for itself many times over.

To get some idea of the benefits that could accrue, let's work through a thumbnail sketch. Say, for example, that after vacations, holidays, and sick days you work 48 weeks per year. Say also that an average of 4 hours a week is spent in debugging. Some weeks you might use all of ten minutes, but then there are those times when you spend days chasing a whopper.

$$48 \times 4 = 192 \text{ hours spent debugging per year}$$

Now let's say that undertaking to improve your debugging skills will reduce your debugging time by a moderate 25 percent. Then we need to estimate the time you will invest reading this book and working to become proficient with its techniques above and beyond actual debugging. Ten hours will be used for this example

$$192 - (.25 \times 192) = 146 \text{ hours}$$

For these 10 hours of investment, 48 hours can be reclaimed in the first year—a net gain of 38 hours or nearly a standard work week. Furthermore, a 25 percent reduction is probably on the low end of what can be expected.

1.6 BASIC APPROACHES TO DEBUGGING

There are about as many different ways to hunt for a bug as there are types of bugs and programmers to hunt for them. But while there are many valid tactics, one universal strategy pervades: to seek and gain useful knowledge until the cause of the problem is understood. This is no different from any other diagnostic practice.

As it is so basic and general, the strategic level requires little more discussion than this brief mention. The actual tactics of debugging are what bear further exploration. Just as the capabilities of a surgeon, carpenter, or any other practitioner are directly affected by the breadth of their knowledge and skill and by the size and quality of their tool sets, so it is with the practice of debugging.

The tactics of debugging can be classified into five major groups roughly based on the amount of effort and the level of invasive manipulations required to implement them. These classifications are shown in the outline that follows.

Locating the root cause of a bug as quickly as possible requires a wise selection of the level to use. For example, if you recognize aspects of the failure and are sufficiently comfortable with the operation of a software debugger, it makes sense to pursue dynamic debugging as the initial approach.

The best level, the best technique, and the best tool to use can change many times in a debugging session. For example, a more invasive level may be helpful at first to isolate the overall section of a program containing a failure. From there, a desk check may be the most productive way to effect a solution.

Furthermore, the grouping used in the following outline is certainly not cast in stone. Quite often, when you conduct a user interview over the phone, it is helpful for both you and the user to be running through the program involved, using clear, careful descriptions to ensure that you stay in step with each other. This would be a mixture of a user interview and testing and experimenting. Various other combinations are also possible.

1. Preliminary Investigations

   User interviews
   Preliminary testing
   Verifying that the problem is actually a bug

2. Static Debugging

   Review of requirements
   Review of design
   Desk check of source code
   Automated analysis of source code

3. Run-Time Observation

   Testing and experimenting
   Analyzing process steps
   Analyzing output

4. Source Code Manipulations

   Applying instrumentation
   Suppression of portions of a program

5. Dynamic Debugging

> Breakpoints
> Single-stepping
> Hardware traps
> Applying custom tools for monitoring and testing

Preliminary Investigations

Preliminary investigations are important to prevent wasting time on wild-goose chases. Before going on into a more detailed layer, double-check your expectations and perceptions by verifying setup parameters, correct installation, and proper operating procedures. Chasing after a "bug" that ultimately proves to be due to a setup problem or a misunderstanding is no fun—not to mention embarrassing.

Static Debugging

Once a determination has been made that the problem is actually a bug, it may be possible to discover the root cause through a static debugging review. Of course, unless the program is quite small, you must know enough about the bug to be able to sufficiently narrow the scope of candidate sections of source code.

If it turns out that more effort is required, time spent gaining an overview knowledge of a system through a static review will rarely be wasted. A good macro-perspective over a system is a powerful complement to the micro-perspective required for the more invasive methods.

Run-Time Observation

Performing run-time tests is one area of debugging that can actually be fun at times. This is where you get to play with a program and conjure up all manner of naughty input to try to uncover its weaknesses. As long as that mischievous gleam in your eyes doesn't impede your perceptions, enjoy.

The poking, prodding, and analysis of run-time tests can also be as frustrating as trying to quell an annoying vibration behind the dashboard of your car. Just as you contort yourself to reach up behind the dash, the darn thing shuts up!

When dealing with intermittent bugs and ones that fail in an inconsistent manner, the redress often involves statistical monitoring and manipulations designed to force that "annoying vibration" to show up often enough for you to locate it. Dealing with defiant and elusive bugs is no fun, so enjoy the ones that aren't!

Source Code Manipulations

In simplest form, applying *instrumentation* to a program means adding statements that cause it to display an indication of its execution flow and internal data values. These statements are also referred to as *event-tracing markers* and *data markers*.

This form of debugging has probably been in use since the days when a computer meant a houseful of vacuum tubes. With this degree of entrenchment, some programmers have come to rely on instrumentation in many cases where other tools, such as a source-level software debugger, would be more appropriate.

Then again, there are cases where instrumentation is a superior method, and still others where it is virtually the only method possible. When one works with processes such as communications and real-time process control, single-stepping of the program code often is impossible, since it would so interrupt the flow of the process as to be a source of failure in itself.

The primary advantage of using instrumentation is that the programmer has a great degree of control over the scope of information obtained. To see a wide view of a process, you can place markers at the entry points to major sections of a program. When it is necessary to trace the execution of each decision within a smaller section of code, instrumentation can be applied accordingly.

Source code manipulation can also be a valuable tactic when chasing an elusive bug. By temporarily removing selected portions of a program, or by converting certain functions to stubs, you can learn more about what is required for the bug to evidence its existence.

Be careful not to presume, however, that the absence of a failure when a certain portion of a program is nullified means that the cause of the failure is in the disabled section. The bug may still exist but be suppressed by the change in conditions. Presumptions are dangerous when debugging.

Dynamic Debugging

The tactics of debugging at this more discrete and detailed level are closely tied to the tools required to implement them. As with all other tactics, the guiding strategy is, of course, the acquisition of useful knowledge about the root cause of a bug. With the greater degree of detail involved at this level, it can be important to avoid accumulating too much information.

Much of the activity at this level centers around the use of different types of breakpoints. A breakpoint is a controlled way to force a program to stop its execution. Single-stepping and hardware traps are basically just special types of breakpoints.

The application of breakpoints has many levels of its own. Although there are exceptions, the following list covers these levels, from the most detailed to the least.

- Manually single-stepping through each machine instruction at the assembler level
- Manually single-stepping through each source line in a higher-level language
- Breaking on software interrupt calls issued by applications for operating system services
- Breaking on each call to a program subfunction
- Breaking at selected points within the program

1.7   TYPES OF TOOLING

A *debugging tool* is anything that provides useful knowledge. The story is told of a computer operator who could use the radio interference generated by a computer as a key in troubleshooting. By leaving an AM radio playing near the computer and getting to know the different types of interference produced, this operator could interpret certain problems, based on the sound pattern. The moral: Be open to as many forms of evidence as possible.

Software Debuggers

When archaeologists of the twenty-fourth century study the records of our era, they might pigeonhole us as the civilization with a penchant for building a better mousetrap. A study of the development of debugging tools is evidence in support of this categorization.

Current debugging tools are much like the ultimate mousetrap. Along with the now almost primitive spring-loaded wire, we have models incorporating the equivalent of constant video surveillance and seismic monitoring capabilities. They detect not only when the varmint is tugging at the cheese but when it is even in the vicinity. (Ironically, these mousetraps are often controlled with a mouse.)

A software debugger enables a programmer to dissect data structures and trace event flow to a nearly infinite degree. Expression evaluation features encourage spontaneity, and complex watch conditions enable precise monitoring. It's like equipping a mousetrap with controls as elaborate as those of a fighter jet.

The primary feature of a software debugger is, of course, the range of breakpoint capabilities it provides. The most elementary of these is the low-level single-step breakpoint, where control is returned to the debugger after each machine instruction. This is actually accomplished by causing the CPU to interrupt itself after executing each instruction. The `INT01` interrupt is dedicated to this purpose.

The next rung on the ladder of sophistication is occupied by the `INT03` breakpoint interrupt instruction. This special interrupt makes it possible for a software debugger to stop a program's execution at selected points while permitting full-speed execution the rest of the time. Temporary and sticky breakpoint commands are made possible through this feature. For a more detailed explanation of the `INT01` and `INT03` interrupts and the internal operation of a software debugger, see Chapter 5.

A number of useful higher-level breakpoint features are predicated upon these two lower-level debugging interrupts. When a source-level debugger for a high-level language single-steps through program statements, the 80X86 single-step `INT01` interrupt is not actually responsible. High-level single-stepping is accomplished through automated placement of the `INT03` explicit breakpoint instruction. The `INT01` interrupt will not work, since a single source-code line in a high-level language usually translates into from several to several hundred assembler-level instructions.

Most software debuggers include a more intelligent type of feature known as a *watch-point* or an expression evaluation breakpoint. A user-specified test is executed after each breakpoint interrupt, and a full program halt is instigated only when the test detects a match.

If managing breakpoints were all that a debugger could do, we would be like pilots trying to perform an instrument landing with only an altimeter. Making it easy to inspect and modify the state of a program's internal variables is another valuable feature of a software debugger. Conveniences such as support for a variety of display formats (e.g., `byte`, `word`, `longint`, `real`, `string`, and `struct` templates) will also reduce the tedium.

The list certainly doesn't stop here. A good debugger will let you search for strings in memory, change the next point of execution, change CPU register values, patch in code changes, make calls to program functions, and perform I/O instructions, along with a variety of similar functions.

Source Language Instrumentation

Instrumenting a program, by adding statements within the source code and recompiling, is an easy way to gain a certain degree of knowledge about its operation. It's easy, because all that is required is the ability to write additional source language program statements and invoke the compiler.

This approach will enable you to get an overall idea of program flow and can help to identify what section of a program is involved with the bug you are chasing. But it is not without its limitations. The extra program statements slow execution and increase the code size. Sometimes either of these changes can be enough to cause a suppression of the very failure you are hunting!

In addition, the range of output destinations for your debug data is limited to what is already available through the language being used. Using the main display monitor has obvious drawbacks in that the normal activity of the program being tested can overwrite your markers. While using a second monitor can help, sometimes the amount of data that can be displayed at one time on a monitor is a serious limitation.

Other destination devices, such as printers and disk files, also have their unpleasant side effects. If very much information must be dumped, the speed reduction caused to the program being tested can become significant. In the case of writing to disk, adding extra disk I/O activity in the vicinity of a buggy portion of a program can increase the chances of disk corruption.

The Instrumentation Driver

Adding instrumentation to a program can be a valuable debugging technique. But the use of only the print output statements of the program's native language is saddled with the limitations described in the previous section.

The use of a debugging tool known as an *instrumentation driver,* can bring benefits of event trace and data markers without incurring the pitfalls. The ROUTER.SYS device driver (included with this book's Companion Toolset) provides exactly this type of functionality.

It is still necessary, of course, to embed instrumentation code within the program being tested. But rather than use native language statements to output debugging information, the embedded instructions make calls to the instrumentation driver.

The primary benefit of this method is that much greater control can be maintained over the processing and eventual destination of debugging information. These embedded calls can make dumps of program status information to the instrumentation driver, or they can command the driver, to change some aspect of its operation.

An instrumentation driver can route debugging information to one or more of the following destinations: the main video display, an alternate display, a serial terminal, a ring buffer, a printer, or another computer linked with a high-speed parallel connection (using built-in parallel ports). The use of each of these destinations, and their benefits and trade-offs, will be covered later in this book.

With this driver acting as a distributor of debugging information, sophisticated features such as pattern recognition and the filtering and annotation of trace information are possible. The conquest of elusive intermittent bugs is also simplified through the use of the driver's ring buffer.

While the addition of any embedded instrumentation code will slow a program's execution and increase the size of the code, this method provides a significant degree of control over these factors.

The Interrupt Intercept Driver

Virtually all application programs make operating system calls. Monitoring these calls with an intelligent tool can be a valuable way to gain insight into a program's operation. While this method does not allow the same degree of selectivity as when markers are encoded into the source, it does provide a good overview at a fairly detailed level of a program's operation. Since this can be accomplished without requiring that the program's source code be modified and recompiled, it is both easier to implement and more secure against undesirable side effects.

The DOS services interrupt INT21 is the one most commonly subjected to this eavesdropping. By monitoring this interrupt, you can follow requests for file I/O, console I/O, interrupt vector assignments, time and date services, disk directory searches, network activity, and other system activities. In addition, you can be learn more about a system's operations by monitoring other interrupts, such as INT10 (video services), INT13 (low-level disk services), or INT15 (misc services).

This bit of magic is accomplished by intercepting system calls and reporting entry and exit conditions. By dumping this information to the instrumentation driver previously described, we can take advantage of all the features it provides, such as the variety of possible output destinations, pattern recognition, and filtering.

The intercept driver can be made to annotate the call with a string identifying the type of call. Relevant entry parameters, such as filenames, and exit parameters, such as completion status, can also be displayed. This extra display information can really help add clarity, especially when you are not very familiar with system interrupt calls.

Observing a program's system call activity while coaxing a bug to show its face can really help you home in on the failure's origin quickly. In some cases, just noting when a failure occurs with respect to the system calls being made will be enough to permit you to identify the cause, go directly into the source, and make a fix. Even when that is not the case, being able to discern the last system call made before the failure occurs will make it much easier to go in with another tool to obtain additional information.

Interrupt intercepts are also valuable as points on which to hang custom test code. For example, if you know, or even suspect, that a certain memory area is being corrupted during a program's execution, you can add custom code to test for this corruption at the entry and exit points of each system call. When the custom test code detects corruption, it can be made to display a signal to the debugging output device or execute a breakpoint.

If the corruption is detected on entry to a system call, you can know that it was caused at some point between the exit of the last system call and the current point. When corruption is detected on exit from a call, you can know that something about the current call is suspect. There are, of course, exceptions to these conclusions, due to variants such as asynchronous IRQ interrupts.

Hardware Monitor Aids

A primary benefit of hardware debugging aids is that the program under test can be run at full speed. Not only does this have the obvious benefit of reducing time spent debugging, but failures that may be suppressed due to the timing changes introduced with other methods will not be so adversely affected.

Suppression of a failure can also result from changes made in the system environment, such as the addition of embedded instrumentation code or the loading of an interrupt instrumentation driver or a software debugger. In such cases, hardware aids that do not incur this liability may be the only answer.

The most common form of hardware debugging aid is what could be referred to as a *CPU intercept*. Just as an interrupt intercept allows software interrupt call activity to be spied on, the CPU intercept causes each transaction between the CPU and the computer's memory and other support circuits to be exposed. When this is used in conjunction with a high-speed trace buffer and software that interprets the captured data, there is virtually no type of system event that can escape detection.

Constraints must be placed on the size of the trace buffer for two reasons. First, the memory required must be capable of very high-speed operation, so it demands a higher price. Second, there is a practical limit to the amount of debug trace information a human can sift through.

Given these constraints, the basic trick when using this type of tool is to know how to stipulate when the contents of the trace buffer should be frozen for inspection—knowing how to detect the failure in very precise terms.

Other diagnostic techniques are often applied as a preface to bringing in this heavy a tool. This is necessary to narrow the scope of possibilities, so that a suitable set of trigger conditions can be fashioned.

Another form of hardware debugging aid is available as a built-in feature to many computer systems: the debugging registers within the 80386 and 80486 CPUs. Many software debuggers take advantage of these. While a high-speed trace buffer is not included (maybe the 80686?), triggering on many types of events can be done with the program running at full speed.

1.8 SUMMARY

What can you expect after going through this book? If you take its techniques to heart and make its tools your arms and legs, there will still be bugs that take you a week to find. But these will be the ones you probably would have had to classify as impossible before. Start scratching some marks on your calendar to track time spent debugging and find out for yourself. It may be a useful statistic when you are up for your next salary review.

Debugging can be a complicated business, but much can be done to pare down the time involved. That's what this book is all about.

CHAPTER 2
The Debugging Mindset

In this chapter, we will examine how to cultivate a mindset that helps one avoid hindrances and gain proficiency in debugging. To debug proficiently, the programmer needs the manager's ability to cope with details, the leader's ability to see the bigger picture, the physician's emotional detachment, and the detective's cool, creative cunning.

2.1 PERSPECTIVE

In the business world, the roles of leader and manager are clearly defined: The manager manages and the leader leads. These roles are filled by separate people in larger companies, but the proprietor of a small business must wear both hats. When you undertake a nontrivial debugging problem, you must also fulfill both the leadership and managerial roles. You must take a leadership position to ensure that the best path is taken. You must also act as a manager to contend with the details involved in the diagnosis and repair of the problem and to move through each stage of the project as efficiently as possible.

Further, you must reassume the leadership role periodically to review the direction being taken, either certifying it as correct or adjusting as needed. This is necessary because, when working as a manager, you can sometimes get so immersed in details that you won't notice when you're straying off course or when a new course would be better.

As with most things in life, the best approach is a balanced one. Too much of either, to the neglect of the other, is almost guaranteed to result in a waste of time.

While neglecting the importance of these two roles is certainly unadvisable, regarding them as completely separate is just as unhealthy. The leader needs the manager's input in order to make informed decisions and the manager needs the leader's guidance to know what information to provide and what processes to manage.

Since you as the programmer must attend to both of these functions and since they both must be carried on simultaneously, it would seem that you need two brains. What a fortunate coincidence that you do have a two-sided brain! Now all we have to do is figure out how to integrate and coordinate the two parts of this tool.

The micro-perspective of the manager maps into the more intellectual left side of the brain, while the macro-perspective required of a leader maps into the more intuitive right side. The more we are able to integrate these two sides the more capable we will be at debugging—or software development in general for that matter. The treatment of mental development techniques is certainly beyond the scope of this book. The point of this discussion is to alert you to the fact that integration of the left brain micro-perspective and the right brain macro-perspective can be beneficial to debugging.

2.2   AVOID PRESUMPTIONS

There are two basic types of presumptions: conscious and unconscious. When you say "Since the problem is occurring during the execution of a standard library function, I will presume that improper input data is being supplied" you are making a conscious presumption. This is simply a hunch—a likely possibility based on experience. You are not ruling out a bug in the library function itself or that the memory used for this function's code and data may be getting corrupted. You have chosen to presume that improper input data is responsible.

There is nothing wrong with conscious presumptions. They can be a useful way to give an idea enough substance to get a feel for how valid it is. The unconscious presumption is the one you have to watch out for and to become conscious of as quickly as possible. When this type of presumption is not seen for what it is, the amount of frustration with which you must contend will rise dramatically.

Unconsciously presuming that the problem you are chasing is due to a software bug can get you into a lot of trouble. To jump right into a micro-perspective debugging session on the premise that a software bug exists will result in a 100 percent waste of time if the problem turns out to be due to a user setup error, a corrupted file, or a hardware problem. The macro-perspective attitude of checking all possibilities in priority order should be adopted.

Sometimes we fall into the trap of thinking that a certain part of our program could not possibly be involved in the failure and therefore neglect it during all further analysis. This usually occurs because we don't pay enough attention to all possibilities. We actually should not rule out this certain portion of the program, but due to a lack of realization, we judge it to be beyond suspicion. This human failing will be considered an unconscious presumption for our purposes, though other terms could be used to describe it.

During the debugging of a program, you will sometimes find more than one indication of failure. If you presume that they are all due to one bug and that correcting this one bug will remedy them all, you could be leaving latent bugs in your program. Rather than make this presumption and risk having to go through further debugging sessions in the future, keep track of all failure indications noticed and retest for each one after making a correction. You may be dealing with multiple bugs.

To drive this point home even more, consider the following two sample cases:

1. Upon a cursory review, the symptoms of a failure seem very similar to another bug you flushed out a couple of weeks ago. This previous debugging session proved to be quite complicated, requiring the use of hardware aids, much custom tooling, and many hours of head-scratching. Judging the current failure to require this same approach, you spend an hour on tooling setup—only to ultimately discover that this bug was readily apparent through a desk check of the source code.

2. If the motor controlling a robot's arm is not being turned off at the right time, to suspect only the software in charge of the motor relay would be a blinding presumption, since the software involved in reading position sensors could also be responsible. Sometimes the absence of a compensating secondary action can make a primary action seem improper. But to judge the primary action totally at fault evidences too limited of a perspective. Time will be wasted as a result.

When it comes to working with bugs that only occur on an intermittent basis, it can be difficult to know when you've effected a complete fix. This is especially true when the time between occurrences is in terms of days or weeks.

If you make a correction and then cannot reproduce the problem, you may have only found part of the problem—or it may be that you've stumbled onto another problem, leaving the original still unaddressed. Even worse, the changes you make may cause the original problem to become dormant.

It can be argued that it is never safe to presume that an intermittent problem is fixed. If you test for it and can still make it occur, you know that you haven't found the right cause yet. If, however, you cannot make it show up, you don't know anything for sure—except that dealing with intermittent bugs can be an uncertain thing.

2.3 CLEAR THINKING

Our goal in this section is to learn how to form a clear description of a problem: one that is free of unconscious presumptions. Note that at this stage, to say that we are going "to form a clear description of a bug" would involve presumption. The *problem* we are confronting may not even be a bug at all.

In simplest form, this process consists of drafting a statement describing the problem and then scrutinizing and revising this statement until you are satisfied that it contains no hidden presumptions or ambiguities. You may find it helpful to go through this editing process in writing, if this practice is new to you or if the problem you are dealing with is especially complex.

Often it is sufficient simply to form one clear statement of known fact. Sometimes, however, you may want to extend this analysis practice to include the listing of all possible causes and relationships you are aware of. You could then rank these by likelihood and ease of testing.

As an example, consider the first draft: "The system crashes when menu choice #3 is selected."

In the first revision, we realize that it is presumptive to say that the system crashes. The actual "crash" may have already occurred before we select choice #3. To be clear, we must refer to what we see as "the first evidence of failure." Further, we should be clearer about the nature of the failure: "The first evidence of failure, a dead keyboard and blank screen, occurs when menu choice #3 is selected."

From here, our next step would be to further qualify what is involved in selecting menu choice #3. If a light-bar type menu is being used, does merely moving the light bar to the 3rd line cause the effect, or is it necessary to press the Enter key to register the choice? The former would suggest a problem in the menu function, whereas the latter points more to the code that handles function #3.

Consider the phrasing in this description: "The bug is in the third section of the payroll module. When the third screen of that module is displayed, the system locks."

Now consider the more open-minded phrasing: "The first evidence of failure, a system lockup, occurs when the third screen of the payroll module is displayed."

Making the distinction between the occurrence of a "bug" and the occurrence of "the first evidence of failure" is important. If your phrase shows that you presume to already know the bug's location, you might slip up and jump into a detail-laden debugging session without benefit of a more comprehensive initial analysis.

When you consciously form a clear statement about a problem using the phrase "the first evidence of failure occurs when . . . ," you are also reminding yourself to be prudent and search for other evidence first. Hopefully, you will discover anomalies that occur earlier and, therefore, even closer in temporal proximity to the actual point of failure.

2.4 REEVALUATE YOUR APPROACH

Debugging is an information-gathering process, and therefore a dynamic process. You must be flexible and not treat your initial observations and judgments as if they're cast in stone. As you make discoveries, it is important to review what you have learned to see if a new direction of research is called for. Certainly, if you are not making any useful discoveries, you should also question your current direction.

This is where the leadership aspect comes in—the right-brain macroperspective. Our managerial side has been busy collecting details; now it's time to review them, asking questions such as:

- What have I learned so far?
- Given what I now know, is my current approach still the best one?
- In an ideal world, what tool would I bring out? What technique would I employ?

Sometimes when you've been immersed in the detail management aspect of a debugging session for awhile, you can become jaded. Go for a walk, get a drink of water, and then sit back and take a fresh look at what you have learned so far. An important piece of the puzzle may have already presented itself to you, but you might not yet see it for what it is.

Even if no startling revelations arise from this review, it's still important to do. A debugging session often involves a number of layers or stages through which you must go to trace a failure back to its source, and different tools and techniques will be needed to deal with these different layers.

For example, when you start a debugging session, you might use a tool that monitors interrupt calls made to the operating system by the application you are debugging. Knowledge gained from this may then lead to the use of a software debugger to analyze the application's activities in between a certain pair of interrupt calls. Information gleaned from this study may indicate that the use of a hardware-based debugging tool is required to go further.

At each of these stages, if you don't reevaluate your situation, you might continue trying to use your current tool when switching to a different type would actually be wisest.

The third question in the foregoing list may sound frivolous, but it actually has a very important purpose. Pretending for a moment that you could instantly develop a magical fix-it-all tool helps keep your creativity alive. Too much micro-perspective thinking and detail management can sometimes stifle your creativity.

What can sometimes result from this indulgence is that you will realize a new way to use existing tools or a way to build a new tool that, while not quite magical, does offer great promise. Keep your creativity alive.

2.5   HINDRANCE AND PROFICIENCY

In current writings on debugging, it is not uncommon to find this practice described as involving an art. But to say that there's an art to it can make it seem elusive and mystic. Sometimes we even hear the phrase "black art." This is unfortunate because it can infer that debugging is too mysterious to approach; that it is something you just have to have an innate sense for, as with clairvoyance or divining. This idea needlessly disenfranchises programmers who don't consider themselves artistic or psychically sensitive.

Now, it is true that debugging does involve mystery—two types of mystery to be precise. But neither of these has anything to do with the unattainable. The first is the basic mystery of the bug itself, embodied by the question "What is the root cause of the failure?" The second type comes in when you feel at a loss to know where and how to begin your search.

Obviously, there is no pat answer for this first mystery. No master reference book of symptoms versus root causes can ever be written, since each piece of software is unique. Indeed, each invocation of the same piece of software can have unique qualities given different input data. Regarding the second mystery, "How and where do I begin searching?" the fact that you are reading this book shows that you are already actively pursuing an answer. Keep reading.

One form of hindrance that bears examination comes up when you regard debugging as a loathsome undertaking—to be avoided at all costs. If you have not taken the time to become familiar with the operation of a software debugger or other types of tools, it can feel like you are treading into very unfriendly territory when you attempt an invasive debugging session. Some programmers react to this by spending a great deal of time proofreading program listings and experimenting with program modifications, trying to find their bugs without having to go in underneath.

If we acknowledge debugging as an inevitable part of software development and view it as a skill to study and practice just like software design and coding, it will become something we spend less time doing. So, if you don't like debugging, become proficient at it.

To gain proficiency at debugging, identify it as a goal. Rather than begrudge it, view it as the "job at hand" and rise to the challenge. It can actually be an interesting process; a time when you get to learn more about lower-level system functions; a time when you get to play detective.

Take a proactive stance. Don't just be driven by the fact that there is this bug in your program and you've got to find it. Adopt an attitude which says, "I want my program to be clean and stable."

As with any skill, practice is the key. Make use of a debugger and other tools as often as practical. Use one to step through test-bed code to verify proper operation. Not only is this an invaluable part of a software test plan, you will become fluent in the use of a debugger much more quickly. You may not like getting thrown in the lake, but if you learn how to swim and train to swim well, you'll make it to shore a lot quicker.

Debugging benefits from a mixture of a systematic approach and creativity, just as programming does. There is nothing mystical involved, no cauldron stirring or crystal ball gazing required.

2.6 SUMMARY

Debugging requires the macro-perspective of a leader to choose the best overall direction to be taken, as well as the micro-perspective of a manager, to contend with the profusion of details typical in a debugging session. The greatest benefit will be realized when you can integrate both of these perspectives through a balanced approach.

When you allow unconscious presumptions to creep into your analysis, increased frustration and an increased expenditure of time and energy will result.

Develop a habit of clear thinking by drafting a descriptive statement about your problem and then reworking it until it is free of presumptions and ambiguities.

Periodic progress reviews are essential during a debugging session to ensure that you maintain a clear understanding of the problem as it changes and that you adapt your approach as necessary.

Viewing debugging as a "black art," as something too mysterious to understand, will only hinder your skill development.

Take a proactive stance. Debugging is simply a practice you employ to produce clean, stable code. The more skillful you become at this practice, the less time you will have to spend applying it.

CHAPTER 3
Making the Journey

This chapter introduces the general phases of a typical bug hunt. As a prelude to the actual hunt itself, the rituals of simplification, stabilization, and definition are covered. Debugging involves enough details as it is, so anything done to simplify the environment can only help. In addition, the fewer the players in a mystery, the easier it is to finger the culprit.

The cyclic process of gaining knowledge and drawing conclusions based on that knowledge is illustrated next. Included is a treatment of that most venerable debugging topic, binary division. This tactic has been used in the troubleshooting of all manner of systems for decades.

As debugging is a process replete with details, methods are presented to help preserve one's sanity and avoid information overload. The final section contains a discussion on how to deal with being stumped—what to do when you think you've tried everything.

3.1 SIMPLIFY

Imagine for a moment that you are the master detective Sherlock Timelord and that you have been called out to the scene of a murder. Early in your investigation, you ascertain that the deceased was visited that day by her nephew Ivan the Greedy, by her accountant, by the milkman, and by the local chimney sweep.

Now imagine that, through some strange and macabre twist of reality, you could replay the day's events over and over again. In your first trial, you could temporarily banish the nephew and the accountant to a nebulous realm early in the morning and then see if the poor woman still meets her demise. By virtue of this fantastic method, you would be able to assign guilt in very short order.

When this process of elimination proves the milkman to be the villain, your job then is to determine exactly how and when he committed his crime.

Since the other three players were nebulized at the time, you can ignore any question of complicity on their part.

The more you can do to simplify a situation from the very start, the easier it will be to solve. This is just as true with crimes within a computer system as it is with those in the human world.

The process of debugging is replete with details. While all you really want is that one key detail that identifies the cause of your problem, you may have to sift through thousands of other pieces of information before it becomes apparent. One very good way of reducing the amount of detail with which you must contend is to eliminate as many system components and operations as possible from the outset. In the practice of debugging, simplification applies to three basic areas:

1. The initial software-based system environment
2. The activities involved in reproducing the failure
3. The hardware environment

The first item refers primarily to any device drivers and TSR (Terminate and Stay Resident) utility programs that may be loaded in a system. It can also include the effect on the system's state due to the actions of internal commands and of utility and applications programs that are run before the failure occurs. The goal is to eliminate all unnecessary software execution and system memory allocation from the time the system is first booted until the time the failure occurs.

A good start is to make copies of your current `CONFIG.SYS` and `AU-TOEXEC.BAT` files and then edit them to trim out all unnecessary actions. If you can reproduce the problem you are chasing without having device drivers loaded to support your network and tape backup unit, TSRs to dial your phone, and so on, so much the better.

Once you clear these auxiliary system components of complicity by proving that the failure will occur without them, you may be tempted to reinstate their use. Resist. While they may not play any direct part in the cause of your problem, their existence may complicate its diagnosis. The simpler the system, the less chance for frustration.

The second item refers to the activities you must go through to make the problem appear. Suppose you are debugging a database program and the end users claim that when they enter a new customer record, print a report on that customer and then print a summary report, the summary contains garbage in certain fields. Your goal should be to distill this sequence of steps down to the minimum necessary to see the problem.

Can you produce the problem by just printing a summary report directly? What if you print a customer report on an existing customer and then a summary? What if you enter a new customer but don't print a customer report? This type of simplification not only reduces the steps you must go through on each successive debugging trial, it helps narrow the field of suspect components. It can sometimes even lead to your shouting "Eureka" without even having to break out your debugger.

The third item, stripping the hardware down to the bare essentials, is obviously not warranted in every case. Removing unnecessary device drivers and TSRs is too easy to neglect, but removing unnecessary hardware is often another matter. This will have to be a judgment call, based on what you know about the bug and your familiarity with computer hardware manipulations. If you suspect hardware involvement and can install the software you are debugging on a second machine, this can be a quick and easy way to effect hardware simplification.

As with many processes involved in debugging, the simplification phase isn't something you go through once and are then done with. As your bug hunt takes various twists and turns, you will be presented with repeated opportunities to simplify. As you reevaluate your approach at regular intervals throughout a debugging session, add the following to your checklist of questions: "Can I simplify and reduce the situation I'm now dealing with?"

A final note: Simplification is often not a black-and-white issue. Changing your `AUTOEXEC.BAT` file to skip the loading of a certain TSR may prevent a bug from appearing, but that doesn't necessarily mean that the TSR is at fault. Without this TSR in the picture, the position in memory of other system components changes and the execution path of the system changes.

The root cause of the bug could still be very much alive in your system. It may just not be causing a form of harm that is noticeable . . . yet! It also could be that something in the TSR is at fault. The key is to keep an open mind and remain aware of all conceivable possibilities while you continue to experiment and collect clues. Don't let presumption cloud your judgment.

Changes made for the sake of simplification can also make a bug change its behavior. If removing system components or changing the steps taken to produce a bug causes it to switch from locking up the keyboard to printing a message in an endless loop, study the bug's behavior in each of these forms and select the one that seems the most consistent and easiest to deal with.

3.2 STABILIZE

The process of stabilization is intertwined with that of simplification, in that they both involve experimenting with a system's operation through variations in the initial environment and the steps taken to produce the failure. They are discussed as two separate topics, since the goals are different. Indeed, you might find a case where the greatest possible degree of simplification results in an unacceptable degree of instability.

When dealing with a bug that exhibits an inconsistent or intermittent behavior, effort invested in stabilization early on can pay for itself many times over during the long run. Consistency will be much more valuable than simplicity when it's time to go underneath a program with a software debugger or other tools.

Since what we're talking about here is a variable type of effect, it can be good to take a statistical approach. As you run through different test trials, write up a chart that lists the test conditions and the resulting buggy behavior. When dealing with numerous variables and test runs and a frustratingly changeable bug, the clarity of written records can really help.

Below are two lists of ideas to consider when experimenting. This summary is by no means exhaustive—it is simply a starting point. The first list, "Outer-Level Manipulations," contains things that can be tried from an operational standpoint, whereas the items on the second list, "Inner-Level Manipulations," usually require making software changes to the program being tested or incorporating custom test code in other ways.

Outer-Level Manipulations

Order and timing of steps within a program
Switch options and parameters used
Installation options used
Load order of resident modules
Activation order of commands and utilities
Memory areas and IRQ lines used for peripherals
Size of data files
Position of files on disk
Type of disk media used
Type and timing of keyboard activity
Time of day value in software clock
Rate of mouse movement
Temperature of computer or peripherals
Electrical noise
Mechanical vibration

Inner-Level Manipulations

Selective exclusion of portions of the software
Timing of main-line software execution and interrupt processes
Position of software entities in memory
Contents of unused memory

3.3   DEFINE THE BUG

When you are just beginning to hunt for a bug, the field of possibilities can be pretty wide open. When this seems too overwhelming, leaving you uncertain as to where to begin, spend some time developing a concise definition of the bug as you understand it at the time.

This can help you get focused and help ease the transition from working with the problem at an exterior, operational level to working at an internal and more invasive level. Here is where you apply the clear thinking method described in the previous chapter.

As with the previous two phases, the main vehicle through which you gain the information you need is through observation and experimentation.

Similarly, the boundary between this bug definition phase and those of simplification and stabilization is not entirely distinct. Through the course of these two previous phases you will often acquire all the information you need to define the problem clearly.

By experimenting with an aim to define, you discover more precisely which parts of a program's operation are affected and which ones aren't. By flexing a system with a variety of input data, especially boundary values, you can sometimes come up with that most valuable of all debugging knowledge: a way to produce a failure at an even earlier point.

Skipping this phase can mean that you take up the detail manager's role before enough time has been spent in the leadership role. Without an adequate overview of the situation, the manager can end up chasing wild geese.

This is also a phase that you will likely visit more than once during a given bug-hunting session (unless the bug turns to be fairly easy to find). As evidence of the failure is uncovered in earlier parts of a system's operation, what you know the bug to be can change dramatically. Bugs can also take on a whole new personality due to changes made by corrections of other problems discovered, changes in load position, changes in debugging tools used, or just general contrariness.

3.4 DEFINE NORMAL BEHAVIOR

If you must work with a program you didn't originally write, it is certainly important to make sure you have a clear understanding of what is normal. If presumption slips in here and you go off thinking you understand what a program is supposed to be doing when you really don't, you'll soon be bleary-eyed. A few minutes of clear thinking from the start can save hours later on.

If possible, set up a version of the program where the failure does not occur. It may be possible to revert to an older version or just disable certain aspects of the current version through installation switches or changes in a configuration file. Without benefit of this method, you may be left to interpret the hopefully accurate source code comments and user documentation to learn what should be happening. The tips presented in Section 4.3, "Keeping Records," may be useful in helping you ensure that the comments you add will be clear and adequate.

3.5 GAIN KNOWLEDGE AND DEDUCE

As can be seen from the bubble diagram in Figure 3.1, this phase is the hub of the debugging process. Research, testing, analysis, decision making, and idea generation all go on here. Within this hub, you must act as the detail manager to run tests, gather data, and do first-cut analysis. You must

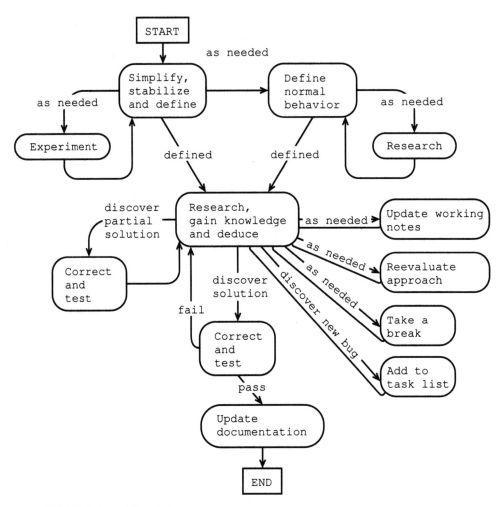

FIGURE 3.1 The debugging process.

also assume the leader's role to review the information comprehensively and make course adjustments.

One approach is to formulate a hypothesis and then seek to prove or disprove it. While it's certainly best if you can prove your idea correct, if you end up disproving it you have at least eliminated one possibility. If you do not actually disprove the idea, be sure to categorize it as indeterminate. Don't let presumption slip in.

As you proceed, always keep the question in mind: "What information do I need?" and then derive ways to obtain that information—using tools and techniques such as those covered in this book. When setting up for a test, call on your macro-perspective: "What is this test going to tell me?" "How reliable will the information be?" and last, but certainly not least, "Is there an easier way to proceed?"

Imagine what type of magical tool you would concoct if reality wasn't a limitation. This will help you open up your creativity and help you better see what can be accomplished with existing tools or ones you can build.

When you're just getting started, you will often have to use some type of debugging tool just to gain enough knowledge to know which tool is best. Tend towards those that provide an overview level of information and are easy to set up. One type that fits this description is the interrupt intercept driver, where DOS and BIOS system call activity is monitored and reported. Also, don't forget about the Tool & Technique Locator Chart in Appendix A.

Quite often, information gained during this process comes in layers. You start out seeking the cause of the symptom you've come to know the bug by. Once found, it turns out to be merely a symptom itself.

For example, in tracing down the cause of a corrupted data file, you discover that a few bytes of the program code that generates that file are being overwritten. This memory corruption is now the new symptom for which a cause needs to be found—it is now the earliest evidence of failure. Tracing back further shows that the memory corruption is due to an array-indexing operation receiving out-of-range data. Some call this *peeling the onion*.

At each layer, you are presented with a bug that is essentially "brand new." This is why it is so important to reconsider the simplification, stabilization, and definition steps. Further, within the hub, it is important to reevaluate your tactics. As you address the problem's different layers, the most appropriate tools and techniques will often change.

3.6 BINARY DIVISION

Binary division is a fundamental debugging tactic. It is often cited as being analogous to the military tactic of divide and conquer. The problem with this simile is that the goal in debugging is not to separate and weaken each part of a program so that each part may be destroyed more easily. Quite the contrary, our purpose is to heal.

A much more accurate analogy can be drawn by examining the maintenance of an underground water pipeline. Figure 3.2 depicts a pumping station and a receiving station connected by a 200-mile run of underground pipe. A sensor at the pumping station reports the water's pressure and flow rate to the operator inside. This same data is measured and transmitted back to the pump station operator from the receiving station and three remote stations spaced evenly along the pipe's run.

When a problem is detected, either a blockage or a breakage, the operator first reads the sensor at point A_2. A good reading instantly rules out the first 100 miles of pipe, throwing the suspicion to the last 100 miles. A bad reading, of course, reverses this binary assignment of blame.

Next, a reading would be taken from the station halfway along the suspect section. Based on this information, the operator would isolate the point of suspicion to a 50-mile section of the pipeline. Obviously, more must be done

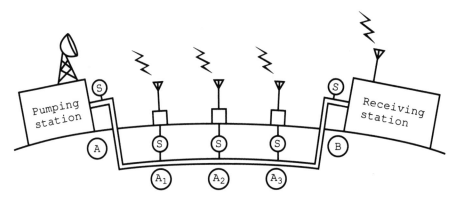

FIGURE 3.2 Maintaining a pipeline in sections.

to isolate the problem, but you are now able to ignore three-quarters of the pipeline's run after only two readings.

Unfortunately, while some computer programs are of the linear, one-pass type, many are not. To carry the pipeline analogy further, many programs involve so many multi-branched, cyclic, and recursive operations that they are like the maze of pipes that tangles around an oil refinery.

Binary division is the basis for many of the techniques discussed in this book. It can be applied to temporal events as well as to sections of a system. It can be a good way to get started in a debugging session when you've got too many things to choose from, too many possible locations for a bug.

Let's further this discussion by examining a sample case. Suppose a program is somehow ending up with one of its memory variables in a corrupt state. You have discovered this corruption to be evident at a certain time in the program's operation: a temporal position we'll label as "Point B."

You elect the binary division tactic and start by testing the variable's integrity at a point halfway between "Point B" and the point where the variable should first be getting assigned, hereinafter referred to as "Point A." Upon finding the corruption to exist halfway between "Point A" and "Point B," you dutifully restart the program and test at a new point that is halfway closer to "Point A." After a number of successive division steps, you finally discover, to your great dismay, that the variable was never assigned correctly at "Point A" in the first place!

What happened here? What is so great about this technique if it lets us down this easily? Actually, there's nothing wrong with the technique. The flaw here was in its application—a presumption was permitted to slip into the works. The state of the memory variable was presumed to be good at the temporal position "Point A" from the very start.

Binary division will only work when the starting and ending points of the range to be studied are in diametrically opposed states. Before binary division can be used, you must first prove that the endpoints of your chosen range satisfy this criterion. Presumptions are dangerous in this business.

Another way to use this technique to isolate a failure's cause is by temporarily nullifying parts of the program. This, of course, requires that the nullification doesn't cripple the program to the point where its operation is too distorted. Further, you must be careful not to presume that a certain section is the cause of a symptom just because the symptom disappears when that section is nullified. Such a reaction should only be treated as a clue rather than anything conclusive.

3.7 MANAGING DETAILS

Within a computer system, not only is the code within your program being executed—processor time is also being given to the library modules linked to your program, to the operating system, to the machine's BIOS firmware, and to any device drivers and TSRs that have been loaded. When required to track and analyze the internal activities of a system, you can find yourself faced with an enormous amount of detail. To avoid becoming bogged down in an information overload, good note-taking habits are a must.

If you are a programmer, you already know what it's like to manage a profusion of details. Debugging involves as many and often more details per unit of time. In addition, if you normally program in a high-level language, the detail level increases by an order of magnitude when debugging requires that you deal with assembly code, hexadecimal numbers, and operating system interfaces.

At the start of a debugging session, list possible explanations for the problem and different tests you could use—a sort of a research task list. Doing this will ensure that you don't forget any of your alternatives after spending hours going down a certain path only to encounter a brick wall. Debugging can be exasperating, and exasperation can inhibit clear thought. Therefore, it is best to plan ahead.

A disciplined approach to note taking is just as important throughout the research process. At this time, it's actually best to maintain separate logs for reference data you accumulate along the way, for tangents and future tasks, and for your working notes. Reference data consists of facts about a program you will need to refer to often, including the addresses in memory of key variables and sections of code and the meaning of different files used by a program.

Keeping reference information separate from your working notes makes accessing it easier. It also frees you to make your working notes in whatever loose style helps you through the process. Working notes are often scratch-pad calculations, small hand-drawn sections of a flowchart (from reverse-engineering a section of code) and small charts of logic states. While it pays to make reference notes clean and clear, working notes should not be saddled by formality.

Regarding notes on tangents and future tasks, completeness turns out to be the most important factor. Through the course of a debugging session, you have to examine the system from many different angles, using various sorts of information filters. The perspective you have when you jot down a note about a future task may be long forgotten by the time you go back to that list, due to the dozens of other perspectives you had to assume in the meantime. Taking another minute to jot down some supporting details is well worth it.

You will encounter points where multiple subpaths are possible within your current path of study. You also will discover other aspects of your program that are suspicious and need further investigation at a later time. You may even discover potential or dormant bugs: defects in the logic that haven't yet yielded any detectable symptoms.

As was already mentioned in the section on stabilization, it is valuable to chart operating conditions versus behavior when dealing with intermittent or variable failure–type bugs. In the case of an intermittent failure, noting the conditions that seem to contribute to the *absence* of a failure is also important.

Your tools should also help you in the management of details. Tools that dump interrupt calls (e.g., DDICEPT.SYS) should display annotation strings and associated data strings to document the function of each call. Having to look up each function call in a book is not acceptable. When selecting commercially available tools, look for convenience. When building custom tools, design for automated detail management as much as is practical.

3.8   BREAKING STALEMATE

When you seem to be treading around in circles, kneedeep in a vat of molasses, there are a number of things you can try:

- *Write to yourself about the problem.* Make a list of all aspects of a system's behavior and all of its components that could be at all related to the problem. Apply the clear thinking method of Chapter 2 to each item to make sure you aren't being limited by an unrealized presumption. Don't presume something isn't related just because it shouldn't be— anything can happen when bugs are crawling around in your code.

  Draw pictures of the process—both in its normal form and in its current buggy state. Talk out loud to yourself about the problem—the strangeness of it can jar you into seeing things you've missed.

- *Talk with someone else about the problem.* Presenting an associate with a stack of listings is usually not a good idea. Rather, start out at a higher level, explaining the normal function of the failing component and then its aberrant behavior. Too much detail too soon tends to produce confusion. Remember, you've been jousting with this demon for a while already and your associate hasn't.

- *Think of different ways to describe the problem.* Conjure up an analogous situation to the program when it is behaving normally. Then ask yourself: "What could cause a problem in this other system that would correspond to the failure I'm seeing?"

- *Get away from the machine for a while.* Take a walk or get a snack. Take your listings and notes into another room to review them—preferably a light, upbeat kind of room.

3.9 SUMMARY

Simplify the environment as much as possible before undertaking any type of invasive bug hunt. This includes the initial software-based environment, the steps required to evidence a failure, and the hardware environment.

Attempt to stabilize a bug as much as possible first. The bug-hunting process can involve a significant time investment even when a bug's behavior is consistent. When a bug behaves in an inconsistent manner, the time involved mounts up rapidly.

Defining a failure in clear and concise terms is valuable as a focusing aid and as a means to help isolate which parts of a program are involved in the failure and which are not.

Defining a program's normal behavior is important when debugging a program you didn't originally write.

The hub of the debugging process consists of research, testing, analysis, decision making, and idea generation. This is where the tools and techniques of debugging are applied to systematically isolate a failure and locate its root cause.

Binary division is a common method of systematic isolation. It can be applied to temporal events and to different subcomponents of a system. This technique is valid only when it is known that the range of events being tested starts with a condition that is the binary opposite of the ending condition.

Given the profusion of details attendant to debugging, a disciplined approach to note taking is wise. A bug hunt can involve numerous branches of program flow, each of which requires investigation. It is also a time when you may discover a variety of tangential issues about a program, other weaknesses, potential and dormant bugs, and unfinished and forgotten sections.

Maintain separate logs for working notes, reference notes, and notes about tangents and future tasks. Working notes should be informal; reference notes should be structured enough to be clear and easy to access; and your future task list should contain enough supporting information to remind you of your perspective at the time you first noticed each issue.

When selecting or designing information-gathering tools, value features that automate or otherwise reduce detail management requirements.

When you become stumped, write and talk to yourself about the problem, talk to an associate, conjure up analogies, and, by all means, take a break to let your head clear.

CHAPTER 4
Resolution

Once a bug is found, the job is still far from complete. The critical phase of the task is just beginning. The correction that you fashion must not only fix the problem, it must not produce any new bugs of its own, and it must also be congruent with the algorithm and higher-level design criteria. This chapter discusses approaches that can help fulfill these requirements.

No less important is the preparation of proper documentation. Record-keeping methods are examined, with the goal of developing one system which supports future development efforts, future debugging and technical support issues.

The final portion of this chapter covers the management of permanent patches, in which corrections are applied to an already released product.

4.1 APPLY CORRECTIONS—NOT BANDAGES

Imagine for a moment that you've just finished working through a multilayered debugging session and have discovered that a certain memory variable is being referenced before being assigned. In short, function A was being called at point B, but variable C (used by function A) had not yet been written to.

Modifying the program to initialize variable C before calling function A produces a bizarre new type of failure, however. What has gone wrong here? Where was the presumption this time? (A good question to ask yourself any time your attempts fail.)

When you find that a section of program logic is misbehaving because an unassigned variable is being referenced, it's normal to suspect that the initial assignment was simply forgotten. But to regard this as the only possibility is a narrow perspective, which will sometimes come back to haunt you.

One presumption here was believing that it was proper for function A to be called from point B in the first place. When the cause of a problem is traced to an uninitialized variable, it is also wise to suspect that the logic referencing it actually has no business being executed at that time in the life of the program. That the program even makes a call to function A at point B could be a mistake.

Note that there are a number of other possible explanations for this type of situation. Here are some of these:

- Variable C does need to be initialized, before function A is called at point B, but the new initialization method is buggy.
- Variable C does need to be initialized, but other variables also hold incorrect values at the time, or other logic is mistakenly coded. In other words, multiple bugs exist within the program.
- The logic within function A should not be referencing variable C in the first place, or the function should be verifying proper initialization first.

You might think that this type of presumption is only likely when you are working with a program with which you are not very familiar. While this is certainly one case, it can also occur when you are *too* familiar with a program. Through a narrowly focused micro-perspective, you might indeed see specific causes for the problems plaguing you, but the most comprehensive solution may really be to start from scratch.

Once you discover the nature of a problem, it's time for some scrutiny— some clear thinking. Ask yourself:

"Is what I've found a self-contained problem within an otherwise correct program?"
"Is it an indication of a bad interpretation of the underlying algorithm?"
"Is the underlying algorithm valid?"

As is obvious, this type of analysis requires a thorough understanding not only of the specific implementation of the program but of the design requirements as well.

4.2 VERIFICATION

Much software is undertested, as testing can be tedious and complicated. Given the number of factors that participate in the execution of a computer system's operation, generating a list of significant permutations of these factors can be a monumental task (sounds like a good job for a computer).

The next difficulty arises when you must create actual tests that produce these different combinations of internal machine states. Making this especially difficult is the fact that, to be realistic, you must produce each of these internal states through external manipulations (e.g., through the user interface and the contents of data files).

One way to verify that the internal machine state is following your prediction during a series of tests is to embed instrumentation code into the

TABLE 4.1 Typical boundary values

Data Item	Bits	Boundary Values
Signed byte	8	−128, −1, 0, +1, +127
Unsigned byte	8	0, 1, 255
Signed integer	16	−32768, −1, 0, +1, +32767
Unsigned integer	16	0, 1, 65535
Signed long integer	32	−2147483648, −1, 0, +1, +2147483648
Unsigned long integer	32	0, 4294967295
Float	—	Depends on size and implementation
Pointer	—	NULL, meaningful value
String	—	Zero length, typical nonzero lengths, maximum possible length based on buffer size.

program. With this method, you can get an indication of program path execution and a report of the states of selected internal variables.

Since this does, however, change the program under test, testing with instrumentation in place can only be considered an intermediary measure. Once you've proven that your chosen external manipulations produce the desired internal effects, you must remove the instrumentation and rerun each test. Implicit in this, of course, is the presumption that there is no strange bug that causes the data to track normally with your predictions when the instrumentation code is active but causes a loss of synchronization when the instrumentation code is removed.

When deriving a list of significant permutations for your selected internal machine states, be sure to identify boundary values as well as normal values and out-of-range values. An out-of-range value is distinguished from a boundary value for cases such as the representation of a month number with an unsigned eight-bit byte. The boundary values would be 0, 1, and 255, but values below 1 or above 12 are out of range. Table 4.1 shows the boundary values for several common data types.

Boundary conditions can also pertain to interactions between a program and the outside world. For user input, typing fast or banging on the keyboard could be significant. Sweeping a mouse quickly across the table while holding down a key while a modem is also transferring data could flush out an instability you should be aware of. Ask yourself: "What conditions can I set up that will stress this system?"

The following list outlines a systematic testing method. This type of testing can be applied on a function-by-function basis to major sections of a program, or to an entire program.

1. List machine states relevant to the bug correction being tested. This could include the state of memory variables, the initial contents of data files, and responses to user prompts.

2. Derive test values for each item, including normal values, out-of-range values, and boundary values.

3. Generate a table of significant permutations, using the selected machine states as the column headings. For each table line, predict what external manipulations will produce the required internal machine states. Then determine the results you expect for each test and add written notes to the table, detailing your predictions and expectations.

4. Order the lines in the table to simplify the steps necessary to run the sequence of tests. For example, in a database or accounting program, you would want to run tests involving empty data files first, then tests involving data entry, then tests involving the management of large data files.

5. Embed instrumentation into the program to report on the machine states you've selected.

6. Run through each test and verify that the resulting internal machine states match your predictions for each line in the table. Correct any bugs or other anomalies found.

7. Remove the instrumentation and repeat all tests, verifying proper operation through external means.

Ideally, a test document of this sort should be generated when a program is initially developed and then saved for later use as part of an overall *test suite*. Whenever changes are made to a program, the test suite should be reapplied. Furthermore, any time you do find and fix a bug, be sure to amend your suite of tests to include a verification of the fix.

Any instrumentation added to effect this type of testing could be left in the source code but simply commented out or deactivated through a conditional compilation feature. However, changes made to a program since its initial development may render this instrumentation code invalid. Be sure to review this situation before you just activate dormant instrumentation code and begin using it. If the tools you use in testing and debugging aren't reliable but you don't realize it, you're in big trouble!

Another method to keep in your bag of tricks is to take the function you've just repaired out of the main program and place it in a small test bed program. How practical this is depends, of course, on the complexity involved in duplicating the data required for the function. Providing this is not prohibitive, using a test bed makes it very easy to flex a function with various combinations of entry parameters.

4.3 KEEPING RECORDS

If you have ever studied software design and maintenance practices, you've no doubt been admonished to document your work. Your teachers were right—do not skip this step. Time invested in clear concise documentation does pay off in the long run. Keeping records of bug fixes will help you in the future when:

- Debugging a recurrence of the same problem
- Debugging a problem that is a side effect of your fix
- Debugging a similar problem
- Adding enhancements to the program
- Doing a major rewrite of the program

You may be the only programmer currently involved in a project, but the history you keep will be priceless to future team members that sign on. Also, unless your memory is infallible, you will often find such historical records useful yourself as well. Six months from now you may encounter a bug that turns out to be a side effect of the correction you've just made. In order to develop a solution for this new problem and not undo your previous correction, you will need to have a very clear understanding of that previous fix.

When documenting a bug fix, it is important to don your macro-perspective hat and consider what information will be required in order for your notes to make sense in the future. To help speed and simplify this process, and to achieve a level of consistency, establish a standard template for each report entry. The following list suggests information which should be included:

- A brief description of the problem, using key words to simplify future searches
- Who reported the problem, who corrected it, and the date
- A specific list of the symptoms and how to recreate the problem
- Your findings as to the cause of problem
- What corrections were made
- Side effects of the change
- Which source code modules were involved, including their revision numbers
- The name of the binary module or modules involved
- The name of the patch created to implement the correction (when applicable)
- The names of any utility or test bed programs created to debug and verify the problem

If the project is comprised of only one source code file, you could keep this change-tracking documentation within the source file itself. In a multi-module project, it is wise to maintain one master change log file and also place a copy of each entry in the source module to which it pertains.

Through the use of the `EXTRACT.EXE` utility program supplied on the companion Toolset Diskette (see Section 8.7, "Tool Management"), it is possible to produce a report, aimed for technical support technicians, that contains a selected subset of the information in the master change log. This could be done by enclosing the general information on the nature of each problem and the corresponding corrective action within extract markers. You should also consider using a database program to manage this type of reporting.

Finally, make the appropriate amendments to the master design documentation—entity-relationship charts, flowcharts, and so on. Keeping this type of documentation within the same revision control system that is used for the source code files is wise. If you need to work with an older version, you'll need access to the master design documentation that matches that version of the software.

4.4 PERMANENT PATCH MANAGEMENT

To *patch* a program is to make corrective alterations to the binary program modules (the executable files). This can be done to effect a change in the machine language instruction code contained within the file or to change the initial value of memory data that is contained within the file. Patches are typically applied through the use of the DEBUG.COM software debugger with a script file, or through a dedicated patching utility.

Patches are simplest to design for programs written in assembly language. For programs written in a high-level language, a good understanding of how the compiler ultimately produces assembler code is required. Notes on developing patches can be found in Appendix E, "Patch Techniques."

The primary advantages of patches are that they are small enough to be downloaded by the end users of your product using a modem and that they can be placed on public access bulletin board systems without compromising security. Placing a corrected copy of an entire binary module on a public BBS can be too great a temptation to would-be pirates, whereas placing patches on a BBS benefits only those who already possess your product.

Patches are not only a useful way to distribute bug fixes, you can also use them to make custom modifications to your product to satisfy clients with particular needs. Another reason to develop a patch is to modify a program for which you do not have source code. This might be done to solve a compatibility problem with other programs you need to use or with certain hardware within your computer.

The advantage of developing a patch based on the use of DEBUG.COM and a script file is that it's reasonably simple to create an adequate script. But being simple and just adequate can also be a disadvantage. This method is far from bulletproof, and since the application of patches is done chiefly by end users, the more user-proof, the better.

Through the use of a custom patching utility, it is possible for the tool to verify that the correct version of the correct module is being patched, that enough memory is available, and so forth. The patching of binary modules with multiple segments can also be dealt with much more easily when a utility is used that is designed to apply patches.

An additional function that can be performed by such a tool is to report which patches have already been applied to a binary module. This information will be valuable to technical support technicians when a customer calls with a problem. This capability can be achieved by including an array of flags within the binary code module, with one flag existing for each patch number anticipated. When each patch is applied, one change made to the file will be that the corresponding flag within the array is set. All that is then necessary to produce a report of which patches have been applied is for the tool to locate and read this array.

To accommodate patching, you must, of course, allocate a patch space within each segment of each binary module from the very beginning. In addition, to accommodate the patch-reporting feature, an array of flags must be allocated within the binary module.

4.5 SUMMARY

When a symptom's cause is found to be due to a reference to an uninitialized variable, while it may be that the initialization of the variable was overlooked, it could also be that the reference shouldn't have been made in the first place. Keep an open mind when designing a correction.

Generating a thorough set of tests for a program is difficult but must not be neglected. By using systematic methods to generate permutations of test conditions, and using instrumentation during an intermediate test trial to verify internal machine states, testing can be made manageable.

When generating a set of test trials, consider normal values, boundary values, and out-of-range values for each significant memory variable, data file record, user interface response, or other component in the machine state.

Testing a corrected function can be made easier by extracting the function from its program and placing it within a test bed program. The viability of this option depends on how complicated it is to fabricate the required data set.

Time invested in writing clear, concise documentation on program corrections does pay off in the long run. Do it!

Consider what information will be needed by yourself or another programmer to understand the reasons for the correction you've just made after a year has passed.

Program patches are a way to distribute program corrections and modifications to end users through a bulletin board without having to worry about piracy.

Producing patches based on a script for use with `DEBUG.COM` is simple but limited to simple cases and not user-proof.

A custom patching utility can be made to verify that the correct version of the correct module is being patched. It can also be made to report which patches have already been applied to a module.

SECTION TWO

Tools

CHAPTER 5
Basic Debugger Operation

5.1 THE SOFTWARE DEBUGGER

This survey of debugging tools will begin with what is easily the most commonly known and commonly used type of tool, the software debugger. The software debugger is the Swiss Army knife of debugging tools, containing features to load and single-step programs, to manage breakpoints, and to inspect and change memory. More sophisticated versions offer symbolic debugging, source level debugging, breakpoints with expression evaluation, and a variety of other features. These advanced features will be examined in the next chapter.

In this chapter the basic internal operation of a software debugger will be explored. The concept behind the single-step and breakpoint features of the 8086 family of CPUs will be revealed, along with the details of how these features are exploited by a software debugger.

One reason for this low-level peek inside is to help you understand more clearly when a software debugger is the best tool for the job. In addition, if the development of custom tools falls within your set of interests or requirements, being intimately familiar with a software debugger's inner workings will be a definite plus. A common type of custom tool is one that serves to extend the breakpoint capabilities of a debugger.

When you arrive at the end of this chapter, you will have made close acquaintance with the INT01 single-step interrupt and its mentor, the trap flag, and with the INT03 breakpoint interrupt. Should you wish to brush up on the operation of interrupts, a review is included in Appendix D, "System-Level Knowledge for Debugging."

5.2   TYPES OF SINGLE-STEPPING

When introducing a new topic, it is usually wise to begin with a definition of terms. This is especially true in this section, because there is more than one type of single-stepping in common use.

If you program in a high-level procedural language such as C, Pascal, BASIC, or a 4GL database language, you are no doubt aware that software debuggers exist that operate at the source level. With this class of software debugger, you can observe the system's operation while stepping through each of your high-level language program statements.

The debuggers built into Borland's IDEs (Integrated Development Environments) for C and C++ and for Pascal are one example of this class of tool. In addition, the stand-alone Turbo Debugger, Codeview, Periscope, and many other debuggers also support high-level languages.

When a program is manually advanced through each of its high-level language statements with a debugger, there can actually be anywhere from one to several thousand discrete instructions being executed. This discrete level of execution is that of the assembler or machine language level. The one-to-many relationship between high-level statements and assembler instructions is, of course, why the former is termed a "high-level" language in the first place.

A prime example of a debugger that operates at the assembler statement level is the DEBUG.COM utility provided with MS-DOS. This type of single-stepping is the only type it is capable of. Many other debuggers, such as Codeview and Periscope, are also capable of this level of operation.

To preserve the distinction, the term "high-level single-stepping" shall be used for the high-level language case, and "assembler-level single-stepping" for the assembler language case. As will be shown in the upcoming sections, the mechanisms used to implement these two levels of controlled cadence are entirely different.

Assembler-Level Single-Stepping

What does it mean to single-step at the assembler instruction level? Is the CPU being forced into a type of suspended animation after it executes each instruction? While it is actually possible to perform single-stepping in this manner (with the help of additional hardware), this is not the way a software debugger operates. Even when assembler-level single-stepping is being done, the CPU continues to execute instructions at full speed without missing a beat.

When Intel developed the 8086 CPU, it included a new kind of single-stepping capability. This new feature enables the CPU to operate with a split personality—where two program threads can execute in parallel. The first of these two threads is the program being debugged, and the second is the program doing the debugging—the debugging monitor program. If you'll forgive the legalese, these will hereinafter be referred to as the *debuggee* thread and the *debugger* thread, respectively.

When this single-stepping feature is in effect, control is automatically transferred to the debugger thread after each instruction within the debuggee thread is executed. The CPU continuously fetches and executes instructions with its usual hard-wired thirst, but the instructions within the debuggee program thread are processed only when the debugger allows, and then only one at a time.

This multithreaded magic is accomplished through a special type of interrupt known as the *single-step interrupt*. Interrupt vector 01 is dedicated to this function and has virtually no other use than to support the operation of a software debugger.

When the proper conditions are established, the CPU will automatically issue an INT01 call after completing the execution of each instruction within the debuggee thread. Since the software debugger establishes itself as the handler of these type 01 interrupts, it is able to assert almost total control over the execution of the instructions within the debuggee thread.

Before the 8086 chip was developed, achieving a software assembler-level single-step type of operation with its predecessors (e.g., the 8080/8085 and the Z80) was possible only through a very inconvenient contrivance. Without benefit of the dedicated interrupt feature, a software debugger was burdened with the task of empirically predicting the next instruction to be executed within the debuggee thread. The debugger would then temporarily replace it with an instruction that would cause a branch back into the debugger. Consequentially, software single-stepping through program code burned into a ROM (read-only memory) chip was impossible.

As you can imagine, the introduction of the single-step interrupt in the 8086 chip was quite welcome to developers of software debuggers. All that was required was to activate this new single-stepping mode and wait until the INT01 calls started coming in. In addition, stepping through program code was just as easy in ROM as in RAM.

The Chicken or the Egg

Within the 8086 CPU, the flags word is a collection of status and control bits. It is also sometimes referred to as the Program Status Word. When the control bit known as the trap flag is set to 1, the built-in assembler-level single-stepping feature is activated. From this point forward, when the execution of each instruction is complete, a call to the INT01 interrupt handler is automatically made.

But wait a minute! How is this flag going to get set? Since the software debugger must set the trap flag in the first place, does that not mean that as soon as it is set, the debugger will start running in single-step mode itself?

Furthermore, when an instruction within the debuggee thread is finally executed and the INTO1 call occurs, will not the instructions within the INTO1 handler be single-stepped, causing recursive INTO1s? Are we not doomed?

There's got to be a better way, and there is. Let's tackle the second problem first, since it suggests the dual dilemma of an endless loop and a stack runaway. What prevents our fall from grace is the way that an 8086 CPU has been trained to behave when an interrupt occurs. After pushing a copy of the current flags word onto the stack, the CPU always clears the trap flag.

This is true regardless of whether the interrupt is caused by an external hardware signal, through the execution of an explicit software interrupt call, or through the automatic invocation of an INTO1 single-step interrupt. Thus, the INTO1 interrupt handler will not be single-stepped itself.

When the INTO1 handler completes its processing and is ready to return control to the next instruction in the debuggee thread, the instruction used is the IRET, meaning Interrupt RETurn. The execution of an IRET will, among other things, cause the CPU to take the flags word, which was pushed onto the stack at the time the INTO1 occurred, and make it the current flags word again. Since this copy of the flags word had the trap flag bit set to 1, single-stepping will resume.

To orchestrate an entrance into this multithreaded mode of execution, some way is needed for the software debugger to transfer control to the first instruction within the debuggee thread and set the trap flag bit at the same time.

In fact, this situation is virtually the same as the foregoing case, where the IRET instruction was used to continue a single-stepping session already in progress. The only difference is that in the previous scenario the stack information expected by the IRET instruction was already laid in place as part of the processing of the INTO1 interrupt call.

One of the interesting things about software development is that you can fake an egg in order to end up with a chicken, which then lays its own egg, which grows into a chicken, and so on. To initiate a single-stepping process, the debugger fakes an egg by explicitly pushing information onto the stack just as would be done by the processing of an INTO1 interrupt call.

To be more precise, a flags word, in which the trap flag bit is set, is pushed onto the stack; then the address of the first instruction within the debuggee thread is pushed. Now, when an IRET is executed, control will be transferred from the debugger to the debuggee and the trap flag will be set. Off we go!

The INTO1 assembler-level single-stepping feature works through branch instructions just as well as through simple straight-line sequences. Further, since it does not require that the code be constantly modified with jump instructions as in the pre-8086 days, instructions within nonwritable memory may be single-stepped.

The Action Taken on Each Single-Step

The most typical action taken when a debugger's single-step `INT01` handler is called is to present the debugger's user interface. A familiar example of this would be the behavior of the venerable `DEBUG.COM`. Each time the `T` command is used to trace through the current instruction, the `INT01` handler within `DEBUG.COM` performs the following steps:

1. Save the state of the CPU's internal registers.
2. Determine the memory location of the next instruction to be executed.
3. Translate the instruction at that location into its assembler mnemonic.
4. Write the current CPU register values and next instruction to be executed to the current display device.
5. Prompt the user for the next command.
6. If another `T` command is entered, restore the registers to their original values and execute an `IRET`.

There are certainly more elaborate styles of user interfaces possible, as exemplified by the watch windows for data and the stack that are supported by more sophisticated tools. But the basic action is the same.

In this text, this type of action will be referred to as manual assembler-level single-stepping. This definition is cast with full recognition that there are several automatic processes involved.

Most of the more sophisticated debuggers provide a feature known as *evaluation breakpoints*. One of the ways this feature can be implemented is through the `INT01` single-step interrupt. What this means is that each time an `INT01` occurs, the debugger will not immediately present its user interface. Rather, it will perform one or more user-defined tests and use the outcome of those tests to decide whether to continue the single-step and test cycle or to stop and report that the test conditions were satisfied.

This can be a powerful tool in the quest for a bug's point of origin. It also places the burden for performing repeated and complicated analysis where it belongs—with the computer. The term for this will be *evaluative assembler-level single-stepping*.

As with all forms of powerful medicine, however, this practice is not without its side effects. Having a series of tests performed by the debugger between the execution of each and every assembler instruction within a program can end up being a slow way to locate a problem in some cases. More on knowing when and when not to use this method, rather than the other possibilities, will be covered in Chapter 11, "Working with a Debugger."

An additional action that is sometimes performed as part of a debugger's `INT01` handler is that of updating a backtrace buffer. This is where a perpetual history of a program's execution path is recorded in a ring buffer within the debugger. When this feature is included within the debugger you are using, the updating action is usually performed for both the evaluative and manual cases.

A final note concerning the operation of assembler-level single-stepping: There is a situation where what amounts to double-stepping will occur. Whenever an instruction is executed that results in a change to the contents of the stack segment register, an INT01 will not occur until after the execution of the next instruction, even if the trap flag is set.

This would explain what appears to be a buggy debugger when you are stepping through a sequence such as the following:

```
mov     ss,[stack_seg]
mov     sp,offset stack_top
mov     bp,sp
```

When the mov ss,[stack_seg] instruction is displayed as the current one and you command your debugger to step through it, it will appear that the debugger has skipped the mov sp,offset stack_top instruction. The current instruction after one single-step will be the mov bp,sp but the new stack pointer value will be in effect, because the mov sp instruction actually did execute.

The reason for this automatic guarding is simple. Since the CPU uses two registers to address the program stack, a two-instruction sequence is required to change from one stack to another (there are exceptions to this in the 80386 and 80486, but they are ignored here). If an INT01 interrupt were made to occur just after the execution of the mov ss,[stack_seg] instruction, there would not be a fully defined stack onto which the interrupt return address could be placed.

5.3 BREAKPOINTS

In the pre-8086 dark ages the only way to accomplish assembler-level single-stepping under software control was by temporarily replacing each subsequent instruction in turn with a branch back into the debugger. Granted that this method pales beside the use of the INT01 single-step interrupt, it is still a very useful and prominent member of a debugging arsenal. This method is known as the *breakpoint*.

Unlike assembler-level single-stepping, breakpoints allow you to select exactly when control is returned to the debugger. Through judicious application of these control points, your debugging sessions will be more effective and will therefore take much less of your valuable time.

Effecting a breakpoint simply means causing a branch from the program being debugged back into the program doing the debugging. While it is possible to cause a transfer of control through different means (e.g., branch instructions, call instructions, and general software interrupt calls), it is much better to use the special INTO3 interrupt call designed for this purpose. The exact reasons for this will be discussed later in this section.

When a software debugger loads itself into memory, it modifies the INTO3 interrupt vector to point to a handler within its own codespace. Then, to instantiate a software breakpoint at a certain instruction within the program being debugged, the debugger temporarily replaces the first byte of that instruction with the INTO3 breakpoint instruction. It is (almost) that simple.

Note that since it requires a temporary rewriting of a program's instructions, the software breakpoint method cannot be used with code burned into a read-only memory. The hardware types of breakpoints available with 80386+ CPUs or with other forms of hardware assist are often the best choice when working with code in ROM. This is covered in the next chapter.

Sticky and Nonsticky Breakpoints

Although there is nothing to stop a programmer from manually implanting INTO3 instructions within a program (indeed, this is a useful technique, and is covered later in this section), in most cases it is preferable to let a software debugger manage the placement of breakpoints.

There are basically two management philosophies that apply to breakpoints. The first method involves a one-time-only replacement of an instruction with a breakpoint. Once a break is made into the debugger, the breakpoint is undone and forgotten. This type will be referred to as a *nonsticky breakpoint* or a *temporary breakpoint.*

The second method makes the breakpoint instruction a semipermanent part of the program being debugged. This type will be referred to as a *sticky breakpoint.* Each time a program's execution is resumed after any breakpoint (sticky or nonsticky) is encountered, all sticky breakpoints are automatically put back into effect.

To clarify, the INTO3 interrupt is used to implement both of these types of breakpoints. The only difference between them is in the way they are controlled. Beginning with the nonsticky breakpoint, let's turn to venerable old DEBUG.COM for a closer look.

Entering a G for the go command at the beckon of this tool's prompt causes the program under test to begin executing at full speed. Qualifying this go command with an address parameter, such as in the command g 0142, will cause the insertion of a breakpoint instruction at the specified address before full-speed execution is begun. When the program being run executes the breakpoint (presuming it does), the program's activities will be put on hold and control will be returned to the debugger.

At this point, DEBUG.COM immediately replaces the breakpoint instruction with the opcode that originally occupied the memory location in question. Then all internal record of the breakpoint is erased. The only way to cause a breakpoint to be reissued for that address is to set another breakpoint there explicitly. Note that it is also possible to specify more than one address after the go command.

Some debuggers emulate the g [address] command method, whereas others support temporary breakpoints through a point-and-shoot method. Using a mouse or the arrow keys, you move a highlight bar to the instruction at which you wish to stop, and then click a mouse button or press a key to indicate your choice.

Sticky breakpoints are remembered and automatically put back into effect by the debugger after breaking. DEBUG.COM doesn't support the sticky breakpoint; SYMDEB was the first Microsoft offering to support this type. Codeview, Periscope, and Turbo Debugger also provide their own versions.

The point where a sticky breakpoint behaves differently than the non-sticky variety is when a program's execution is being resumed. The next section will further illustrate the behavior of this second type.

The Action Taken on a Breakpoint Interrupt

The explanation being tendered in this section is, by necessity, a generalized one. If you were to delve into the inner workings of five different software debuggers, you would no doubt uncover five different variations on this basic theme. Fortunately, the level of understanding that is useful to gain proficiency in debugging can be achieved without that much detail.

In our generalized model, when a breakpoint occurs, all breakpoints being managed by the debugger will first be replaced by the corresponding original instructions. To achieve this cleanup, our model must maintain two lists: one to record the location of each nonsticky breakpoint and the corresponding original opcode, and another to record the location and original opcode for each sticky breakpoint.

Once the list of temporary breakpoints has been processed, its useful life is over. Conversely, the list of sticky breakpoints is destined to be called upon again a little later on in this scenario.

This cleanup is necessary before the debugger displays a disassembly view of the current instruction or a window full of disassembled instructions. If this were not done, your view of the program would be skewed by the presence of these "guest" INTO3 instructions.

At this point, if the breakpoint is not of the evaluative type, the user interface will be presented. The next action then depends on the commands entered by the operator. If instead the breakpoint is an evaluative one, the specified test is performed. A true conclusion of this test causes the specified action to take place, whereas a false conclusion signals that full-speed execution is to be resumed automatically.

Certain preparatory steps are involved in this resumption if the debugger supports a backtrace buffer, or if the breakpoint was of the sticky variety. First, the INTO1 single-step feature is used to execute the current instruction.

This must be done so that the resulting machine state can be recorded (for the backtrace buffer case) or so that a breakpoint instruction can be reasserted over the instruction (for the sticky breakpoint case). Next, any other sticky breakpoints are reasserted. Finally, control is passed to the program, which resumes full-speed execution until the next breakpoint is hit.

Some debuggers offer a feature to count breakpoints and present the user interface only after a certain number occur. For our purposes in this section, this will be considered an evaluative breakpoint with an intrinsically defined test condition.

Breakpoints of Convenience

Now that we have gone down into the 8086 CPU's basement and inspected the plumbing of the INT01 and INT03 debugging features, let's step back upstairs and explore some of the conveniences that can be built on this foundation. Assembler-level single-stepping is such a hard-wired behavior that there is little more enhancement to be made beyond the evaluative single-stepping already covered. Where convenience can really be gained is through automatic placement of INT03 interrupt calls.

Given the degree of tedium often involved in the use of a debugger any conveniences quickly come to be viewed as necessities. The first of these convenient necessities to be examined is what is known as a step-over or step-around type of function. This is useful when the next instruction to be executed is a call to a subprocedure and you do not wish to single-step through it. Rather, you wish to have it executed at full speed and arrive back in control beginning with the instruction immediately following the call.

To accomplish this, the debugger writes a temporary breakpoint over the instruction following the call and then resumes full-speed program execution. As soon as the subprocedure completes its operations and returns to the point of call, control will return to the debugger and the temporary breakpoint will be replaced with the original instruction.

DEBUG.COM implements this function through its P command, whereas Periscope provides a more intuitive J, for "jump around." Other debuggers offer a function key to produce this step-over action.

Another time saver is high-level single-stepping. It would be a sure bet that most programmers who work in a high-level language have little desire to become involved with the assembler-level aspect of their work. Through careful orchestration of INT03 breakpoints, a debugger makes high-level single-stepping a reality. The result is a form of single-step execution that insulates the operator from the code's underbelly.

To make this possible, the compiler must divulge the correspondence between each high-level language statement and the resulting assembler code. The debugger uses the compiler's concordance list to determine automatically where temporary breakpoints should be placed.

Importance of Single-Byte Replacement

Many instructions within the 8086 instruction set consist of more than one byte of opcode or operand information. Although other instructions could be used to implement a breakpoint, the INTO3 instruction is especially well suited for this purpose, because it requires only one byte.

This is no small coincidence since acting as a breakpoint is the purpose of this instruction. The fact that Intel devoted silicon to features such as the special-purpose single-step and breakpoint interrupts certainly attests to the fact that debugging is a significant aspect of software development.

To understand more clearly the critical significance of the fact that the INTO3 instruction was designed to require only a single byte, let's examine the example case where a single-byte instruction is temporarily overwritten with a two-byte interrupt call. Normally, the first byte of the next instruction follows immediately after the single-byte instruction where the breakpoint is to be asserted; but once the breakpoint is written, this subsequent instruction will be corrupted by the operand of the temporary interrupt call. During the execution of the program under test, a branch could be made to the address normally occupied by this now damaged piece of code. The results will vary, depending on the exact contents of memory in this wounded area, but they will never be desirable.

Another useful spinoff effect of having a breakpoint instruction that occupies only one byte is that unused memory areas can be filled with this byte to help catch a runaway program. If a program jumps off into space and encounters a memory area filled with breakpoints in this way, it will bomb out to the debugger so that an analysis of the situation can be performed.

If the breakpoint interrupt instruction were composed of more than a single byte, this type of runaway trapping could not be done with any reliability. If a program that was jumping off into space happened to land on some other byte in the breakpoint instruction than the first, no benefit would be gained—the crash would simply have a different flavor.

5.4 LOADING PROGRAMS—A QUIRK

When a program is loaded for execution by DOS, one of the tasks performed is the preparation of a private copy of the *environment string block*. This buffer is where DOS's command processor records strings such as the command search path, the prompt, and any strings assigned with the SET command. When a program is loaded by a debugger, this task must, of course, be emulated.

Beginning with Version 3.0 of DOS, an extra, hidden string is placed at the end of this buffer, denoting the complete drive, path, filename, and extension of the program. Some programs use the drive and path portion of this string to locate associated data and overlay files—presuming them to be in the same directory that the program's main executable file was loaded from.

One quirk, which some debuggers exhibit, is the environment that they build for the program to be debugged still contains the drive/path string from where the *debugger* was loaded. If a program extracts what it thinks is its home drive and path from this special environment string, things can get confused when the debugger is in another directory.

If a program is unable to find its auxiliary files when loaded by a debugger, suspect this anomaly. One method of compensation is to install your debugger in the same directory as the program you are debugging. Should that not be practical, the remaining choices are to modify the string using the debugger's memory-editing capabilities, or to obtain a different debugger. If you choose to edit the string, make sure enough memory is available before expanding it.

5.5 SUMMARY

The `INT01` single-step interrupt makes it possible for a software debugger to run as a separate thread of execution alongside the program being debugged.

When the `INT01` feature is used to step through each instruction, this is known as assembler-level single-stepping.

The `INT03` interrupt is specifically designed as a breakpoint instruction. Breakpoints allow more selective control over when a program's execution is stopped, and the program can run at full speed until a breakpoint is executed.

Nonsticky breakpoints are temporary, whereas sticky breakpoints are automatically reasserted by the debugger each time full-speed execution is resumed.

The most common action taken by a software debugger when either an `INT01` or `INT03` interrupt occurs is to present its user interface.

An evaluative breakpoint makes the debugger perform a test on each break and resume execution until the test is satisfied.

A debugger will update its backtrace buffer on each breakpoint, whether a full stop is done or an evaluative test is done and not satisfied.

High-level single-stepping is effected through the use of source-line-to-address information, supplied by the compiler, to manage the automatic placement of temporary breakpoints.

CHAPTER 6
Advanced Debugger Features

This chapter takes us on a tour of some of the capabilities offered by more sophisticated debuggers. It is intended to help you do the following:

1. Know what is available—what is possible
2. Select the best tool for each situation
3. Understand how to interface custom code to this class of tool when necessary

The usual end-of-chapter summary is not included this time. Instead, a summary of the advantages and consequences for each topic is presented at the end of each section.

6.1 SYMBOLIC DEBUGGING

Symbols are the mnemonics we use to represent addresses and data values in a program. Assemblers and compilers make it easy to associate names with memory storage locations, numeric constants, and positions in the code. But ultimately the CPU only understands the pure numbers of its machine language. The names you make up are abstractions, meaningful only to your assembler or compiler and, of course, to anyone reading the source code (or so you hope).

The small assembler language program in Listing 6-1 contains three symbols: START, MSG, and BEGIN. The remainder is comprised of directives to the assembler, literal data, instruction mnemonics, and operands for the directives and instructions.

```
_TEXT    segment para public 'CODE'
         assume  cs:_TEXT,ds:_TEXT,es:_TEXT,ss:_TEXT
         org     0100H

         public  start, msg, begin

start:   jmp     short begin

msg      db      'Hello',13,10,'$'

begin:   mov     ah,9
         mov     dx,offset msg
         int     21h
         mov     ax,4c00h
         int     21h
_TEXT    ends
         end     start
```

LISTING 6-1 The file X.ASM.

Loading the machine code for this program into DEBUG.COM, you could produce the disassembled version as shown in Listing 6-2. This is termed a *raw* disassembly, since it contains only the base information that can be derived from the machine code. This view of the code is devoid of all English-like abstractions.

The only symbolic information a debugger can provide when given a binary file containing machine instructions are the assembler mnemonics. The symbolic representations we used for data and code position labels are gone. For a debugger to associate raw machine code numbers with the symbolic information you used when you developed the program, it must be provided

```
1ADB:0100 EB08          JMP     010A
1ADB:0102 48            DEC     AX
1ADB:0103 65            DB      65
1ADB:0104 6C            DB      6C
1ADB:0105 6C            DB      6C
1ADB:0106 6F            DB      6F
1ADB:0107 0D0A24        OR      AX,240A
1ADB:010A B409          MOV     AH,09
1ADB:010C BA0201        MOV     DX,0102
1ADB:010F CD21          INT     21
1ADB:0111 B8004C        MOV     AX,4C00
1ADB:0114 CD21          INT     21
```

LISTING 6-2 Raw disassembly of X.COM.

with a crib sheet—a list of symbol names and their corresponding memory locations.

Listing 6-3 gives an indication of what can be done when a debugger is supplied with a symbolic concordance list. If you're not familiar with assembler, the benefit this annotation brings to the listing may not seem like much. If you are familiar with assembler, you know that while this simple a program only benefits a little, support for symbols can make a very significant difference in a larger real-world program. The annotation makes the program more readable and self-documenting. It also establishes a link to the source code, making the disassembled view more familiar-looking.

There are two ways to provide a debugger with symbol information for a program: through a .MAP file and through information encoded into the resulting .EXE file. Both of these are produced by the program linker with information from .OBJ files. The compiler or assembler you are using must be instructed to place debugging info in .OBJ files.

The process of generating an .OBJ file from a source file for the assembler and C language cases is basically the following:

$$.\text{ASM source file} \quad \rightarrow \quad \text{Assembler} \quad \rightarrow \quad .\text{OBJ file}$$
$$.\text{C source file} \quad \rightarrow \quad \text{Compiler} \quad \rightarrow \quad .\text{OBJ file}$$

In the case of assembler language, the assembler includes symbolic information in the .OBJ module by virtue of PUBLIC statements in the .ASM source module. Each symbol so declared in the source module will be identified with a record within the .OBJ module, known as a PUBDEF record. An explicit PUBLIC statement must exist within the .ASM module for each symbol you want exported to your debugger.

```
              START:
1ADB:0100 EB08         JMP      BEGIN
              MSG:
1ADB:0102 48           DEC      AX
1ADB:0103 65           DB       65
1ADB:0104 6C           DB       6C
1ADB:0105 6C           DB       6C
1ADB:0106 6F           DB       6F
1ADB:0107 0D0A24       OR       AX,240A
              BEGIN:
1ADB:010A B409         MOV      AH,09
1ADB:010C BA0201       MOV      DX,0102      ; MSG
1ADB:010F CD21         INT      21
1ADB:0111 B8004C       MOV      AX,4C00
1ADB:0114 CD21         INT      21
```

LISTING 6-3 Annotated disassembly of X.COM.

```
Start  Stop    Length Name              Class

00000H 00115H 00116H _TEXT             CODE

 Address           Publics by Name

0000:010A        BEGIN
0000:0102        MSG
0000:0100        START

 Address           Publics by Value

0000:0100        START
0000:0102        MSG
0000:010A        BEGIN
```

Program entry point at 0000:0100
Warning: No stack

LISTING 6-4   The file X.MAP.

When working with high-level languages, the exportation of symbol information from the source module to PUBDEF records in the .OBJ file depends on the compiler. For example, in the C language all function names and global variables are made public by default. The static storage class specifier must be used in a declaration to make a symbol private.

The typical function of a linker is to process one or more .OBJ files and library files and produce an executable binary module in the .EXE format described later in this section. Some linkers can also output other formats, such as .COM, .SYS, and overlay modules. Otherwise, an EXE2BIN-type utility is required to generate these alternate forms.

```
.OBJ and .LIB files  →  Linker  →  .EXE file
.OBJ and .LIB files  →  Linker  →  .EXE file and .MAP file
```

The "old standard" way of making symbolic information available to a debugger is through a text file known as the .MAP file. This is basically a summary report output from the linker, showing how it resolved various details of combining .OBJ modules and library modules to form the executable binary module.

Listing 6-4 shows the .MAP file for the X.ASM program. This was produced using Borland's TASM and TLINK products using the command sequence:

```
tasm x
tlink /m x
```

Note that the symbols listed in the sections marked "Publics by Name" and "Publics by Value" are precisely those that were included in the public statement within the source file, X.ASM. A symbolic debugger will read this .MAP file and build its lookup table using the information contained in one of these lists.

While the information carried by a .MAP file can certainly be helpful when debugging, it is limited. No means is provided to represent the type of the data—only the symbol name and the starting address. For example, in the .MAP file in Listing 6-4 there is no differentiation between the symbol MSG, used to denote the start of a string, and the symbol BEGIN, a code label. The debugger cannot discern whether MSG represents the start of a string, a code position label, or the base of an array of 10,000 records.

Why is this important? The primary reason has to do with the display and manipulation of a program's data by a debugger. When you need to inspect the contents of your program's memory variables, you don't need to be burdened with the translation of a raw hex dump.

To circumvent this limitation, the producers of software development products have derived a different way to channel debugging information from the source file to the debugger. When so instructed, the assembler or compiler will generate additional COMMENT type records in the .OBJ module, which describe the type of each symbol and the amount of memory associated with it.

When the linker is instructed to process this extended debugging information, it will translate these special .OBJ COMMENT records into a special block of data within the .EXE module. Note that while this does increase the file size of an .EXE module, the base memory requirements of the program do not increase. The extra information is only for the sake of a debugger that is designed to read it. That these bloated .EXE files take up more space on a disk cannot, however, be denied.

To get a better idea of the importance of this feature, consider the following two storage declarations. The first pair of lines are assembler statements and the second two are the corresponding C declarations. In each case, the variable named file_handle is being allocated one 16-bit word of storage, and the variable named flag_array is allocated a block of eight bytes:

```
file_handle  dw  ?
flag_array   db  8 dup(0)
unsigned int file_handle;
unsigned char flag_array[8];
```

Through a .MAP file, a debugger could know only the beginning address for the file_handle and flag_array symbols. By using instead the extended information embedded within an .EXE file, the disassembly and memory dumps performed by a debugger can be made much more intelligible. The extended .EXE debugging information would not only represent the starting address of each of these variables, but also the data type and total number of elements for each.

Through the extended-.EXE method, it is even possible to pass information to a debugger about stack-based variables, which are local to a function. The debugger must, of course, be designed to know how to apply this data.

The steps required to generate the extended-.EXE form of debugging information will vary among different assemblers, compilers, and linkers. The steps for TASM and TLINK are shown here. The /zi switch instructs the assembler to place debugging information in the .OBJ file, and the /v switch tells the linker to build it into the .EXE file:

```
tasm /zi x
tlink /v x
```

When the final form of the program you are working with is not an .EXE file, (e.g., a .COM, .SYS, .BIN, or .OVL file), a separate .MAP file is the only way debugging information can be made available to a debugger. But since more information can be passed to a debugger through an .EXE file, it is a good idea to do as much initial development as possible in the .EXE form and then switch to the final form after all testing is done.

Note that while the issue of symbols only applies to debugging at the assembler level, it is certainly not limited to programs written in assembler. Most high-level language compilers and linkers can be made to produce a .MAP file containing symbols for the names of functions and key code position labels.

FEATURE:

Symbolic Debugging

ADVANTAGES:

Disassembled code is easier to understand when labels and variable names appear as they do in the source code.
Setting breakpoints and viewing and changing data locations is easier when names can be used rather than raw address values.

CONSEQUENCES:

Memory must be allocated by the debugger to store symbols.
Symbol information must be made available during the compile and link steps.

6.2 SOURCE-LEVEL DEBUGGING

Source-level debugging is "just like being there." Rather than having to wind through a disassembled view of your program, you are able to see your very own source code, including comments. What the debugger needs to accomplish this feat is a list showing the memory address that corresponds to each line in the source code file. This information can be provided through the .MAP file method or the extended-.EXE method.

The following commands would produce line number information in a .MAP file using Borland's parlance. Listing 6-5 shows the .MAP file produced from the X.ASM program introduced in Listing 6-1.

```
tasm /zi x
tlink /m /l x
```

To produce line number information in an extended .EXE file, use the same method as already shown in the previous section:

```
tasm /zi x
tlink /v x
```

To prevent confusion when working with high-level language, do not combine more than one statement on a line. For example, in the following C language excerpt, when you single-step through the if statement, there would be no simple way to know whether the resulting assignment was made. When the current line pointer or highlight bar advances from the second

```
Start   Stop   Length Name              Class

00000H 00115H 00116H _TEXT             CODE

  Address            Publics by Name

0000:010A           BEGIN
0000:0102           MSG
0000:0100           START

  Address            Publics by Value

0000:0100           START
0000:0102           MSG
0000:010A           BEGIN

Line numbers for x.OBJ(X.ASM) segment _TEXT

    7 0000:0100   11 0000:010A   12 0000:010C   13 0000:010F
   14 0000:0111   15 0000:0114
Program entry point at 0000:0100
Warning: No stack
```

LISTING 6-5 X.MAP, including line number information.

statement to the third, you can't determine whether the calc_payroll() function was called unless you use a step-into type of single-stepping rather than a step-over, or you use some other form of determination such as a breakpoint.

```
day = get_day();
if (day == friday) calc_payroll(total_hours, rate);
report_hours();
```

Now, you hope you know when it's Friday, but in the general case, it can be simpler to structure your code as shown in the next example. This way, there is no ambiguity. When you step through the if statement, you'll either land on the calc_payroll() line or on the report_hours() line. Simple and direct.

```
day = get_day();
if (day == friday)
  calc_payroll(total_hours, rate);
report_hours();
```

Note that it is often necessary to disable optimization when generating a debugging version of a program. You must do this to achieve a one-to-one correspondence between the line number information and the actual machine code. You must then hope that this change does not make the bug you are chasing go into hiding or change in some other undesirable way.

Since the debugger must be able to make DOS INT21 calls to read the source file, source-level debugging may not always be possible when working with resident code such as device drivers and TSRs, where DOS reentrancy can be a problem.

FEATURE:

Source-Level Debugging

ADVANTAGES:

Being able to see the actual source code as you step through a program, complete with comments, is very helpful.
Setting breakpoints and viewing and changing data locations is easier when names can be used rather than raw address values.

CONSEQUENCES:

Memory must be allocated by the debugger to store line-number information.
Memory must be allocated by the debugger to buffer a portion of the source code file.

It must be possible for DOS file I/O calls to be made by the debugger to access the source code information.

Line-number information must be made available during the compile and link steps.

It may be necessary to disable compiler optimizations to ensure proper correspondence between the machine code and the lines of source code.

You can miss seeing things that would be evident on inspection of the underlying machine code.

6.3 PROTECTED MEMORY BOARD

When you're working with a buggy program, it can be especially frustrating when the bug causes damage to your debugger. But when a debugger is loaded into the same system RAM as a buggy program, it is fair game. Not only can the debugger's code or data areas be overwritten, but the interrupt vectors, which the debugger must manage, can also be changed—either inadvertently or intentionally.

One method some debuggers use to combat this problem is known as a *protected memory board*. When you install the debugger, it loads itself into the special memory board and then activates a latch to establish a write-protect state, effectively closing the door behind it. The process being debugged, however, can still damage any read/write memory required by the debugger, including interrupt vectors.

FEATURE:

Protected Memory Board

ADVANTAGES:

The debugger's code is protected from damage by buggy software.

Main memory is not reduced, enabling large programs to be debugged.

The load position of the program being debugged is not affected by the debugger.

The protected memory board can be made to appear as an adapter card ROM. This means that the debugger can gain control during the power-on self-test (POST) part of the boot-up process.

CONSEQUENCES:

A free address region is required between the 640K and 1M points.

An adapter card slot is required.

6.4 PROTECTED MODE

Certain debuggers are designed to load into extended memory and run in the processor's *protected mode*. This is only possible on 286 and 386/486 systems. The protection offered by this method is powerful. The program being debugged has virtually no access to the code and data of the debugger. Further, a protected mode supervisor program (e.g., the debugger) will always receive control on an interrupt before less privileged programs (e.g., the program being debugged). An unruly program can tromp on the INTO1 and INTO3 vectors with impunity, but the debugger will continue to function.

FEATURE:

Protected Mode

ADVANTAGES:

The debugger's code can be loaded into extended memory.
The debugger's code is protected from damage by buggy software.
Main memory is not reduced, enabling large programs to be debugged.
The load position of the program being debugged is not affected by the debugger.
No special adapter card is required.
The I/O trapping feature permits breakpoints to occur on I/O operations while the program runs at nearly full speed (386/486 systems only).

CONSEQUENCES:

Enough extended memory must be available to meet the debugger's needs.
The simultaneous use of memory manager products, which also rely on VM86 mode, will work only if the debugger has been designed to coexist with them (386/486 systems only).

6.5 REMOTE-CONSOLE DEBUGGING

Having a debugger load itself into a protected memory board offers some measure of isolation. Taking advantage of protected mode improves this isolation by a couple of steps. But another form of isolation becomes important when debugging: contention for the keyboard and display.

When you must debug a graphics-based program or a keyboard interrupt handler, you need a debugger that can function through a remote console rather than share the target's keyboard and display. One method is to connect a dumb ASCII terminal to a serial port on the target machine. A second computer that emulates a dumb terminal can also be used, of course.

FEATURE:

Remote-Console Debugging

ADVANTAGES:

Permits graphics based programs and keyboard interrupt handlers to be debugged.

The application's screen is always present on the target system's monitor.

CONSEQUENCES:

Additional hardware is required (a free serial port, a cable, and a terminal or second computer).

The maximum baud rate for most dumb ASCII terminals is 38,400. This will slow the debugger's operation when much display updating is being done.

6.6 REMOTE/HOST DEBUGGING

In the remote/ host configuration, the bulk of the debugging code is moved off to a separate *host computer.* A high-speed serial link, connected between the target and host systems, lets the host communicate with a small software *control stub,* which remains within the target system.

This control stub contains just enough code to process communications with the host, to handle the low-level details of `INT01` and `INT03` interrupts, and to read and write target memory through the link.

In addition to providing the same benefits as the remote-console method described above, remote/ host debugging can make it possible to work with programs that require too much memory to be loaded under a full software debugger. A typical control stub consumes from 4K to 8K of memory, whereas a typical debugger consumes anywhere from 50K to 200K.

FEATURE:

Remote/Host Debugging

ADVANTAGES:

Permits graphics-based programs and keyboard interrupt handlers to be debugged.

The application's screen is always present on the target system's monitor.

More memory is available for the application being debugged.

CONSEQUENCES:

Additional hardware is required (a free serial port, a cable, and a second computer).

6.7   386/486 DEBUG REGISTERS

When Intel's engineers designed the 80386 CPU, one of them had the foresight to say, "Including a small amount of debugging circuitry within this chip will not only make our development task easier, but it will be a great feature for everyone!"

The basic circuit element they used is known as a *digital comparator*. A 32-bit version of this logic element is illustrated in Figure 6.1. The output of this circuit assumes the "on" (logical 1) state only when the 32 bits of the test input match the 32 bits in the reference buffer.

Through the coordination of supporting logic circuitry, a digital comparator can be made to interrupt the CPU at the precise instant a 32-bit address value is generated that matches the contents of the reference buffer. The coordinating logic makes it possible to qualify this interrupt based on

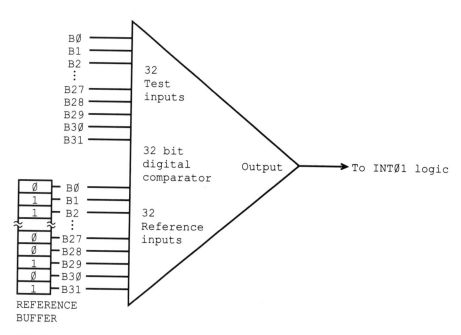

FIGURE 6.1   Digital comparator, used to trigger an interrupt.

whether the match occurs during an instruction fetch operation, a memory write operation, or a memory read or write operation.

The power of this feature is in the speed it affords. Somewhat similar breakpoint capabilities could be provided through the evaluative single-step approach described in Chapter 5. But whereas evaluative single-stepping can easily result in a thousandfold reduction of program throughput, the CPU can be made to watch itself with built-in hardware with little or no speed degradation.

In actuality, the 80386 includes four of these silicon sentries. The reference buffers are accessed as debugging registers DR0, DR1, DR2, and DR3, while hardware debugging registers DR6 and DR7 are used to manage the actions of these four watchdogs.

Each digital comparator can be independently controlled through software instructions to watch addresses for operations involving one, two, or four bytes. This means that a range of 16 bytes could be monitored if all four debug registers are used in conjunction, providing proper alignment conditions are met.

For data breakpoints, the CPU's prefetch pipelining feature must be disabled, resulting in a slight slowdown. If the CPU were allowed to fetch instructions ahead of data read or write operations, the offending instruction would have already been executed by the time a breakpoint could be generated. Indeed, from four to six more instructions could have been processed in the meantime.

When a hardware breakpoint is set on an instruction fetch, the address used must be that of the first byte of the instruction, including any prefixes. Although the underlying reasons are different, this is the same rule as with the INT03 software breakpoint.

FEATURE:

386/486 Debug Registers

ADVANTAGES:

The software being debugged runs at full speed (in real mode).
Breakpoints can be set within ROM.
Breakpoints are not lost when an overlay is loaded.
Breakpoints can be set on memory read, read/write, and execute operations.
By setting a breakpoint on the read of an interrupt vector, you can maintain a
  breakpoint on the corresponding interrupt handler even if an intercept
  or replacement handler is established.

CONSEQUENCES:

Due to limited range, you must have a specific idea of what you are after.

6.8   BUS INTERFACE CARD

A *bus interface card* is an adapter card that plugs into a computer's mother-board just like a memory board, disk controller, or dozens of other types of peripheral interface cards. As with the 80386 hardware debugging registers, one of the basic circuit elements used on such a card is the digital comparator.

Through the circuitry on this type of hardware adjunct, a debugger can instigate a breakpoint interrupt based on a wide variety of system conditions. A trigger can be established on the system's address, data, and control signals, not only for matching conditions but for comparison tests such as greater than, greater than or equal, or less than.

FEATURE:

Bus Interface Card

ADVANTAGES:

DMA signals can be monitored and triggered on.
Installation is much simpler than with a CPU intercept pod.
More information is provided than with a software-only debugger.
The target system runs at full speed.
Through the inclusion of memory chips on the interface card, a perpetual audit trail of bus state information can be maintained. This is known as a *hardware trace buffer.*

CONSEQUENCES:

This type of interface is not useful on fast systems. Machines with a clock rate faster than 8 Mhz use a separate bus for memory accesses.
Since more information is provided, there can be more to sift through.
When using bus signals, you can't directly know the contents of the CPU's registers.

6.9   CPU INTERCEPT POD

While the use of a CPU intercept pod provides many of the same features of the bus interface card, it surpasses it in one very important area—the 8 Mhz system clock limitation of the ISA bus. Because a CPU running at a quicker clip must forsake this bus for a private memory bus, intercepting address, control, and data signals directly at the CPU socket becomes the only practical alternative.

Most products in this class also support a hardware trace buffer and some even include a powerful feature known as a *state machine* or *multi-stage trigger.* This latter feature can be especially valuable when dealing with intermittent and stray-bullet type problems. For example, a state machine can make it possible to invoke a breakpoint when a memory write is done to a certain range of memory, with a certain data value, when and only when the current point of execution is within a certain function.

The signals available to this type of tool include memory addresses, memory read/write signals, data bus values, I/O port read/write signals, interrupt signals, interrupt acknowledge, instruction fetch, halt, and shutdown. Depending on the implementation, either these signals can be selected as trigger-point criteria or their state may be recorded within the hardware trace buffer.

FEATURE:

CPU Intercept Pod

ADVANTAGES:

When configured for remote operation, no debugger code exists anywhere within the target machine. Full isolation can be achieved.

Any aspect of the target's operation can be monitored, including transitions to and from protected mode.

CPU signals can be captured in a hardware trace buffer.

The target system runs at full speed.

More information is provided than with a software-only debugger.

A pod can be used with non-DOS system (e.g., an embedded 8086 system).

With a hardware trace buffer you can set the hardware to break when the trigger event is at the start of the buffer, at the end, or in the center. This lets you see how the break condition arose and what happened immediately afterwards.

CONSEQUENCES:

The system's CPU must be removed and a CPU intercept pod installed—a nontrivial exercise in hardware manipulation.

DMA signals are unavailable.

Internal CPU register states cannot be read and written.

Since more information is provided, it can mean more to sift through.

CPU-specific pod hardware is required.

6.10   IN-CIRCUIT EMULATOR (ICE)

An in-circuit emulator goes several steps further than the CPU intercept pod. It also commands a much higher purchase price. Rather than simply intercept the existing CPU and enable the state of external signals to be tested and recorded, this type of tool makes it possible to enter the domain of machine states within the chip.

While running at full speed, an ICE permits you to specify trigger conditions involving not only external CPU signals but the values of the general registers, values within control registers, and values within memory.

FEATURE:

In-Circuit Emulator (ICE)

ADVANTAGES:

Any aspect of the target's operation can be monitored, including transitions to and from protected mode.
Full isolation is achieved between the target system and the ICE control system.
Internal CPU register states can be read and written.
Target memory can be read and written.
More information is provided than with a software-only debugger.
The target system runs at full speed.
An ICE can be used with a non-DOS system (e.g., an embedded 8086 system).

CONSEQUENCES:

The device is very expensive.
The system's CPU must be removed and a CPU intercept pod installed—a non-trivial exercise in hardware manipulation.
Since more information is provided, it can mean more to sift through.
CPU-specific pod hardware is required.

6.11   NMI BREAKOUT SWITCH

When the 8086 was first introduced, the proclaimed reason for its non-maskable interrupt (NMI) signal was to accommodate catastrophic conditions such as an imminent power failure. The main use of this interrupt within a PC/XT/AT or Micro Channel computer system is to alert the user to a memory failure known as a *parity error.*

This interrupt has also found much favor with debuggers. By connecting a switch to a CPU's NMI signal line, it is possible to break into an NMI-compliant debugger no matter what state the system is in (as long as the NMI vector hasn't been overwritten). This can be especially valuable when a system's keyboard is completely dead and you need to find out why.

Figure 6.2 presents a simplified rendition of an NMI breakout switch and its connection to an ISA-type computer. For a Micro Channel system, the edge connector pin number is B32.

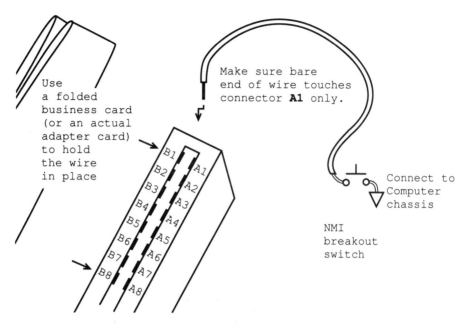

FIGURE 6.2 Installation of NMI breakout switch.

FEATURE:

NMI Breakout Switch

ADVANTAGES:

It is possible to regain control of a hung system.

CONSEQUENCES:

Extra hardware is required (a breakout switch).
Installation requires careful insertion of a wire into an edge connector (or soldering onto an adapter card).
Some video EGA/VGA display adapters make use of this interrupt (INT02), which can cause compatibility problems.

6.12 EXCEPTION HANDLERS

A *processor exception* occurs when the CPU encounters an instruction that attempts to break the rules. Even the now-primitive 8086 supports an exception through its divide-by-zero interrupt, INT00.

With the introduction of the 80286, several exception conditions were added that apply to real-mode execution, and many more were added for that chip's protected mode. The 80386 brought with it an even greater number of exception-handling features.

A prime example of an exception that pertains to debugging is the *invalid instruction* exception. In a 286, 386, or 486, the attempted execution of an invalid opcode will cause the automatic generation of an INT06 interrupt. When you use a debugger that traps these interrupt calls, your chances of finding more bugs more quickly take a distinct upward turn.

An exception condition that can be caught by a debugger supporting the INT0D general protection exception interrupt is best illustrated by the following program excerpt:

```
xor     ax,ax
mov     di,0ffffh
cld
stosw
```

When the CPU attempts to execute the last instruction in this sequence, the STOSW, an abnormal condition will occur. The normal action of this instruction would be to write the word in the AX register to the memory location addressed by ES:DI and then leave the DI register advanced to the next word in memory. To break this down, the byte in the AL register should be written to memory location ES:DI, and the byte in the AH register should be written to the next higher address, ES:DI+1. Then this instruction should leave the DI register pointing to the next higher memory address.

When the initial DI register value upon execution of the STOSW happens to be FFFF, it is not possible to advance DI to the next memory location. Incrementing a 16-bit register containing FFFF will produce a new value of 0. Rather than let this action slip by, the CPU automatically generates an INT0D. This condition could also occur with the other forms of string instructions, the CMPSW, MOVSW, and SCASW, as well as their 32-bit counterparts, STOSD, CMPSD, MOVSD, and SCASD.

There are certainly many other types of operational errors which will produce similar exceptions. Many involve protected-mode operation, but some also pertain to the VM86 mode, supported on the 386 and 486 processors. Some examples are the following:

Load an invalid selector	286+	Protected mode
Segment limit violation	286+	Protected mode
Segment type violation	286+	Protected mode
Privilege violation	386+	VM86/protected mode
Memory protect violation	386+	VM86/protected mode
Page not present	386+	VM86/protected mode

FEATURE:

Exception Handlers

ADVANTAGES:

A debugger that supports exception handling provides a built-in way to detect certain failures as soon as they occur.

CONSEQUENCES:

None (maybe there *is* a free lunch sometimes!)

6.13   THE PERISCOPE TOOLS

To give this discussion of advanced tool features a grounding in reality, this next section will take a quick look at the Periscope line of debugging tools. Periscope, produced by The Periscope Company, Inc., was chosen because, in its various models and configurations, it supports most of the features examined in the previous sections. It is well suited for debugging application programs, TSR utilities, device drivers, and even operating systems.

Here are some of the features it provides:

- User-customizable window interface
- Keyboard emulation of Codeview or Turbo Debugger
- On-line help
- Command recall and editing
- Macro keys
- Symbolic debugging
- Source-level debugging
- Hardware debugging registers in 386 and 486 systems
- Remote/ host debugging
- Remote-console debugging
- Software backtrace buffer
- Hardware-assisted debugging support

Periscope Models

Model I   The Model I system includes a protected memory board, the Periscope software, and optional breakout switch. The board can support up to 1M of RAM and requires a 32K footprint between 640K and the 1M boundary.

The card can be made to look like a ROM chip on an adapter card (as with the ROM on a display adapter or disk controller). This allows you to pop up Periscope and debug the ROM BIOS bootup process. This is also known as the POST time, for Power-On Self-Test.

Model II With this model you get a breakout switch and the Periscope software. The breakout switch connects to a motherboard edge connector and can be used with an already-occupied slot.

Model II-X The Periscope software, with no breakout switch, makes up this model.

Model IV The most capable, complex, and expensive, this model includes the software, a breakout switch, and an adapter card with a high-speed real-time trace buffer and sophisticated hardware breakpoint capabilities, including multilevel triggering (a state machine). The adapter card intercepts the CPU through a pod and works with 80286, 80386DX, 80386SX, and 80486DX systems at speeds up to 33 Mhz.

Periscope/EM The /EM feature enables Periscope to load into extended memory, providing that a suitable memory management utility is used. For systems with extended memory, this model can provide a functional equivalent to the protected memory board of Model I without any extra hardware investment.

6.14 PERISCOPE'S SOFTWARE BREAKPOINTS

One of the most important capabilities a debugger can have is the ability to manage breakpoints. DEBUG.COM, the debugging tool supplied with DOS, supports only temporary breakpoints. Issuing the command G 1234 results in a breakpoint instruction being placed at offset 1234 within the current code segment. When the break occurs at this offset, DEBUG replaces the original opcode. This is termed as a temporary breakpoint, since the original instruction is restored and then left alone from then on.

In Periscope, temporary breakpoints of this type are supported along with a new type known as sticky breakpoints (see Chapter 5). The BC command is used to set sticky breakpoints at selected positions within an application's code. Once one or more sticky breakpoints have been set, you can simply enter a G command directly. When a break occurs, the original opcode is replaced automatically so that the disassembly display makes sense. However, as soon as you issue another go command, all active sticky breakpoints are automatically reasserted.

One place a tool like Periscope really shines is in its ability to handle complex breakpoints. The following list summarizes the breakpoints available within the software version of this tool.

BA   Displays current breakpoint settings. Can also be used to clear all software breakpoints or to enable or disable them.

BB   Break when a specified byte of memory meets test conditions.

BC   Break on a specified point of execution.

BF   Break on a certain flags condition.

BI   Break on a specified interrupt.

BL   Break on a specified line (for source level debugging).

BM   Break when a specified range of memory is read, written, or executed.

BP   Break when a specified range of I/O ports will be read or written.

BR   Break when a specified register meets test conditions.

BU   Break when user written code detects desired conditions.

BW   Break when a specified word of memory meets test conditions.

BX   Break on procedure exit (when a RET, RETF, or IRET is executed).

Periscope also supports additional forms of the go command, GA, GT, and GM, which are used in conjunction with the foregoing breakpoints. The GT command, short for Go Trace, causes Periscope to check for a breakpoint match after each single step. Single-stepping is automatically continued until a match occurs. It's as if a robot is operating the keyboard, entering T commands until certain conditions are met. This is one form of evaluative single-stepping.

This single-stepping method affords great flexibility in the choice of break conditions. But due to the added overhead of the hundreds or even thousands of debugger instructions that must be executed for each actual program instruction, a significant slowdown of the process under test will occur. In certain cases, such as telecommunications or other real-time event processing, this slowdown could easily be prohibitive.

The GA command, short for Go All, is similar to GT, except that it traces into all interrupt calls. If breakpoints you've set are not occurring and you suspect that they may be within an interrupt handler, try the GA command. As you'd expect, the slowdown factor with GA is even greater than with GT. Note also that the GT command does allow for selective interrupt tracing through a /T option.

Each time Periscope traces an instruction with its T or J commands, or when evaluative single-stepping is done with one of the enhanced go commands, a record of the machine state is deposited in the software backtrace buffer. This record may be reviewed on-line or sent to a printer for further analysis.

Periscope's J command jumps around calls. It is equivalent to DEBUG's P command.

The third and final form of enhanced go command is the GM command. GM stands for Go Monitor and must be used in conjunction with *monitor breakpoints*. Monitor breakpoints are all those listed previously except the BA and BC types. The use of GM also requires that one or more sticky code breakpoints be set. GM does essentially the same thing as GT, except that it only tests for a match with monitor breakpoints on each sticky code breakpoint.

6.15 A SOFTWARE BREAKPOINT CASE STUDY

Considering the variety of monitor breakpoints supported, and considering that the time of evaluation may be controlled through the selection of one or more sticky code breakpoints, rather complex test conditions may be established. For example, consider the case where you know that the point within a program you wish to reach follows the opening of a certain file using function 3D of INT21.

To set a sticky breakpoint on calls to interrupt 21, the DOS system call interface, the following shorthand notation may be used:

```
bc {0:21*4}
```

The curly braces mean "use the contents of memory addressed by the far pointer within the braces." In other words, read the INT21 interrupt vector and set a sticky code breakpoint at the address to which it points.

Now, rather than simply issuing go commands until you reach the particular 3D call you're interested in, you could issue the following commands:

```
br ah eq 3d
gm
```

Internally, Periscope will break on each INT21 call and test for a value of 3D in the AH register. Each time the evaluation condition is satisfied and control is returned to the console, you can determine which file is being opened by dumping the filespec pointed to by the DS:DX register pair.

The DZ command, one of many dump commands, displays data in ASCIIZ string format:

```
dz ds:dx
```

One obvious result of using GM is that overall program execution can occur at a much faster rate than with GA or GT. In addition, the information obtained can be tailored to your needs. Manually tracing through program code using the T, J, and G commands while continually evaluating program conditions can be very tiring—a form of information overload.

If very many 3D calls must be stepped through before the one you are interested in, you can join these commands together on one line by using the semicolon character:

```
gm ; dz ds:dx
```

Each time this pair of commands doesn't produce the results you're looking for, simply press F4 to cause the last command to be repeated.

6.16 PERISCOPE'S HARDWARE BREAKPOINTS

As mentioned above, Periscope does support the use of the debug registers built into 386 and 486 CPUs. The following list shows this command along with the hardware breakpoint commands for the Model IV hardware-assisted debugging system.

BD Break using the 386/486 debug registers.
HC Used to control the breakpoint hardware (Model IV).
HD Break when a certain data value is accessed (Model IV).
HM Break when a certain memory address is used (Model IV).
HP Break when a certain I/O port is accessed (Model IV).

The HC command controls various aspects of Model IV hardware breakpoint operation. It provides subcommands to do the following:

- Apply a pass count to breakpoint events
- Gate buffer capture on and off
- Activate a cycle-counting feature
- Cause a breakpoint to occur when the trace buffer fills
- Enable triggering from an external probe input
- Enable selective capture, so only events that cause a break are recorded in the trace buffer
- Assign the trigger location as buffer top, center, or bottom
- Exclude certain trigger levels from trace buffer recording

For the HD, HM, and HP breakpoints, up to eight of each type can be defined at any one time; they can all be used with the multi-level trigger feature; and ranges can be used for each. For example, the following generates a breakpoint when an input or output is done to any of the port addresses in the 03F8 to 03FF range:

```
hp 03f8 03ff i
hp 03f8 03ff o
```

The go command used to activate hardware breakpoints is GH. Note that any active software breakpoints will also be effective when this form of the go instruction is used. Furthermore, when a software breakpoint is taken, the hardware trace buffer will hold a valid chronology, just as in the case where a hardware-generated breakpoint was taken. The hardware trace buffer holds 16K of bus states (actually, different boards are available, with 2K, 4K, and 16K trace buffers).

The HR, HU, and HT allow the hardware trace buffer to be examined in raw, unassemble, and trace mode respectively. Additional features provide for the filtering of trace buffer information, searching for specific types of operations, and counting CPU cycles between selected points.

6.17   A HARDWARE BREAKPOINT CASE STUDY

In this section, we will examine how Periscope's Model IV hardware can be used to deal with a stray-bullet type of problem. What is required is to identify the memory area that is being crashed and then identify all points within the program that are supposed to be able to write to that area.

When the memory being crashed holds program code, identifying the points that are supposed to write to that area should be easy: There shouldn't be any unless the program uses self-modifying code, overlays, or other code-swapping techniques. To add a twist to the example to be studied, it will involve the case where an aberrant write is randomly being done to what is actually a read/write memory buffer.

Listing 6-6 shows a conjured-up test program, TRAP.ASM. This program contains a data buffer named BUF, a subprocedure named FUNCTION_X, that writes to the data buffer, and a main section of code after the label BEGIN.

When the keyboard input loop of the main section detects that the x key has been pressed, a call to FUNCTION_X will be made. When the y key is pressed, an instruction is executed that also writes to the buffer. This second instruction is the "random" offender—our conjured-up bug.

Our goal, then, is to set up breakpoint conditions so that a break will occur on the first write to BUF that occurs outside of the code of FUNCTION_X. To accomplish this, Periscope's hardware breakpoints and its state machine will be employed.

The normal resting state value of its state machine is #0. To handle this type of case, state #1 will be used to identify the times when writes to BUF should not cause a break. Breakpoint statements will be designed such that state #1 is established whenever code is executing that should be permitted to write to BUF.

In some cases, it is possible to set a breakpoint on the execution of an instruction at the beginning of a function to establish state #1. Likewise, an execution breakpoint would be set on an instruction at the end of a function to cause a return back to state #0.

```
_TEXT    segment para public 'CODE'
         assume  cs:_TEXT,ds_TEXT
         org     0100H
start:
         jmp     begin

buflen   equ     100
buf      db      buflen dup(0)

function_x:
         push    dx
         mov     dx,200h              ; signal ps iv
         out     dx,al
         pop     dx
         cld
         mov     ax,cs
         mov     es,ax
         mov     cx,buflen
         mov     di,offset buf
         mov     al,'a'
         rep     stosb                ; normal buffer write
         push    dx
         mov     dx,201h              ; signal ps iv
         out     dx,al
         pop     dx
         ret

begin:
         mov     ah,1
         int     16h
         jz      begin
         mov     ah,0
         int     16h
         cmp     al,'x'
         jne     t1
         call    function_x           ; normal buffer write
         jmp     begin
t1:
         cmp     al,'y'
         jne     t2
         mov     byte ptr [buf+1],2   ; crash buffer
         jmp     begin
t2:
         mov     ax,4c00h
         int     21h
_TEXT    ends
         end     start
```

LISTING 6-6 TRAP.ASM, used to exercise Periscope Model IV.

There is a problem, however, with this approach, given the structure of the sample program and the 386's pipelining execution feature. This is that the last instructions within FUNCTION_X will have already been executed before the normal memory operation is done from the REP STOSB instruction. Our breakpoint would be triggered falsely.

To circumvent this problem, the program was modified to contain output instructions to address ports 200h and 201h, thus giving us something on which to trigger. When making use of this method, be sure to select I/O ports that are known to be unused. Alternatively, writing to memory at segment F000 can also be used as a trigger event.

Here are the Periscope commands to be used:

```
hp 200 o (0,1)
hp 201 o (1,0)
hm buf 164 w (0,!)
gh
```

The first statement says, "When an output to port 200h is detected, change the state machine from state #0 to state #1." The second statement will cause a transition back to state #0 when the output to port 201h is done. The third statement says, "Break when a write is done to BUF and the current state is #0." The GH command activates the hardware breakpoint functions and begins full-speed execution of the program.

If you were to set up this example, you would find that pressing the x key would not cause a break into Periscope but that pressing the y key would. Once the break occurs, the HT command can be used to review the contents of the hardware trace buffer, allowing you to determine the cause of the aberrant memory write.

CHAPTER 7
The Companion Toolset

7.1 USE OF THE COMPANION TOOLSET

This book's Companion Toolset consists of tools that primarily support the instrumentation method of debugging. With a little creativity, these tools can also be used to supplement a debugger in numerous situations. With that said, let's get right to the introductions. This chapter will cover the following:

- Instrumentation logic for direct inclusion within a program
- The ROUTER.SYS instrumentation driver
- The calling macros and functions used to communicate with ROUTER.SYS
- The CHANNEL.EXE data capture utility

The code for the direct inclusion instrumentation logic is printed in Appendices G and I through N in addition to being included on the Companion Toolset Diskette. Regarding the other tools, they are available only on the diskette. The Companion Diskette also contains design notes, the debugging tool program library, and a set of program templates. Source code is provided for all tools and the program library so that you can adapt them to suit your specific needs. The next chapter will delve into these goodies.

There are a number of possible output destinations for the output produced by instrumentation code, each with its own particular advantages and tradeoffs:

- A Packetized Ring Buffer (PRB)
- Direct video
- A serial port to which an ASCII terminal is connected
- A parallel port to which a printer is connected

- A high-speed binary serial link to second machine
- A high-speed binary parallel link to second machine

A ring buffer is an excellent storage medium for debugging data, because it is fast and can hold a large amount of data. But using a ring buffer within the target system is next to worthless when the failure you are chasing causes the system to lock up, reboot itself, or crash in some other manner.

As you will see, there are ways to get your valuable debugging information off of the target system so that it can be stored in a ring buffer in a second computer. This approach is beneficial for another reason as well: With the memory requirements for the ring buffer moved from the target to the remote system, it is practical to use a larger buffer.

Writing directly to a video display adapter's memory is another very fast way to make debugging information available for inspection. Some drawbacks inherent in this method include limits on the number of characters which can be viewed at once (2000 for an 80 × 25 display), vulnerability to overwrite by a program's normal display activity, and vulnerability to overwrite when a program crashes. The use of a second video display adapter and monitor can help with the second of these three concerns and will be of benefit with the third issue in many cases.

Shipping instrumentation data out through a serial port to where it will be displayed on a dumb ASCII terminal avoids video collisions with the main display output of the program, but it is still limited to 2000 characters for an 80 × 25 display. Most terminals will operate at a maximum baud rate of 38,400. This will suffice for many situations, but it may be too much like treading through molasses when a heavy amount of data output is involved.

The use of a printer as a destination for debugging information is a study in extremes—extremely high data storage, limited only by available paper, but the low data throughput will make this a choice for only the more casual debugging situations.

Connecting a special null-modem type of serial cable between two computers to facilitate the transport of debugging information opens up a whole new world of possibilities. Moving debugging data off the target system as soon as possible is highly valuable when dealing with a crash that blanks the screen and hard-locks the machine. With a baud rate of 115,200, the throughput load on the program under test is reasonably light.

An even faster way to move your debugging data to a second computer is to connect a parallel version of a null-modem cable between them. In this case, as in the high-speed serial link case, the CHANNEL.EXE data capture utility would be used within the second computer to gather the data and route it to the selected destination. The construction of the special cables needed for the serial and parallel binary links is covered in Appendix F.

For the case where instrumentation code is included directly within the program being debugged, Figure 7.1 depicts the routing alternatives for the resulting instrumentation output. Note that only one of these routes would typically be used in a given situation.

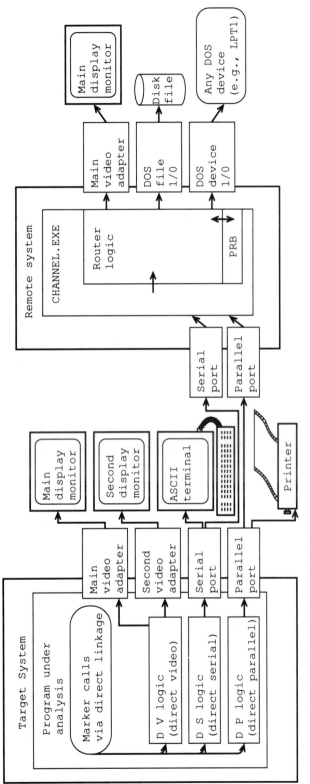

FIGURE 7.1 Routing in the direct inclusion case.

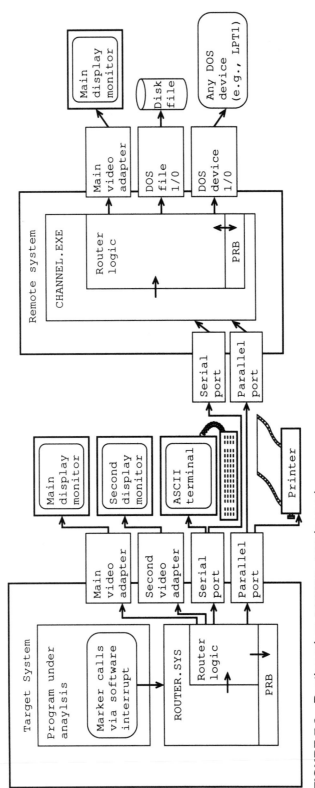

FIGURE 7.2 Routing when ROUTER.SYS is used.

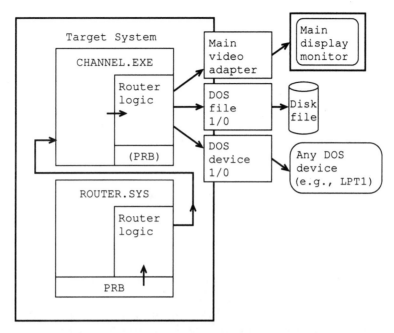

FIGURE 7.3 Using CHANNEL.EXE to fetch PRB data.

Figure 7.2 illustrates how this data routing landscape changes when the ROUTER.SYS instrumentation driver is used. In this case, software interrupt calls are embedded into the program under analysis, and the logic within ROUTER.SYS takes care of processing the raw data from the program and transmitting it to the desired destination. One important difference with the use of ROUTER.SYS is that the PRB (Packetized Ring Buffer) becomes available as a destination.

In these first two configurations (as represented by Figures 7.1 and 7.2), the mission of the CHANNEL.EXE utility is to pick up debugging information sent across a high-speed binary link to a second computer and display it on the screen, write it to a file, or output it to any DOS device, such as LPT1. Intermediate storage within a ring buffer (PRB) is also a possibility.

If the ROUTER.SYS driver is used in the target system to store debugging data within its ring buffer, how is that information retrieved? The CHANNEL.EXE utility is designed to fulfill this need in addition to its capabilities as a remote capture tool. Figure 7.3 shows how this works.

There are certainly other tools included on the Companion Toolset Diskette. One of these is the DDICEPT.SYS intercept driver. Since this driver must be configured through reassembly, detailed discussion of it is left for the next chapter. However, a set of ready-made versions of this driver are included on the diskette:

DDICEPT.10   To report on INT10 system calls for video output
DDICEPT.13   To report on INT13 system calls for disk I/O
DDICEPT.17   To report on INT17 system calls for printer I/O
DDICEPT.21   To report on INT21 system calls for DOS services

With this intercept driver, it is also possible to build a version that will monitor multiple interrupt calls. A driver such as this can also be a good place to install custom test code, such as instrumentation that watches for a certain sequence of interrupt calls and invokes a breakpoint when that sequence is detected.

7.2 GENERAL INSTRUMENTATION MACROS AND FUNCTIONS

Using macros for instrumentation makes life easier. Even in a high-level language, where a call could be made to a debugging function in one line, macros can still be useful. Listing 7-1 shows how the define statement of C can be used to create a macro that simplifies the task of adding instrumentation.

Rather than enter an unwieldy printf() statement at each point where you require information be dumped, simply enter a line such as the one that follows. This type of convenience helps you to stay more focused on your debugging analysis.

```
shid(widget_count);
```

(When a # symbol precedes a macro argument, it causes the parameter of that argument to be treated as a string.) The output produced would be the following:

```
widget_count = 25
```

The use of macros also makes it easy to incorporate conditional compilation controls into your instrumentation. It can often happen that you will need or want to deactivate all instrumentation temporarily for testing purposes. It's much easier to change one conditional compilation control variable than it is to locate each piece of debugging code and comment it out.

The SHMACS.H file on the Companion Toolset Diskette contains a set of instrumentation macros such as this one. A copy of these macros is also

```
#ifdef debug
#define shid(x)  printf(#x " = %d\n",x)
#else
#define shid(x)
#endif
```

LISTING 7-1   The SHID (SHow Integer in Decimal format) macro.

printed in Appendix G, "Printf Macros." These macros will simplify the reporting of the following:

- The source module name and line number
- An immediate message string (e.g., "at point A")
- A character variable's name and value
- A string variable's name and value
- A byte variable's name and value (unsigned char), displayed in hex or decimal format
- A word variable's name and value (unsigned integer), displayed in hex or decimal format
- A dword variable's name and value (union of 2 words), displayed in seg:ofs or longint format

Designing Assembler Macros

When developing instrumentation macros in assembly language one must consider more details. First, debugging macros should make no presumptions as to the state of the CPU registers (except that SS:SP points to a valid stack) and should not change any registers or memory locations unless done as a specific part of the macro's design. Second, such macros should not make use of any BIOS or operating system services to produce its output. Reentrancy problems could occur, causing additional buggy behavior.

Listing 7-2 presents a small assembler program containing a macro called dv_chari (Dump to Video, CHARacter Immediate). This macro is designed to display a single character by writing directly to the video display adapter's memory buffer. Since no provisions are included for scrolling the display, this simplistic type of tool can be used only where the amount of information required is small.

In the program mock-up shown in Listing 7-2, four instrumentation markers have been implanted in the main section. It can be helpful to make your debugging code stand out by indenting it differently from the normal program code.

If the program runs without error, the letters abcd will appear on the screen. If the setup function returns a carry flag, the letters ad would appear. The reason for the dv_chari c line is to provide confirmation that a normal return is made from the process function.

Note that this type of macro cannot presume that either the DS or ES register holds anything meaningful. For this reason, all accesses to the [vidseg] and [vidofs] memory variables are coded using an explicit CS override. The placement of data within a code segment is possible and even common in real-mode assembler debugging code. Should this type of code need to be adapted to an environment where code and data cannot be mixed, arrangements would have to be made for access to a data segment where the video pointer is stored.

```
_TEXT     segment para public 'CODE'
          assume  cs:_TEXT,ds:_TEXT,es:_TEXT,ss:_TEXT
          org     0100H
start:
          jmp     begin

debug     equ     01

if debug eq 1
vidptr    label   dword
vidseg    equ     0b800h     ; change to 0b000h for monochrome
vidofs    dw      0
endif

dv_chari macro    p1
if debug eq 1
          pushf
          push    ax
          push    di
          push    es
          les     di,cs:[vidptr]
          cld
          mov     ah,7
          mov     al,'&p1&'
          stosw
          mov     cs:[vidofs],di
          pop     es
          pop     di
          pop     ax
          popf
endif
          endm


;==== main section of program


begin:

    dv_chari a

          call    setup
          jc      bad_setup
```

LISTING 7-2 An assembler macro.

```
        dv_chari b

            call    process

        dv_chari c

bad_setup:

        dv_chari d

            mov     ax,4c00h
            int     21h

_TEXT   ends
        end     start
```

LISTING 7-2 *(Continued)*

An example of such a situation would be where one common block of code is used by multiple program threads, where each thread uses its own data segment. If the debugging data in question needs to be thread-specific, a copy of the data would need to be allocated in each thread's data segment. You would then either have to design your macros to expect a certain segment register to hold the required value, or include code within the macro to establish the necessary segment register value.

Since most programs make extensive use of the display screen themselves, this type of direct video output can often result in conflicts. Your debugging code will just have sent important information to the screen when it is overwritten by the normal display output activities of the program you are analyzing.

One way around this problem is to install a second video display and monitor in your system. For example, if your main console is of the CGA, EGA, or VGA type, you can install a simple monochrome card and monitor to be used for debugging output. To adapt the program in Listing 7-2 for this, simply change the initial value for the [vidseg] variable from 0B800h to 0B000h.

It is not uncommon to embed dozens of instrumentation markers throughout a program when chasing a bug. An additional limitation to this simplistic type of macro is that each one expands to a significant amount of code. The larger each macro is, the more likely that a large enough change in code position will occur to cause your bug to behave in a different manner.

Listing 7-3 presents a version of this instrumentation technique where the code within the body of the macro makes a call to a common dumping

```
if debug eq 1
char2vid:
        push    di
        push    es
        les     di,cs:[vidptr]
        cld
        mov     ah,7
        stosw
        mov     cs:[vidofs],di
        pop     es
        pop     di
        ret
endif


dv_chari macro  p1
if debug eq 1
        pushf
        push    ax
        mov     al,'&p1&'
        call    char2vid
        pop     ax
        popf
endif
        endm
```

LISTING 7-3   Reducing the in-line code with a common function.

function named char2vid, thus reducing the amount of code for each macro
expansion. Note that this common function is controlled by the same conditional assembly directive as is the code within the macro.

At this point, an additional refinement is in order. We need to be able
to fill the screen with information and then have scrolling occur rather than
let the offset portion of the video pointer run away. Listing 7-4 presents an
expanded version of char2vid that scrolls the screen and also responds to
the carriage return and linefeed control characters.

Listing 7-4 also contains a new function called vid_init, which will use
the current video mode to determine the location of the video display buffer.
A call to this initialization function would be placed in the startup section
of the program being debugged. Note that when a monochrome display is
installed as the dump monitor along with a CGA, EGA, or VGA main console,
the call must be replaced with an instruction such as mov cs:[vidseg],
0b000h.

```
cols      equ    80                    ; # of cols on display
rows      equ    25                    ; # of rows on display
rowbytes  equ    cols*2                ; bytes per row
scrbytes  equ    rowbytes*rows         ; total bytes in screen

vidptr    label dword
vidofs    dw     0
vidseg    dw     ?


;===========================================================
; vid_init
;
; in:    none
;
; out:   cs:[vidseg] is defined
;
;===========================================================
vid_init:
          push   ax
          push   es
          mov    cs:[vidseg],0b000h
          mov    ax,40h
          mov    es,ax
          cmp    byte ptr es:[49h],7
          je     vs1
          mov    cs:[vidseg],0b800h
vs1:
          pop    es
          pop    ax
          ret


;===========================================================
; char2vid - direct video output with scrolling
;
; in:    al = the character to display (or cr or lf)
;        ah = the attribute (unless al == cr or lf)
;        uses cs:[vidptr] globally
;
; out:   all registers preserved (except flags)
;        [vidofs] updated
;
;===========================================================
```

(continued on next page)

LISTING 7-4 The DV_ASM.INC file, with a more complete direct video logic.

```
char2vid:
        push    ax
        push    di
        push    es
        cmp     al,13
        jne     chv1                    ; if a carriage return
        mov     ax,cs:[vidofs]          ; calc start of row
        push    bx
        push    dx
        xor     dx,dx
        mov     bx,rowbytes
        div     bx
        mul     bx
        pop     dx
        pop     bx
        mov     cs:[vidofs],ax
        jmp     short chv5
chv1:
        cmp     al,10
        jne     chv2                    ; if a linefeed
        add     cs:[vidofs],rowbytes    ; calc next line
        xor     ax,ax
chv2:
        les     di,cs:[vidptr]          ; if vidofs > lim,
        cmp     di,scrbytes             ; scroll the screen
        jb      chv3                    ; and reset [vidofs]
        push    ax
        push    cx
        push    si
        push    ds
        mov     si,es
        mov     ds,si
        mov     si,rowbytes
        xor     di,di
        mov     cx,(scrbytes-rowbytes)/2
        rep     movsw
        mov     di,(scrbytes-rowbytes)
        mov     cx,cols
        mov     al,20h
        mov     ah,7
        rep     stosw
        mov     di,(scrbytes-rowbytes)
        pop     ds
        pop     si
```

LISTING 7-4   *(Continued)*

```
        pop     cx
        pop     ax
chv3:
        or      ax,ax               ; if not linefeed
        jz      chv4                ; display the char
        mov     ah,7
        stosw
chv4:
        mov     cs:[vidofs],di      ; update offset
chv5:
        pop     es
        pop     di
        pop     ax
        ret
```

LISTING 7-4   *(Continued)*

One final issue to be addressed is the conversion of numeric data from a binary form to a displayable form. Listing 7-5 contains a set of functions to display the hexadecimal representation of byte and word values. A pair of calling macros are shown in Listing 7-6. The dv_byte and dv_word macros each expect one parameter: The register or memory location containing the value to be displayed. As shown in the following examples, the form of this parameter can be the same as the operand for the mov al,? or mov ax,? instructions, with one exception:

```
dv_byte dh
dv_byte al
dv_byte 0c4h
dv_byte [total_widgets]
dv_byte <byte ptr es:[17h]>
dv_word si
dv_word es
dv_word 0f2a9h
dv_word [widget_class]
dv_word <word ptr es:[0]>
```

Any parameter composed of more than one term must be surrounded by the < and > characters to cause it to be treated as a single macro parameter. The use of byte ptr and word ptr are the primary cases where this exception will apply. Since it can be easy to forget about this special exception, error-checking logic has been incorporated into these macros. The macro directive .errnb <p2> will generate an assembler error if the macro processor sees a second parameter.

```
;==================================================================
; al2axhex
;
; in:   al = byte to lookup hex chars for
;
; out:  ah = hex char for high nibble of entry al
;       al = hex char for low nibble of entry al
;
;==================================================================

hxtbl    db        '0123456789ABCDEF'

al2axhex:
         push     bx
         push     cx
         mov      cl,al
         xor      ch,ch
         and      ax,000f0h
         shr      ax,1
         shr      ax,1
         shr      ax,1
         shr      ax,1
         mov      bx,ax
         mov      ah,cs:[hxtbl+bx]
         and      cx,0000fh
         mov      bx,cx
         mov      al,cs:[hxtbl+bx]
         pop      cx
         pop      bx
         ret

;==================================================================
; bw2v_helper
;
; in:   al = byte to convert and display
;
; out:  none
;
;==================================================================
bw2v_helper:
         push     ax
         call     al2axhex
```

LISTING 7-5   Hex conversion code, to be added to DV_ASM.INC.

```
        push    ax
        mov     al,ah
        mov     ah,7
        call    char2vid
        pop     ax
        mov     ah,7
        call    char2vid
        pop     ax
        ret

;===========================================================
; byte2vid
;
; in:   al = byte to convert and display
;
; out:  none
;
;===========================================================
byte2vid:
        call    bw2v_helper
        push    ax
        mov     al,' '
        mov     ah,7
        call    char2vid
        pop     ax
        ret

;===========================================================
; word2vid
;
; in:   ax = word to convert and display
;
; out:  none
;
;===========================================================
word2vid:
        xchg    ah,al
        call    bw2v_helper
        xchg    ah,al
        call    byte2vid
        ret
```

LISTING 7-5   *(Continued)*

```
dv_byte macro p1,p2
if debug eq 1
.errnb <p2>
        pushf
        push    ax
        mov     al,p1
        call    byte2vid
        pop     ax
        popf
endif
        endm

dv_word macro p1,p2
if debug eq 1
.errnb <p2>
        pushf
        push    ax
        mov     ax,p1
        call    word2vid
        pop     ax
        popf
endif
        endm
```

LISTING 7-6 Macros for hex conversion code.

Installing the Assembler Instrumentation Code

The Companion Toolset Diskette includes a file named DV_ASM.INC, which contains a more complete rendition of the code in Listings 7-4, 7-5, and 7-6. Also included are the DS_ASM.INC file for direct serial port output and DP_ASM.INC for direct parallel port output. The C versions for each of these files are DV_C.H and DV_C.INC; DS_C.H and DS_C.INC; and DP_C.H and DP_C.INC. These files also appear in print in Appendices I through N.

The placement of the include statement within the program being debugged does require some attention. Since these files contain live code and data in addition to macros, the include statement must appear in a position within the program where live code and data are appropriate. In addition, any SET statements (for assembler) or #define statements (for C) required to cause the instrumentation code to be activated must appear before the include statement.

Also included with the Companion Toolset is a set of text files, which contain the statements needed for each of the .INC and .H files containing instrumentation code. These text files are also printed in the aforementioned

TABLE 7.1 General instrumentation files and associated text files

Instrumentation Code File	Text File Containing Include Instructions
DV_ASM.INC	DV_ASM.TXT
DS_ASM.INC	DS_ASM.TXT
DP_ASM.INC	DP_ASM.TXT
DV_C.H & DV_C.INC	DV_C.TXT
DS_C.H & DS_C.INC	DS_C.TXT
DP_C.H & DP_C.INC	DP_C.TXT

appendices. Table 7.1 shows the name of the text file corresponding to each instrumentation code file. To make use of one of these files, use your editor to read its contents into the source code module to which you are applying instrumentation.

In the sample assembler program in Listing 7-7, the contents of the DV_ASM.TXT file have been merged into the program's source code module just after the first jump instruction. This way, the instrumentation macros can be used within any of the program's functions as well as within the main section of program code.

It is important to note that the assembler include files contain no assume directives to control segment register use. All segment register use must be controlled by direct specification using segment override prefixes. Since this type of include file must be placed within a "live" code position within a source module, the existence of any assume directives could affect the segment register usage of code within the source module after the include statement.

The use of these instrumentation include files requires certain initialization steps. In the direct video case (DV_ASM.INC) the segment of the video buffer must be assigned in one of two different ways. The vid_init function within the include file can be called from within the start-up section of the program being debugged. This will automatically cause the main console display buffer to be used. If you wish to have instrumentation output directed to an alternate display, define the appropriate segment address with the dv_addr variable and do not call the vid_init function.

In the case of direct serial port output, the ds_addr variable must be assigned the address of the serial port to be used, and a call to the ser_init function must be made one time within the program's startup code. This function expects the divisor for the baud rate as an entry parameter. This initialization call must, of course, be made before any instrumentation calls are made that would attempt output to the port.

To initialize the direct-to-parallel instrumentation tooling, the dp_addr variable must be assigned the appropriate parallel port base address. There is no need for an initialization function.

```
_TEXT    segment para public 'CODE'
         assume  cs:_TEXT,ds:_TEXT,es:_TEXT,ss:_TEXT
         org     0100H
start:
         jmp     begin

;$$$$$$$$$$$$$$$$$$$$$$$$$$$$$$$$$$$$$$$$ from dv_asm.txt $$$$$
if1
%out !!!!!!!!!!!!!!!!!!!!!!!!!!!!!!!!!!!!!!!!!!!!!!
%out !!!!!!!!!!!!!! dv_asm.inc included !!!!!!!!!!
%out !!!!!!!!!!!!!!!!!!!!!!!!!!!!!!!!!!!!!!!!!!!!!!
endif

; minimum setup requirements:
; the segment of the display buffer must be initialized
; either by calling the vid_init function or by using the
; dv_addr variable.

dv_active = 01
dv_cli    = 01
;dv_addr  = 0b800h

include c:\xtools\dv_asm.inc
;$$$$$$$$$$$$$$$$$$$$$$$$$$$$$$$$$$$$$$$$ from dv_asm.txt $$$$$


        ... program data and functions ...


;==== main section of program

begin:
         call vid_init


        ... main program code ...


         mov     ax,4c00h              ; terminate
         int     21h
_TEXT    ends
         end     start
```

LISTING 7-7 Locating the `include` statement.

Some enhancements you might wish to add to the direct video logic would be functions and corresponding macros to clear the screen and support the addressing of specific portions of the screen (kind of like a set-cursor-location function, but the cursor never moves in this case). Given an 80-column by 25-line display and zero-based X and Y coordinates (where location 0,0 is in the upper left corner) the following formula will produce the offset to be used when writing to the video display buffer:

$$\text{Video offset } = (X * 2) + (Y * 160)$$

Installing the C Instrumentation Code

To install the C instrumentation functions, merge the corresponding text file (DV_C.TXT, DS_C.TXT, or DP_C.TXT) into the source code module you are working with. A copy of one of these files, for the direct video code, is shown in Listing 7-8.

The first section, which ultimately includes the DV_C.H header file, should be located near the top of the C program being instrumented. The second section, which contains the include statement for the DV_C.INC file, may need to be relocated depending on your program's structure. The DV_C.INC file contains the code and data for the instrumentation functions and must, therefore, be positioned where it will compile correctly.

Configuring the C Functions as Stand-Alone

It is possible to use the functions within the C files as precompiled code within an .OBJ module. These modules can then be specified to the linker within

```
/*$$$$$$$$$$$$$$$$$$$$$$$$$$$$$$$$$$$$$$$$$$ from dv_c.txt $$$$$*/

#define dv_active 01
#define dv_access static
#include "c:\xtools\dv_c.h"

/*$$$$$$$$$$$$$$$$$$$$$$$$$$$$$$$$$$$$$$$$$$ from dv_c.txt $$$$$*/

/*$$$$$$$$$$$$$$$$$$$$$$$$$$$$$$$$$$$$$$$$$$ from dv_c.txt $$$$$*/

#include "c:\xtools\dv_c.inc"

/*$$$$$$$$$$$$$$$$$$$$$$$$$$$$$$$$$$$$$$$$$$ from dv_c.txt $$$$$*/
```

LISTING 7-8   The DV_C.TXT file.

your program development environment, added to your project's make file, added to an existing library module, or placed in a new library module.

To produce a precompiled .OBJ module, do the following:

1. Copy the D?_C.INC file to a new file named D?_STAND.C (where the ? character represents a V for the DV_C.INC case, an S for DS_C.INC, or a P for DP_C.INC).
2. Load this new file, D?_STAND.C, into your programming editor.
3. Delete the word static in the line that reads:

   ```
   #define d?_access static
   ```

4. Save the file and exit your editor.
5. Use your compiler to produce an .OBJ module. With Borland's BCC.EXE version 2.00 (their command line C++/C compiler), enter the following:

   ```
   bcc -c d?_stand.c
   ```

From this point, to use these instrumentation functions within a program, you would read in the contents of the D?_C.TXT file but delete the second section.

IRQ Handlers

The first rule is that when any markers are placed where they could be executed as part of an IRQ handler's processing, all markers within the module must be protected from interruption. This applies to all markers that can be called from within IRQ handlers as well as those encoded into the main flow of the program logic.

The reasons for this are as follows:

1. Instrumentation data could be lost.
2. Your desired display order for groups of markers could be subverted, making it confusing to interpret the output.

To understand the first reason more clearly, consider what would happen if an interrupt were to occur during the middle of an output to a parallel port by a marker macro. This type of output operation requires that the data value be written to the port and then that the strobe signal be toggled to cause the receiving device to take notice. If a marker executing from within the main flow of the program logic has just written its data to the port but is interrupted before the strobe can be toggled, and if the interrupt handler does its own output to this same port, the first data will be overwritten. In fact, the data byte written to the port by the interrupt process would be strobed twice.

Regarding the second reason in the foregoing list, when you are using instrumentation to dump data values, it is often helpful to precede each data dump with a marker letter to help you identify each piece of data at analysis time. If this is being done by portions of a program which can interrupt each other, the marker output can become interlaced. To avoid this problem, interrupts would need to be disabled around each set of marker calls.

Care must be taken when adding interrupt control statements to a program. If you know for sure that interrupts will always be enabled when the section of code containing your multiple-marker sequence will be executed, the following approach would be safe:

```
cli
dv_chari a
dv_byte [total_widgets]
sti
```

But if the code in this section of the program could sometimes be entered with interrupts already disabled, the addition of an sti instruction would introduce a dangerous change. To be safe in all cases, an instruction sequence such as the following should be used:

```
pushf
cli
dv_chari a
dv_byte [total_widgets]
popf
```

When interrupts are being disabled, it is important to use the fastest possible type of instrumentation. The use of a slower destination device, such as a printer or serial terminal, may cause interrupt loss problems. Your fastest choices are direct video, a ring buffer, and a parallel link to a second computer. A serial link to a second computer, running at a baud rate of 115,200, will work in many cases.

7.3 ROUTER.SYS

The ROUTER.SYS device driver provides a variety of instrumentation support functions within one concise package. It is installed within a system just like any other device driver: Through the use of a device= statement within the CONFIG.SYS file. Here is a sample line:

```
device=c:\xtools\execute\router.sys /vi /cc=m /ss
```

The primary function of the router logic is to accept data dump request calls and route the dump output to specified destinations, translating binary data to a text format when necessary. A number of testing and control functions are also supported. Switch parameters are used to designate how debugging data is to be routed. See Appendix O, "Switch Parameters for ROUTER.SYS," for a summary of these switches.

The router logic is a group of functions that are incorporated into the ROUTER.SYS device driver. The CHANNEL.EXE data capture utility also makes use of them. This group of functions could also be used within other debugging tools, since they are included within the program development library on the Companion Toolset Diskette. The next chapter will cover the use of the program development library in more detail. In the following descriptions of the features of this router logic, the context of ROUTER.SYS is assumed.

The device driver format was chosen so that the services this tool provides could be made available to other device drivers (e.g., if you are developing a device driver). Being resident in memory from boot time, this tool's services are also, of course, available for use by application programs. If you wish, you could convert ROUTER.SYS to a TSR format and make it able to be un-installed when it is no longer needed.

When instrumentation-processing functions are located within a device driver, it becomes practical to support many features that wouldn't be practical to encode directly within a program. But more features do mean a larger amount of code. In many cases, therefore, it is better to use the direct inclusion method when working with IRQ handlers. See the discussion of DV_ASM.INC, and related include files, in the previous section.

With the majority of the instrumentation code installed as a device driver, all that must be included within the program being instrumented are calls to this driver. The desired function and appropriate data are supplied as parameters to the call. A software interrupt vector is used as the method of communication, so any high-level language that supports interrupt calls can make use of this driver.

The INTFF vector is the default vector for ROUTER.SYS's calling interface. Should this conflict with interrupt vector use by some other driver, TSR utility, or application, it may be changed. See the file DESNOTES.TXT in the Companion Toolset for details.

Output Destinations

Instrumentation dumps can be directed to any of the destinations described in this chapter's opening section. Furthermore, once instrumentation calls to ROUTER.SYS have been implanted within a program, the routing applied to the resulting output can be changed by simply editing the ROUTER.SYS parameter line. No changes to the program under test would be required.

It is also possible to specify multiple destinations, but only one of each type of output can be specified. For example, you can direct output to the main video display and to a ring buffer, but you can't dump to the main video display and to an alternate video display. Likewise, you can only use the parallel port dump feature for a printer or for a link to another computer, but not both simultaneously (even when two ports are available).

To restate, only one type of output can be done for each type of device, but output can be routed to multiple devices. You could activate dumping to the main display (direct video) *and* to a serial port, a parallel link, and a ring buffer. A typical case in which using multiple outputs would be helpful is where data is routed to a ring buffer (where there is high data retention) and also to a video display (where you can monitor the dumping in real time and watch for patterns in the marker output).

Types of Processing Functions

ROUTER.SYS provides three different types of function calls through its software-interrupt-vector calling interface:

1. Data conversion and output functions
2. Data-testing functions
3. Driver control functions

The best way to call on this driver for these services is to use the calling macros for assembler or the calling functions for C. The next section details their use, and they are, of course, included in the Companion Toolset.

The types of data supported are the following:

- ASCII character
- Newline
- ASCIIZ string
- Byte
- Word
- Doubleword, seg:ofs format
- Doubleword, longint format
- CPU flags word
- Full CPU register set
- Debug style memory dump (similar output as when DEBUG.COM's D command is used)

Two data-testing functions are provided. For simplicity, these will be referred to by their assembler macro names:

- dr_dwatch
- dr_seqchk

The equivalent C functions for these assembler macros are dr_dwatch() and dr_seqchk(). A typical use of dr_dwatch would be to monitor a certain section of memory for overwrite by a type of bug known as a *stray bullet* (see Section 13.2, "Stray Bullets"). The `dr_seqchk` testing function is used to detect when a certain sequence of events has occurred. Sequence detection can be useful when chasing an intermittent failure (see Section 13.7, "Intermittent Bugs").

The driver control functions provide control over

- The gating of all `ROUTER.SYS` activity
- The gating of each type of output
- Single-stepping of dump output
- Breakpoint invocation

When you are chasing an intermittent problem, where program trace markers and data values are perpetually being recorded in a ring buffer or written to a video display, it is important to be able to gate off all further dump processing when the bug finally does rear up its head. `ROUTER.SYS` supports gating control through a software call as well as through keyboard input.

Other control functions exist to enable and disable specific data output destinations, to dictate when marker output will be single-stepped and to dictate when a breakpoint will be issued. The initial state of many of these control functions can be established through the use of switch parameters. The next section describes how these features can be controlled through the calling interface.

The Control Console

`ROUTER.SYS` supports a control console feature to permit some measure of control over the dumping process.

These control measures include the following:

- Gating of debugging data output/capture
- Single-stepping of data output calls
- Setting of a breakpoint flag for use with a debugger

Two different types of control consoles are supported. The *master control console* refers to the use of certain keys on the target system's keyboard. The *serial control console* refers to the case where the keyboard of an ASCII terminal is used to control the aforementioned operations. The main keyboard would be used as the control console when dump output is being routed to a video display, to a printer, or to a second machine through the binary parallel link. Using a serial terminal's keyboard as the control console is possible only when the serial terminal is already being used to capture marker output.

When the `CHANNEL.EXE` capture utility is being run in a second machine using the binary serial link, it is possible to use the keyboard of that second machine as a control console, just as in the case where a dumb ASCII terminal is used. This is not possible, however, when the binary parallel link is used between two computers. Due to the number of circuits available in the parallel port interface, this is a unidirectional data transfer method, so keyboard feedback from the remote machine back to the host is not possible.

Note that the use of this feature is optional. If you can exert sufficient control over the data collection process by other means, you can leave this feature inactive.

The initial state of the single-stepping feature defaults to free-running mode. A switch parameter is provided (/ss=1) which will make ROUTER.SYS start in single-step mode. This can be helpful when you need immediate pacing control over dump events.

One keystroke combination on the control console is made to set an internal breakpoint flag within ROUTER.SYS. When this flag is set, a breakpoint instruction will be executed if and when an instrumentation service call is made to the router by the application under test. It is up to you, when applying instrumentation to a program, to decide if you want to use this feature and, if so, at what locations you wish breakpoints to be possible.

The Master Control Console

When the main system keyboard is defined as the control console, certain keystroke combinations will be sensed by ROUTER.SYS. If this special use conflicts with the hot keys used within the application being tested or with hot keys used by TSR utilities, you may wish to connect a second computer or a dumb terminal and use the serial control console method.

Following are the master control console keystroke combinations:

Scroll-Lock	Toggle dump gate
RightShift–LeftShift	Toggle between single-step and free-running mode
LeftShift	Advance each single step
Cntrl–LeftShift	Set the internal breakpoint flag

As you can see, your typing habits will need to change somewhat when it comes to entering uppercase characters and symbols where a shift key is required. You must use the right shift key for such operations when single-step dump mode is active, since the left shift key has a new purpose.

When you want to toggle the single-step/free-run mode, press down the right shift key first and then the left one. Otherwise, ROUTER.SYS will see the left shift key down by itself for a moment and do a single step.

The master control console feature is activated through the use of the /CC=M switch parameter.

The Serial Control Console

When a serial terminal or second computer is used as the serial control console, the controlling keystrokes are as follows:

G	Toggle dump gate
T	Toggle between single-step and free-running mode
J	Advance each single step
B	Set the internal breakpoint flag

Note that both the upper- and lowercase version of these characters can be entered. The serial control console feature is activated through the use of the /CC=S switch parameter.

Output Control Gates

ROUTER.SYS has three different types of gates to control its activity. Two gates control overall dumping activity, and individual gates control dumping to each specific type of output destination.

The master gate, also called gate1, defaults to the open state, which means that ROUTER.SYS responds to requests for data output services and to calls to the other testing and control functions. One of the control functions supported enables you to open and close the master gate. When the master gate is closed, only three function calls are recognized:

1. A set-gate1 call (so you can open the gate again)
2. A call to get the size of the PRB
3. A call to read the contents of the PRB

The second and third function calls are used by the CHANNEL.EXE utility.

As will be explained below, the /G1=0 switch parameter can be specified to cause the initial state of the master gate to be closed. This can be useful when you are using direct video dumping to the main display and want display output to occur only when your instrumentation logic determines that conditions are right.

The secondary gate, also referred to as gate2, is the one that can be controlled through a keystroke on a control console. This gate has an open and closed state as well as an active and inactive one. When the control console feature is selected using the /CC switch, the secondary gate feature defaults to the inactive state. This is to allow the master control console to be used in cases where the scroll-lock key is already assigned a purpose by the program being analyzed.

To activate this secondary gate and have it start out in the closed state, the /G2 switch must be included. Using /G2=1 would activate this gate and cause it to start out in its open state. When this gate is active and in its closed state, no data dumping is done. Internal control function calls are still made so that the gate can be opened again when the appropriate key is pressed.

Each output destination has a gate of the third type, which can be opened and closed by software calls to ROUTER.SYS. This is primarily for use by the CHANNEL.EXE utility, but it could also be useful in other cases. For example, you might direct ROUTER.SYS to output to a ring buffer (e.g.,

/PR=2000) as well as to a serial terminal (/SR=03f8,38). When your custom debug code triggers, it can call ROUTER.SYS to close the gate on further output to the ring buffer but let the serial output continue. You can continue to monitor the program's activity but have the current contents of the ring buffer frozen until you are able to use CHANNEL.EXE to retrieve and process the information it holds.

Sample Cases of Switch Parameter Use

Following are a number of sample parameter lines for ROUTER.SYS, with a quick summary for each describing the resulting configuration:

```
device=c:\xtools\execute\ROUTER.SYS /vi
```

- Output to direct video using the main video display and monitor.

```
device=c:\xtools\execute\ROUTER.SYS /vi /cc=m /ss /g2
```

- Output to direct video using the main video display and monitor.
- Use the main keyboard as a control console.
- Activate the single-stepping feature, where the initial state is free-running mode.
- Use the scroll-lock key to control the secondary gate, with this gate initially in the open state.

```
device=c:\xtools\execute\ROUTER.SYS /vs=b000
```

- Output to direct video, writing to the video buffer used by a monochrome display adapter.

```
device=c:\xtools\execute\ROUTER.SYS
        /pp=0378 /cc=m /ss=1 /g2=0
```

- Output to a parallel printer.
- Use the main keyboard as a control console.
- Activate the single-stepping feature, where the initial state is single-step mode.
- Use the scroll-lock key to control the secondary gate, with this gate initially in the closed state.

```
device=c:\xtools\execute\ROUTER.SYS /pb=03bc
```

- Output to the parallel port at port address 03BC using the binary link protocol.
- The special parallel link cable must be used to connect this port to a parallel port in a second computer, where CHANNEL.EXE will be run in its binary parallel link configuration.

```
device=c:\xtools\execute\ROUTER.SYS
        /pr=6000 /vi /cc=m /g2
```

- Allocate a ring buffer of 6000h bytes and activate it as the destination for data dumps.
- Also activate dumping to the main video display adapter.
- Use the main keyboard as a control console.
- Use the scroll-lock key to control the secondary gate, with this gate initially in the open state.

```
device=c:\xtools\execute\ROUTER.SYS /sr=03f8,38
```

- Output to the serial port at port address 03F8, setting this port to a baud rate of 38,400.
- The output data format will be character mode, for use with a dumb ASCII terminal.

```
device=c:\xtools\execute\ROUTER.SYS
        /sr=02f8,19 /cc=s /g2 /ss
```

- Output to the serial port at port address 02F8, setting this port to a baud rate of 19,200.
- The output data format will be character mode, for use with a dumb ASCII terminal.
- Use the serial terminal's keyboard as a control console.
- Use the scroll-lock key to control the secondary gate, with this gate initially in the open state.
- Activate the single-stepping feature, where the initial state is free-running mode.

```
device=c:\xtools\execute\ROUTER.SYS /sb=03f8,11
```

- Output to the serial port at port address 03F8 using the binary link protocol.
- The special serial link cable must be used to connect this port to a serial port in a second computer, where CHANNEL.EXE will be run in its binary serial link configuration.

```
device=c:\xtools\execute\ROUTER.SYS
        /sb=03f8,11 /cc=s /g2 /ss
```

- Output to the serial port at port address 03F8 using the binary link protocol.
- The special serial link cable must be used to connect this port to a serial port in a second computer, where CHANNEL.EXE will be run in its binary serial link configuration.
- CHANNEL.EXE should also be configured to activate the second computer's keyboard as a serial control console.

- Use the scroll-lock key to control the secondary gate, with this gate initially in the open state.
- Activate the single-stepping feature, where the initial state is free-running mode.

7.4 INSTRUMENTATION MACROS AND FUNCTIONS FOR `ROUTER.SYS`

This section will cover the installation of the `ROUTER` assembler macros and C functions into a program as well as guidelines for their effective use. For a complete description of the assembler calling interface, see the comments within the `\XTOOLS\DR_ASM.INC` file. For the C calling interface, see `\XTOOLS\DR_C.INC`. If you are interested in developing a set of `ROUTER`-calling functions for a different language, see the file `DESNOTES.TXT` in the Companion Toolset for relevant considerations.

For the sake of simplicity, this section will discuss the use of the assembler interface macros for `ROUTER`. Unless the text stipulates otherwise, assume that each discussion applies equally to the C interface functions for `ROUTER`. Further, this section is written assuming the typical case, where you do have source code for the program being debugged and will be rebuilding it with instrumentation calls embedded. If source code is unavailable but you do want to use instrumentation, it would be possible to develop a TSR tool containing the macro calls you need and dynamically patch the program to use them.

Installation

As was the case in Section 7.2, the include file for the `ROUTER` macros or functions must be installed at a position where live code can exist. Also as in that previous case, text files are included within the Companion Toolset, which contain the instructions necessary to activate the instrumentation code.

Table 7.2 shows the name of the text file that corresponds to each instrumentation code file. To make use of one of these files, use your editor to read the text file's contents into the source code module to which you are applying instrumentation.

TABLE 7.2 Instrumentation files and associated text files for use with `ROUTER`

Instrumentation Code File	Text File Containing `Include` Instructions
`DR_ASM.INC`	`DR_ASM.TXT`
`DR_C.H` & `DR_C.INC`	`DR_C.TXT`

```
/*$$$$$$$$$$$$$$$$$$$$$$$$$$$$$$$$$$$$ from dr_c.txt $$$$$*/

/* note: if the dos.h header file is not already included,
un-comment the following line. */

/* #include <dos.h> */

#define dr_active 01
#define dr_access static
#include "c:\xtools\dr_c.h"

/*$$$$$$$$$$$$$$$$$$$$$$$$$$$$$$$$$$$$ from dr_c.txt $$$$$*/


/*$$$$$$$$$$$$$$$$$$$$$$$$$$$$$$$$$$$$ from dr_c.txt $$$$$*/

#include "c:\xtools\dr_c.inc"

/*$$$$$$$$$$$$$$$$$$$$$$$$$$$$$$$$$$$$ from dr_c.txt $$$$$*/
```

LISTING 7-9   The DR_C.TXT file.

When you need to use markers in more than one source module of a multimodule program, simply merge a copy of DR_ASM.TXT or DR_C.TXT into each module. As long as the names of these functions will not be made public, duplicate copies can exist without causing the linker to complain about multiple uses of the same procedure name. This is the purpose of the dr_access term within the C debugging functions.

In the C case, the DR_C.TXT file contains two sections. A copy of this file is shown in Listing 7-9. The first section, which ultimately includes the DR_C.H file, should be located near the top of the C program being instrumented. Note that the code within DR_C.INC requires that the DOS.H header file be included for the sake of the INT86X() prototype.

The second section, which contains the include statement for the DR_C.INC file, may need to be relocated depending on your program's structure. The DR_C.INC file contains the code and data for the ROUTER instrumentation functions and must, therefore, be positioned appropriately.

Configuring the C Functions as Stand-Alone

It is possible to use the functions within the DR_C.INC file as precompiled code within an .OBJ module. This module can then be specified to the linker

within your program development environment, added to your project's make file, added to an existing library module, or placed in a new library module.
To produce a precompiled .OBJ module, do the following:

1. Use the DOS COPY command to copy the DR_C.INC file to a new file, named DR_STAND.C.
2. Load this new file, DR_STAND.C, into your programming editor.
3. Uncomment the line that reads

   ```
   /* #include <dos.h> */
   ```

4. Delete the word static in the line that reads

   ```
   #define dr_access static
   ```

5. Save the file and exit your editor.
6. Use your compiler to produce an .OBJ module. With Borland's BCC.EXE version 2.00 (their command line C++/C compiler), enter the following:

   ```
   bcc -c dr_stand.c
   ```

From this point, to use these instrumentation functions within a program, you would read in the contents of the DR_C.TXT file but delete the second section.

ROUTER Instrumentation Usage Notes

Once the include files have been installed, simply place instrumentation calls at strategic locations within the areas of the program you need to analyze. Be careful when placing calls within loops, or you might find yourself flooded with output.

When dumping markers to denote the entrance and exit of a function or interrupt handler, using character pairs such as [and], { and }, or (and) can make the interpretation easier. The < and > characters can be used but won't work directly with the dr_chari macro in the assembler case, since the macro preprocessor regards these characters as having a special meaning. The following code fragment is one work-around for this limitation:

```
push    ax
mov     al,'<'
dr_charal
pop     ax
```

If you are using instrumentation that produces a hexadecimal representation (e.g., dr_byte or dr_word), it is best not to use uppercase letters in the range A through F for character markers. The mixture can get confusing when it comes time to interpret output.

When the inclusion of dump macros causes the assembler to complain about conditional jumps being out of range, you may use the zj? set of long-jump macros, which are located at the end of the DR_ASM.INC file. Using the beginning letter of z makes it easy to find modified lines when it is time to remove the instrumentation code.

Video Lead Strings

When ROUTER.SYS is configured to write its debugging output directly to a video buffer (where the /VI or /VS switch was used), it is possible to control certain aspects of the video display. This includes clearing the screen, defining the video attribute to be used for future writes, and defining the screen coordinates to be used for the next write.

These special functions are accomplished by transmitting special strings using the dr_str_rg assembler macro or the dr_str() C function. What makes these strings special is that they begin with a byte containing the value FF. Successive bytes within the string identify the operation to be performed and the parameters to be used. The format of these strings is shown in Table 7.3.

This video control method can be used to make a status monitor type of display, where labeled fields are perpetually updated in constant positions rather than having a continuous stream of dump information scrolling across the screen. This method will work not only when ROUTER.SYS is made to do direct video output itself but also when a binary serial or parallel link is connected to a second computer. In this latter case, the router logic within the CHANNEL.EXE data capture utility must be configured for direct video output.

Using dr_dwatch

The dr_dwatch assembler macro calls a service function within ROUTER.SYS that simplifies the task of watching a certain memory area in order to catch a change. There is also a corresponding C function, named dr_dwatch().

TABLE 7.3 Video lead strings

FF 03 01	Clear the screen (using the current attribute).
FF 04 02 *aa*	Establish a new current video attribute byte (where *aa* is the new attribute).
FF 05 03 *xx yy*	Establish a new video writing position (where *xx* is the X coordinate and *yy* is the Y coordinate).

TABLE 7.4 Record structure for `dr_watch`

Field Name	Data Type	Description
hit_flag	byte	Set to ! = □ when a change is detected
once_flag	byte	Set to ! = □ after the first call
data_ptr	dword	Far pointer to the memory area to watch
data_size	word	Number of bytes to watch
delta_ofs	word	Offset of the first difference
buffer	? bytes	The reference buffer

For each memory area to be watched, a reference buffer of equivalent size must be allocated. In addition, a handful of memory variables must be allocated, which will be used by the router logic to manage the data-watching process. These tracking variables must be located immediately before the reference buffer. The structure of this record is shown in Table 7.4.

In the assembler case, the `dr_wdef` macro can be used to allocate and initialize this storage area. In the event that the memory required for the tracking variables and reference buffer is so large that a dynamic type of memory allocation must be done, don't forget to include program statements to initialize the tracking variables. The `hit_flag` and `once_flag` fields must be set to zero, the address of the memory area to be watched must be written to the `data_ptr` far pointer field, and the number of bytes to be watched must be written to the `data_size` field. No initialization is required for the `delta_ofs` field or the reference buffer.

Once the data setup is taken care of, a call to the `dr_dwatch` macro should be placed at each point you wish to monitor for a change. The first time this service is called, the reference buffer is simply initialized with the current state of the area to be monitored. From then on, each call to `dr_dwatch` will compare the bytes within the reference buffer with those in the memory area being watched. The macro returns a nonzero flag state when a change is detected.

When a difference is detected, several different actions can be taken:

- A formatted byte dump of the entire reference buffer and the area being monitored could be done. See the `dr_fmbyte_rg` and `dr_fmbyte_at` macros.
- A dump of the area around the first point of change could be done using the `delta_ofs` field.
- The `dr_dwarept` macro could be used to report the address and contents of the first byte found to be different.
- Custom code could be executed to invoke a breakpoint, freeze the contents of the PRB within `ROUTER.SYS`, or close ROUTER's master gate.
- Additional instrumentation code could be added to reset the `hit_flag` and `once_flag` for the case where the memory change has been

found to be inconsequential. Calling `dr_dwatch` again right after re-setting these flags will update the reference buffer to the new state of the memory area being watched.

The process of preparing the tracking variables and reference buffer for the C case can be simplified through the use of the program fragments within the `DRDWATCH.TXT` file. The comments within this file will direct you to replace the generic variable names with ones specific to your situation and to locate the data declarations and code fragments in the appropriate sections of your program.

Using `dr_ifbrk`

The `dr_ifbrk` macro (or the `dr_ifbrk()` C function) is intended to be used when ROUTER's control console feature is active and a debugger is also loaded underneath the program being analyzed. When you wish to break into your debugger, press the B key on the serial terminal or press Cntrl–LeftShift on the main keyboard. The next call to `dr_ifbrk` will result in a hard-coded breakpoint instruction being executed.

Note that it is up to you to include calls to this instrumentation service at selected points within your program. Just having the control console feature active and pressing the breakpoint key will not invoke a breakpoint. On the other hand, if you have embedded `dr_ifbrk` calls and do activate them through the control console hot key but have forgotten to load your debugger, you're inviting a crash. What happens next depends on where the `INTO3` interrupt vector happens to be pointing.

Once you break into your debugger, you will probably have to manu-ally advance the IP register's value by 1. Most debuggers cannot step ahead through a hard-coded breakpoint instruction. From here, you will have to trace through a few instructions to reach the end of the assembler macro code or C function.

Using `dr_seqchk`

The `dr_seqchk` assembler macro calls a service function within `ROUTER.SYS` that simplifies the task of detecting when a certain sequence of events has occurred. There is also a corresponding C function named `dr_seqchk()`.

For each sequence to be tested for, a data record must be prepared, containing the total number of events in the list, an internal tracking variable, and the actual list of event words. Upon each call to this testing service, the address of this data record must be passed to `ROUTER.SYS` along with the current event value. The structure of this record is shown in Table 7.5.

TABLE 7.5 Record structure for `dr_seqchk`

Field Name	Data Type	Description
tot_evts	word	The number of event words in the list
evt_ofs	word	Internal tracking variable for current event
evt_list	? words	The list of event words

In the assembler case, a simple DW directive can be used to define this list (just make sure that the initial value for the second word, the `evt_ofs` field, is zero):

```
seq1    dw      5,0,03c00h,04400h,04000h,03e00h,04c00h
```

To prepare a sequence list record for the C case is similarly simple. For an explanation of the word data type in C, and other related data types, see Appendix H "The ASMTYPES.H Data Structures."

```
word seq1[] = {5,0,0x3c00,0x4400,0x4000,0x3e00,0x4c00};
```

Once the event list record has been prepared, all that is left to do is place the call. Entry parameters needed are a far pointer, which locates the event list record, and the current value of the event word. In the assembler case, the DS:SI register pair must point to the list, and the AX register must hold the current event value. For the C version, the parameters are normal function parameters. The DR_C.H file contains the prototype of this function, and the DR_C.INC file contains the function itself.

For the assembler case, a CPU flags value of ZR (where the zero flag is set) indicates that a sequence match has occurred. For the C case, a function return value of 0 indicates success.

Should the event values you need to monitor be only bytes rather than words, simply place the byte value into one-half of a word-sized variable or CPU register and zero out the other half. Just be sure that you form the values in the event list in the same manner.

If you find yourself needing to track doubleword values, simply make two calls at a time to the sequence-tracking logic. For example, if the memory variable `widget_status` is a doubleword field, the following code fragment shows how this could work:

```
        mov     ax,word ptr [widget_status]
        mov     si,offset seq_list
        dr_seqchk
        jnz     no_match
        mov     ax,word ptr [widget_status+2]
        dr_seqchk
        jz      got_a_match
```

7.5 CHANNEL.EXE

We first met the CHANNEL.EXE data capture tool in Section 7.1, "Use of the Companion Toolset," and have had additional details leaked in the succeeding sections. Now is the time to summarize all of the capabilities of this tool in one place.

As you have seen, this tool can be used to capture instrumentation output in one of two basic ways:

- From a PRB within ROUTER.SYS on the target system (to collect a postmortem type of dump)
- From a second computer to which output is transmitted from the target system across a high-speed binary link using serial or parallel ports

Controlling CHANNEL.EXE involves a juggling of parameters in a similar way as with the ROUTER.SYS driver. Both fixed-position parameters and switch parameters are used to designate how debugging data is to be routed and what additional processing is to be done. See Appendix P, "Parameters for CHANNEL.EXE," for a summary of these parameters.

To give this flurry of parameters some grounding in reality, take a look at the following sample cases. One parameter switch, the /IR switch, will be left for discussion in Chapter 8, where the DDICEPT.SYS intercept driver is explained.

When CHANNEL.EXE is used in a second computer to gather data sent across a high-speed binary link, the most important thing to remember is to have CHANNEL.EXE already up and running before the first instrumentation output is made by the target system. If the target attempts transmission before the remote system is ready, the target will become locked and a reboot will be the only remedy.

Note that when this tool is directed to store its captured data temporarily within a PRB, a final destination must be specified. This final output can be made either to direct video, to a file, or to any valid DOS device such as LPT1. Whereas in ROUTER.SYS the sizing of the PRB is left to you, with CHANNEL.EXE the largest PRB possible is used. This is typically in the range of 56K bytes.

The /C switch is specified when the input data stream from a serial or parallel port is to be in character mode rather than binary mode. This would be the case when the direct inclusion type of instrumentation is used to do serial or parallel output (e.g., DP_ASM.INC, DP_C.INC, DS_ASM.INC, or DS_C.INC).

When ROUTER.SYS is the source of the data, do not use the /C switch. For ROUTER.SYS to communicate with CHANNEL.EXE across a serial or parallel link, the binary transmission protocol must be used. This means using the /SB or /PB switch with ROUTER.SYS and not using the /C switch with CHANNEL.EXE.

Note that in the case of character mode serial reception, the /SK switch is not allowed. The purpose of this switch is to make the remote system's keyboard act as a serial control console. The direct inclusion serial code doesn't support a control console—this only applies when ROUTER.SYS is running within the target system. The /SK switch and the /C switch are mutually exclusive.

Sample Cases of Parameter Use

```
channel  prb, dv
```

- This would be a use of CHANNEL.EXE within the target system rather than within a remote system.
- Read the contents of the PRB buffer within the ROUTER.SYS driver and output the information to the video display.

```
channel  prb, log1.txt  /w
```

- This would be a use of CHANNEL.EXE within the target system rather than within a remote system.
- Read the contents of the PRB buffer within the ROUTER.SYS driver and write the information to the file LOG1.TXT.
- The /W switch will cause a newline code to be written to the file after every 80th character.

```
channel  ser, dv  /sb=03f8,11
```

- This would be a use of CHANNEL.EXE within a remote system.
- Gather data from the serial port at address 03F8.
- The serial port will be initialized to a baud rate of 115,200.
- Data received from the serial port will be written to the main video display.

```
channel  ser, dv  /sb=03f8,11  /sk  /f=T
```

- This would be a use of CHANNEL.EXE within a remote system.
- Gather data from the serial port at address 03F8.
- The serial port will be initialized to a baud rate of 115,200.
- Data received from the serial port will be written to the main video display.
- The remote system's keyboard will be activated as a control console for the router logic running within the target system.
- The character marker T will be watched for and further dumping will cease if it is found.

```
channel  ser, prb, log1.txt  /dv  /sb=02f8,38
```

- This would be a use of CHANNEL.EXE within a remote system.
- Gather data from the serial port at address 02F8.
- The serial port will be initialized to a baud rate of 38,400.
- Data received from the serial port will be written to a PRB within CHANNEL.EXE.
- The /DV switch will cause a copy of the data to be output to the main video display as it is received, as well as to the PRB.
- When the escape key is pressed to end the data capture, the current contents of the PRB will be written to the file LOG1.TXT.

```
channel  par, log1.txt  /dv  /c  /pb=03bc
```

- This would be a use of CHANNEL.EXE within a remote system.
- Gather data from the parallel port at address 03BC.
- The /C switch will cause character mode to be used.
- Character mode is for the case where the direct inclusion type of instrumentation code is being used within the target.
- Data received from the parallel port will be written to the file LOG1.TXT.
- The /DV switch will cause a copy of the data to be output to the main video display as it is received, as well as to the file.

```
channel  par, prb, lpt1  /w  /pb=0378
```

- This would be a use of CHANNEL.EXE within a remote system.
- Gather data from the parallel port at address 0378.
- Data received from the parallel port will be written to a PRB within CHANNEL.EXE.
- When the escape key is pressed to end the data capture, the current contents of the PRB will be written to the printer connected as the LPT1 device.
- The /W switch will cause a newline code to be written to the printer after every 80th character.

7.6 SUMMARY

The output destinations supported by instrumentation code are the following:

- A Packetized Ring Buffer (PRB)
- Direct video
- A serial port, to which an ASCII terminal is connected
- A parallel port, to which a printer is connected
- A high-speed binary serial link to a second machine
- A high-speed binary parallel link to a second machine

A ring buffer is fast and can hold a large amount of data, but is vulnerable to the actions of a bug.

Writing to a video display is fast, but only one screenful of data is available at a time for historical study. On an 80 × 25 display, only 2000 characters can be shown. A crash can blank the screen.

Writing to a serial port isn't very fast, and an ASCII terminal's display is also typically limited to 2000 characters. But the actions of a bug will only ruin the display in rare cases. If the occurrence of the failure causes a stream of garbage to be sent out through the serial port, stand ready to yank out the serial cable.

Writing to a printer is slow, but the data retention is excellent.

Moving data off to a second computer through a high-speed serial or parallel binary link is the best way to capture debugging data.

Instrumentation code can be included directly within a program (e.g., `DV_ASM.INC`), or it can be located within a device driver such as `ROUTER.SYS`. In this latter case, calls to this driver are embedded within the program being instrumented, typically using a software interrupt vector.

When assembler macros are used as instrumentation tools, all CPU registers must be preserved, especially the CPU flags. Further, no reliance on the values within the segment registers should be made for addressability (unless you know the program very well).

The best way to use direct video writing as an instrumentation destination is to install a second video adapter and monitor. This will avoid video collisions with the display output of the program being debugged.

When include files are used to hold assembler macros, related debugging code, and data, no `assume` statements should be used. Depending on where the `include` statement is located, this can change the assembly of the program you are analyzing.

If any of the instrumentation points you are working with can be executed as a result of an IRQ handler, all points must be protected from interruption. Surrounding the marker code with a `pushf/cli...popf` is the recommended method.

`ROUTER.SYS` supports three different types of control gates. The first is the master gate. It can be closed by a call from custom code that triggers when a bug is detected. This will freeze all debugging information gathered so far. The second is a manually controlled gate, operated by a hot key on the control console. The third type consists of the individual gates for each output destination.

The control console feature allows a keyboard to be used to control the flow of instrumentation output. The possible choices are the target system's keyboard, the keyboard on a serial terminal, and the keyboard on a remote system (when `CHANNEL.EXE` is being used with a binary serial link).

The bracket-type characters: [,], {, }, (,), ‹, and › are useful in identifying entrance and exit to a function or interrupt handler. Their graphic nature can make interpreting the dump output easier.

Through the use of video lead strings, a direct video instrumentation display can be cleared, the video attribute can be defined, and the coordinates of the next point to be written can be specified. This makes it possible to set up a perpetual status-monitor type of display.

The dr_dwatch macro/function is used to monitor a region of memory for change. A reference buffer must be allocated that is just as large as the region being watched.

The dr_ifbrk macro/function will invoke a hard-coded INT03 breakpoint instruction if the breakpoint flag within ROUTER.SYS has been set by the control console.

The dr_seqchk macro/function is used to detect when a certain sequence of events occurs.

The CHANNEL.EXE data capture tool is run within the target system when data is to be retrieved from the PRB within ROUTER.SYS. The information from this ring buffer can be written to direct video, to a disk file, or to any DOS device such as LPT1.

CHANNEL.EXE can also be run within a remote computer to gather data transmitted from the target system across a serial or parallel link.

CHANNEL.EXE can be used to collect serial or parallel link data sent from ROUTER.SYS (binary mode) or from the direct inclusion type of instrumentation code, such as that in the D?_ASM.INC and D?_C.INC files (character mode).

CHAPTER 8
Rolling Your Own

One thing that distinguishes humans from other animals is that we are able to use the tools we currently possess to make more advanced tools. We learned to use flint to make fire, fire to cast metal, metal to build machines, and machines to land us on the moon.

So it is also with software development. In the early days, programs had to be manually assembled and their binary machine code values entered into the computer through switches or jumper wires. From there, we progressed to punched cards and then to on-line terminals. Now program development can be as simple as dragging icons around on the screen with a mouse.

When it comes to the analysis and repair of software faults, if the tools currently available to you will suffice, then by all means get on with it. But in many cases building a new tool specifically tailored for the task at hand will be worth the time required. In other cases, the construction of a custom tool can mean the difference between spending days taking potshots at an intermittent problem and exposing it within a few hours.

Of course, if you must start from scratch to build each custom tool and its construction alone will take a day or more, using them will rarely be practical. Through the use of the program templates and function library included on this book's Companion Toolset Diskette, the development of custom debugging tools can become a practical avenue. This chapter's goal is to enable you to use an existing set of tool components to make new tools.

8.1 USES FOR CUSTOM TOOLING

Awareness is the first step. The greater your awareness of what is possible in terms of custom tooling, the better you will be able to judge when their use is appropriate. Do not think for a minute, however, that the examples presented in this chapter are all-encompassing. That would be like trying to list all of the possible combinations of moves in chess—technically possible but not much fun to read. The important thing is to keep your imagination in its on-line mode.

Here are some uses for custom debugging tooling:

- To augment a software debugger (custom debugging code can be embedded within a program, or hooked in through interrupt intercepts or patching, to effect complex breakpoint triggers)
- To trigger freezing of a ring buffer's contents or gating of instrumentation output
- To monitor the interrupt calls a program makes—spying on the system calls made to the operating system and to the BIOS
- To monitor the hardware interrupt calls that occur within a system
- To serve as a test bed, used to flex a function that is involved in a failure by sending it a conjured-up set of input data—making it much easier to see how well it deals with boundary conditions
- To serve as a simple model, which performs only a certain sequence of operations that is involved in the failure of a large program, in order to replicate the bug in a simpler environment
- To exercise significant permutations and boundary conditions in each functional aspect of a resident module such as a device driver or TSR
- To generate input files quickly for a program to see how it acts with different data
- To serve as a data file browser, which displays the records within a data file in the format used by the program
- To flex hardware that you suspect is to blame for your woes by presenting it with a variety of test conditions, in order to prove or disprove this theory
- To serve as data verification tooling, embedded within an application or loaded as a TSR underneath an application, to trace linked lists, inspect other data structures, and report when the first sign of damage is found

8.2 PROGRAM FORM AND STRUCTURE

Custom tooling can take one of four different forms:

1. Code that is embedded directly within the program being analyzed
2. A stand-alone utility program
3. A TSR utility
4. A device driver

Directly Embedded Code

This is most often effected by introducing additional source code language statements into the program being analyzed and then reassembling or recompiling the program to produce a new executable module. The fact that you are using the same language in which the program is written carries advantages and disadvantages. While this is a language that you are familiar with, many high-level languages make it difficult (on purpose) to interact directly with the computer's memory, CPU registers, interrupts, and so on.

Custom debugging code can also be directly embedded within a program by patching it in with a debugger. While it's not practical to use this approach for more than a small amount of code, it can be a valuable method when you must apply instrumentation to a program that is sensitive to changes in the positions of its components.

This patching could be done by modifying the program's executable file (static patching) or by modifying the program's code after it has been loaded into memory (dynamic patching). See Appendix E, "Patch Techniques," for a further discussion of this topic.

The Stand-Alone Utility

This program form would be used for a test bed environment, data file generator, or exercise utility for a resident module or hardware, as discussed in the list in the previous section.

When constructing tools such as a test bed environment, a data file generator, or a data file browser, it is wise to place the record format declarations within include files so that they can be used by both the actual program and associated debugging tools. This way, when changes are made to a program's data structures, you need only recompile your tools.

Maintaining duplicate copies of data structures within the program and these types of tools is dangerous. An error that slips in when you are updating a duplicate copy of a data structure within the tool can lead to false analysis. Forgetting that the tools contain a duplicate copy is also a danger. When a common include file is used, the make file used to build your application can be modified to keep its associated tools up to date as well.

The TSR

The TSR is a type of program that is installed in the computer's memory in such a way that it stays resident even when it is not executing. There are numerous advantages to making debugging code which remains resident in memory. It becomes possible to establish intercepts of system call interrupt vectors, to monitor the keyboard for the pressing of a hot key, to watch for changes in memory in other parts of the system, and so on.

To many computer users, the term *TSR* conjures up an image of a utility that can be made to pop up a window when a hot key is pressed. The design of this type of tool involves saving and restoring screen memory, intercepting the INT09 or INT16 keyboard interrupts, preventing DOS reentrance, and a number of other messy compatibility issues, such as how to coexist with other, badly behaved TSRs.

The application of this program form to the construction of debugging tools must involve a much simpler scenario. The last thing you want a debugging tool to do is introduce new compatibility problems. TSRs designed as debugging tools should use hot keys that don't require keyboard interrupt intercepts (see Section 8.6, "Control Interfaces") and should make use of the instrumentation methods presented in Chapter 7 rather than use a pop-up window or operating system calls.

The Device Driver

The device driver form is similar to the TSR in that it results in a module of binary program code permanently installed within the computer's memory. For debugging work, character mode device drivers will be used almost exclusively. The block device type of device driver has only very few applications in a debugging context (e.g., when you are developing an operating system's file I/O logic).

The string chosen for the 8-character device name within the device driver's header often doesn't matter. When it is necessary for other modules to communicate with the driver, it is usually simpler to make the driver establish an interrupt handler using a free interrupt vector (see Section 8.6, "Control Interfaces").

However, there can be advantages to using the standard character device interface. Nearly all languages provide the capability to open a DOS device for input and output, but not all high-level languages support the ability to issue software interrupt calls.

For example, you could develop a character device driver which goes by the device name of DUMP. From within a program, you could then initiate communications with this tool using very ordinary program statements, such as these:

```
DUMPOUT = fopen("dump","w");
fprintf(DUMPOUT,"widget_count = %d\n",widget_count);
```

One interesting project would be to construct a driver that relays the strings it receives through the standard character device interface on to ROUTER.SYS. This would make the features of this instrumentation driver available to languages that do not support a software interrupt–calling interface.

One tip when developing a device driver—never use a device name that is the same as the filename of the source module. When this driver is loaded through CONFIG.SYS, you would then not be able to edit its source code module or perform any other file operations on it. For example, if your device driver's code is contained within RINGBUFF.ASM and the device name RINGBUFF is placed within the device driver's header, when you try to load RINGBUFF.ASM for editing, DOS will find the RINGBUFF device name to exist and will issue a read request to it rather than open the file RINGBUFF.ASM. To avoid this problem, use a device name such as _RINGBUF or $RINGBUF.

TSR or Device Driver?

To help you decide between these two program forms, consider the following:

- A TSR can be de-installed, but a device driver cannot.
- You can decide to load a TSR at almost any time after booting. The only requirement is that you be at the command prompt (note that this means at the parent command processor level—not shelled out of an application). To change the loading status of a device driver requires that you edit your CONFIG.SYS file and reboot.
- A device driver can introduce debugging code that can be applied during the loading of another device driver (e.g., when you are developing a device driver) or during the installation of a replacement COMMAND.COM command processor shell (e.g., when you are developing that type of program). A TSR cannot be loaded this early in the boot-up process.
- A device driver can be communicated with through the standard device interface, whereas a TSR cannot (actually, a TSR can be made to patch itself into the device driver chain, but it does require extra steps and the use of undocumented operating system calls).

Resident and Nonresident Code

The TSR and the device driver program forms are similar in that they both consist of an initialization section and a resident processing section. TSRs and device drivers almost always overlay their initialization code with data buffer space (when a data buffer is required by the resident section), or they simply do not include this startup code in the portion of the module that is retained in memory.

The purpose of the initialization code is basically the same for a stand-alone program, TSR, or device driver. It assigns values to global variables; processes command line parameters; installs interrupt intercepts and interrupt handlers; programs hardware to a known state; reads the hardware to determine the operating environment; and makes any other preparations required to launch the resident portion of the module.

In the case of a stand-alone utility, the initialization code typically makes a direct entry into the main process portion of the module. In the case of a TSR or device driver, this code returns to the operating system with a report of the amount of memory to be reserved for the resident portion. The code of the resident portion is then entered through an interrupt or through the standard character device interface.

Languages

As you've probably noticed, the debugging tools and templates included on the Companion Toolset Diskette and the tool-building techniques described within this book are written in a mixture of C and assembler. This is done because it brings the best of two worlds.

Debugging tools typically require a very direct interface with the hardware and with the system-level operation of a computer. C is an excellent choice for debugging tools, since it supports high-level coding but can also interface with low-level aspects of a system. Its high-level nature makes tasks such as parameter processing, file I/O, and display formatting much easier to accomplish. Its low-level capabilities make it possible to do direct video output, I/O port operations, validation of memory blocks, and so on.

Assembler code is invaluable for the startup portions of TSRs and device drivers and for use in interrupt handlers, interrupt intercepts, and stack switching. It would, of course, also be called for when the utmost in execution speed or program compactness is required.

It now becomes important to distinguish between the mixing of C with assembler and that of assembler with C. Taking a stand-alone C program and writing time-critical or interface-critical functions in assembler is a case of mixing assembler functions with a C substrate. Your C compiler's startup code is being used so calls can be made to functions within the Standard C Library.

When it comes to making TSRs and device drivers, the use of C functions with a substrate of assembler is a good approach. But since your C compiler's startup code is not being used in this configuration, it is not possible to use any of the Standard C Library functions unless you have intimate knowledge of their implementation. Therefore, it is safer to write your own library functions so you know that they will operate correctly in your configuration. A starting set of these is provided with the Companion Toolset.

Although some developers have devised ways to modify the startup code of certain C compilers to fit the format of a TSR or device driver, this isn't a portable practice. Such methods are compiler-dependent and, indeed, dependent on the version of the compiler as well.

Fundamentals of Linking

When an assembler or compiler processes the source code statements you write, it stops short of producing pure binary code in ready-to-execute form.

Instead, an intermediate form of binary code file is produced, known as the *object module*. The object module file generated from a given source code module typically has the same filename as that source module but uses the `.OBJ` extension (e.g., assembling `XYZ.ASM` produces `XYZ.OBJ`; compiling `ABC.C` produces `ABC.OBJ`).

Using this intermediate form makes it possible to construct a program from a collection of precompiled and preassembled modules (object modules). This speeds development, especially in a larger project, because as changes are made, only the affected sourcecode modules must be recompiled or reassembled. It also makes it possible to develop a single program from more than one language (e.g., those mixtures of C and assembler mentioned above).

When it comes to building a program from separate object modules, there are three fundamental truths. Unfortunately, they are not entirely compatible:

1. Placing commonly used object modules within a library makes working with them much more convenient.
2. When building a device driver or TSR, link order control of the sections of the program is important. All parts of the program that will remain resident must be located within the first part of the final executable module, and all nonresident initialization code must be positioned at the end.
3. No direct means exists to control the link order of library modules.

When individual `.OBJ` modules are specified to the linker utility, it is possible to control the link order of the sections of the code these modules represent. In simple terms, the contents of the first object module listed as an input to the linker will occupy the first position in the final output file, the second object module's contents will come next, and so on, until all have been accounted for.

But when a library file (typically carrying the `.LIB` extension) is listed as a source of input to the linker utility, there is no simple way to control the position that the linker will assign to the contents of each object module pulled from that library module.

You could keep a collection of `.OBJ` modules that contains the common types of functions that you would normally find collected within a library. For each program you build, you would then have to manually identify the `.OBJ` modules that contain the functions you need and then build an ordered list of these modules to supply to the linker. You could also go back to using punched cards!

In the construction of tools such as device drivers and TSRs, the order of the functions within the executable module is critical. What is needed is a way to use a library of common functions while still maintaining control over the link order of the final product. The advantages of using separate object modules are just too important, and the convenience of being able to collect a set of object modules within a library is just too desirable, for efficient program development.

To clarify how critical this requirement is, consider the simplified model of a TSR-type program shown in Listing 8-1. Within this tool, two functions are referenced with `call` instructions, where the code for these functions is not included directly within the same source module. The `display_data` and `parse_parameters` functions are located within a `.LIB` library file, because they are modular functions, designed for reuse.

When the linker pulls the object modules containing these functions from the library, what will most likely happen is that all library functions will be located after the functions within the main code module. In other words, the function named `interrupt_handler` will come first, then `init_tsr`, followed by `display_data` and `parse_parameters`.

Now imagine that this tool has been installed resident in memory and the first interrupt call is made to its interrupt handler. Although the address the linker wrote as the operand to the `call display_data` instruction was technically correct with respect to the binary module as a whole, this address is after the `end of resident section` point.

```
org 100h
jmp init_function

resident data

   interrupt_handler

 call display_data

 iret


end of resident section

   init_tsr

 call parse_parameters

 establish the interrupt handler

 terminate and stay resident
```

LISTING 8-1 A pseudocode model of a TSR.

The final task of the init_tsr function is to terminate to the operating system, causing only the memory that comes before the end of the resident section to be retained. As a result of this action, the memory that initially contained the display_data function is "given back" to the operating system. If a tool that is malformed in this way should happen to be installed, the best you can hope for is a quick and clean crash—as opposed to one where the disk drive light comes on and strange noises hail the scrambling of your less-than-fully backed-up hard disk.

To restate our goal one last time, what we need is the ability to reference a common library function from either the resident or nonresident section of a tool and have the linker position that function in the appropriate section of the final executable module. Further, any data associated with a resident function must be located before the end of resident section point, and any data associated with a nonresident function must be located after that same point.

Library-Based Link Order Control

The solution to this puzzle involves a combination of three techniques:

1. *The use of multiple code and data segments* within all programs to be developed under this library method. The resident code and data segments (one code, two data) are given the names RTEXT, RDATA, and RBSS, with the corresponding nonresident segments given the names _TEXT, _DATA, and _BSS.
2. *The use of macros to modify the names* ultimately used for library functions—so that a different final name results depending on whether the reference is made from within the resident section or the nonresident section.
3. *The existence of two copies of each library function* within the .LIB file, where the segment names and function name of one copy have been modified for the resident case and those of the other copy being set for the nonresident case.

The following summary of multisegment linking will suffice for the sake of this discussion at this time. The rull range of peculiarities involved is beyond the scope of this book; for more details on these "peculiarities," consult the user's manual for the linker portion of your chosen compiler or assembler.

To get an idea of the linking process involved when multiple code and data segments are being used within multiple object modules, it can be helpful to think of a game of cards. In this game, there are two players, a dealer, a playing table, and, of course, a deck of cards. Player #1 is the resident section of the final program and player #2 is the nonresident section. The dealer, in this analogy, is the linker, and the playing table represents the code and data from the main source code module of the program being constructed. Last, but not least, the deck of cards represents the function library.

The dealer (the linker) begins by picking up the freshly shuffled deck of cards (the function library—where the functions can be located in any order within the .LIB file). The dealer then inspects a wish list that player #1 has presented and searches through the deck for the cards in that list, placing those found in a stack on the playing table in front of player #1. After that, it's player #2's turn to present its wish list and have its stack built.

When the dealing is finished, what you have is a playing table with two neatly ordered stacks of cards on it. Viewing the table and card stacks as their real-life counterparts, you now have a properly formed program, where functions have been pulled in from a library file and located in the correct portion of the final executable module.

The dealer orders the stacks correctly because the name-modifying macros and multiple-segment configuration force it to. In the simpler model described in Listing 8-1, the dealer did not have the benefit of the extra information made possible through this method. As a result, the entire set of cards (library functions) in the wish lists of both players was placed in one stack on player #2's side of the table (the nonresident section of the program).

In the assembler case, the lcall macro is responsible for the function name manipulations. While this method is transparent to the programmer for the most part, a small concession is necessary on the part of a programmer using this tool construction system. Any call made to a function within the Companion Toolset's function library must be made using the lcall macro instead of the normal call instruction.

In the following example piece of code, the nonlibrary function, local_function, is still called using the normal call instruction, but the la_word2hex function is located within the Companion Library and must be referenced using the lcall macro instead. Actually, this can be thought of as a form of documentation, since it provides anyone reading this source code with a useful bit of information: the location of the called function.

```
mov     ax,[widget_class]
call    local_function
mov     bx,[total_widgets]
mov     si,offset dgroup:buffer
lcall   la_word2hex
```

The lcall macro, located within the file \XTOOLS\LA_MACS.INC, works in conjunction with an assembler SET variable named reslib. This SET variable must be assigned the value of 1 at the start of the resident section of the main program's source code module and then reassigned the value of 0 at the start of the nonresident section. This detail has already been taken care of in the template files described in the next section.

This macro produces a call instruction where a t (for "transient") is appended to the end of the specified library function for the nonresident case. This occurs because the SET variable reslib holds a value of 0. When reslib holds the value of 1, an r (for "resident") is appended to the specified function name. In either case, an underscore character is prefixed to the specified name. This is done for compatibility with the C language's function-naming convention.

Thus, even though you code an `lcall` statement to a function named `la_word2hex`, there is actually no library function with that exact name. Rather, there are two library functions: one named `_la_word2hexr` and another named `_la_word2hext`. In addition, the resident version, `_la_word2hexr`, is coded within a module using the RTEXT, RDATA, and RBSS segments. Likewise, the `_la_word2hext` function is coded to use the _TEXT, _DATA, and _BSS segments. To revisit the card game analogy briefly, the name manipulation causes the dealer to find the right card for the wish list being processed, and the corresponding segment names make sure that the dealer places the card in the right stack.

Note that when a stand-alone assembler program is being developed, where there are no resident and nonresident sections, you still must use the `lcall` macro. Fortunately for you, by using this macro you can remain largely oblivious to this naming manipulation.

One further detail that must be attended to when functions are used from the Companion Library is that another macro must be used when the function is declared as external. This macro is named `lextrn` and is also located within the file \XTOOLS\LA_MACS.INC. Whereas with a normal `extrn` statement, you must supply an ending term such as `near`, with `lextrn` this is not necessary:

```
reslib = 1
lextrn la_word2hex
```

Were you to inspect the actual expansion text for the foregoing use of this macro, here is what you would see:

```
extrn _la_word2hexr:near
```

In the C case, due to the nature of its macro preprocessor, life with this library technique is even simpler. To use a function from the library requires nothing special; all you have to do is reference the function in the normal manner. For example, the following call uses the `lc_word2hex()` function to convert a word value to its hexadecimal representation within a text buffer:

```
lc_word2hex(&buffer[5],total_widgets);
```

As long as the header file \XTOOLS\TLIBDEFS.H is included within your program (as it is in the program templates of the Companion Toolset), the naming manipulation will be taken care of in a transparent manner. The macros within this header file manipulate the function name based on the current value of the #defined variable `reslib`, just as in the assembler case.

8.3   USING THE PROGRAM TEMPLATES

The Companion Toolset contains source code template files to handle the most common tool-building situations. These files are located within the \XTOOLS\WORK\STOCK directory and are also listed in this section.

Any assembler- or C-based functions within the Companion Library can be used with any of the tool forms represented by these templates, providing the proper calling interface is coded. The naming technique used within the library must also be observed.

To access a C function from assembler, use the lcall macro and be sure to specify the function name without a leading underscore character. The lcall macro will append the r or t character to the end of the function name and prefix an underscore.

To access an assembler function from within C, where the assembler function has been included within the TLIBDEFS.H file, is simple and direct: Just reference the function as you would any other, using the base name (not appending an r or t character). If the function has not been included within the TLIBDEFS.H file, you can either include it within that file or explicitly add the ending r or t character. Since all assembler functions within the library begin with an underscore character, this part of the C function-naming convention will always be satisfied.

These are the template files:

```
STANDA.ASM
TSR.ASM
SYS.ASM
STANDC.C
DDXXXXX.ASM
DDXXXXXT.C
DDXXXXXR.C
DDXXXXX.MAK
```

All of these template files are contained within the directory \XTOOLS-\WORK\STOCK.

The STANDA.ASM template is designed to produce a stand-alone program from assembler source code. An executable binary file of the .COM type is the intended result.

The TSR.ASM template is designed to produce a TSR program from assembler source code. An executable binary file of the .COM type is the intended result. C code modules could be compiled into separate .OBJ modules and linked in with this module (note how the MODOBJ.EXE utility is used to modify segment naming in the case of the DDXXXXX set of templates). But library functions from the Standard C Library should not be used, since the compiler's startup code is not being included by the linking process.

The SYS.ASM template is designed to produce a device driver from assembler source code. An executable binary file of the .SYS type is the intended result. The `SYS.ASM` template is for the case where the entire device driver will be coded in assembler.

The `STANDC.C` template is designed to produce a stand-alone program from C source code. An executable binary file of the `.EXE` type is the likely result (depending on your chosen C compiler). Since this module will contain the compiler's startup code, Standard C Library functions may be used. In addition, assembler code modules could be assembled into separate `.OBJ` modules and linked in with this module.

The `DDXXXXX` set of template files is for use when you wish to build a device driver using C code. Note that since your C compiler's startup code will not be linked in, functions from the Standard C Library should not be used. An executable binary file of the `.SYS` type will result.

The `XXXXX` portion of the filenames of each of these modules is to be replaced with a descriptive string of characters of your choosing. The `.MAK` file must also be edited, as it contains one line where this `xxxxx` string must be replaced with your descriptive name. The batch file `GETSTOCK.BAT`, explained below, automates this detail (except for the editing of the `.MAK` file).

The `DDXXXXX.ASM` module contains the assembler startup code for the driver. The `init` function, located at the end of this module, makes a call to a `parse()` function, which is written in C and located within the `DDXXXXXT.C` module. See Section 8.6, "Control Interfaces," for more details on the parsing logic. If any additional C functions are required by the initialization logic, they may also be placed within the `DDXXXXXT.C` module. Be aware that any code and data placed within this module will not be retained in memory when the initialization process completes.

The `DDXXXXXR.C` module is to be used for any C functions that are to be retained resident in memory. Note that it is not necessary to place any functions or data within this module. You may simply want to take advantage of the parsing logic within `DDXXXXXT.C` and code the entire resident portion of the driver in assembler within the `DDXXXXX.ASM` module.

Should you wish to develop an interrupt handler or an interrupt intercept written in C, the `TLIB.INC` file contains two macros designed to make this easier. The intercept would be established through the placement of two macro lines within the `DDXXXXX.ASM` module, and the C function that should be given control on each interrupt call would be located within the `DDXXXXXR.C` module, where the C code would remain resident in memory. See Section 8.5, "Stack Switching and More Intercepts," for an example of each case.

To use any of these template files, make a copy that uses a filename of your choosing, edit in your code, and process the resulting file with your assembler or C compiler. The following set of batch files is provided within the `\XTOOLS\BATCH` directory to simplify this process in many cases:

```
MC.BAT
MS.BAT
CLC.BAT
```

Producing a .COM file from an assembler source code module is the function of the MC.BAT batch file (its two-letter name stands for "Make.COM"). It would be used with files derived from the STANDA.ASM and TSR.ASM templates. At minimum, one parameter is expected: the filename of the .ASM module to process. If a d is specified as a second parameter, debugging information will be produced during the assembly and linking process (for use with a source-level or symbolic debugger).

The MS.BAT batch file is intended for use with source modules derived from the SYS.ASM templates; its filename stands for "Make.SYS." The parameter conventions for this batch file are the same as for MC.BAT.

The CLC.BAT (Command Line Compiler) batch file is designed to be used with files copied from the STANDC.C template. The parameter conventions for this batch file are also the same as for MC.BAT.

To produce a device driver from the DDXXXXX set of template files, use the DDXXXXX.MAK make file. Note that there is one line within this file where the xxxxx string must be replaced with your descriptive name.

The process of making copies of these template files can be simplified through the use of the GETSTOCK.BAT batch file. This file is located within the \XTOOLS\BATCH directory. For example, when you want to build a TSR named WATCHER, use GETSTOCK as follows:

```
getstock tsr watcher
```

Similar application of this tool would be made when dealing with the other template files. See the documentation within GETSTOCK.BAT for further details.

Coding Conventions

In both the C and assembler cases, the small memory model is being used. Actually, a qualification must be added to this statement, because the code segment(s) are included within the same group as the data segments. Some refer to this as the *tiny* model.

One consequence of using two code segments within an assembler program, where both are contained within the same group, is that any statements using the offset directive must include a specification of the group name. For example, the following statement would not produce the correct results if it was encoded within the nonresident code segment (_TEXT):

```
mov    si,offset buffer
```

What this statement would do is render the offset of the memory variable buffer with respect to the start of the segment within which it is located. In most cases, what you actually want is the offset of the variable with respect to the start of the entire program. To produce this result, the statement must be modified as follows:

```
mov     si,offset dgroup:buffer
```

Although this treatment would not be required of statements within the resident segment of a multiple-segment program (the RTEXT segment) or within the only code segment of a stand-alone program (named _TEXT), it is good practice to use the dgroup: modifier in all cases.

8.4 INTERRUPT INTERCEPT BASICS

First, a word of warning: The examples of interrupt intercepts shown within this section are simplistic. This is necessary to approach this topic in workable steps. As a result of their simple nature, these early examples will not be appropriate for all cases. Please read through this section and the next section, "Stack Switching and More Intercepts," before employing any of the examples in a tool.

What does it mean to intercept an interrupt? Let's begin by considering the case of an interrupt that was designed to be intercepted: The INT1C timer interrupt. Within a PC- or AT-class machine, the 8253 clock chip generates an IRQ0 hardware interrupt at a rate of 18.2 interrupts per second. This gives control to the interrupt service routine (ISR) that the INT08 vector points to.

One of the actions taken by the INT08 ISR within the ROM BIOS is to issue a software interrupt call to INT1C. This is done just in case any software modules within the system have established an intercept. If no intercepts have been established, the default contents of the INT1C vector point to an iret instruction within the ROM BIOS, so that a null action results. The following code fragments should help make this a bit clearer:

```
---- Part of the INT08 ROM BIOS code
      int     01ch
---- Another part of the ROM BIOS, at address F000:9876
F000:9876  iret
```

When the software interrupt call to INT1C is executed, the CPU will fetch the contents of the corresponding interrupt vector and make an interrupt-style call to the code at that address. In this example, the INT1C vector would contain the address F000:9876.

Now let's say that you are developing a program where you need to gain control on a regular basis to perform some type of maintenance operation. To establish an intercept of the INT1C timer service, you could use code such as that shown in Listing 8-2.

```
---- Storage for the original vector

ilc_orig        dd      ?

---- The INT1C intercept

ilc_icept:
      sti
      call    do_maintenance
      jmp     cs:[ilc_orig]

---- Establishing the intercept

      mov     ax,351ch
      int     21h
      mov     word ptr cs:[ilc_orig],bx
      mov     word ptr cs:[ilc_orig+2],es
      mov     ax,cs
      mov     ds,ax
      mov     dx,offset dgroup:ilc_icept
      mov     ax,251ch
      int     21h
```

LISTING 8-2 Intercepting INT1C.

Beginning with the third section, where the intercept is established, the call to function 35h of INT21 will return the current contents of the INT1C vector in the ES:BX register pair. It is necessary to record this address in a location that will be accessible to the intercept handler. In this case, the ilc_orig memory variable is located within the same code segment as the intercept handler, so a CS override type of addressing can be used.

Once the current vector contents have been recorded, it's time to pirate control of INT1C calls away from the current handler and funnel them through our intercept first. This is accomplished by the call to function 25h of INT21, where the DS:DX register pair contains the address of the new interrupt handler.

As soon as this second initialization call completes, the code at the label ilc_icept will be executed upon each tick of the timer. Note that the do_maintenance function must preserve the state of any of the CPU registers it makes use of. Note also that unless measures are taken to control reentrance, the execution time incurred by this function must not be longer than the interval between timer ticks.

Once this maintenance function completes its operations and returns, a jump instruction transfers control to the previous handler in the chain. This is necessary, since other intercepts may have been established previous to yours. To presume that yours is the only one and end your intercept with an iret

```
i1c_icept:
      sti
      push    ax
      push    bx
      mov     ax,cs:[widget_color]
      mov     bx,23
      call    do_maintenance
      pushf
      cli
      call    cs:[i1c_orig]
      pop     bx
      pop     ax
      iret
```

LISTING 8-3 An INT1C intercept.

instruction would deprive any previously established intercepts of their time in the CPU limelight.

With IRQ-based interrupt calls such as INT08 and INT09, and with related calls such as INT1C and INT1B, the important thing is to make sure that all CPU registers are preserved and that proper stack balance is maintained. But since there are no defined entry conditions for an IRQ-based ISR, it is not necessary for the original entry register states to be established when passing the interrupt call on to the previous vector holder. Therefore, it would be allowable to use an intercept of the form shown in Listing 8-3 for the INT1C case, or for any other IRQ-based intercept.

In this intercept handler, a simulated interrupt call is made to the previous ISR rather than branching directly to it. This is the purpose of the pushf and cli instructions. Since an interrupt event such as INT1C has no input requirements, the fact that the AX and BX registers have been changed from what their original values were at the time the INT1C call was first issued is not of consequence.

Preserving Entry and Exit Registers

In the case of a software interrupt service such as INT21, INT13, INT16, or INT17, the design requires entry parameters to be supplied in certain CPU registers. Likewise, certain CPU registers will hold exit parameters when the ISR makes its return to the caller. When an intercept is to be established on an interrupt handler of this type, care must be taken to pass these parameters on to the previous vector holder and to pass the exit parameters of that pass-on call back to the original point of call.

The intercept handler presented in Listing 8-4, intended to dump information on INT10 calls to a debugging monitor, shows an example of this register preservation. In this fictitious example, the instrumentation logic

```
i10_icept:
        sti
        push    ax
        push    bx                      ; save entry regs
        push    es


        . . . . .
          (dump logic for entry state)
        . . . . .


        pop     es
        pop     bx                      ; restore entry regs
        pop     ax
        pushf
        cli
        call    [i10_orig]
        push    bp
        mov     bp,sp
        pushf                           ; transplant exit flags
        pop     [bp+6]
        push    bx
        push    es                      ; save exit regs


        . . . . .
          (dump logic for exit state)
        . . . . .


        pop     es
        pop     bx                      ; restore exit regs
        pop     bp
        iret
```

LISTING 8-4 An INT10 intercept.

required the use of the AX, BX and ES registers, so they had to be temporarily saved on the stack. But since the BIOS INT10 handler expects entry parameters in the CPU registers, all registers must hold their original values when the interrupt call is passed on.

On the exit side of this INT10 intercept, another register preservation detail must be considered. Not only must the state of the general registers be carried from the exit point of the pass-on call back to the original point of call—the CPU flags word must also be carried back.

This requires some extra attention, due to the way that the flags word is handled in an interrupt call. The flags word that will ultimately be delivered

```
        call    [i10_orig]
        pushf                           ; save exit flags
        push    ax
        push    bx
        push    es                      ; save exit regs

        .....
          (dump logic for exit state)
        .....

        pop     es
        pop     bx                      ; restore exit regs
        pop     ax
        popf                            ; restore exit flags
        retf    2
```

LISTING 8-5   An alternative way to deliver the return flags.

back to the original caller must come from the stack, because that is how the
iret instruction works, and this intercept ends with an iret.

But the actual return flags that the original caller needs to see are the
flags that are returned from the pass-on call. In the INT10 intercept shown
in Listing 8-4, the BP register is used to transplant the return flags from the
pass-on call to the position on the stack where a flags word will be pulled off
by the final iret instruction.

The code fragment within Listing 8-5 is an alternative method of making
sure the original caller sees the flags value returned from the pass-on call.
In this case, a different type of return instruction is used at the end of the
intercept. The retf 2 instruction will discard the flags word placed on the
stack by the original interrupt call and return to the original calling point
with the current flags state intact.

Caveats and Finer Points

If you would use instructions that count on the state of the direction flag
within an intercept (e.g., movsb or stosw), be sure to use a cld or an std
instruction first. Although the direction flag is commonly set to the up direction within an interrupt intercept or interrupt handler, there is no guarantee
of this.

Even if your intercept's processing will be very short, you should still
begin the intercept with an sti instruction. Otherwise, a strange side-effect
could cause problems. If a sloppily designed program disables interrupts, performs a critical operation, and then makes a software interrupt call, counting

on that interrupt call to enable interrupts, an intercept could subvert this action if the intercept doesn't begin with an sti instruction. Without this leading sti in your intercept, when a return is made to the point of call, interrupts would still be disabled. This is not necessary when a direct jump is made to the previous vector holder.

If you would establish interrupt intercepts from within a stand-alone program rather than a resident module such as a TSR or device driver, you must ensure that your program does not terminate before all intercepted vectors can be restored to their original values. If a vector is left pointing to the abandoned memory space where the program was previously loaded, a crash is sure to happen on a future use of that interrupt.

Where an intercept is established for the purpose of issuing a breakpoint when certain conditions are detected, a reentrance control flag should be used to prevent a repeated invocation of the breakpoint. For example, say that an INT21 intercept has been established to invoke a breakpoint when a certain section of memory is found to be corrupt. When the test code triggers and you break into your debugger, the debugger is likely to issue INT21 calls of its own. If this results in your intercept executing the breakpoint again, you will have a breakpoint that causes a breakpoint that causes a breakpoint...

A reentrance control flag is not needed as long as the trigger to execute a breakpoint automatically resets itself and doesn't fire again while the debugger is being used. When using the dr_ifbrk macro (from DR_ASM.INC) within an intercept, as long as you don't press the b key on the control console again while within the debugger, there will be no reentry problem.

If you are designing a TSR-based tool that contains intercepts and that will be removable, you must verify that another intercept has not been established since your tool was installed. If the interrupt vectors your tool has hooked do not still hold the values it placed into them, the removal process must be aborted.

When you are building a new intercept tool to monitor a common system service such as INT21, begin by making your tool intercept an unused vector at first, such as INTF0. Then construct a test program that issues INTF0 calls as if they were INT21 calls, stepping through the process with your debugger to verify proper operation. When working with an unused vector like this, make sure that it is pointing to an iret from the start, or your tool will cause a crash when it passes the call on to the previous vector holder.

An Interrupt-Pacing Tool

The program exhibited in Listing 8-6 serves as an example of several of the ideas discussed in the previous sections of this chapter, as well as a couple of new ideas. Its purpose is to force INT21 system calls to be paced on INT08 timer tick interrupts. This can be a helpful technique when trying to stabilize a bug which seems to be timing dependent.

```
dgroup  group   RTEXT,RDATA,RBSS,_TEXT,_DATA,_BSS

;==== resident code segment

reslib = 1
RTEXT   segment para public 'RODE'
        assume  cs:dgroup,ds:nothing,es:nothing,ss:nothing

include c:\xtools\tlib.inc

        org     0100H
start:
        jmp     begin

;==== i08_icept, write a 1 into the had8 flag on each timer tick

i08_orig        dd      ?
had8            db      ?

i08_icept:
        mov     cs:[had8],1
        jmp     cs:[i08_orig]    ; pass on to previous vector holder

;==== wait8, wait for the next int8 interrupt to occur

wait8:
        mov     cs:[had8],0
xx1:
        cmp     cs:[had8],0
        je      xx1
        ret

;==== chk_scrl, return flags == nz if scroll-lock is toggled on

chk_scrl:
        push    ax
        push    es
        mov     ax,40h
        mov     es,ax
        test    byte ptr es:[17h],10h
        pop     es
        pop     ax
        ret
```

(continued on next page)

LISTING 8-6 Pacing INT21 calls in INT08 events.

```
;==== i21_icept, if scroll-lock is on, pace int21 calls in int08

i21_orig        dd      ?

i21_icept:
        sti
        call    chk_scrl
        jz      xx3
        call    wait8
xx3:
        pushf
        cli
        call    cs:[i21_orig]       ; call previous vector holder
        retf    2                   ; return with current flags

RTEXT   ends

RDATA   segment para public 'RATA'
RDATA   ends

RBSS    segment para public 'RSS'
RBSS    ends

;==== initialization code segment

reslib = 0
_TEXT   segment para public 'CODE'
        assume  cs:dgroup,ds:nothing,es:nothing,ss:nothing

endres  label   byte
        nop

begin:
        hook_vect 08
        hook_vect 21
        mov     al,0                ; errorlevel 0
        mov     dx,offset dgroup:endres+15
        mov     cl,4
        shr     dx,cl
        mov     ah,31h
        int     21h

_TEXT   ends
```

LISTING 8-6 *(Continued)*

```
_DATA    segment para public 'DATA'
_DATA    ends

_BSS     segment para public 'BSS'
_BSS     ends
         end      start
```

LISTING 8-6 *(Continued)*

First of all, this tool was derived from the `TSR.ASM` program template. For the sake of brevity, unused lines have been deleted. A complete version of this program is available on the Companion Toolset Diskette under the filename `\XTOOLS\WORK\PACE2108.ASM`. Use the `MC.BAT` batch file to generate `PACE2108.COM`. For example:

```
mc pace2108
```

Note that within the `INT08` intercept, at the label `i08_icept`, there is no need to push any registers onto the stack. The only operation carried on by this intercept is to set the `had8` flag. Since this can be done using code segment relative addressing (i.e., the CS segment prefix in the `mov cs:[had8],1` instruction), none of the general-purpose registers will be affected.

The `INT21` intercept, which begins at the label `i21_icept`, makes calls to two functions but leaves the preservation of any CPU registers up to these functions. The first of these two functions, `chk_scrl`, does use a pair of registers and does, therefore, have to save and restore these registers through `push` and `pop` instructions. The purpose of this function is to enable you to use the Scroll-Lock key to turn this tool on and off. See Section 8.6, "Control Interfaces," for more information on this type of gating.

Although a `jmp cs:[i21_orig]` instruction could have been used to pass the interrupt call on to the previous vector holder, the `pushf/cli/call` method was chosen instead. This was done because it is possible that, when this tool is put to use in a debugging session, additional testing code may need to be placed within this intercept. Remember that if any additional tests are placed between the `call cs:[i21_orig]` instruction and the `retf 2` instruction, the state of the CPU flags register must be preserved.

```
pushf
        cli
        call     cs:[i21_orig]
        pushf
        call     check_for_failure
        popf
        retf     2
```

```
hook_vect macro inum
        pushset ax,bx,dx,ds,es
        mov     ah,35h
        mov     al,0&inum&h
        int     21h
        mov     word ptr [i&inum&_orig],bx
        mov     word ptr [i&inum&_orig+2],es
        mov     dx,offset dgroup:i&inum&_icept
        mov     ax,cs
        mov     ds,ax
        mov     ah,25h
        mov     al,0&inum&h
        int     21h
        popset  ax,bx,dx,ds,es
        endm
```

LISTING 8-7　The hook_vect macro to establish an intercept.

Now let's take a look at the initialization logic in the nonresident section of this program—the section which starts just after the begin: label. Since the process of establishing an interrupt intercept is common in the construction of debugging tools, the steps involved have been distilled down to a macro. The hook_vect macro, shown in Listing 8-7, can be found within the file \XTOOLS\TLIB.INC. This macro will simplify the task of establishing an interrupt intercept as long as a few simple rules are observed:

1. The interrupt number must be supplied as a parameter to this macro. It must be the hexadecimal value of the interrupt number, but do not use an h at the end. Two hex digits must always be used: this entails the use of a leading zero for interrupts 0 through F.
2. A doubleword of storage must be allocated to hold the original contents of the interrupt vector. The name used for this memory variable must be of the form ixx_orig, where the xx is replaced with the two hex digits for the interrupt involved (e.g., i08_orig for INT08).
3. The label that defines the start of the intercept must be of the form ixx_icept where the xx is replaced with the two hex digits for the interrupt involved (e.g., i08_icept for INT08).

8.5　STACK SWITCHING AND MORE INTERCEPTS

The interrupt intercept examples illustrated in the previous section were fairly simple cases. It was reasonably safe to assume that enough stack depth would be available no matter when the interrupt call occurs. There will be cases, however, where it will be desirable to perform more complex types of operations from within an intercept. For this reason, and to make it possible to call functions coded in C from within an intercept handler, it's time to take a look at the practice of *stack switching*.

In the most basic sense, all that is required is that the current values within the SS:SP register pair be saved somewhere and that new values be assigned. This would, of course, be done right at the start of an intercept handler, with a corresponding restoration of the previous SS:SP values done at the end. But, as you may have surmised from skimming ahead and noting the size of this section, there's a little more involved than this "most basic" idea.

Stack-Switching Safety

A PC/AT type of machine is designed to make use of a number of hardware interrupts. About 18 times a second, the 8253 timer asserts an IRQ0 interrupt, causing the INT08 handler to gain control. Every time you press or release a key, an IRQ1 interrupt occurs (vectored to INT09). In addition, IRQ-type interrupts are caused by disk drives, mice, video display adapters, and a number of other peripherals. The NMI type (Non-Maskable Interrupt) must also be included in this category.

Whenever it is possible for a hardware interrupt to occur, a valid stack must exist on which the return address and current flags values can be placed. Most interrupt handlers will also require stack space to save the original values within the general-purpose CPU registers that must be used by the handler. This same consideration applies equally to intercepts that are established on hardware interrupts.

Since two registers are involved, SS and SP, establishing a new stack means that two instructions must be executed (actually, the 80386 CPU did introduce an lss sp, [memvar] instruction). If it were possible for an interrupt to occur in between these two instructions, the memory used for the stack by that interrupt would not be a proper stack. It would be whatever memory was pointed to by the *transitional* SS:SP stack pointer value, where one of the registers held a new value and the other still held an old value.

To make sure that the process of loading SS and SP is secure against any type of interrupt, including NMI, the 80X86 type of CPU was designed so that loading a new value into the SS register automatically makes the next instruction immune from interruption. The intention, of course, is that this next instruction be the one that loads the SP register with its new value. For example:

```
mov     ss,[newss]
mov     sp,[newsp]
```

Occasionally, you'll find a program where the designer felt they needed to perform additional operations in between the loading of SS and SP. Realizing that switching stacks was a sensitive operation, they attempt to guard the stack switch from interruption by disabling interrupts:

```
cli
mov     ss,[newss]
sub     [newsp],stk_bias
mov     sp,[newsp]
sti
```

While this method will prevent problems with the normal type of hardware interrupt, if an NMI interrupt should occur in between the sub [newsp],stk_bias instruction and the mov sp,[newsp] instruction, the collective SS:SP value would be invalid and a crash would occur.

Given that the normal use of the NMI within a PC/AT system is to signal a memory parity error, this flaw may be of little consequence. But problems can also occur when this type of code is traced using a debugger's assembler-level single-step feature. When you trace through the instruction that loads the SS register, the next instruction will automatically be skipped.

This will place you at the mov sp,[newsp] instruction...if you're lucky! Remember from Chapter 5 that when the CPU is doing assembler-level single-stepping, an INT01 will automatically occur after each instruction. In this case, however, the stack used by the INT01 instruction will be half-baked. Whatever memory happens to be pointed to by the new SS and the old SP will be overwritten by the stack usage implicit in the execution of the INT01 interrupt.

The moral of this story is to keep your stack-switching code clean and safe. Always make use of the automatic interrupt-guarding feature provided when a new value is loaded into the SS register.

Now for the strange part: Even though you design your stack-switching code to work with the automatic guarding feature, you should also surround each stack switch with cli and sti instructions. There are reportedly some early versions of the 8088 CPU in existence that contain a flaw (a hardware bug) whereby this automatic stack guarding doesn't always work. Therefore, to avoid problems on older machines, here's the final recipe:

```
cli
mov     ss,[newss]
mov     sp,[newsp]
sti
```

A First-Cut Attempt

Listing 8-8 shows a first-cut attempt at incorporating stack switching code into an intercept. Note that the prologue code does make use of the au-

```
i21_icept:
        mov     cs:[savess],ss
        mov     cs:[savesp],sp
        push    cs
        pop     ss
        mov     sp,offset top_of_lcl_stk
        sti


        .....
          (1st section of intercept logic)
        .....

        pushf
        cli
        call    cs:[i21_orig]
        pushf


        .....
          (2nd section of intercept logic)
        .....

        popf
        cli
        mov     ss,cs:[savess]
        mov     sp,cs:[savesp]
        retf    2
```

LISTING 8-8 Intercept stack switching (not stable, see text).

tomatic interrupt-guarding technique, since the loading of a new SP value immediately follows the loading of a new SS value.

Where this first-cut attempt falls short is in its handling of reentrance. Interrupt handlers are notorious for being reentered. When this happens, the prologue portion of the handler is executed once for the original entry and is then executed again before the first entry is balanced with an exit. In other words, while the system is executing within an interrupt handler, some action occurs that causes another call to be made to that same interrupt. Consequently, any intercept logic you write should be designed to account for this possibility.

What would happen if the intercept handler within Listing 8-8 were reentered? First of all, the [savess] and [savesp] memory variables would be reused by the second entry before their values would serve their purpose to the first entry. When this nesting of calls finally unwound to the point where the original entry was concluding, the stack restoration logic at the end of the intercept would end up using the SS:SP values saved on the second entrance rather than those saved on the first.

If this weren't enough, all information placed on the local stack by the first entrance will be overwritten by the second entrance. This would occur because when a local stack is provided for the second entrance, the same stack offset is used as for the first entry.

So we've got some problems here. Before attending to solutions, let's deal with the question: "How can reentrance occur in the first place?" It's always good to have a clear understanding of a problem before you set out to find its cure.

There are a number of ways that reentrance can occur. First of all, it can be an intentional recursive-type call. In the INT10 video BIOS logic, function number 13h is provided to write a string of characters to the display. In some BIOS implementations, this function performs its task by itself making INT10 calls. The AH function selector values used in these recursive calls are for some of the lower-level functions, such as 09h (write character) and 02h (set new cursor position). If you set up an INT10 intercept and a call is made to function 13h, your intercept handler will be reentered, due to the actions of these recursive calls.

Reentrance could also occur due to the actions of a previously installed intercept handler. Say that you have a tool that is intercepting INT21 calls, and when your intercept logic makes its pass-on call, another INT21 intercept gains control. This handler could set a reentrance control flag and then issue INT21 calls as part of its intercept-processing activities. Even though this previously installed intercept has set a flag to let its own entrance logic know that a recursion will occur, your intercept will be reentered, with no knowledge of this flag.

Making additional INT21 calls during from an INT21 intercept is safe and is not uncommon in debugging tools, CD-ROM redirector drivers, and network redirectors. It is often done to get and set the current PSP (functions 50h and 51h) or to record details of the original INT21 call within a file. Note that a better way to make INT21 calls from within an INT21 intercept is to execute a pushf and cli and then make a far call to the previous INT21 vector, which your intercept driver will have already recorded.

Another way reentrance could occur involves those pop-up window–type TSR utilities (e.g., phone dialers or calculators). Such a utility could be hooked into the INT08 or INT1C timer interrupt, watching for an acceptable time to pop up by checking the INDOS flag. This timer interrupt could occur just after your intercept logic has switched to its local stack but before the INT21 call has been passed on to DOS. Therefore, the INDOS flag will be clear and the TSR will pop up. When this utility issues its first INT21 call, your intercept logic will be reentered. Refer to books on constructing this type of utility for more details on the INDOS flag.

Interrupt handler reentrance can also occur with IRQ-type interrupts. It may be that the amount of time required to process certain interrupt events will be so long that another one of those same interrupts occurs before the previous one has completed. As long as this only happens occasionally and the code has been designed to expect it, there is nothing intrinsically wrong with this scenario.

Actually, the underlying issue is not reentrance into the same interrupt handler but reuse of the same stack space. If you were to develop a tool with an `INT21` intercept and an `INT10` intercept, where the same local stack was switched to upon entry to each handler, you would be in trouble when you intercepted an `INT21` call that happened to issue an `INT10` call. The `INT10` intercept would overwrite the stack information that the `INT21` intercept was counting on.

A Better Way

The intercept shown in Listing 8-9 doesn't represent a complete solution, but it is a step in the right direction. In this version, the original SS:SP values are stored within the ES:BX register pair. The contents of the ES:BX register pair is then saved on the new stack for the duration of the intercept.

While this version does store the entry SS:SP values in a way that is resilient to reentrance, the second problem previously noted still remains. Should a reentrance occur, all data placed on the local stack by the first entrance will be overwritten by the second.

Another difference between this intercept method and the intercept handlers previously presented in this chapter is that the values of certain registers aren't directly accessible any more. Extra steps would be required to fetch the entry values for the ES and BX registers before the interrupt call is passed on to the previous vector holder. In some interrupt intercept tools, it is also necessary to locate the CS:IP return address from the entry stack so that the location of the interrupt call can be determined and dumped to an output display. Note that after the stack switch, the ES:BX register pair does point to the caller's stack where these values are located.

Further, after the pass-on call is made to the previous vector holder, the current values of ES and BX registers and the CPU flags register must be transferred back to the original point of call. Since ES and BX must also be used to restore the original SS:SP values, some nontrivial cross-stack manipulations would be required to transplant the returning ES, BX, and flags values.

One idea for dealing with the reuse of the same area of the local stack would be to detect when a reentrant call is being made and use a lower point on the local stack. A method sometimes used to detect a reentrance is to test the value of the SS stack segment register upon entry to the intercept. If it is the same as that of the local stack, a reentrance is being made.

The problem with this method is that it isn't foolproof. The fact that a reentrance is possible means that some other software entity (e.g., an IRQ handler) has gained control during a time when your local stack was in effect. This other entity could have switched to its own local stack before making this call, preventing your test of the SS register from working properly.

```
i21_icept:
        push    bx
        push    es
        mov     bx,ss
        mov     es,bx
        mov     bx,sp
        push    cs
        cli
        pop     ss
        mov     sp,offset top_of_lcl_stk
        push    es
        push    bx
        sti


        .....
          (1st section of intercept logic)
        .....

        pushf
        cli
        call    cs:[i21_orig]


        .....
          (2nd section of intercept logic)
        .....

        cli
        pop     bx
        pop     ss                      ; pushed as es
        mov     sp,bx
        pop     es
        pop     bx
        iret
```

LISTING 8-9   Storing SS:SP on the stack (still not stable).

Listing 8-10 shows a trio of functions and a data structure which have been taken from this book's Companion Library. These functions are designed to support reentrance within interrupt intercepts and also provide easy access to the full set of entry registers without the problems just described.

These functions require that a variable named [ld_lstk] exist to hold the offset to be used for the local stack. Although not shown here, the actual library module from which these functions were taken includes both a declaration of this word-sized field and a function that would be used to assign the initial value to this field. For the sake of this discussion, assume that

```
regset  struc
osp     dw      ?
oss     dw      ?
obp     dw      ?
oes     dw      ?
ods     dw      ?
odi     dw      ?
osi     dw      ?
odx     dw      ?
ocx     dw      ?
obx     dw      ?
oax     dw      ?
onret   dw      ?
oip     dw      ?
ocs     dw      ?
oflags  dw      ?
regset  ends


;=============================================================
; la_local_context
;
; in:    registers = interrupt calling registers
;        fl, cs and ip on stack from int call
;
; out:   caller's registers in save area on caller's stack
;        es:bx -> register save area
;        ss:sp -> local stack
;        ds = cs -> dgroup
;        interrupts disabled
;
;=============================================================
        assume  ds:nothing,es:nothing,ss:nothing
lname la_local_context
        push    ax
        push    bx
        push    cx
        push    dx
        push    si
        push    di
        push    ds
        push    es
        push    bp
```

(continued on next page)

LISTING 8-10 Stack functions from the Companion Library.

```
            push    ss
            mov     ax,sp               ; can't just do a 'push sp'
            push    ax                  ; since its 8086 action
            cli                         ; != 80286+ action
            mov     ax,ss
            mov     es,ax
            mov     bx,sp
            mov     ax,cs
            mov     ds,ax
            assume  ds:dgroup
            mov     ss,ax
            mov     sp,dgroup:[ld_lstk]
            push    es:[bx].onret
            ret


;============================================================
; la_adjlstk
;
; in:    ax = amount to be subtracted from ld_lstk
;        ds -> dgroup  (ds == cs == ss)
;        interrupts disabled
;
; out:   [ld_lstk] -= entry ax
;        interrupts enabled
;
;============================================================
            assume  ds:dgroup,es:nothing,ss:nothing
lname la_adjlstk
            sub     dgroup:[ld_lstk],ax
            sti
            ret


;============================================================
; la_orig_context
;
; in:    es:bx -> register save area
;        ax = amount to be added to ld_lstk
;
; out:   caller's registers restored
;        ss:sp -> caller's stack
;
;============================================================
```

LISTING 8-10 *(Continued)*

```
        assume  ds:nothing,es:nothing,ss:nothing
lname la_orig_context
        pop     es:[bx].onret  ; xfer near return address
        cli
        mov     ss,es:[bx].oss
        mov     sp,es:[bx].osp
        add     sp,2            ; skip orig ss
        mov     bx,cs
        mov     ds,bx
        assume  ds:dgroup
        add     dgroup:[ld_lstk],ax
        pop     bp
        pop     es
        pop     ds
        pop     di
        pop     si
        pop     dx
        pop     cx
        pop     bx
        pop     ax
        ret
```

LISTING 8-10   *(Continued)*

this memory variable has been seeded with the offset of the top of the local stack buffer. The library source code module that contains these functions is named \XTOOLS\LIBSRC\CONTEXT.ASM.

The way these routines deal with the problems involved in local stack switching and reentrance is by throwing memory at them. There's actually nothing else you can do, unless you can prevent the reentrance in the first place or detect it early on and skip the processing of nested events.

To use these functions, you must first determine how much stack memory must be allocated to handle each entrance level and how many levels of reentrance are possible. This first factor is referred to as the stack block allocation. Together, these two factors determine the total size of the local stack.

For instance, assume that the interrupt intercept–processing code will require a stack of 256 bytes to cover all code executed by the interrupt intercept as well as a reasonable margin for any other interrupts that might occur while this stack is in effect. Assume also that eight reentrance levels are to be supported. From this, you can determine that 2048 bytes would be required for the local stack buffer (256 × 8).

Each time an entrance is made to an intercept where this stack-switching code is used, the current value of the [ld_lstk] memory variable is used to

```
i21_stkblk        equ      256         ; stack block allocation

i21_icept:
        lcall    la_local_context
        mov      ax,i21_stkblk
        lcall    la_adjlstk

; 1st section of intercept logic)

        .....

        mov      ax,i21_stkblk
        lcall    la_orig_context
        STl
        pushf
        cli
        call     cs:[i21_orig]
        push     bp
        mov      bp,sp
        pushf
        pop      [bp+6]
        pop      bp
        lcall    la_local_context
        mov      ax,i21_stkblk
        lcall    la_adjlstk

; 2nd section of intercept logic)

        .....

        mov      ax,i21_stkblk
        lcall    la_orig_context
        iret
```

LISTING 8-11 An interrupt intercept with two stack switches.

set the top of the local stack. Then the stack block allocation is subtracted from this memory variable before interrupts are enabled. This way, if a reentrance should occur, a lower section of the local stack buffer will be used, leaving the stack block in use by the previous entrance layer unchanged.

Listing 8-11 shows how these functions would be used within an interrupt intercept. Note that in this case a switch back to the local stack is made just before the interrupt call is passed on to the previous vector holder. Upon return from this pass-on call, another switch is made back to the local stack.

Then, when the final section of the intercept logic is finished, a switch is made back to the local stack just before the `iret` is done.

This approach does three things for you. First, the switch back to the local stack just before the pass-on call restores the original calling registers, so the previous interrupt handler will see the conditions it expects. Second, in the event that an interrupt handler expects entry data to be on the caller's stack, everything will be in the proper position, just as if the intercept wasn't hooked into the calling chain (the intercept logic described previously would not work in this type of situation). Third, the transplantation of all return registers from the pass-on call is taken care of automatically by the second pair of stack switch calls.

Accessing the Caller's Registers

While the local stack is in effect in the first part of the intercept handler, accessing the original values of the entry registers is simple. Upon exit from the `la_local_context` function, the ES:BX register pair is pointing to a section of the caller's stack where all of the caller's registers have been placed. This includes the CS:IP and CPU flags register values that were automatically pushed onto the stack as a result of the software interrupt call.

The `regset` structure for assembler, shown at the top of Listing 8-10, is included within the file `\XTOOLS\TLIB.INC` on the Companion Toolset Diskette. Using this structure in conjunction with the ES:BX register pair, addressing the caller's entry registers is as simple as

```
cmp     es:[bx].osi,1234h
```

It is also possible to write new values to these fields, which will be applied to the corresponding register when the switch is made back to the caller's stack with the `la_orig_context` function. Access to the byte-sized registers (AL, AH, BL, etc.) can be done as well. A common use of this type of access would be to test the AH function selector for an interrupt call. For example:

```
cmp     byte ptr es:[bx].oax+1,40h
```

Providing that the ES:BX register pair would always be maintained as the pointer to the caller's register set, a set of equate statements such as the following could be crafted to simplify register access:

```
_AX     equ     es:[bx].oax
_AH     equ     byte ptr es:[bx].oax+1
_AL     equ     byte ptr es:[bx].oax
_BX     equ     es:[bx].obx
_BH     equ     byte ptr es:[bx].obx+1
```

and so on. It would then be possible to reference the caller's registers with a more simple form of instruction, such as the following:

```
mov     cx,_CX
cmp     _AH,32h
mov     _DL,cs:[new_dl]
```

A complete set of these equate statements is included within the \XTOOLS-\TLIB.INC file.

Placing the Stack Switch Calls

The call to the la_local_context function must be the first thing in terms of stack depth. No push instructions can be placed before this call, unless they are counterbalanced by corresponding pop instructions before la_local_context is called. Similarly, the call to la_orig_context has to be the last operation performed before the final iret in terms of stack depth.

In the following code fragment, the use of the ES register was required before the call to the la_local_context. Since the original stack depth is restored before this function is called, there is no problem with this type of filtering code.

```
        push    es
        mov     es,cs:[xyz_segment]
        cmp     ax,es:[xyz_data]
        pop     es
        je      skip_intercept
        lcall   la_local_context
        .....
           (intercept handler goes here)
        .....
        lcall   la_orig_context
skip_intercept:
        iret
```

By the same token, the following code would work, since no registers are changed and no stack depth changes occur:

```
        cmp     ah,43h
        jne     skip_intercept
        lcall   la_local_context
        .....
           (intercept handler goes here)
        ......
```

```
        lcall    la_orig_context
skip_intercept:
        iret
```

The following method would not function correctly. The existence of the BX register on the stack before the call to la_local_context has distorted the stack positioning that this structure was designed to expect:

```
        push     bx
        mov      bx,cs:[xyz]
        cmp      ax,bx
        je       skip_intercept
        lcall    la_local_context
        .....
           (intercept handler goes here)
        .....
        lcall    la_orig_context
skip_intercept:
        pop      bx
        iret
```

The Stack Pocket Technique

When you design interrupt intercepts, the need can arise for the second section of the intercept logic to have access to information derived during the first section. Let's say that you want to construct an INT21 intercept where entry and exit conditions are reported for each call, including the parameters specific to each call.

A call such as function 47h (get current directory) can pose a small problem. This call accepts a drive number in the DL register and a pointer to a text buffer within DS:SI. Upon completion, this operating system service will write a string in the text buffer that identifies the current directory for the specified drive.

It will be up to the logic in the second section of intercept logic (after the pass-on call has been made) to dump this string, but how will the second-section logic determine when the function being called is 47h? Upon completion of this call, DOS changes the AX register (0100h seems to be a typical value). The logic within the second section needs access to the caller's AX value that was extant during the first section.

Listing 8-12 illustrates how a *pocket* can be formed on the local stack during the first section of an intercept so that data can be passed to the exit section. In this example, the only logic shown within the first section is that which saves the caller's entry AX and CX values, and the only logic shown for the second section is that which accesses these entry values. In an actual

```
i21_stkblke    qu      256      ; stack block allocation
i21_pocket     equ     4        ; bytes in section-to-section pocket

i21_orig       dd      ?

i21_icept:
        lcall   la_local_context
        mov     ax,i21_stkblk
        lcall   la_adjlstk
        sub     sp,i21_pocket    ; setup addressability
        mov     bp,sp            ; to pocket

; 1st section of intercept logic

        mov     ax,es:[bx].oax   ; save entry ax
        mov     [bp],ax
        mov     ax,es:[bx].ocx   ; save entry cx
        mov     [bp+2],ax

; adjust the stack while preserving the pocket

        mov     ax,i21_stkblk - i21_pocket
        lcall   la_orig_context
        pushf
        cli
        call    cs:[i21_orig]
        push    bp
        mov     bp,sp
        pushf
        pop     [bp+6]
        pop     bp
        lcall   la_local_context
        mov     ax,i21_stkblk
        lcall   la_adjlstk       ; setup addressability
        mov     bp,sp            ; to pocket

; 2nd section of intercept logic

        mov     ax,[bp]          ; recover entry ax
        mov     cx,[bp+2]        ; recover entry cx

; adjust the stack, freeing up the pocket

        mov     ax,i21_stkblk + i21_pocket
        lcall   la_orig_context
        iret
```

LISTING 8-12 Preserving stack information between sections.

intercept handler there would, of course, be additional logic that would put this information to use.

In this example, a pocket of four bytes is required to make the entry AX and CX values accessible to the second section of the intercept logic. This is defined by the i21_pocket equate statement. If your situation involves a large amount of pocket space, be sure to account for this when determining your stack block allocation value.

A working copy of this intercept handler is supplied in the file \XTOOLS\WORK\POCKET.ASM. This copy uses INTF0 instead of INT21, since working with an unused interrupt is better when testing. Install the F0IRET.COM TSR first, so that when the pass-on call is made, your system will not crash.

Interrupt Handlers and Intercepts in C

Through the use of the DDXXXXX set of template files, it is relatively simple to build a device driver containing an interrupt handler or interrupt intercept coded in C. This is exemplified by the following set of files (found within the \XTOOLS\WORK directory):

```
DDCICEP.ASM
DDCICEPR.C
DDCICEPT.C
DDCICEP.MAK
```

Note that this sample program does not serve any useful function as a debugging tool. Its purpose is to illustrate the following points:

- How C code can be used within a device driver
- How C code can be used for an interrupt intercept function using the c_icept macro, which is contained within the file \XTOOLS\TLIB.INC
- How the caller's registers can be accessed and manipulated within an intercept handler (Note that with this form of intercept handler, preserving entry registers for use by code after the pass-on call is simple: Automatic, that is, stack-based, variables within the C intercept-handling function hold their values during the pass-on call)
- How data can be shared between the resident and nonresident C modules. The word variable named x_option is declared within the DD-CICEPR.C module, since it must be available to the resident code (and, therefore, resident itself). An extern statement is used for this variable within the DDCICEPT.C module so that the parsing logic can set this flag when the /x switch is detected.

This technique can also be applied to the use of the TSR.ASM template in conjunction with the same pair of C modules. In fact, this has been done.

See the files `TTCICEP.ASM`, `TTCICEPR.C`, `TTCICEPT.C` and `TTCICEP.MAK` within the `\XTOOLS\WORK` directory in the Companion Toolset.

8.6 CONTROL INTERFACES

Conversing with a Resident Tool

A TSR or device driver type of debugging tool will often need to provide an interface, through which its actions can be controlled and its services made available. The easiest way to effect this communication is through the use of an interrupt vector. That way, you can encode software interrupt calls to the driver within the program you are debugging, and you can craft stand-alone utility programs that call upon the driver to retrieve data it has captured or to alter its behavior in some way.

Regarding the selection of an interrupt vector, the following are good choices:

```
INT60 through INT66
INT86 through INTF0
INTF1 through INTFF
```

Interrupts 60 through 66 and F1 through FF are documented as user interrupts. Interrupts 86 through F0 are documented as being reserved for the BASIC interpreter. As long as you are not using this dinosaur, there is no reason not to make use of these vectors. There is, of course, always the chance that some other software entity installed within your system is already making use of some of these vectors. See Section 9.5, "Memory/Device Map Utilities," for information on utilities that can help you identify which vectors are in use.

Where software interrupt calls may be made to a debugging tool from within the program being debugged or within a setup utility, it is safest to preface each call with a signature check. This would be done to avoid the crash that would result if a call were made when the debugging tool's interrupt handler had not been installed.

This, of course, entails additional code and an increased execution time. If that will cause problems, directly encode the interrupt calls and realize that you cannot run a modified program without having the tool installed (or at least a nullified interrupt handler).

See the signature-checking method used by the instrumentation code within the file `\XTOOLS\DR_ASM.INC`. This is done to verify that `ROUTER.SYS` is loaded before a call is made to that instrumentation driver.

Hot Key Detection

Consider, for a moment, the case of a bug that is so elusive that it will only occur once every several days, but when it does rear up, it brings your client's operations to a halt. You cannot afford to spend weeks in direct pursuit of it, but you also cannot afford to ignore it.

One approach can be to craft a custom debugging tool that is perpetually capturing a history of the last several hundred program events within a ring buffer. As soon as the failure occurs, you would want the program's operator to be able to press a special hot key, which would cause this tool to output its precious cargo to a printer.

Since simpler is always better when it comes to debugging tools, the suggested hot key method involves the use of special combinations of shift keys. The advantages to this method are that no keyboard interrupt intercepts are necessary (e.g., INT09 and INT16) and that the information required is already maintained within a common memory location.

This location is the byte at address 0040:0017, the keyboard shift-state status byte within the BIOS data area. This same byte is returned in the AL register from a call to function 2 of the INT16 BIOS interrupt. Through inspection of the bits within this byte, the state of the shift keys can be determined. See Table 8.1 for details.

Each time your tool processes a debugging event, make it poll the state of this shift-state byte and test for a certain combination of shift keys. Here are some combinations that shouldn't occur during normal keyboard use:

> Cntrl–RightShift
> Cntrl–LeftShift
> Alt–RightShift
> Alt–LeftShift
> Cntrl–Alt–RightShift
> Cntrl–Alt–LeftShift
> LeftShift & RightShift
> Cntrl–LeftShift & RightShift

If it could happen that you would need your tool to respond to the hot key during a time when no debugging event calls are being made to it, establish a timer interrupt intercept by hooking INT08 or INT1C. On each

TABLE 8.1   Shift state bit definitions

Bit	Key
0	Right Shift
1	Left Shift
2	Control
3	Alt
4	Scroll-Lock
5	Num-Lock
6	Caps-Lock
7	Insert

timer interrupt, poll the value of the shift-state byte to check for your chosen combination.

Note that when this method is used, your debugging dump process should not make use of any DOS interrupt services unless you deal with the attendant reentrance issues. In general, it is preferable to avoid this complication by using the direct inclusion type of instrumentation code presented in Chapter 7. Calls to the ROUTER.SYS instrumentation driver could also be used.

The following code fragment shows how a test could be established for the Cntrl-RightShift case:

```
            push    ax
            push    es
            cmp     cs:[once_flag],0
            jne     wait_release
            mov     ax,40h
            mov     es,ax
            mov     al,es:[17h]
            and     al,00000101b
            cmp     al,00000101b
            jne     not_hot_key
            mov     cs:[once_flag],1
            call    hot_key_process
wait_release:
            test    byte ptr es:[17h],00000101b
            jnz     not_hot_key
            mov     cs:[once_flag],0
not_hot_key:
            pop     es
            pop     ax
```

The once_flag is necessary to prevent retriggering of the hot key event from two different sources:

1. When this polling logic can be entered through a timer intercept, further timer intercepts that occur during the execution of the hot_key_process function must not be allowed to reenter that function.
2. When the hot_key_process function completes its execution before the shift keys have been released, another entry to this logic should not cause a retriggering.

Manual Gating Control

There are a number of cases where it is helpful to be able to control when certain debugging tests will activated from the keyboard. A heavy amount of instrumentation dump output may be required once you arrive at a certain point within a program, but having it active when the program is going through its startup operations may waste too much time.

What is needed is a simple way to gate a debugging process based on a key. This key should be of the toggle variety, and it should not be used by applications programs, so that no conflicts will occur. As it happens, the Scroll-Lock key fits this description rather nicely.

As with the hot key logic shown above, the basic technique is to establish a far pointer to the shift-state status byte at 0040:0017 and test the appropriate bit. For example:

```
            push    ax
            push    es
            mov     ax,40h
            mov     es,ax
            test    byte ptr es:[17h],00010000b
            pop     es
            pop     ax
            jz      scroll_lock_off
            call    debugging_function
scroll_lock_off:
```

This type of test can also be done with C code. Through the use of the dword data type within the file \XTOOLS\ASMTYPES.H, the following code fragment will perform the same function as in the foregoing assembler version (see Appendix H "The ASMTYPES.H Data Structures," for more information):

```
dword shift_state;
SETDWORD(shift_state,0x40,0x17);
if(*(shift_state.bptr) & 0x10) debugging_function();
```

Parameter Parsing

The Companion Toolset Library includes a comprehensive set of parameter-parsing functions. This section presents a summary of the parsing logic's features. To get a further taste of the use of this logic, examine the examples within the following files, which are all located within the \XTOOLS\WORK directory:

Stand-Alone Programs

```
EXTRACT.C
ADDHEAD.C
CHANNEL.C
PARSTEST.C
MODOBJ.C
```

TSRs

`TTCICEP.C`

Device Drivers

`ROUTERT.C` (part of the source for `ROUTER.SYS`)
`DDCICEPT.C`

The parsing logic supports fixed-position parameters, position-independent switches, and position-dependent switches. Switches can be single- or double-character.

Response files are supported. If the first term of a parameter line begins with a @ character, the remainder is treated as the name of a file from which the actual parameter line is read. Note that this feature should not be used from within a device driver, as file I/O is not supported.

User-defined recognition functions provide for the verification and conversion of a wide range of parameter types. They can be applied to both fixed- and switch-type parameters.

A set of functions are supplied within the library to handle

- Switch parameters involving a hex number (e.g., `/pb=03BC`)
- Switch parameters involving a filename (e.g., `/d=widgets.txt`)
- Switch parameters involving a character (e.g., `/c=r`)
- Fixed parameters involving a hex number (e.g., `1F29`)

Either a `/` or a `-` may be used to denote a switch parameter. The matching of switch parameters can be made case-sensitive or case-insensitive.

Fixed parameters are tokenized, leading and trailing delimiters are trimmed off, and each term is zero-terminated. Optional fixed parameters may be skipped by a double comma. A pointer to each fixed parameter is recorded within the parameter data structure so that the parameter may be used at any time during the program's execution.

For switch parameters, once they are processed the parameter's text will be blanked out of the buffer. Therefore, if more data must be stored about a parameter than simply its existence, a recognition function must be set up.

The position of each switch parameter and each fixed parameter is recorded to support position-dependent switches (see `PARSTEST.C`).

Two separate functions are provided, one for switch parameters and another for fixed parameters. The `lc_parse_sw()` function is the parent function for parsing switch parameters, and the `lc_parse_fx()` function is the parent function for the processing of fixed-type parameters. You may find it useful to use only the `lc_parse_sw()` function to parse switches and then use the `lc_process_src_parms()` function to step through the fixed parameters. See the file `EXTRACT.C` for an example of this approach.

The process of initializing the parse engine's data structures has been set up to be almost as simple as filling out a table. It ends up being self-documenting—easy to understand at a glance.

These parsing functions are largely independent of the Standard C Library functions. They can be used in a device driver, where the Standard C Library functions should not be used, by simply changing the three display functions to make their output by some other means than `printf()`. This is taken care of within the `DDXXXXX.ASM` template file through the inclusion of the file `\XTOOLS\XLIBDISP.INC`. See the comments above this `include` statement within `\XTOOLS\WORK\STOCK\DDXXXXX.ASM`.

The only other difference between using this logic in a device driver and using it in a TSR or stand-alone tool is the source of the parameter line string. In a stand-alone program or TSR, the tail portion of the command line is found within the program's PSP data structure, beginning at offset 0080h. In the case of a device driver, the address of the `DEVICE=` line from the `CONFIG.SYS` file is passed to the driver's `init` logic through a field in the request header data structure. Further, as mentioned above, the response file feature should not be used from within a device driver.

If a recognition function detects an error, it should report it using the `lc_disp_error_lead()` and `lc_disp_str()` functions. The recognition function should then return with a nonzero return value. This will cause the parent parsing function to return with a nonzero return value.

Some errors are detected within the parent parsing function. When this occurs, the parent function will emit a report of the condition and return a nonzero return value to the caller.

Internal error checking and reporting are done for the following cases:

- A required parameter is skipped.
- Too many parameters are given.
- A switch parameter is duplicated.
- A proper delimiter doesn't follow a switch parameter.
- A switch is detected that hasn't been defined.

Thus, when your calling code receives a nonzero return value from `lc_parse_sw()` or `lc_parse_fx()`, the specific error has already been reported. This can be a good time to display a screen explaining proper parameter syntax.

8.7 TOOL MANAGEMENT

One side effect of the program templates and function library provided on this book's Companion Toolset Diskette is that it becomes easy to develop a large collection of tools. After a while, when the need arises for a new tool, you will have already built something similar, from which sections could be cloned. But when you need a tool, you don't want to have to squint at a directory of a hundred or more arcane eight-character filenames to find what you're looking for.

One approach that can help is to create separate directories for each type of tool. For example, off of the `\XTOOLS\WORK` directory, you could create individual directories for stand-alone utilities, TSR utilities, and device drivers:

```
\XTOOLS\WORK\UTILS
\XTOOLS\WORK\TSR
\XTOOLS\WORK\DD
```

Another alternative would be to use directory names that categorize tools by their function rather than by their form:

```
\XTOOLS\WORK\ICEPT
\XTOOLS\WORK\TESTBED
\XTOOLS\WORK\FILEDUMP
\XTOOLS\WORK\FILEGEN
```

The EXTRACT.EXE Utility

To simplify the task of finding the tool you need among many, yet another tool is provided in the Companion Toolset: EXTRACT.EXE. This one is designed to scan each source file within a specified set and extract specially marked comments. Extracted comments from each file within the set are written out to one central index file. When it's time to search your collection, all that need be done is to browse through this central index. Using the search function of your editor or browsing tool will make short work of the task of locating a particular tool.

To accommodate this method, write up a comment header block, describing the program's intended purpose, and place it at the top of the source file. Listing 8-13 shows an example of a comment block intended for an assembler program. Listing 8-14 shows the arrangement used for a C program's comment header block. You have probably noticed that each of the program template files contains this type of block.

```
comment ^
,hs

$.
        An explanation would be written here to describe
        the overall function of the source code module.
,he

=============================================================
^
```

LISTING 8-13 Comment block for an assembler program.

```
/*
,hs

$.
        An explanation....
,he
===============================================================
*/
```

LISTING 8-14 Comment block for a C program.

When EXTRACT.EXE begins scanning a file, it will be on the watch for a line beginning with the ,hs metastring. A line starting with this metastring marks the header start point, and the ,he metastring marks the header end. Since these marker lines will appear in the same position for both the assembler and the C case, the EXTRACT.EXE utility will have no trouble finding them.

When the starting marker is found, this text-processing tool will begin copying all successive lines to the specified output file. This copying stops as soon as the tool finds a line beginning with the ,he ending marker.

The advantage of this method is that all documentation on a program can be kept within the program's source code files, but it can be extracted and placed into other summary files. When all program documentation of a summary type is located at the top of the source code module, it is much easier to make updates to this summary when maintenance changes are made to the code (and therefore it is more likely to be actually done).

The more detailed you make this beginning comment block, the clearer your understanding of the program will be some months later when you are browsing through the index text file produced by this extraction method.

EXTRACT.EXE must be supplied with a specification of the set of files to be scanned. This can done in two different ways. First, one or more explicit filenames can be named on the parameter line:

```
extract file1.asm file2.asm  /d=asm.idx /m=h /b
```

Alternatively, one or more of these file specifications may contain wildcard characters:

```
extract *.asm *.c   /d=asm.idx /m=h /b
```

Explicit directory names may also, of course, be included:

```
extract *.asm tsr\*.asm  /d=asm.idx /m=h /b
```

Finally, by starting a file specification with the # character, you can tell this scanning utility to open the corresponding file and regard it as a list of the files to be processed:

```
extract #asmfiles.txt /d=asm.idx /m=h /b
```

For an example of this list-file method, see the files \XTOOLS\LIBSRC-\GENINDEX.BAT and \XTOOLS\LIBSRC\GENINDEX.DAT.

The use of this list-file method enables you to be selective about which files are scanned and to order the scanning process. It does, however, create an additional maintenance task in that you must remember to update your list file whenever you add, delete, or rename a tool in your collection.

In addition to extracting comment header blocks, this tool can also be made to produce an index containing the comments within function header blocks. This will work as long as comment header blocks of the form contained within the files \XTOOLS\WORK\STOCK\PROCHEAD.ASM and \XTOOLS\WORK\STOCK\PROCHEAD.C are used and the /m=f switch is specified to EXTRACT.EXE.

EXTRACT.EXE recognizes one more metastring: the $. string. Whenever this is encountered within a comment header during the scanning process, the filename and extension of the module being scanned is written to the index file in its place. This way, if you rename a file, you don't have to edit the comment header block.

The ADDHEAD.EXE utility is provided to simplify the addition of comment header blocks to your existing set of program source modules.

8.8 THE COMPANION LIBRARY

The Companion Library contains functions to support the following areas:

- Parsing Logic
    Parsing fixed and switch parameters
    Supporting response files
- File-Processing Logic
    File find loop processing
    The list file method
- Packetized Ring Buffer Logic
- Stack-Switching Logic
    Switch to local stack
    Switch back to caller's stack
    Pass-on call to previous vector holder
- ROUTER Logic
    Functions to build the ROUTER.SYS instrumentation driver (can be used to incorporate the router logic into other tools)
- DDICEPT Logic
    Functions used to build the DDICEPT.SYS intercept driver

- Parallel Link Logic
    Functions to read and write data through the parallel machine-to-machine link
- Parallel List Logic
    Functions to support the building of parallel lists, such as is done within DDICEPT.SYS
- String/Memory Logic
    Copy blocks of memory
    Fill memory
    Copy/fill strings
    Measure the length of strings
    Check for character inclusion in a string
- Display Logic
    Display characters and strings
- I/O Logic
    Input a byte from a port
    Output a byte to a port
- Conversion Logic
    Convert binary to decimal ASCII
    Convert binary to hex ASCII
    Convert text ASCII to hex
    Convert character to uppercase
- Miscellaneous Logic
    Derive a program's home path
    Compare doublewords
    Enable and disable interrupts
    Manipulate segment registers

The source code modules for the library have been designed to work with the EXTRACT.EXE utility. The batch file \XTOOLS\LIBSRC\GENINDEX.BAT will put an index of all functions within the library into a file named \XTOOLS\NDXLIB.TXT.

Within the set of library functions, the following naming conventions are used:

- Functions prefixed with la_ (e.g., la_setlstk) are designed to be called from within assembler programs.
- Functions prefixed with lc_ (e.g., lc_passon()) are designed to be called from within C programs.

Of course, it is possible place to calls to a function designed for C from within an assembler program, as long as the proper stack parameters are prepared before the call and cleared after the call. Where registers are used to pass entry parameters to a function designed for assembler and this function needs to be called from within a C program, it is best to design a C-based function, written in assembler, that translates between C's stack parameters and the register parameters of assembler.

8.9 DDICEPT.SYS

The DDICEPT.SYS intercept driver provides a supporting framework for the construction of tools that intercept and report on system calls. These would include interrupts such as INT10, INT13, INT17, and INT21. A set of ready-made versions of this driver are included on the diskette:

DDICEPT.10   To report on INT10 system calls for video output
DDICEPT.13   To report on INT13 system calls for disk I/O
DDICEPT.17   To report on INT17 system calls for printer I/O
DDICEPT.21   To report on INT21 system calls for DOS services

The detail provided in this reporting is what makes this a valuable tool. For each call, the hex value of the entry and exit registers are dumped. In addition, this tool also looks up and displays a text string that identifies the purpose of each function. It also determines the input and output string parameters for each function and includes them in the dump output, along with identifying annotation. For example, when an INT21 function 3D call is made to open a file, this tool will display the filename string to which the DS:DX register pair points.

DDICEPT.SYS makes calls to ROUTER.SYS to dump its information. Therefore, its output can be stored within a ring buffer or written to direct video, to a printer or serial port, or to another machine, where the CHANNEL.EXE utility will be used to collect the data.

The DDICEPT.ASM source module contains the basic scaffolding upon which the interrupt-specific code is placed. The code and data specific to each interrupt supported is placed within a module whose name has the form IIMXX.INC, where the XX is replaced with the two hex digits which represent the interrupt involved. For example, the include file containing the intercept code and data specific to INT21 is named IIM21.INC.

Near the very end of the DDICEPT.ASM file is the point where the IIMXX.INC modules are to be included. Note that it is possible to include several such modules at one time. For instance, you could make one version of DDICEPT.SYS that would intercept and report on INT21, INT13, and INT15.

The IIMSTOCK.INC module is provided as a template from which new IIMXX.INC can be made. More detail on this is provided within the file \XTOOLS\DOC\DESNOTES.TXT.

To build a version of DDICEPT.SYS, simply use the MS.BAT batch file as follows:

```
ms ddicept
```

It is a good idea to rename the resulting .SYS file to something which will identify the particular version of the driver which results. While most device drivers have a file extension of .SYS or .BIN, this is a convention rather than a requirement.

The `SETDDIC.EXE` utility is provided to control the setting and clearing of the filter flags for each function. Filtering can be helpful when you want to see most of the function calls being made but skip "busy" calls, such as keyboard polling.

One advantage of having a collection of `IIMXX.INC` modules available is that the intercept-handling logic contains documented hook points where custom test code can be added. This can be useful for cases where you want to issue a breakpoint when a certain sequence of interrupt calls occurs, or when you want to have a certain memory region validated before and after each system call.

The `ILMRCFXX.BIN` Modules

When this intercept driver outputs its information into a packetized ring buffer or across the serial or parallel binary link to another machine, the data is in binary form. The entry and exit register values only require a word of storage each rather than the five bytes involved in their ASCII representation (the four hex digits and following space).

The text string identifying the call need not be stored at all within the binary data packet, since it is based upon the value of one of the entry registers, typically the AH register. The same is true of strings that annotate error conditions and those that preface parameter strings by telling which register pointer is used. The only text strings that must be stored within the binary data packet are the entry and exit string parameters themselves.

By using the binary format, significantly more information can be retained within a given size of ring buffer, and transmission throughput across a serial or parallel link to another machine is higher. But once this data leaves the `DDICEPT.SYS` driver in its binary form, how are the various annotation strings obtained when it's time to convert this binary data to a displayable form?

The `CHANNEL.EXE` data capture utility has been designed to work in concert with `DDICEPT.SYS` . By using the `/ir` switch with `CHANNEL.EXE`, you can specify that a special copy of the lookup tables that `DDICEPT.SYS` uses be loaded into memory. The module containing this copy of the lookup tables is produced from the same `IIMXX.INC` modules that are incorporated into `DDICEPT.SYS` .

For example, to use `DDICEPT.SYS` to monitor `INT67` calls to an EMS memory management driver, you would create a module by the name of `IIM67.INC` for inclusion within the `DDICEPT.SYS` scaffolding, ultimately producing `DDICEPT.67` . Before you put this tool into use where the data will be stored in a binary form (in a ring buffer or across the machine-to-machine link), you must also run the `GENILR.BAT` batch file, which is located within the `\XTOOLS\BATCH` directory. Note that the parameter must be simply the two hex digits corresponding to the interrupt. An h should not be used:

```
genilr 67
```

This process will use the `IIM67.INC` include file to produce a binary code module named `ILMRCF67.BIN` . Now, when you use `CHANNEL.EXE` to retrieve binary data from a ring buffer or capture binary data from a serial or parallel link, use its `/ir` switch to specify the `ILMRCFXX.BIN` module you want it to load. As shown in the second example line following, if you are working with a version of `DDICEPT.SYS` which is intercepting more than one interrupt, multiple hex numbers can be specified after one `/ir` switch:

```
channel prb, capture.txt   /ir=67
channel prb, capture.txt   /ir=67,21,15
```

When its `/ir` switch is used, `CHANNEL.EXE` will look for the corresponding `ILMRCFXX.BIN` module(s) within the current directory first. If not found there, the directory from which `CHANNEL.EXE` was execed will be searched. This way, you can keep `CHANNEL.EXE` and all `.BIN` modules within the `\XTOOLS\EXECUTE` directory and operate in any other directory you wish.

8.10 Summary

Custom tooling can be used to do the following:

- Augment a debugger
- Trigger and gate instrumentation code
- Monitor interrupt calls
- Provide a test bed environment
- Produce a simple model of a problem
- Generate test versions of data files
- Display the contents of data files
- Flex hardware

Custom tooling can take one of four different forms:

- Code that is embedded directly within the program being analyzed
- A stand-alone utility program
- A TSR utility
- A device driver

A TSR can be de-installed, but a device driver cannot.

You can decide to load a TSR at almost any time after booting, but to change the loading status of a device driver you must edit your `CONFIG.SYS` file and reboot.

A device driver can introduce debugging code at a much earlier point than a TSR can.

A device driver can be communicated with through the standard device interface.

The TSR and the device driver both consist of an initialization section and a resident processing section.

Placing commonly used object modules within a library makes working with them much more convenient.

When building a device driver or TSR, control over link order of the sections of the program is important. All parts of the program which will remain resident must be located in the first part of the final executable module, and all nonresident initialization code must be positioned at the end.

The program templates and function library included within the Companion Toolset use naming techniques for functions and segments to ensure that functions referenced by logic within the resident section are linked into that section, and likewise for the nonresident section.

In the assembler case, the `lcall` macro must be used to call a library function, and the `lextrn` macro must be used to declare these functions as external.

The `STANDA.ASM` template produces a stand-alone assembler program.

The `STANDC.C` template produces a stand-alone C program.

The `TSR.ASM` template produces a TSR assembler program.

The `SYS.ASM` template produces a device driver assembler program.

The `DDXXXXX` set of templates produces a device driver containing an assembler substrate where C functions can be used.

The `STANDA.ASM`, `TSR.ASM`, and `SYS.ASM` templates can be used to build assembler programs where C functions are linked in. The `STANDC.C` template can be used to build a C program where assembler functions are linked in.

The `MC.BAT` batch file will produce a `.COM` file from an assembler source module derived from the `STANDA.ASM` or `TSR.ASM` template.

The `MS.BAT` batch file will produce a `.SYS` file from an assembler source module derived from the `SYS.ASM` template.

The `DDXXXXX` set of template files includes a `.MAK` file for use with a make utility.

When coding an assembler statement within a source module derived from one of the templates, you must use the `dgroup:` modifier for all statements where an offset is involved. For example:

```
mov     si,offset dgroup:buffer
```

To intercept an interrupt is to record the current address within the corresponding interrupt vector and then replace it with the address of a new interrupt-handling function. This new function will ultimately pass control on to the previous vector holder.

With an IRQ-based intercept, the important thing is that the intercept preserve all CPU registers that it will change. When a pass-on call is made to the previous vector holder, the registers do not have to be restored as long as they will be restored when the intercept executes its final `iret` instruction. In the event that an intercept passes control on to the original vector holder through a far jump instruction, all registers must be restored first.

When an intercept is established for a software interrupt handler such as `INT21`, care must be taken to restore the registers to their original entry state before passing the call on to the previous vector holder. In addition, the register values that result from the pass-on call must be delivered back to the original point of call. This can also mean that the exit flags word must be planted onto the stack, where the intercept's final `iret` instruction will pull it off.

When an intercept handler will perform any complex operations or make calls to C functions, a switch to a local stack should be done.

Always take advantage of the automatic interrupt-guarding feature of the 80X86 class CPU when switching to a new stack. The next instruction after any instruction that loads the SS register is protected from interruption.

The library functions `la_local_context` and `la_orig_context` manage stack switching in a reentrant resilient manner and support easy access to the caller's registers.

The best way to establish a communications link with a resident code module is to make use of a free interrupt vector. To be safe, all logic that makes calls to this vector should check for a signature first.

When you need to make a debugging tool respond to a hot key, the simplest approach is to take advantage of the shift key status information maintained in the byte at address 0040:0017.

When you need to implement a gating control key, the simplest way is to use the Scroll-Lock key. The toggle state of this key is also maintained in the byte at address 0040:0017.

The library contains a set of functions to handle the parsing of fixed parameters, position–dependent switch parameters, and position–independent switch parameters. The same logic can be used within stand-alone programs, TSRs, and device drivers.

To manage a growing collection of debugging tools and other utility programs, use the `EXTRACT.EXE` utility to create an index from comment headers, which are located at the top of each tool's source code module.

The Companion Library contains functions to support parsing, file processing, packetized ring buffers, stack switching, the router logic, the `DDICEPT.SYS` driver, parallel links, parallel lists, string and memory operations, display output, I/O operations, numeric conversion, and other miscellaneous operations.

The `DDICEPT.SYS` intercept driver, with its associated `IIMXX.INC` modules, provides a framework from which annotating interrupt intercepts can be built. Since intercept drivers produced from this framework make their output through `ROUTER.SYS`, the final output can be displayed or recorded in any of the ways that `ROUTER.SYS` supports.

When `DDICEPT.SYS` and `ROUTER.SYS` are configured to store interrupt intercept information in binary form (such as when a ring buffer or machine to machine link is used), the `CHANNEL.EXE` utility must be supplied with `ILMRCRXX.BIN` modules that correspond to the interrupts being monitored.

CHAPTER 9
Other Tools

This chapter examines the debugging use of a variety of commercially available tools. This group consists of those tools not already covered elsewhere in this book. For example, software debuggers are covered in Chapters 5, 6, and 11; event-tracing tools are covered in Chapters 7 and 12; disassemblers are covered in Chapter 13; and so on.

The set of tools covered in this chapter is also confined to those that can be used in an after-the-fact manner. Whereas tools such as CASE environments, documentation extraction utilities, and revision control systems can be very helpful when it comes to debugging, their initial setup requirements usually make them impractical to bring in at the point where debugging is being done.

9.1 SOURCE CODE ANALYZERS

Someday, maybe we'll be able to feed our source code into an all-knowing tool and, a few seconds later, receive a report showing the exact location of all bugs. Then again, when tools of the all-knowing class are possible, they'll be used to write the code in the first place!

In the meantime, tools are available that approach this ideal. A prime example is the `lint` type of utility used to analyze C programs (similar tools also exist for Assembler and other languages). This class of tool parses through your source modules watching for the types of coding errors that most compilers just aren't able to pick up. While ANSI C, with its function-prototyping conventions and similar requirements in the name of clarity, goes a long way toward ensuring clean coding, the time it takes to apply a `lint`-type utility can still more than pay for itself.

Here are some of the errors that `lint`-type utilities can pick up:

- Assignments that result in a loss of precision
- Mixed use of signed and unsigned variables and constants

- Switch blocks with missing `break` statements
- The use of variables that have not been initialized
- Inconsistent declarations and uses of functions and variables across multiple source modules

This type of watchdog tool will typically produce many more warnings than are actually pertinent to your situation. The trick is, then, to sift through them and discern which are meaningful to your situation and which aren't. *You* have to supply the "all-knowing" part. For example, there are cases where it is useful to omit `break` statements within a switch block or to assign a `long` to a `short`. Note that to speed this sifting process in the future, it can be a good idea to add documentation to the source to explain why rules are bent.

9.2 CHARTING AND LISTING UTILITIES

This group includes utilities that produce the following output:

- Calling hierarchy charts to illustrate the calling relationships between functions graphically
- Flowcharts and action diagrams to illustrate the procedural logic of each function graphically
- "Pretty-printed" versions of a source module to make the names of program variables appear in bold print or otherwise clarify the code
- A version of a source module where a uniform indentation style has been enforced
- A program listing where high-level language statements and the corresponding assembler statements have been merged together
- A version of a BASIC source module where unreferenced line numbers are filtered out

It's a universal principle: The clearer your road map is, the sooner you'll be able to find your way. Given the availability, low cost, and ease of use of the tools in this category, there's basically no excuse not to use them. These source code clarifiers are nothing short of invaluable when you must analyze a program that was written by someone else, or code that you wrote long ago.

The new perspective they provide can also be helpful when you must debug your current project. You may think your understanding of your current project to be so clear that applying this type of tool would be unnecessary. But let's face it: If you are being visited by bugs, things can't be as clear as they could be. When you have been closely involved with a project for a period of time, your perspective can benefit from a tool that helps you review your code at more of an overview level—a macro-perspective level.

Seeing a report of the module-calling hierarchy could alert you to a way that a certain function could be involved in the problem you are chasing where you had previously presumed it couldn't or shouldn't be involved. Seeing an action chart diagram of your code may help you understand a structural anomaly that you've been overlooking. Using a utility to merge your high-level source statements with their assembler counterparts can reveal subtle effects that could otherwise require hours of backtracing to pin down.

9.3 CROSS-REFERENCE GENERATORS

Which source modules reference the variable total_widgets? Which module contains the declaration for the count_widgets() function? While you can seek the answers to these types of questions using a grep-type utility, a text file browser, or the search commands of your editor, having a cross-reference listing generated makes the task much simpler.

Some cross-reference utilities work by scanning the source code statements themselves; some operate on special cross-reference data files produced by a compiler or assembler; and still others generate their reports by processing the object (.OBJ) modules produced by a compiler or assembler.

When it comes to debugging, not only will a cross-reference table make it easier to find where variables and functions are declared and referenced; it can also enable you to identify points of suspicion. When a function has no callers or a variable has no references, it is a strong indication that something has been forgotten.

9.4 EXECUTION PROFILERS

There are times in the debugging of a program when it can be very helpful to know where the program spends most of its time. When you must reverse-engineer a program for which no source code is available, this knowledge will help you know where your analysis efforts are best spent. Likewise, when you need to understand a program you didn't write, knowing which portions of it are the most active gives you a good indication of which portions of the source to review first.

If you were to print a copy of a program's source or a disassembly listing and then begin studying it from front to back (for lack of better insight), you could easily end up expending a great deal of energy analyzing portions of the program that aren't very important. By keying in on high-activity areas of a program, you are more likely to develop an understanding of the most important parts of it more quickly.

One exception to this rule pertains to a program's initialization logic. Understanding how a program prepares its data structures and performs its initial startup tasks is certainly important, but this section of a program will usually consume only a relatively small amount of total execution time.

A profiler can use any of several operating methods. A common one is to intercept the timer tick interrupt (also known as IRQ0 or INT08) and determine what the current point of execution was when each of these hardware interrupts occurred. The profiler makes this determination by examining the return address on the stack and comparing it to a table that holds the addresses of key points within the program. A "hit counter" is incremented for each event for which a match can be found in the table.

Another method is to embed breakpoint instructions within the program being studied. Once these breakpoints are installed, the profiler acts in fashion similar to a debugger. When it processes an INT03 breakpoint call, it replaces the breakpoint instruction with the original opcode, uses the INT01 single-stepping feature to execute the original instruction but stay in control, reasserts the breakpoint instruction, records the event in its profile database and then resumes full-speed execution of the program.

When this technique is applied in conjunction with the debugging information normally intended for a source-level debugger, namely, the list that shows the correspondence between source file line numbers and binary module addresses, a profiler can generate a report of the time spent in each section of a program down to the source-line level. In addition to this automatic placement of breakpoints, explicit placement specifications are also usually supported.

9.5 MEMORY/DEVICE MAP UTILITIES

This group includes tools that report on the following:

- The contents of interrupt vectors
- The state of the BIOS data area beginning at address 40:0
- Internal structures within DOS, such as the MCB chain, the SFT (System File Table) chain, the chain of installed device drivers, and the PSPs and memory allocations associated with installed TSRs
- Memory allocation statistics from XMS and EMS drivers

To be robust for use in a debugging situation, utilities that trace linked list–type data structures should always try to verify the chain's integrity before advancing to the next node. Otherwise, you will have to determine when a corrupt point has been found by more empirical means, such as noticing when the screen becomes littered with happy faces.

When you must determine which of a set of programs is responsible for the corruption of a certain memory area, where the corruption occurs only on an intermittent basis, it can be helpful to run an array of structure-dumping utilities after each invocation of each of the programs.

9.6 HARDWARE DIAGNOSTICS

It's always a shame when you discover, only after hours of debugging, that the intermittent bug you've been chasing is being caused by flaky hardware rather than flaky software. If only you'd run a memory diagnostic first, you might have saved yourself some unnecessary frustration.

Hardware diagnostic utilities are available that will analyze a system's CPU, memory, IRQ signals, I/O operations, serial ports, parallel ports, video display adapters, disk drives, and other features. In addition, external hardware devices may be used to monitor serial communications traffic between two devices.

Some of these diagnostics also enable you to manipulate a system's peripheral circuitry through explicit specification. This can be helpful when debugging to play out a hunch. For example, if you notice that a bug results in a certain strange video mode being established, you might want to manipulate the display adapter into that mode yourself to understand better what would be required for your program to effect the same action.

SECTION THREE

Techniques

CHAPTER 10
General Diagnosis

In this chapter, it is time to start applying the fundamentals covered in the preceding two parts. This chapter examines the more preliminary and non-invasive types of techniques. Whenever possible, it only makes sense to cure an ailment with the simplest approach that will work.

10.1 CHECKING FOR CORRUPTION

A program can be as correct as possible in terms of its design, its encoding, and its operating data, but still exhibit buggy behavior. One way this can happen is when the media on which a program and its data are stored becomes corrupt. When a program that was working satisfactorily only a short time ago suddenly falls very ill, corruption is a likely explanation.

Often, such corruption can be detected by disk diagnostic tools. But since this isn't an iron-clad rule, other testing methods bear discussion.

Regarding media failure on a hard disk, a disk crash can occur when small particles of dust come between a disk head and the platter or when a mechanical shock causes a head to collide with the platter. The magnetic coating on the platter can also deteriorate due to age or extremes in temperature. In addition, electrical noise or power-on and -off transitions that occur while the disk heads are riding over the media can cause unwanted changes in the information stored on the drive.

Regarding diskettes and other removable media, improper handling is the biggest concern. Touching or bending a disk's surface, or subjecting it to heat, water, or magnetic flux, is also an invitation for disaster. Dirty, worn, or misaligned diskette drive heads are another source of trouble.

As was mentioned above, the first line of defense against this type of problem is to run disk diagnostic utilities. But even when these tools report no problems, suspicion of file corruption can still be warranted.

Other Sources

Another way a program can become corrupted is when it is downloaded through a modem or transferred through another form of communications media, such as a local area network (LAN) or satellite link. While almost all communications systems incorporate some level of error checking, nothing is perfect, and corrupted files can slip through undetected at times.

Unfortunately, intentional sources of corruption cannot be ignored. Deliberate mischief may have been played out at the location where the problem is being experienced, or you may be seeing the effects of a virus that originated on another continent.

A final source to be considered is accidental corruption. Someone may have unknowingly copied a binary file using a utility intended for a text file. The utility would be monitoring the data stream for the text-mode end-of-file character (the byte value 1Ah) and stop copying when this code is detected. This can cause a truncation in binary files, where the byte 1Ah can be an opcode, an operand, or a piece of data.

Someone may have run a data conversion program and specified the wrong input file name or used a wildcard file specification that was too encompassing. The program you are experiencing problems with may have had one of its overlays or data files run through a wringer!

When you suspect that you have a corrupt code or data file, it is time to install a fresh version from the original master disks. First, take care to preserve the current copy. If you know without a doubt that the package's installation program allows you to specify a different directory name or hard disk volume letter, then this is no problem. Otherwise, use a utility to rename the directory or copy the current set of code and data files off to another directory first.

Your next task is, of course, to determine whether the new copy is free of the problem. One approach is to run the new program through the same sequence of operations that exhibited a failure in the original installation. Care must be taken to be sure that you are actually replicating the original conditions fully. If the program uses data files, you will need to regenerate them too.

You may be tempted simply to use the set of data files from the original installation. This can be done as long as you realize that doing so will not always produce conclusive answers. For example, if using new code files and original data files results in no evidence of the failure, corruption of the original code files is likely. But if the problem still occurs, it could be either that the original data files are corrupt or that there is a previously undiscovered bug in the code.

Binary File Comparison

Another approach is to use a binary file comparison utility. Some caveats apply, however, since differences may exist between the old and new versions for a legitimate reason. If this is actually the case, but it is not seen for what it is, you can wind up going on a wild-goose chase and making an improper diagnosis.

Some packages include a utility that lets you customize a program's colors, default choices, and so on by patching changes directly into data areas within the executable file. In this situation, the newly installed copy would have to be configured to be the same as the original before a binary comparison could be a valid test. How can you know when this is the case? Being aware of the possibilities is often your best hope.

Any patches applied to the original version that were not also applied to the master copy will also cause a binary file compare utility to report differences. As in the previous case, maintaining an awareness of what is possible, combined with a healthy suspicion, is wise. If the directory entries for the file's date and time are different between the freshly installed copy and the original, this can sometimes be a tip-off. It just depends on the type of file copy operation done by the package's installation program.

If you do discover that patches were applied to the original program, it can be wise to suspect a side-effect bug. Providing that you can operate at all without having the patches applied in the new version, try running without them first. Does the problem only show up in the newly installed copy when it is patched in the same way as the original?

Analysis

If after observing these prerequisites, a difference still exists between the old and the new, take a close look at the values of the bytes that constitute the difference. In looking for clues, the position in the file and the size of the differing section can also be important. For example, if the differing region begins on a 512-byte boundary relative to the start of the file and is a whole multiple of 512 bytes in size, suspect that cross-linked clusters either exist now on the disk or may have existed on a disk from which this file was previously copied.

Using DEBUG

It can sometimes be instructive in the pursuit of clues to load the corrupted file into DEBUG.COM for a closer examination. As a first step, if the file is of the .EXE type, temporarily rename it to have a different extension such as .BIN. This will make DEBUG treat this file the same as any other with regards to the initial values for the segment registers.

When a file is loaded into DEBUG, the file's first byte is located at offset 100h with respect to the current segment register values (the values for the DS, ES, SS, and CS segment register values should all be the same). This convention was established because DEBUG is typically used with files of the .COM type.

Most file compare utilities, however, report the location of the differing section as a zero-based offset relative to the first byte in the file. Therefore, your next step is to adjust DEBUG's DS register to match. Adjusting a segment register to account for an offset of 100h is done by adding 10h to its current value. An example should make this clearer.

In the first of the three lines shown here, the first character, the -, is DEBUG's command prompt. The command entered in this case is rds, which allows the DS register's value to be changed. The <cr> at the end of the line means to press the Enter key to enter this command.

```
-rds <cr>
DS 3AA6
:3AB6 <cr>
```

The second line is DEBUG's report of the current value within the DS register. The value of 3AA6 is merely an example. The first character of the third line, the :, is another one of DEBUG's prompt characters. Following that, the 3AB6 value is what you must enter (or whatever value corresponds to the value shown on the second line, plus 10h).

From this point, whenever you use DEBUG's data dump command d or unassemble command u, simply specify the DS register before the offset. For example, if the binary file compare utility reported a difference at file offset 509A, enter the following command to browse this area within DEBUG:

```
-d ds:509a <cr>
```

If the file offset reported by the compare utility is greater than 64K (0FFFFh), an additional adjustment of segment values will be required. See Appendix B for tips on dealing with hexadecimal numbers.

Wrap-Up

In the event that you are unable to draw any conclusions regarding the source of the corruption, write it off to a power-line glitch or gamma particle collision and keep the freshly installed new version. But be sure to save the corrupted copy for future reference, along with a copy of your notes detailing the nature of the problem, the differences found, and the steps required to derive those differences. If the problem occurs again, being able to compare the first corruption with the second may help you identify the cause.

10.2   TESTING PROCEDURES

When you first discover a bug, it can be tempting to begin immediately using invasive types of techniques. While there is certainly nothing wrong with this approach, providing that you are fairly familiar with the problem, going in too deep too soon can be a problem when you don't have a strong hunch. You can end up missing important details.

In such cases, it is usually best to spend more time experimenting with the program from the outside. You may learn how to make the bug occur with more consistency or how to find an evidence of failure at an even earlier point. You may even learn that more than one type of failure is occurring, indicating either multiple bugs or multiple manifestations of the same bug. You may even see enough to get a flash of inspiration, where you will be able to determine the exact cause of the bug.

The first step is to try to identify the section of the program where the failure is occurring. When the bug is of the consistent type and you are familiar with the program, you will often be able to readily identify the function or module involved. When this is not the case, qualify a location based on the menu choices and other program actions that take place immediately preceding the failure. With intermittent or variable types of bugs, this isolation phase will, of course, be much more difficult.

Once you are able to isolate a failure to a certain section of a program, identify the significant data items involved, such as memory variables, the contents of data file records, and the state of I/O ports. Then list boundary values, out-of-range values, and nominal values for each (see Section 4.2, "Verification," for more information on boundary values and permutations).

Next, derive a set of combinations of these data items which seems likely to be involved with the problem—a set of suspicious permutations. If you are fairly familiar with this section of the program and its associated data, you may be able to do this by mulling this data over in your mind. Otherwise, consider generating a formal set of permutations. Be sure to save any charts and notes generated during this phase, as they will be useful once you've made a correction and must test again to verify it.

In addition to considering the possible states for entry data items (e.g., the state of a function's entry parameters and the initial state of global variables referenced by a function), you must also consider what is required to produce boundary values and out-of-range values in intermediate data variables as well as output data variables. Similarly, consider each branch that could be taken and each exception condition that could occur within the section under scrutiny, and derive a set of entry conditions that will exercise these different actions.

Your goal in this exercise is to produce a script from which a series of tests can be run to invoke each data state. As described in Section 4.2, "Verification," it can be useful to apply instrumentation to determine whether the actual conditions match your expectations. When discrepancies exist, it could be that you overlooked something in your test design, or it could be a clue—a manifestation of the bug you are chasing.

When developing a set of permutations, be aware that combinations where more than data item is driven to an out-of-range value may be of limited use. If producing this type of condition within the program does flush the failure out, you probably won't be able to make a direct assignment of fault.

In the course of running a program through its paces to try to find the easiest way to produce a failure, don't overlook the use of different installation options. These often come in the form of parameter line switches, environment variables, and parameters within a configuration file.

While running a series of tests, it is important to keep track of what you are doing. If you've been flexing a program for some time, working at a feverish pace to try to flush out a frustrating intermittent bug, will you be able to remember exactly what steps you just went through when it finally does occur and fills the screen with garbage?

Maybe if you repeat the last 10 or 20 steps you went through just before the crash, you'd be able to produce the failure again. The only way to know is to recreate the exact sequence of events. But the fatigue of prolonged testing can tax even the sharpest of memories. What is needed is a form of real-time data acquisition system.

Pausing to jot down each step you take as you exercise a program is certainly a possibility—though not a very attractive one. When you must resort to this approach, developing a shorthand notation can help somewhat (e.g., writing "mm5" when you select item #5 from the Main Menu).

There are some other alternatives that will help you keep your speed up when stepping through a series of tests. Installing instrumentation to record keyboard input, and possibly display output, is one. Since the time when you need access to the collected data will be after the program has crashed, it is often best to set up a serial or parallel link and store the data on a second machine (e.g., using ROUTER.SYS).

Another alternative is to run a tape recorder in record mode while you execute your tests, announcing each step as you do it. Finally, if you have a video camera and tripod, you could set it up to watch over your shoulder, with a view of the keyboard and the computer's monitor.

10.3 UNDERSTANDING THE CODE

When seeking to understand a section of source code, you must be especially careful to seek the real intent of the code. Sometimes this must be done *in spite of* the source code's comments. Comments that have fallen out of synchronization as modifications were made to the code can be hazardous!

Consider using a profiler prior to undertaking an analysis of an unfamiliar program. This will help you prioritize your analysis efforts by ensuring that you don't waste time studying sections of the program that aren't even involved in the operations you are working with.

A more direct form of profiling can be achieved by adding instrumentation markers to the source that report when each function is entered and exited. Further, when you use this method to gain a better understanding of the code, you will often discover a lot more about the bug's behavior in the process.

Using a utility that charts a program's calling hierarchy can give you an important perspective on how it conducts its internal operations. There can also be times when having this information will cut your debugging session short. You may discover that it is possible for the section of the program you are studying to make a call to a certain low-level function that could account for the failure you are chasing. If you had previously ruled out any involvement by this function, believing that it wasn't even accessible from the section of the program you are studying, this type of discovery could save you a lot of time.

When studying unfamiliar code, a utility that produces a formatted listing of a program's source can be very valuable. Such a utility (sometimes called a "pretty-print" program) should enforce consistent indentation of the source statements, enforce consistent alignment of comments (to improve readability), and print line numbers at the left edge of the paper.

If the source code is littered with conditional compilation statements, where the same source is used to build more than one product, see if your compiler can produce a listing that contains only the statements which are actually being used in the version you are studying. Reducing this clutter can make the program much easier to interpret. If such a feature is not provided, you might consider loading a copy of the file into your editor and trimming out the conditional code that isn't being used.

Do not overlook the value of a printed listing. Reviewing source code on the display screen does have certain advantages, such as being able to search for all occurrences of a certain name, but when doing a line-by-line examination of a program, using a display screen, it is easy to gloss over important details. Having a printed listing makes it easy to sketch lines to check for proper matching of braces and parentheses, to scribble additional comments and data values, and to get away from the computer console for a change of perspective.

A tool that automatically produces a flowchart or action chart version of a program's source code can also be worth a lot during this stage. In lieu of this type of tool, it can be worthwhile to sketch a flowchart of selected portions of a program manually.

Do not worry about using a formal diagramming method where decision diamonds and process boxes are drawn with a template. A simple, freehand, pseudocode sketch is best. As these types of sketches tend to sprawl off in hard-to-predict directions, it is wise to start in the middle of a large note-pad. See Listing 10-1 and Figure 10.1 for an example.

Be sure to keep all notes that you generate through the course of studying a bug. Then, when the search is over, make time to go back and update any source code comments and data dictionary entries that you found to be incorrect or that have been made out of date by your work. You'll thank yourself six months from now when you have to come back into this same part of the code to make another change.

```
        mov     si,offset list_1
top_of_loop:
        mov     ax,4
        call    function_a
        cmp     bx,20
        ja      too_large
        call    function_b
        add     si,8
        cmp     si,limit
        je      exit_handler
        jmp     top_of_loop
too_large:
        mov     dx,offset msg1
        call    write_string
        jmp     exit_handler
```

LISTING 10-1   Sample program code for chart in Figure 10.1.

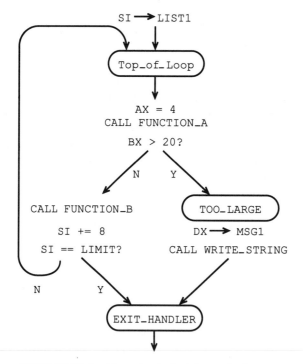

FIGURE 10.1   Flowchart sketch made from source code in Listing 10-1.

To help ensure that this important step is not overlooked, plan for it from the start. When your boss or client asks for a time estimate of project completion, include time for documentation editing.

10.4 STATIC REVIEW

Once you've identified a section of a program as suspect, it can often be effective to apply a static review process to the code. Whereas in the previous section the goal was to discover the meaning and intent of the code, performing a static review requires that you view the code as the CPU does—completely literally, with no preconceived notions as to the intent.

Even if this exercise doesn't net you a cause for your bug, or even a decent clue, you will come out of it with a much more detailed understanding of the code. This will be of great value throughout all further analysis of this part of the program, as well as other sections which interact with this one.

As mentioned in the previous section, working with a printed listing is strongly recommended. It is also very useful to have a listing where line numbers are printed in the leftmost column. If you don't already possess a utility capable of doing this, it should be a simple project to write a program that reads each line of a text file and copies it, prefaced by a line number, to a printer.

The preliminary phase of this review process involves examining each statement to verify that it belongs and to verify that it is performing the correct operation on the correct data. Leftover sections of code can sometimes result when certain features of a program are dropped but not all supporting code is found and removed. Sometimes these orphaned bits of logic impose strange side effects on the rest of the program.

When a program works with hardware interrupt handlers and communicates with them through common data fields, it can become critically important to examine each instruction (at the assembler level). At each point where interrupts are enabled and any common data is being operated on, you must ask yourself, "What if an interrupt occurred right here?" Note that this common data can include interrupt vectors and internal CPU registers.

If, as you are examining a section of code, you see literal constants hard-coded into an instruction, a bell should go off in your head. Using symbolic names for constants is much more reliable. The use of explicitly hard-coded constant values carries with it the danger that when a change is required, not all cases will be found. It also can indicate that a presumption was made in the design of the program.

When working with assembler code, it is important to verify that each function only changes those CPU registers it is documented as changing and that the code surrounding each function call is designed to expect this documented action. The registers used and changed by a function should be described within its function header comment block. Unfortunately, comments can sometimes fall out of date as changes are made to the code.

For each function, examine the push instructions that appear at the top of the function and make sure they are counterbalanced by pop instructions at the function's exit point (watch for multiple exits). Then, providing that stack manipulations (intentional or accidental) are not changing these saved registers while they are on the stack, it should be safe to ignore them and focus on each register for which no push and pop instruction is given.

From this set, you can eliminate any registers that are already documented as carrying return parameters or as being changed. Finally, examine each statement to check for any changes to the remaining set of registers—updating the documentation and calling code as necessary.

Another, more exacting, phase of the static review process involves performing an on-paper simulation run of a section of code. Each significant data item used within the section of code being analyzed must be identified here, as was the case in Section 10.2, "Testing Procedures," and Section 4.2, "Verification." Construct a chart in which each data item is given its own column. Reserve the leftmost column for the line number from the source listing corresponding to each state. Reserve the rightmost column for descriptive notes.

Before the simulation run can begin, you will need to determine the initial values for each data item. Of course, different combinations of entry conditions will generate different effects as the program code is manually executed. Once you've prepared your chart, you may want to run it through a photocopier to prepare for multiple runs.

When running this type of simulation, it can be instructive actually to run the program and break into it with a debugger to determine the initial states for the data items you're working with. Instrumentation can also be used to gain this information. Not only will this provide you with a set of actual values, it may reveal important facts about the failure. If certain of the entry conditions don't make sense, you have probably just identified an earlier evidence of the failure. The function you were about to examine may not be the problem—the code that calls it may be feeding it garbage.

To carry out a simulation, jot down in the leftmost column of a row the line number of each line you mentally execute. Then fill out the remainder of the columns, based on your derivations while acting in place of the CPU. Remember to ignore any preconceived notions you have about what each line is "supposed" to do—your job is to process the instructions just as the CPU would.

When working with a high-level language, this exercise requires that you have a clear understanding of the precedence of operations (e.g., is a logical evaluation done before or after a mathematical one?) Likewise, when working with assembler, you must understand how each instruction can affect the internal registers, the contents of memory, and the state of the hardware. For example, even though the instruction div cx contains no references to the AX or DX registers, its execution will result in changes to both.

If you don't discover any clues using this approach, save your state chart. If you later find yourself tracing through this code with a debugger, having a set of predictions available can serve as a useful reference. This is where you will get to see how well the ideal matches with the actual. It may help you uncover rounding errors and unexpected combinations of events.

10.5 COMPARING VERSIONS

When you discover a bug during the development of a new program or while doing maintenance on an existing one, it can be very illuminating to be able to test several previous builds to determine exactly when the problem first appears.

When major changes are being made to a program, establishing an internal reference build once each week may be necessary. Under less volatile circumstances, establishing a reference build once every two to five weeks should be reasonable.

Care must be taken when using previous builds as a basis for determining a bug's origin. Sometimes a bug will exist within an earlier version but be dormant. Changes in code position or in position-relative data may be involved.

To be able to make use of this method, clear records must be maintained describing the changes made between each reference build. Without this information, you will have to resort to tedious line-by-line comparisons of the source code modules corresponding to each build—not an inviting prospect.

Also be sure to maintain clear records of any changes in the file format of any associated data files. If you back up to a previous build but keep your current set of data files, unpredictable operation will result if that previous build has "different ideas" regarding the data file format.

If you don't have a revision control system (RCS), save the source files corresponding to each reference build, using an archive utility to compress them into one file. Then seriously consider getting an RCS as soon as you can.

If you do have an RCS, each time you make a reference build, mark each source file revision with a corresponding version number. If your RCS can store binary files, use it to store each reference build as well. Otherwise, save the binary files in a directory reserved for that purpose and rename the file's extension to a sequence number. For example, the first build of `MYPROG.EXE` would be renamed to `MYPROG.001`.

When you set out to test a series of reference builds, the use of binary division is often wise. First, select the range of builds you will consider and then start by testing the oldest member of that set. For example, if you elect to test the last 10 monthly builds, test the 10-month-old one first to verify that the failure is not evident in it. Then, providing this first condition is met, test the 5-month-old build next. If the problem appears in that one, the build made in the seventh or eighth month would be your next choice.

In the event that the problem still shows up when you first test the 10-month-old build, you would, of course, need to back up even further.

When libraries are used and the libraries undergo changes as well, this brings in a new variable. Save a copy of the binary for the library with each set of source. The source code corresponding to each version of the library should be kept in its own RCS. But having the binary version available will save a lot of time should it be necessary to de-archive the source code for an older build to add instrumentation or to test hunches.

Providing you fully understand the changes made to the libraries and how they will interact with different versions of the program being tested, you may discover clues by rebuilding a version of the program using an old version of the program code and a new version of the library and vice versa.

10.6　INTERVIEWING USERS

Sometimes you have to go after a bug that you haven't personally seen. In such cases, the debugging tool that you must apply first is the user interview.

It is up to you to take the lead in this dance, to guide the user through a meaningful information-gathering process. Try to get a feel for the user's comfort level with computer operations early on and pace yourself accordingly. Pay attention to your vocabulary, avoiding the programmer's jargon of "byte alignment" and "memory allocation fragmentation" —this will only confuse them.

Bear in mind that many users feel intimidated by computers, seeing them as mysterious and fragile gadgets deserving no small amount of contempt. Others are overwhelmed by the amount of strange details involved in their operation.

In spite of these interface issues, you must be sure to get a fully accurate description. Any phrase that is vague can result in a lot of wasted time. If the user says, "It turns green when I press F4," you need to find out just what turns green: the whole screen, or a specific portion of it—or is it the LED indicator on the disk drive? From there, "What color was it before F4 was pressed?" and so on.

As with other debugging techniques, presumptions are dangerous and to be avoided at all costs. Unfortunately, when two or more people are involved in the process of gathering information and making judgments, presumptions have many more ways to arise.

One of your initial goals is to ascertain if the problem is due to user error or a software problem. But take pains to avoid anything that rings of an accusatory approach. Don't cause the user to close off to you.

It can help to clear the air if you open with a simple statement of purpose: "I have no interest in pointing any fingers; I just need to understand what happened so I can find a solution. That said, I would appreciate any observations you could share."

It can also help set them more at ease if you phrase your questions in terms of "What did this darn machine do this time?" This is the "us against them" approach where you are on the user's side. Further, you might try phrasing things in terms of "Well, I must have missed something when I wrote this program; let's see if we can figure out what it is." Humility can help open up the channel of communication.

As the interview progresses, create a sequence list—a step-by-step description of the events preceding and following the failure. Once you have a fairly complete set of notes, read them back to the user, asking for confirmation. Read at a slow to moderate pace and pause occasionally—you want to give them a chance to digest what they're hearing and possibly come up with additional details they hadn't remembered the first time.

Be sure to ask if they are aware of any recent changes to their system. Was a new operating system, network, or hard disk recently installed? Are they using any TSR utilities? Even changing the BUFFERS= statement in the CONFIG.SYS file could be important, since it can change the load position of applications. Have them tell you the date and time stamp on their AUTO-EXEC.BAT and CONFIG.SYS files to see when the last edit was done.

While it is obviously preferable to make this contact in person, quite often this process will take place over the telephone. When you must work over the phone, try stepping through the procedure with the customer, running a parallel session on your system as they tell you what menu choices they're picking and so on. Note also that there are a number of remote-console utilities available, which enable one computer to control another through a modem.

Keep in mind when it would be wise to have the customer send you a copy of their current data files as well as their code modules so you can check for file corruption or unexpected combinations of data. Make sure that they send a copy of the code from their actual working disk, rather than using DISKCOPY on the original distribution diskettes.

Finally, be careful of jumping to conclusions (which is just presumption by a different name). Just because a user doesn't follow the written operational specifications doesn't always mean they are wrong and that the alleged bug is due to user error. Users will often discover better ways of doing things. Alternatively, they may be forced to adopt seemingly strange conventions to work around compatibility conflicts with other software or hardware in their system.

10.7 DON'T FORGET COMPILER OPTIONS

A compiler is a great tool that takes care of a lot of drudge work for you. But most compilers are capable of providing a lot more information than they are commonly called on to produce—information which can be very useful in a bug hunt.

While you may normally run with options such as array bounds and stack overflow checking disabled to produce smaller, faster code, it's important to remember that these capabilities exist and use them when bugs arise.

Activating your compiler's run-time analysis features is like having a built-in type of instrumentation automatically added to your program.

Consequentially, the same side effects that attend other forms of instrumentation apply here. It may happen that these changes will cause the bug to change its personality or disappear from sight altogether. Therefore, you may have to familiarize yourself with the bug all over again, or even start hunting for evidence of it anew. Nobody ever said this would be easy!

Some compilers will generate an assembler version of your program. Proofreading a troublesome section of code at the assembler level can help you see problems that otherwise evade detection. For example, consider the following two assignment statements:

```
regs.x.dx = (unsigned int) buffer_ptr;
regs.x.dx = (unsigned int) &buffer_ptr;
```

The first statement causes the contents of the buffer_ptr pointer to be assigned to the regs.x.dx field, while the second one actually causes the address of the buffer_ptr variable to be assigned rather than its contents.

These are both valid statements and they both deal with addressing manipulations. But if your program needs the first statement and you've coded the second, or vice versa, strange behavior is bound to occur. Because they look very similar to each other, this is a type of error that can be easily missed during a walk-through inspection. Examining an assembler listing can make this type of error stand out.

Here are these same statements along with their assembler equivalents for a small model C program where the buffer_ptr variable is of the automatic storage class. Variations will occur depending on the type of variables used and the compilation model.

```
regs.x.dx = (unsigned int) buffer_ptr;
        mov     ax,[bp-02]
        mov     [0290],ax
regs.x.dx = (unsigned int) &buffer_ptr;
        lea     ax,[bp-02]
        mov     [0290],ax
```

10.8 VERIFYING THE HARDWARE

There are three scenarios where hardware verification usually becomes a practical undertaking:

1. After you've painstakingly checked every aspect of the software and can find no explanation for a bug
2. When there is some reason to suspect that hardware may be involved, such as frequent disk errors, system errors during boot-up, memory parity errors, strange noises from the disk drives, or flickering in the video display

3. When hardware verification is easy because you have more than one computer available

The simplest way to determine whether something about a certain machine's hardware is responsible for a failure can be to install the same program on another machine. Providing that the same version of the same operating system, with the same CONFIG.SYS and AUTOEXEC.BAT files, can be used, and no other significant differences exist (such as one machine having an EMS board and the other having none), this can be a useful test.

To make this test meaningful, it is important that the load position of the program be the same in both machines. The next load position may be determined using a memory/device map type of utility or by noting the initial value assigned to the CS register when you load DEBUG with no filename parameter. When comparing two different machines, make sure the same copy of DEBUG is being used in each.

When a DOS-type operating system is used, where the OS kernel, disk buffers, device drivers, and command processor load within the lower part of the 640K base memory, using the same CONFIG.SYS file should result in the same program load position between the two machines.

If, however, a memory management driver is used to load some of the operating system components into upper memory areas (above the 640K boundary) then differences in the program load position could exist more easily. Different machines will have differing amounts of the upper memory areas available for this type of use depending on the type of video display adapter used, the type of disk controller, and so on.

Note that certain types of program failures could be sensitive to the type of video display adapter used or to the type of keyboard connected. If one machine has a monochrome adapter and an 84 key-keyboard while the other has a VGA and an enhanced keyboard, the validity of your tests should be questioned.

Moving these components between the machines in different combinations can be very helpful, though. For example, if you can demonstrate that the failure will occur in either machine only when the VGA adapter is used, you might be on to something.

There is also the possibility that a program could consistently fail in machine A and consistently work in machine B, where both are the same model with the same options installed, and still be due to a software problem. When a pointer error causes a reference to be made to an unused memory address, the data read could tend to have different values in different machines, even though they are otherwise identical.

A final reminder when testing on a second machine: In your eagerness to run your tests and pronounce the hardware at blame, do not forget that this is a potentially buggy piece of software you're dealing with. Take the time to run a fresh backup on the second machine before using it as a guinea pig.

When another machine is not available, simplify your system by removing any unnecessary adapter cards and then test again. Next, run diagnostic programs for memory, disk drives, the CPU, serial ports, and the rest of the hardware components. Arrange for these test programs to run in a continuous cycle while you tap on various areas of the system's circuit cards with a plastic or wooden stick. This can help flush out any problems due to loose connections.

10.9 SUMMARY

Corruption can happen from any of the following sources:

- Disk failure
- Transmission errors through a modem download or network transfer
- Intentional tampering
- The effects of a virus
- Accidental processing of files by a conversion utility

Buggy behavior due to corruption could occur from damaged data files just as it could from damaged code files.

When installing a new copy of a program, generate new data too. If the failure does not appear, then try the new code with the old data files. Trying the old code with the new data files can also be helpful in isolating the cause.

When installing a new copy, a binary file compare utility could report a difference due to different setup configurations or patches that were only applied to one copy.

DEBUG.COM loads files at offset 100h (except .EXE files). To make it simpler to work with zero-based file offsets, adjust DEBUG's DS register by adding 10h to the initial value. From then on, specify ds: in each unassemble and dump command.

If you are unable to draw any conclusions from the difference when a corrupt file is found, save the corrupt copy. It could provide useful information should the new copy become corrupt in the future.

Experimenting with a program from the outside (e.g., through its user interface) is a valuable way to learn more about a bug. You can often discover other ways to evidence the bug, which will make your job easier when you do make the transition to more invasive debugging techniques.

One approach is to identify the data involved in the failing section of the code and derive tests which will drive these data to their boundary and out-of-range states.

Another approach is to identify the different decisions being made by the code in the failing section and derive tests to flex each one.

Using tests that force too many boundary and out-of-range states to occur at the same time can be of limited use. There is no distinct association between the failing behavior and the manipulated machine states.

When running through a series of tests, it is important to keep track of the inputs your are using to drive the program. If you've been supplying a series of random responses to the program's menus and prompts and the failure does occur, retracing your steps may be difficult.

When seeking to understand a section of code, remain aware that the source code, the source code comments, and other documentation may be out of step. It is important to seek the intent of the code in spite of the comments.

When you seek to understand a section of code, there are a variety of utility programs which can be helpful:

- Execution profiler: helps you prioritize your analysis efforts
- Calling hierarchy: illustrates interactions between functions
- Pretty-print: improves readability
- Preprocessor: removes unused conditional source statements
- Reverse charting: illustrates logical structure

Reviewing code with a printed listing makes it possible to draw annotation lines and write additional comments. It is also possible to see more lines of code at a time.

When your analysis shows a program's comments to be out of date or otherwise inadequate, schedule time to update them from your working notes.

When performing a static review of a section of code, it is important to remain detached from your understanding of the program's intended function; you must view it with the stark and literal perspective of the CPU. This requires a solid understanding of the order of evaluation used by your compiler and the register usage rules of assembler.

During a static review, it is important to maintain a healthy suspicion about each line of code. Just because lines of code are present in a source file doesn't mean that they belong. The bug you are chasing may be caused by "leftover" code.

When hardware interrupt handlers are involved, you must ask, "What if an interrupt occurred here?" for each point where any sensitivity could exist.

In the process of scrutinizing a piece of code, watch out for explicitly hard-coded constants. These are inflexible (in contrast to symbolically represented constants) and often indicate presumptions.

Proofreading assembler code involves verifying that each function clearly documents the registers that it actually preserves and changes and that each use of each function is designed accordingly.

Another phase of the static review process involves performing an on-paper simulation of a section of code. This is done by charting the data values that result as each statement is manually executed. Having line numbers added to a printed listing is especially valuable here, since they are plugged into one of the chart's columns.

A quick way to isolate a bug during program development and maintenance is to identify when it first occurs. This is facilitated through the maintenance of a collection of reference builds.

As with many tests, this is not always conclusive, since an earlier version may contain the bug you are chasing but in a dormant state.

Clear records must be maintained describing the changes made between each two reference builds. Any changes in the format of data files must also be tracked.

A clear linkage must also be established between each reference build and the corresponding revisions of the source code modules. The use of a revision control system is strongly recommended.

The binary division technique can be applied to the testing of reference builds.

When libraries are involved, where changes have been made to the libraries across different reference builds, saving binary copies of the libraries in an archive will save a lot of time if rebuilding an older version of the program becomes necessary.

Regarding user interviews, be sensitive to the user's position. Don't overwhelm them with technical jargon, and avoid any phrasing which carries an accusatory tone.

Watch for ambiguous phrases. Don't automatically substitute your own meanings for the missing portions—clearly and calmly explain what you need to know.

When working over the phone, set up a similar system as the user's and step through the sequence of events they are describing in parallel with them.

Create a sequence list of the steps involved in producing the bug, based on the user's descriptions, and then review it with them at the end.

Inquire about recent changes to their system. Have them check the directory date and time for the CONFIG.SYS and AUTOEXEC.BAT files.

If you require the user to send a copy of their software to you, clarify that you need a copy of the code and data they are currently using, not a duplicate of their installation diskettes.

Compiler options can be useful when bugs arise. Activate all checks, such as array bounds checking and stack overflow checking.

Proofreading a high-level language program can be augmented by having your compiler produce an assembler listing.

Although it doesn't happen as often as programmers would like, sometimes it is the hardware's fault. Set up the same program on another machine, one as similar to the first as possible. One of the most important factors in setting up this type of test is to ensure that the program's load position is the same.

Remain aware that the failure you are analyzing may be sensitive to differences in the video adapter, in the keyboard, or in ROM BIOS memory contents.

Before testing a potentially buggy program on another machine, or any machine for that matter, make sure it is freshly backed up.

When another computer is unavailable, remove all unnecessary hardware and test again. Running hardware diagnostic programs is another good approach.

CHAPTER 11
Working with a Debugger

In Chapter 5 we took a good look at the plumbing within the CPU that makes the breakpoint possible. Now it's time to see what's involved in putting this feature to use.

The primary objective in debugging is to gain enough useful knowledge about a failure to make its repair evident. Applying breakpoints is a way of asserting control over a program—reining it in and forcing it open for exploration.

In an ideal debugging session, once you identify the problem, a light goes on over your head. After setting one well-chosen breakpoint, you run the program and all the information you need is before your eyes. While this is not an impossible scenario, it doesn't happen very often. But the more you know about breakpoints, the closer you can get to this ideal.

There are two basic ways to apply breakpoints. The first is by setting traps in the direct pursuit of a bug, based on either predicted or observed behavior. The second approach, more indirect, is to use breakpoints to gather history. This is typically done early in a debugging session, when you don't know much about the failure and need to qualify its location in the overall scheme of things.

Other tools are available that make the gathering of historical data simpler. A driver such as `DDICEPT.SYS`, which intercepts common software interrupts and reports the associated entry and exit parameters, is a typical example. But you may not always have access to such tools, and having an interrupt intercept tool loaded can also cause suppression. Therefore, you should also know how to use a debugger to gather overview-level information.

11.1 BENEFITS OF BREAKPOINTS OVER SINGLE-STEPPING

Using breakpoints is beneficial for two basic reasons: speed and reduction of detail. Manual single-stepping is invaluable when you are close to the point of failure, but too much of it will make you old before your time. Evaluative single-stepping is similarly indispensable, but the corresponding reduction in the program's execution rate just isn't practical in all situations.

When hardware interrupts or other forms of interaction with external devices are involved, it can often happen that a bug decides to become dormant when changes are made in a program's execution rate. In lieu of having hardware debugging facilities, judicious placement of breakpoints may be your best hope.

Single-stepping is expensive, not only because of the time it requires but also because of the amount of detail with which you must contend. Whether your immediate goal is to home in on the failure through a series of successively refined traps or just to get an overview idea of the program's action, the wise use of breakpoints will condense these minutiae into a more palatable form.

11.2 CONSIDER YOUR APPROACH

When selecting breakpoint locations and the types of breakpoints to use, it is important to step back and ask, "What is this going to tell me?" and "What else will I need to know once the break occurs?" Equally important, "Is my current approach the simplest and most direct?"

Conjuring up a complex evaluation breakpoint specification is actually a form of programming, and crafting custom breakpoint code can be considered nothing else but. Yet these software creations cannot afford to suffer from bugs. When you can't rely on your tools, you're as good as lost.

The more complicated the test, the more carefully it should be reviewed. As with any system, simpler is more reliable. If you make up a complex debugging test that happens to have bugs of its own, the fact that you are working in a buggy environment in the first place might make it very difficult to realize that your tool is keeping you in the dark.

Debugging is not most people's idea of a good time. Consequently, applying creativity in devising tests can be a bright spot in an otherwise dark day. There's also a thrill in "getting to play detective" and "rising to the challenge." To the extent that these perspectives help you wade through the swamp, they're great. But care must be taken not to overindulge.

Sure, you might be able to envision an elaborate evaluation breakpoint scheme or custom tool that is very interesting and seems like it would do the job. If there is a simpler way, however, you want to have the clarity to see it and take advantage of it. Jot down a note about the more elaborate tool and build it later.

Not only must each test be intrinsically correct, it must also provide meaningful information—and as much of it as possible. When you finally manage to break in at a point where you can see damage occurring, your quest is still a long way from over if you can't tell how you arrived at that point.

Therefore, when devising a set of breakpoints, it is wise to consider how a "trail of bread crumbs" can be left. Not allowing for an execution chronicle from the start can mean having to restart a debugging session. When the failure in question is difficult to produce, this won't be welcome news. The next section in this chapter, "Getting an Overview History," covers this topic in further detail.

There will also be situations where your history-gathering attempts will be thwarted, and other times when it just isn't practical to go through the setup. Section 11.12, "Getting Your Bearings," discusses techniques to help you at least determine where you "are" when you hit a breakpoint. From there, you will have to use your knowledge of the system and the current machine state to reverse-infer the course taken.

11.3   GETTING AN OVERVIEW HISTORY

Breakpoints can be used to gather a trace history of a program's execution. This can be a useful way to gain an overview knowledge of a program's operation. Having access to a record of execution flow can also be valuable when a program is snared by a breakpoint designed to detect the failure you are chasing.

There are a number of ways that breakpoints can be used to gather history. If your debugger sports a backtrace buffer, logging window, or similar feature, learn how to use it. In lieu of such conveniences, you may have to revert to manual note taking. Having a debugger's display output echoed to a printer is another possibility.

Although the use of breakpoints is the current topic, you should remain aware that there are other tools that make the job of historical tracing easier. Utilities such as those included in this book's Companion Toolset may be used in conjunction with the breakpoint capabilities of a software debugger. Still, there will be times when the only tool you have available is a debugger, so it's important to know how to make it jump through this particular hoop.

11.4   PASSIVE BREAKPOINTS AND BACKTRACE BUFFERS

A good debugger will let you select the action associated with each breakpoint you set rather than just automatically stopping the program each time a breakpoint is executed. A *passive* breakpoint is one whose execution only makes an entry in the software trace buffer rather than presenting the debugger's user interface.

By specifying one or more passive breakpoints at key locations within a program or within the system as a whole, you can ensure that when something is done to finally stop the program and present the debugger's user interface, the history gathered will be in terms of these passive breakpoints. This "something" that does finally stop the show can be a nonpassive breakpoint that you've implanted as a failure trap, or it can be the pressing of a hot key or breakout button.

One way to set up a passive breakpoint is to use an evaluative type where the expression used can never be true. In Periscope, this could be done with the following set of commands:

```
bc 1234
bc 2468
br cs eq 0
gm
```

The two `bc` commands specify sticky code breakpoints for two addresses where evaluations are to be carried out. The test done in this case is for a CS register value of 0, a very unlikely occurrence. The net result of these high jinks is that once the `GM` (go monitor) command is issued, the system will run at nearly full speed, pausing only long enough to make a backtrace buffer entry each time either of the two breakpoints is hit.

When one of your nonpassive breakpoints finally triggers or when you finally break in to the debugger manually, it's time to take a look at your collection of "bread crumbs." While we don't really have to worry about forest creatures following along behind consuming your valuable morsels of information, buffer overflow is a common problem.

If one of your passive breakpoints happens to have been executed from within a loop, it can easily fill the buffer and leave you with a meaningless monotony. Then again, don't be too quick to dismiss such cases as totally useless. If you avoided placing your passive breakpoints in tight loops, the fact that looping seems to have taken place can be a clue as to the nature of your gremlin.

Should the monotony prevail, and the attainment of an execution history still be necessary, it's time to get crafty. The use of an evaluative breakpoint that marks the backtrace buffer only when the last break hit was a different one may put you in a better standing. Pattern detection logic may also be appropriate. Last, but certainly not least, try to allocate a larger trace buffer.

Should all these tricks fail, there's yet another to be tried. As mentioned above, embedding instrumentation calls into a program can make the collection of history easier. The hitch is that it's much easier to set breakpoints than it is to implant markers, recompile the program, and then hope that the resulting changes to the binary code module don't suppress or significantly alter the failure.

This final trick is to wed these two techniques into one. The software debugger will be enlisted to do what it does best: set breakpoints. The instrumentation driver will be assigned the task of collecting, filtering, and annotating event trace markers—its particular forte.

This alliance is accomplished by setting passive breakpoints that call a user routine that just happens to make marker calls to an instrumentation driver. For the nitty-gritty on this, refer to Section 12.1, "Instrumentation."

11.5 BREAKING ON SYSTEM CALLS

Setting breakpoints on certain software interrupt calls is an excellent way to get an overview of a program's operations. The INT21 DOS services interrupt is probably the most universally useful of these, with BIOS interrupts such as the INT13 (disk services) and INT16 (keyboard services) useful for specific cases.

Note that to set a breakpoint on a ROM BIOS interrupt handler (when hardware breakpoints are not available) requires that the entry point for the handler be located in RAM. This can be done through the use of a simple interrupt intercept—one that does nothing more than pass the call on to the original vector holder.

Using interrupt calls as breakpoint landmarks is an easy way to get information without having to know details of the program under test, because you don't have to determine where to place breakpoints within the program code in order to gain knowledge. The tracing of system calls is a subject in itself, so you'll need to check Section 12.2, "System Call Tracing," for the particulars.

11.6 TRACING INTO A CRASH

The best way to experience the crash of a computer system is in slow motion. Theatrics aside, when you can single-step up to the point of a failure, you are in the best position to investigate the conditions involved. If fortune smiles upon you, you will have a sudden flash of understanding and proceed directly on to making a fix. At other times, you will have only gained an intermediate piece of the puzzle.

Since it is rarely practical to begin a program's execution in single-step mode, how can you know when to enter this mode? One way to accomplish this is to repeatedly cause the system to exhibit its failure while you measure how far it gets before it dies. Were computers not inanimate, such a gruesome practice would surely get us in all sorts of trouble.

By taking this measurement with increasing precision on each successive death run, you will eventually arrive at the point where you can single-step right up to the edge of the cliff. The mechanics of this process involve applying breakpoints in a layered approach. The first layer is to use a breakpoint or breakout switch to let the program run as far as possible at full speed where you can still stop before the failure occurs. Note that, as always in debugging, "the failure" at any given point is actually the *earliest evidence* of failure available at the time.

If you stopped by using a breakout button or hot key or through the use of an evaluative breakpoint (e.g., break on memory change), you may find yourself within the middle of a BIOS or DOS call or within an interrupt handler or device driver routine. Often the best way to move the point of execution ahead to where you are running within the program being debugged is to break on the next call to INT21. Using an evaluative breakpoint that tests for a value in the CS register falling within the range of your code is another alternative.

Once the situation is normalized, it's time to start applying layered breakpoints. Another name for this technique is *step over/step into*. For the sake of simplicity, this description will assume that the failure being chased results in a full system crash—a lockup. With minor modifications, this same technique can be applied to cases where the failure is less final.

The basic idea is to use your debugger's step-over command to jump around subroutine calls until you step over one from which there is no return. Although there can be exceptions, most often the failure can be said to be due to some action that takes place within that last subroutine. What you now need to do is reboot, recover to the position just before stepping around the subroutine, and then step into it rather than over it. Once you've gone down into this new layer, if the failure's exact origin is still a mystery, repeat this process by stepping around successive subroutine calls until you again come to one from which there is no return.

The term *layered breakpoints* is used because you may encounter several layers of code through which you must apply this technique. The cycle of "step over, crash, reboot, recover, step into" may have to be repeated through several dozen iterations in certain cases. It all just depends on how deeply nested the subroutines are in the area where the failure is occurring.

If your gremlin results in a full-scale lockup, rebooting is, of course, your only choice. In cases where the crash is less severe, it may be possible to terminate the errant process and arrive back at the DOS command prompt. Reboot anyway. Any time you run a process through a known failure, do not rely on the system being stable. Critical sections of the operating system's code and data are sitting ducks when a buggy program is being run.

Keeping Track

Recovering a previous position in a debugging session when a crash occurs is a practice that warrants a section to itself, which will be given later in this chapter. This is the point to discuss a related topic: keeping track of just what that previous position was.

The methods described in Section 11.3, "Getting an Overview History," are all applicable here, with one qualification: You cannot rely on any information that resides within the read/write memory of the system being exercised. Several software debuggers support a remote mode, where backtrace buffer information is maintained in a second computer. If you can't go this route, a product that locates itself in extended memory may suffice.

While Murphy's Law could still visit you, having your debugger's output spooled to a printer should be very reliable. A devil's advocate may argue that a failing program could send enough garbage out the printer port to cause a printer to backfeed the paper and then write on top of your trace data. But then again, lightning could strike and vaporize your note pad, so nothing is 100 percent safe.

Dealing with Inconsistency

When you do come to a subroutine call from which there is no return, while the chances are good that the cause of the failure lies within the confines of that routine or any routines that it calls, the influence of asynchronous IRQ-type interrupts can be a red herring. If, upon reboot and recovery, you find that you can step over all functions within the suspect routine without crashing, suspect an interrupt interaction.

To help confirm this inconsistent behavior, reboot, recover, and step over the same function call several times in a row. If you make it through to the other side on any one of the trials, interrupt interaction is likely. Setting breakpoints within known interrupt handlers or applying instrumentation to make them report their activity can be helpful. In certain cases, temporarily masking off selected IRQ interrupts can also be done. See the discussion of this in Appendix D, "System-Level Knowledge for Debugging."

Another possible explanation for an erratic behavior is memory corruption. Within this idea, there are three variations: stray-bullet code glomming, stray-bullet data glomming, and stray references. Additionally, the possibility of flaky hardware must not be ruled out.

When some portion of a buggy piece of software is overwriting areas of memory it ought not, this is referred to as the *stray-bullet* effect. This is most likely to occur with products developed in languages such as C and assembler, where the use of pointers is more prevalent, but there are ways to make other languages self-destruct similarly. The point of impact and the degree of damage caused by these stray memory writes can vary wildly. Section 13.2, "Stray Bullets," will delve into techniques for dealing with this particularly maddening form of failure.

Stray references are also related to the use of pointers. They are kind of the inverse of stray bullets. With this form of error, a memory value is read or tested using an improper address. Depending on the values that happen to be found in the memory tested, and the testing criteria, the subsequent actions carried out can vary from near-normal behavior, to operations being done too many times or too few, to the execution of "code" that isn't really code.

With a stray-reference problem, providing there is only one such problem in a program, either the erratic behavior will occur when the corresponding subroutine is executed or the program will appear to function normally. It all just depends on what happens to be sitting in the memory area that is improperly referenced.

In the case of stray-bullet memory corruption, the erratic behavior will typically be that when the failure doesn't occur in one place, it will occur in another, or it totally changes its characteristics. Further, the erratic behavior may occur much later than the origin of the failure.

There are, of course, as many exceptions to these guidelines as there are computer programs and combinations of memory addresses and memory values (read: incalculable). In summary, dealing with stray references is usually done by patiently working through a step-over/step-into technique.

A parting thought for this section: Certain compilers produce code that isn't pure code—rather, it's a strange hybrid of code and data. A common form used is for an offset word to be placed after a software interrupt call. The interrupt handler compensates for this action, but since nobody tells the debugger, it ends up corrupting the offset word with its breakpoint. More on this unfortunate choice of language implementation can be found in Section 13.3, "Working with Compiled Code."

Recovering a Previous Position

When you set out to optimize a program's performance, streamlining the execution of loops with high iteration rates is one of the first tasks deserving attention. When you need to apply the step-over/step-into technique of debugging, the process of rebooting and recovering your last known position can be like a high-frequency loop. This section will examine what can be done to optimize what can be a tedious process.

The Need to Reboot

The need to reboot after a failure occurs was already covered in the previous section, but it's important, so you're going to receive further admonition. Any time even one byte of code or data within a computer system is corrupted, or any time an error within a program causes it to make an incorrect memory reference or an incorrect calculation, you are at risk. The contents of your hard disk can become encrypted with a security key known only to Lucifer himself. Certain video monitors can even be permanently damaged when driven into an improper video mode.

Reboot as soon as you know a failure has occurred. As the keyboard will be nonresponsive in many cases, the use of a computer with a built-in hardware reset switch is preferable. Repeatedly powering a computer on and off is a practice that invites its own form of hardware damage.

The importance of staying well backed up when dealing with a bug should also be self-evident. However, the pressure of the situation, and an eagerness to go just that one step further when you think you are getting closer, can displace wisdom at times. Back up your system!

While you are working through a debugging session, you will often make incremental changes to your source code and update your debugging notes and task list. Therefore, running a differential backup after each change is necessary if you value this information.

This may sound like too much hassle to be practical, but it's nothing compared with having to restore your hard disk to its last backed-up state and then still have to recreate the last several hours of work. Write a batch file that makes running a differential backup as easy as pressing two keys. Back up your system often!

Streamline the Boot Process

The removal of unnecessary device drivers from your CONFIG.SYS file and unneeded TSRs from your AUTOEXEC.BAT should have already been done in the simplification and isolation processes described in Chapter 3. Indeed, the execution of all nonessential utility programs from within AUTOEXEC.BAT should be prevented. Even utilities that set default screen colors or modify the default keyboard repeat rate can influence a bug's behavior.

Additional tricks may still be possible to speed the rebooting process. For each program that must be executed from within AUTOEXEC.BAT, specify the full drive and path name before the program name. This will prevent the operating system from having to step through each directory in the command search path to search for the program.

Having your debugger loaded by AUTOEXEC.BAT can be another time saver. Having it start the application you are debugging should also be done when possible.

Full-Sequence Recovery versus Shortcuts

At first glance, it might seem that recovering your last position before the most recent crash should be as simple as setting a breakpoint at that position and running until it's hit. While it can be that easy at times, it often isn't.

So what can happen to prevent this simplistic approach from working? First, the point in the code you have identified may actually have been executed dozens of times in the previous trial before you encountered it. The following pseudocode example should help make this clearer.

```
procedure abc
 call ghi
 call xyz
 return
procedure main
 call    abc
 call    def
 call    abc
 terminate
```

Within the `main` procedure, suppose that stepping around the first two calls is successful, but there is no return when a step-over is attempted for the third call to procedure `abc`. Suppose further that after recovering to the point of this third call and stepping into it, you then find that the call to procedure `xyz` is not cooperative. If you reboot and then recover by setting a temporary breakpoint on the second call within procedure `abc`—the nonreturning call to `xyz`—when you break in, you have not really recovered.

The first call within the main procedure is also a call to `abc`. You have stopped at the `xyz` call within the first `abc` call, not the second. Now in a case as simple as this, what is happening is easy to see. In a real program, it won't be this simple. Using a nonqualified shortcut like this can end up causing a lot of confusion. You will come to regard the bug as exhibiting erratic behavior when this may not really be the case.

One solution is to recover by religiously repeating each and every step you took in each previous trial. Another is to use a technique to qualify a shortcut. Given point X within a program as the location to which you wish to recover, set a sticky breakpoint at point X and then go through the full recovery sequence one time. If you make it through the full recovery without hitting the breakpoint at location X before you arrive there normally, using a shortcut to reach that point is probably safe.

Before using a shortcut, check to make sure the code you would short-cut to is actually in memory at the time. If you were to go through the full recovery sequence, you might be causing the loading of an overlay or a chaining of control to another code module through the operating system's `exec` function. When a load operation is necessary, a two-step shortcut is the best you can hope for. A memory-change type of breakpoint could be helpful in identifying the point at which the code in question is loaded.

This type of case is another reason why a full reboot is necessary between trials. Without a reboot to clear the system's memory, you may check for the existence of the code you wish to shortcut to and find an old copy of it still sitting in memory. Not realizing that this isn't the final copy of this code, you would set your breakpoint and issue a `go` command to your debugger. When the overlay is officially read in, your breakpoint instruction is lost and you again see a misleading, "erratic" behavior.

Alas, there will be times when the bug you are chasing will act honestly erratic. Forgoing shortcuts may help, but you may also need to peruse the techniques in Section 13.8, "Variable Types of Failure." If you can find no other reliable means of recovery, you might be able to set up a reloadable keystroke macro sequence in your debugger to automate the process.

11.7 EVALUATION BREAKPOINTS

Evaluation breakpoints can save you a lot of time, because they place more of the burden of detail management where it should be—with the computer. If your debugger supports this type of breakpoint, spend some time practicing with it. If it doesn't, seriously consider upgrading.

Debugging is not unlike gunslinging. If a gunfighter of the Wild West wanted to be efficient at his job (i.e., staying alive), rehearsing his "fast draw" was essential. If you want to be able to lay bugs to rest quickly, the evaluation breakpoint is one member of your arsenal worth the investment of drill time.

Design Approaches

An evaluation breakpoint consists of two basic components: the test to be performed and a resulting action. Some debuggers let you specify the test in terms of your target language, and some have their own mini-language for this. Regardless, the ultimate outcome of this test is a binary value—a "go" or "no go" signal.

The most commonly used resulting action is to stop the execution of the program and present the debugger's user interface. Another is to increment or decrement the state number for a debugger that supports a state machine.

Regarding the design of the test statement, there are three approaches:

1. Test for the absence of good conditions.
2. Test for the existence of a certain failure condition.
3. Test for suspicious conditions that may be involved with the failure.

A distinct advantage of the first approach is that you can sometimes end up with a pleasant surprise: The discovery of some aspect of the failure that occurs earlier than any you've previously seen. When you are just testing for a certain set of failure conditions (the second approach), opportunities to detect the failure in a more primordial state can be missed.

Unfortunately, distilling "the absence of good" into an expression suitable for use with an evaluation breakpoint can be a Herculean task. We will have to be more like a beaver, which fells a tree one bite at a time. For example, on one trial, you might check for a stack pointer value below a certain limit:

```
if (sp < stack_bottom+margin) break
```

Another possibility would be to select key data items used in the section of the program where you suspect the problem lies and apply tests that validate their contents. Care must be taken, however, to not let this turn into taking potshots. A good basis for judgment is how related the test is to your suspicions about the problem.

Introducing a state-machine feature into a debugging session can help bring "absence of good"–type testing into manageable scope. If your debugger doesn't intrinsically support a state-machine feature, adding one isn't that difficult. It does, however, require the capability of breakpoint code splicing or the addition of a small amount of custom code to the program being debugged.

To give this concept substance, consider the implementation of the test "Break if not conditions X and Y when within procedure T (or any procedure called by T)." If code-splicing breakpoints are available and your debugger permits new variables to be created, set a breakpoint, on the first statement within procedure T, that simply assigns a value of 1 to the new global variable Z. Then set another code splice–type breakpoint, on the exit of procedure T, that resets Z back to zero. Now the test can be entered as follows:

```
if (z != 0 && !(x && y)) break
```

This example is simplistic and will not work properly with recursive procedures. If this is a problem, or if your debugger does not support global variables and code splicing, you may wish to take the custom code route. To do this, first add a global variable like Z to your program and then encode a statement to increment it upon entry to the procedure in question and decrement it again upon exit. The danger here is, of course, that changing the source code and recompiling may affect the bug.

Evaluative Breakpoints and Hardware Breakpoints

This technique examines the use of writes to video memory as a key in getting closer to the origin of a failure. Some debuggers may implement all of the features discussed as hardware breakpoints, and some may employ evaluative software breakpoints in conjunction with hardware breakpoints.

Many a crash is accompanied by a screenful of happy faces and assorted Greek characters. But while this may be the earliest known evidence of failure you currently have, simply setting a memory write breakpoint within the video display memory region will net you a lot of breakpoints in most programs— one for each character displayed.

If the garbage always appears in the same location, calculating the specific video memory addresses involved and using them in a memory write test can help. If the garbage characters always have the same value, qualify the memory write test with those values and you're almost sure to be successful.

If the garbage appears in random locations or fills the screen so quickly that you can't determine if any one location is always hit first, a different approach is needed. Assuming your program has just one low-level routine charged with putting characters on the screen, as any well-designed program should, you could apply a state-machine type of test to trigger on any writes to the video buffer that occur outside of that routine.

Should it be that the rogue in your code is unabashedly using your very own low-level video driver to deliver the garbage, you'll have to get even craftier. If the routine accepts a pointer to a string or buffer full of data to be displayed, doing a range validation on both the pointer passed and the data pointed to is worth trying. If the low-level driver accepts only a character at a time, range validation of that character is your only option.

This assumes that the garbage characters include byte values outside the range of those normally used. If the garbage happens to be regular alphanumeric codes, or if your program makes regular use of the extended character set, it gets trickier. If there is any consistency to the point of failure, refer to Section 11.6, "Tracing into a Crash." If not, see Section 13.7, "Intermittent Bugs," or Section 13.8, "Variable Types of Failure."

11.8 CUSTOM BREAKPOINT CODE

A debugger that supports evaluative breakpoints that can make calls to custom code outside of the debugger itself is offering you a power too tempting to ignore. These calls may be made to procedures within the program being tested or to custom debugging code loaded into memory from a device driver or TSR.

When a debugger opens itself to sharing the evaluation process in this way, it does expect a return. Either the custom subprocedure that is called must return the "go" or "no go" signal directly or it must return information that the debugger can use to derive this result. In the following example test statement, the custom routine `calc_total` is actually returning an integer value. It is the containing expression which ultimately produces the binary indicator:

```
if (calc_total() > 130) break
```

An entirely different way to apply custom breakpoint code is to introduce new source statements within the program itself or introduce testing through an interrupt intercept. When the testing done by this code is satisfied, entry into the debugger is achieved through the execution of a hard-coded breakpoint.

Not only will custom code of this type allow you to extend the evaluative breakpoint capabilities of a debugger, it can introduce this valuable feature where it would not otherwise exist. If a simple-minded debugger such as

DEBUG.COM is all you have available, but your situation begs for the use of an evaluative breakpoint, the custom code approach can be your way in.

On the down side, the same attendant "gotchas" are possible with this method as with any other technique that involves the introduction of new code. The resultant change in timing or code position may force the bug into hiding or cause it to change its behavior so as to invalidate your previous testing. As long as this new behavior is consistent enough to deal with, you may be able to proceed. But if further code changes are deemed necessary to continue the bug hunt, and these changes transform the behavior again, please consider another approach before reaching for that hammer.

Tracing Linked Lists

Custom code really shines when your bug involves the corruption of a linked list. This type of data structure is often too dynamic for hardware memory write breakpoints to be of any help, and verifying a list of even a few nodes by hand while manually stepping from breakpoint to breakpoint is downright unhealthy.

One linked list present in any machine running a PC-DOS type of operating system is the chain of memory control blocks (MCBs). When you see a message such as "Memory Corruption, System Halted" upon terminating a program, some gremlin has caused damage to this list.

A good way to begin isolating this problem is by crafting a custom test routine that runs a verification of this list. Placing calls to this test routine at key locations within your program will help you narrow down the portion of the program involved. Using an interrupt intercept tool to introduce this test upon the entry and exit of each call to the INT21 DOS services interrupt is also helpful. The tradeoff is that while it is an easier type of test to setup since no source code changes are required, you have only limited control over when the tests are performed.

Within the Companion Toolset, the DDICEPT.SYS intercept device driver is designed to implement MCB testing. Refer to Chapter 7 for more information. For a discussion of the structure of the MCB chain and the verification procedure, see Appendix D, "System-Level Knowledge for Debugging."

To state the obvious, verifying a linked list requires some way to distinguish a good node from a bad one. One way can be to validate the value of the next-node pointer itself. If the next-node pointer is supposed to be a normalized far pointer, then the offset portion should never be above 0Fh. With near pointers and unnormalized far pointers, there are, unfortunately, only a few ways to know for certain that the next-node pointer is faulty.

The method used with the MCB chain verification technique relies on each node containing a signature. If the next-node pointer's signature can't be found when it is used to dereference the next node, then the list is corrupt.

Thus, no matter what type of next-node pointer is used, if it's been mangled, chances are that it will not be referencing a point in memory containing the appropriate signature.

It is also possible for each next-node pointer to be valid and for the signatures all to be intact, but for some other portion of a node to be corrupt. Adding a checksum to each node would provide a means of detecting such damage.

For this signature/checksum method to be possible, you must, of course, modify your linked list–building code as well as considering the increased storage requirements per node. You might be able to get away with making this level of change as part of a bug hunt without significantly affecting the bug. You can hope that the changes will be minor and that you can simply relearn the bug. Otherwise, if you work with linked lists a lot, this is a good technique to adopt from the start.

When running a verification process on a linked list, you must understand when changes in the link order can occur. If an IRQ-type interrupt can cause linking changes, your verification code will have to run with interrupts disabled—and be fast. Otherwise, your verification logic could fetch a next-node pointer that would be retired before you could make use of it.

11.9 SEQUENCE TRACKING

The sequence-tracking breakpoint technique is well suited for dealing with intermittent bugs. If, through the use of history-gathering techniques, you can determine that a certain sequence of operations always precedes the failure, a sequence-tracking type of breakpoint can help you break in on the system just before it goes down. You may also find other applications for sequence tracking besides dealing with intermittent bugs. If the recovery steps required in a step-over/step-into debugging session are particularly rigorous, it may be worth setting up the custom logic shown here.

This technique is basically an application of an evaluative breakpoint that uses custom code to implement a state machine. Note that the ROUTER.SYS driver included with this book's Companion Toolset does provide a function to support pattern detection. However, this section will take a more general approach in order to ensure that the fundamentals are thoroughly covered.

Design Approaches

First of all, when designing a sequence detection test, it is important to be sure that the sequence of events you have seen leading up to the crash is consistent. Then there must be something distinct about these events. For the sake of example, assume that only three events are involved, *A*, *B*, and *C*. Say also that the only time that these events occur in the sequence *B, C, A, A,*

B, A is just before the crash. If we can only get your debugger to gain control when that final event occurs, chances are that we could single-step right up to the precipice.

The first step would, of course, be to write the sequence-tracking logic and get it loaded into the computer—but assume for now that this has been done. What then, is required to set this bit of trickery in motion? First, an evaluation breakpoint that calls a user-defined function would need to be set on a point within the program that was indicative of event *A* occurring. Likewise, similar breakpoints would be established for events *B* and *C*.

Note the use of "similar" as opposed to "duplicate." When the same user-defined breakpoint function is called for each of these three events, there must be some way for the custom logic to determine which event is occurring. If your debugger supports compound evaluation expressions, then statements such as the following ones should do nicely. The first statement would be specified as the action for the event *A* breakpoint, the next for event *B,* and the last one for event *C*:

```
dbg_event = 'a'; if (dbg_seq_track()) break
dbg_event = 'b'; if (dbg_seq_track()) break
dbg_event = 'c'; if (dbg_seq_track()) break
```

The variable dbg_event is a global data item which is used by the logic within the dbg_seq_track() procedure. If your debugger supports the passing of parameters to a user-defined evaluation function, your life has just been made a bit easier. You could then use the simpler form:

```
if (dbg_seq_track('a')) break
if (dbg_seq_track('b')) break
if (dbg_seq_track('c')) break
```

Now that we've got the debugger making the necessary calls to the common sequence tracking function, it's time to examine the heart and soul of this custom logic. This logic must be supplied with a list of the event sequence it must watch for and a static variable to track progress. In this instance, the term "static" means that the variable will hold its value between calls to the sequence-tracking function. If your language doesn't support static local variables, a global variable will fill the bill.

The progress-tracking variable, dbg_track_stage, must be initialized to a zero value before the first call to dbg_seq_track is made. This assumes that the event list will be treated as an array with a zero-based index, for that is precisely what dbg_track_stage is: An array index. A pseudocode example is shown in Listing 11-1.

The first two statements are assignments that must be done once when the program starts and then never again. A declaration of the global variable dbg_event must also be made, although its initial value is unimportant.

```
dbg_event_list = b,c,a,a,b,a,0
dbg_track_stage = 0


  procedure dbg_seq_track

    if (dbg_event == dbg_event_list[dbg_track_stage])
    dbg_track_stage = dbg_track_stage + 1
    else
    dbg_track_stage = 0
      if (dbg_event == dbg_event_list[dbg_track_stage])
      dbg_track_stage = dbg_track_stage + 1


    if (dbg_event_list[dbg_track_stage] == 0)
    return(1)
    else
    return(0)
```

LISTING 11-1 Sequence-tracking pseudocode.

Within the dbg_seq_track procedure, the first if/else test decides whether the tracking index variable, dbg_track_stage, can be advanced or if it must be reset to the start, returning the logic to its initial hunt mode. Then a check must be done for a match with the value of dbg_event and the first list element.

The second if/else test is checking to see if the end of list marker might now be the current list element addressed by the index variable. If it is, a nonzero return value is passed back to the debugger's evaluation logic to invoke the specified action.

11.10 MYSTERIOUSLY MISSED BREAKPOINTS

"Now, I'm sure that the calc_totals() function is executing, because I can see output that only it could produce. Why can't I get a breakpoint placed in that part of the code to trigger?"

There can be a variety of explanations for this type of mystery. First, take a careful look at the evidence you are seeing that leads you to believe that calc_totals() is getting called. If seeing messages displayed on the screen or output to the printer is your basis, consider that this display may be due to other code specifying the wrong message string to the display output or printer output function. Presumptions will sneak up on you if you don't keep your guard up!

Although this next possibility sounds a bit wild, remember that these are bugs you're dealing with, so anything is possible. You may be executing the function you think you are, but it may not be where you think it is. If your program uses overlays, disk swapping, or memory paging, or otherwise relocates portions of its code in memory, an old leftover copy of the code in question could be getting control rather than the new copy.

Even if your code doesn't relocate itself, certain portions of your code can exist in duplicate within memory in the operating system's disk buffers. How do you deal with such a bizarre situation? One option many consider at times like this is early retirement. A less evasive tactic is to suspect duplicate code as behind the mystery of the missed breakpoints and use your debugger's memory search function to check it out.

If you do find that duplicate code is getting control, reboot and recover to the point where you first placed the breakpoints that were missed and place them in the duplicate instead. Then, to discover how entry is being made into this leftover code, instigate execution of the program with a go/trace method so that the software backtrace buffer will let you see how the program is jumping off into space.

11.11 THE HARD-CODED BREAKPOINT

There are several situations where it can be helpful to apply hard-coded breakpoints. A common one is when working with an overlay type of code module while using a debugger that isn't designed to manage moving code.

There are also special cases where a stand-alone program must be run from within a certain batch file for the bug to show up. Since this precludes loading the program directly with your debugger, you must resort to having your debugger already loaded resident in memory and embedding a hard-coded breakpoint at the start of the stand-alone program. When the batch file completes its initial setup operations and then finally invokes the stand-alone program, you will find yourself popped into your debugger, ready to begin sleuthing.

Dealing with code that relocates itself within memory can also be made easier through the use of hard-coded breakpoints. The use of any type of breakpoint automatically managed by a software debugger can actually be dangerous when code is being relocated. If a breakpoint is set when the section of code you are studying is located at address A, but it doesn't happen to be executed until after that piece of code has been relocated to address B, guess which address the debugger will use when it writes back the original opcode?

Further, if memory at address A (where the opcode restoration will take place) is currently being used for a new section of code or data, your debugger may have just corrupted it with that original opcode (a good debugger would pretest for the 0CCh opcode first). If you aren't aware that the program you are working with uses code relocation, this can be quite confusing. Although not foolproof, a key point to watch for is when a hard-coded breakpoint is hit when you didn't specify any.

In environments where code relocation is known to be typical, use a debugger that is prepared to deal with it. Microsoft Windows is a prime example of this situation.

There are three basic ways that hard-coded breakpoints can be introduced:

1. Directly poking them into code already loaded into RAM
2. Adding INT03 calls to a program's source code and reassembling or recompiling
3. Using a debugger to embed them directly into a binary code file

Poking a Breakpoint Call into Code in RAM

The first thing to do when poking a breakpoint directly into code already in memory is to *carefully* select the proper location. This requires working at the assembler level and understanding what constitutes the very first byte of an instruction. Confusion arises most often when segment override prefixes are involved. Consider the following disassembly output from DEBUG.COM:

```
0CE2:0100 B83F00          MOV AX,3F00
0CE2:0103 26              ES:
0CE2:0104 8B1EC903        MOV BX,[03C9]
0CE2:0108 BAE575          MOV DX,75E5
0CE2:010B CD21            INT 21
```

This piece of code shows the setup and calling of the handle read function. In the third line, the handle number is being loaded into the BX register from a memory location with offset 3C9h. If this instruction were chosen as the point for the hard-coded breakpoint, you might think it as simple as jotting down the current opcode at address 0CE2:0104 (which is 8B) and then overwriting it with the CCh opcode of an INT03 call.

Whoa! Let's take a closer look at this instruction—in particular, the effect and involvement of the preceding line. This is what is known as a *segment override prefix* and it is actually part of the instruction shown on the third line. It is unfortunate that DEBUG.COM's limited logic disassembles these on separate lines. The proper location for the INT03 opcode is at address 0CE2:0103, where the 26h prefix will be overwritten.

When a break does occur at this point, you would then need to overwrite the CCh opcode with the original 26h opcode. Note that if you need this to be a sticky breakpoint, you will have to step ahead to the next instruction and then manually replace the 26h with a CCh again. Aren't you glad your debugger manages all this automatically in all other cases?

Adding a Breakpoint Call to the Source Code

The nice thing about implanting hard-coded breakpoints directly within a program's source is that you don't have to keep track of and replace the original opcode. Note that when you do break into a debugger due to a hard-coded breakpoint, trying to step ahead with either the step-over or step-into commands will not behave as you have come to expect. Most debuggers simply refuse to advance past a hard-coded INT03 instruction. Some, strangely enough, will let you step into the INT03-handling logic of the debugger itself. The solution is to advance the instruction pointer by one manually when you want to advance.

In assembler, introducing a breakpoint call at the source-code level is a snap—simply add the following line:

```
int     3
```

In C, there are a couple of possibilities. The int86() library function can be used, or an in-line assembler statement can be coded. Here are examples of both of these:

```
int86(3,...);
asm int 3;
```

If your language doesn't support a software interrupt–calling function or in-line assembler, you might consider generating a new library function that is written in assembler but is designed to be linked in with your high-level source. Adding the .OBJ module produced from this assembler module to one of your program libraries would eliminate the need to make any custom specifications to the linker.

This assembler module need contain nothing else but an INT03 instruction followed by a RET to return back to the point of call. The exact form of this return instruction depends on the calling conventions used by your compiler.

How to Poke into a Binary Module

To enter a breakpoint into a binary file requires loading the file into memory with a debugger, determining where the breakpoint should be placed, recording the current opcode at that location, poking the INT03 call into memory, and writing the code file back out to the disk. To digress just a moment: The first and most important step is to make a copy of the file in its original state.

Entering a breakpoint into code that is loaded in RAM was already covered above. The part of this process that isn't always simple is writing the modified code back to disk. In the case of a .COM file, it is simple. For the sake of example, that common denominator of a debugger, DEBUG.COM, will be used.

To load the file XYZ.COM is as simple as

```
debug xyz.com
```

Then, assuming you want to break when the first instruction of this file is executed, you would enter the commands shown in Listing 11-2 at DEBUG's dash prompt.

The first command, D, dumps the first 128 bytes of the program, which lets you see the first byte and record it in your notes. In any .COM file, the opcode of the first instruction is located at address CS:0100. The first opcode in the above example is the byte BAh.

Next, use DEBUG's enter command, E, to poke the breakpoint instruction's opcode into CS:0100. Then invoke the write command, W, to update the disk file image of this program. Finally, enter a Q to quit DEBUG and return to the DOS command prompt.

If you need to introduce a hard breakpoint at some other point within the module, follow the instructions above for poking a breakpoint call into code in RAM.

To embed a breakpoint within a .SYS file (a device driver) involves the same steps as with a .COM file, except that locating the initial entry point is a different story. The details involved in reverse-engineering a device driver are beyond the scope of this section. Refer to Appendix D, "System-Level Knowledge for Debugging."

The .EXE file format is one that DEBUG.COM cannot handle directly. It can, however, be tricked into doing our bidding. What is required is to rename the file to have a different extension, patch a breakpoint into the clone file, and then rename it back to its original extension after updating the disk file.

To derive the address of the initial load point when the renamed version is loaded involves calculations on the hexadecimal values within certain fields of the file's EXE header. Refer to Appendix D, "System-Level Knowledge for Debugging," for a treatment of this topic.

Don't Forget

Once a binary file has been modified to include hard-coded breakpoints, you are obliged to always provide that program with a resident debugger before letting it be loaded for execution. If you forget that a module contains a

```
-D CS:100
4FA2:0100  BA 0C 01 B4 09 CD 21 B8-00 4C CD 21 68 65 6C 6C   ......!..L.!hell
4FA2:0110  6F 20 77 6F 72 6C 64 00-00 00 00 00 00 00 00 00   o world.........
4FA2:0120  00 00 00 00 00 00 00 00-00 00 00 00 00 00 00 00   ................
4FA2:0130  00 00 00 00 00 00 00 00-00 00 00 00 00 00 00 00   ................
4FA2:0140  00 00 00 00 00 00 00 00-00 00 00 00 00 00 00 00   ................
4FA2:0150  00 00 00 00 00 00 00 00-00 00 00 00 00 00 00 00   ................
4FA2:0160  00 00 00 00 00 00 00 00-00 00 00 00 00 00 00 00   ................
4FA2:0170  00 00 00 00 00 00 00 00-00 00 00 00 00 00 00 00   ................

-E CS:100 CC
-W
-Q
```

LISTING 11-2 Setting a hard-coded breakpoint.

hard-coded breakpoint and run it without a debugger, the results will be un-predictable. If you added the breakpoint in the source code and recompiled, and if the INTO3 vector happens to be pointing to an IRET instruction, you will be safe. When the INTO3 vector points to anything else, a nice quick, clean lockup is the best you can hope for (as opposed to a slow, agonizing crash where your disk drive light comes on).

In the case where a breakpoint was patched into a binary code module, you still aren't safe even if the INTO3 vector happens to point to an IRET. The instruction that was overwritten with the INTO3 opcode is unable to play its normal part in the program's execution. Don't forget!

11.12 GETTING YOUR BEARINGS

When you break into a program with a breakout switch or by virtue of a hardware or evaluative breakpoint, you can end up inside a portion of your program that is unfamiliar to you. It is also not uncommon for this type of breakpoint to occur when code outside the confines of your program is executing. Getting your bearings when this happens is what this section is all about.

"Finding Yourself" within the System

One of the handiest utilities to come along in quite awhile is the memory dump tool. You know the type—it tells you where all your device drivers and TSRs are loaded, how much memory is left, and what the next program load point is. Further detail on this debugger's helper can be found in Section 9.5, "Memory/Device Map Utilities."

The most important thing about using such a utility is to remember to use it before you load the program being debugged and set your breakpoints. Once you've hit a breakpoint, you don't want to have to reboot to run a utility—you want to be able to take a good look around at the particular portion of your system's underbelly you happen to find yourself in.

When you break into a strange neighborhood, have a look at the value in the CS register. When it holds a value of F000, you've broken in on the execution of a ROM BIOS call. While the upper addresses from C000 to F000 are usually occupied by ROM memory devices, exceptions do exist (don't they always?). Through the use of a memory management driver or memory management hardware, it is possible to have read/write memory allocated to addresses within this region. This opens up all kinds of possibilities for what may be located at these upper addresses; device drivers, TSRs, and similar systems components are prime examples.

Another place you'll often find yourself when you're not within the Tran-sient Program Area (TPA) is within the operating system kernel or within its command processor. A good way to get familiar with where these entities are located is by inspecting the segment values in certain key interrupt vectors. Providing interrupt intercepts aren't in effect, the segment of DOS should be found within the vectors for INT21 and INT28. The vectors for INT23 and INT24 are good indicators of the command processor's location.

If you aren't in the high-memory area and you aren't down below the transient program area, then you must be within the TPA. In most cases, the case of breaking within a TSR utility's resident code (which will be within the TPA) should be covered by the use of the memory map utility. It can happen that a TSR is loaded by a batch file just before that same batch file invokes the main application. Upon exit from the main application, this same batch again gains control and calls upon the TSR to uninstall itself. Your best way to know when this is happening is to peruse the batch file from the outset.

Using .MAP and .LST Files with a Nonsymbolic Debugger

If you have a .MAP file or .LST file available for the program you're working with, the task of "finding yourself" is usually much easier. There can still be a number of cases where you'll be "off the map," however. Typically, you will only have listing files for the portion of your program for which you have source code. Any linked-in library modules will exist as mysterious sections of machine code. Fortunately, almost all language systems will show the names and addresses of library functions within a .MAP file.

When your program is made up of a number of code segments, correlating a listing file to the machine code in memory requires a bit of hexadecimal gymnastics. The information at the start of the .MAP file tells you the position of each segment with respect to the first segment. Providing you know the address at which the program's first instruction was loaded and which program segment contains that point, you can determine the actual segment load values for each of the program segments. Therefore, it's a good habit to jot down the initial load address of a program before you set your traps and begin tracing.

Check the Vectors

Have a look at the interrupt vectors. If your debugger supports formatted data dumps, display the interrupt vector table, which begins at address 0:0 in word or dword format. The first word is the offset of the INT0 vector and the subsequent word is the segment. This pattern repeats for each of the 256 doubleword interrupt vectors.

If you find that the segment portion of any vectors matches the segment of your current position, look up the definition of the associated vector.

When making inferences from this, remember that the existence of interrupt intercepts can change the landscape.

For example, if you find the segment of the INT23 vector to match, you may conclude that you've broken into a portion of the command processor. Unfortunately, it is very common for both TSR utilities and applications programs to intercept this vector. Memory map tools can help identify which resident utilities have which interrupt vectors hooked. To track the intercepting of interrupt vectors by an application requires tracing through its code, watching for calls to function 25h of INT21.

Disassembly

Browsing through the machine code in the area near where you've broken in is one way to shed some light on things. Having a debugger with a window-type interface is a definite plus when it comes to browsing through machine code. With a non–window-oriented debugger, such as DEBUG.COM, disassembling in the forward direction is relatively painless, but going backwards involves the entirely nonintuitive process of guessing what address to specify.

When you are using a symbolic debugger but happen to have broken in at a point for which no symbols exist, try browsing ahead or back until you find the first function for which symbols do exist and then count the RET instructions between that point and the point where you broke. The Periscope debugger sports a /N command option, which simplifies this process. This feature searches the symbol table and reports the values nearest to your current point.

A malady that often befalls those who browse is the loss of synchronization that occurs when code and data are mixed together in memory. Unfortunately, without benefit of symbols or source code, differentiating between code and data can require a trial-and-error approach. This is done by issuing disassemble commands with incremental addresses until code appears that seems reasonable.

Note that the mixing of code and data is not the only possible explanation for a loss of sync. If a program contains a mixture of 80X86 real-mode code and 32-bit protected-mode code aimed for an 80386/80486 CPU, your debugger will become confused. Some more sophisticated debuggers do support disassembly of 32-bit native-mode code.

Once you determine how big a pocket of data seems to be, jot this info down in your permanent set of notes—you never know when you'll need to browse through this section again. It can also be helpful to do a memory dump of the area of memory you are trying to disassemble. If the disassembly is getting confused due to ASCII message strings, a data dump can sometimes make it easier to identify the end of the data area. If your need to differentiate is critical, see Section 13.1, "Reverse Engineering/Disassembling."

Inferring the Past by Moving Ahead

In some cases, the easiest way to determine where you are is to begin stepping forward through the program and see what you have to go through to arrive at a familiar point. Using your debugger's step-over command rather than step-into will speed this process along. Take note of how the program unlayers as you execute RET instructions and move back up the calling hierarchy.

Placing a sticky breakpoint on the INT21 interrupt handler, as well as other interrupt services you deem likely to be involved, can be useful. As you step over call instructions, any interrupt breakpoints that occur will reveal what goes on within a function.

Searching Binary Modules

When working with a program comprised of multiple modules that are loaded by means of program chaining or overlays, you may have to resort to using a debugger's search command on each code module to find a code sequence matching the one at the point where you've broken in. When working with .EXE-type programs, be aware that the memory image and the file image of a program can be different due to the effects of code relocation processing.

An easier method can be to browse through memory in the area near where you've broken and look for ASCIIZ strings. If the content of such a string isn't revealing enough by itself, use a hex dump tool to browse for it in each module or use a debugger's search command.

This method does, of course, mean that unless you have another computer available, you will have to exit your debugging session to get to a point where you can load the code modules for inspection.

11.13 SUMMARY

Breakpoints can be used to set traps for a failure or to gain familiarity with a program's internal operation.

Using breakpoints is faster than single-stepping and reduces the amount of detail with which you must contend.

Review and testing are important when developing a complex breakpoint test.

Gathering historical data on a program's operation may be done through the use of a backtrace buffer and passive breakpoints or by setting up breakpoints that call a user function, which then emits markers to an instrumentation driver.

Setting breakpoints on software interrupt vectors used by DOS and the BIOS is a good way to monitor a program's operation. To break on ROM BIOS calls requires either a hardware breakpoint or a simple intercept driver.

To trace into a crash, step over function calls until the crash occurs. Then reboot, recover your position, step into that call, and resume stepping over until the problem is sufficiently isolated.

Erratic behavior when recovering a previous position may be due to the effects of IRQ interrupts, stray bullets, stray references, or a mixture of code and data that is set up by certain compilers.

Rebooting is essential after the occurrence of a failure.

Making a proper recovery to a previous position in the code may require replication of the full sequence.

When designing evaluation breakpoint tests, strive to test for the absence of good conditions rather than a specific bad condition.

Using hardware or evaluative breakpoints to test for video memory changes can be helpful in tracing video garbage bugs.

Custom breakpoints can be implemented when a debugger supports the calling of a user routine or when custom code is embedded that executes a hard breakpoint when a test is passed.

Verification of linked lists can be accomplished with custom code, and it benefits from the inclusion of a signature and a checksum.

Sequence-tracking and state machines can be effected with custom code.

Mysteriously missed breakpoints can occur when duplicate copies of a piece of code exist within memory and the wrong copy is being executed.

Hard-coded breakpoints are useful when working with relocated code, code loaded from an overlay, and resident code. They can be introduced by poking them directly into code in memory, modifying a binary module, or inserting them into the source code and rebuilding the executable module.

When poking a hard-coded breakpoint into existing code, be careful to watch for segment overrides and other instruction prefixes.

Most debuggers will require you to advance the instruction pointer past a hard-coded breakpoint manually.

Before loading a program with a debugger to begin a bug chase, use a memory-mapping utility to determine the initial load segment. You might also want to print out source, .LST, and .MAP files or copy them to another computer for ready access.

Inspecting the values within interrupt vectors can be helpful in getting your bearings.

When a disassembled section of code doesn't look like valid code, it might be data mixed in with the code, corrupted code, or 386 native-mode code.

Inferring your position within a section of code is often easier when you step forward through the code and note the path taken.

Inspecting memory in the vicinity of your current position can reveal ASCIIZ strings that will be helpful in getting your bearings.

CHAPTER 12
Invasive Techniques

Whenever you can locate a bug without having to place a program on the table and cut it open, all the better. Everyone involved is back in business sooner with more time available for productive work. But there are times when the external indications are too vague or inconsistent; when the only way to find out what's going on is to take scalpel in hand and go in for a look.

12.1 INSTRUMENTATION

When you apply instrumentation to a program, you are making it report on its internal activities in a manner of your choosing. These reports can provide information on the current state of selected data within the program as well as information on the program's execution flow.

This approach allows the programmer to pinpoint areas of concern with great precision. For this to be effective requires an understanding of the program's normal function, an understanding of the language and environment being used, and a reasonable suspicion of the nature of the software fault. It also can be easy to generate a large amount of such data, so care must be taken not to create a flood.

Different Ways to Implement Markers

There are a number of ways to introduce instrumentation into a program. The simplest method is often to add additional program statements and re-compile:

```
PRINT"at point a"        (BASIC)
writeln('at point a');   (Pascal)
printf("at point a\n");  (C)
```

Other methods include adding calls to an instrumentation driver (e.g., ROUTER.SYS) and recompiling; patching in calls to an instrumentation driver (e.g., when source code is unavailable); or using breakpoint markers as described further in this chapter.

Instrumentation markers can be made to dump single characters; strings; discrete data values such as bytes, integers, and floats; CPU register contents; the contents of the stack; and selected blocks of memory. Information can be displayed in character format, converted to decimal or hexadecimal, or displayed in a debug-style dump (e.g., the format used by the D command of DEBUG.COM). Several types of instrumentation were introduced in Chapter 7, "The Companion Toolset."

A typical debugging session in which instrumentation is used can involve a number of edit/compile/test cycles. Information gained by a study of the marker output of one run will often dictate new locations for the instrumentation statements. Effort spent making macros that simplify the task of implanting debugging code will easily amortize out during these repeated trials.

It also can be worthwhile to retain markers in the source code but in a dormant form. You may want to leave markers permanently within the source code to identify when an entry and exit is made from each function—adding additional markers specific to each problem. In addition, it can be helpful to be able to turn off all instrumentation during certain tests and then turn it back on again without having to comment out each marker statement individually. The conditional compilation technique shown in Listing 12-1 can address this need.

```
#define debug 01


#if debug == 1

  #define showchar(x) dumpchar(x)

  void dumpchar(char dc) {

    putchar(dc);
    }

#else

  #define showchar(x)

#endif
```

LISTING 12-1 Conditional compilation of debugging code.

Instrumentation versus the Debugger

When a bug appears to be fairly consistent in its behavior, it is often best to attack it with a software debugger. The extra edit/compile/test cycles inherent to instrumentation are usually practical with this type of bug only when no debugger is available or the only one available is too primitive (e.g., DEBUG.COM).

Situations that call for instrumentation include programs with intermittent bugs, problems involving IRQ handlers, and cases where you must study a large number of events or a sequence of events widely spaced in time (where single-stepping is too tedious).

Especially when used in conjunction with a ring buffer or similar storage device, the ability to gather history using instrumentation can be a powerful weapon when you must tackle a problem about which you know little. While some debuggers do sport logging windows and trace-back buffers, the range of operations supported can be too limited for many situations.

A primary difference is that instrumentation only tells you what you make it tell you, whereas single-stepping with a debugger provides you with a very complete picture of a program's operation. The selectivity made possible by instrumentation can be good or bad, depending on the circumstances. Dealing with a select set of information, delivered to you in a form of your choosing, involves much less tedium than using a debugger to step through a program. On the other hand, by not using a debugger, you could miss important details that would take longer to uncover with instrumentation.

Using an Instrumentation Driver

In the methods discussed above, all debugging code was included directly within the application being instrumented. By using a separate instrumentation driver such as ROUTER.SYS, the only code that must be embedded in the application being debugged are the calls to that driver at each point where positional or data value information is required.

This configuration reduces the chances of bug suppression due to major code position shifts within an application. It also becomes more practical to support a wider variety of instrumentation features.

Direct-inclusion instrumentation code can still be required when working with processes that must execute at a very high speed, which would be adversely affected by the extra overhead involved in the use of a driver like ROUTER.SYS. Providing extra features does involve more processing to route the data to its destination, performing the necessary conversions and buffer housekeeping along the way.

The benefits of using an instrumentation driver are often quite valuable, however. The ability to have information recorded in a large ring buffer or written to a file can greatly simplify the management of large amounts of instrumentation output.

Placing Instrumentation Markers

First and foremost, always make a backup copy of a source file before adding instrumentation or any other type of debugging code. This not only makes it easier to back out debugging code; it also eliminates the danger of accidentally deleting too many lines when deleting marker instructions. We certainly don't want any *new* bugs to show up!

Thought must be given to what execution flow patterns and what data values within the program are significant to the problem you are studying. Look carefully at the portions of the program that you assume still work correctly, and implant instrumentation to verify this. Then, by all means, identify and instrument all areas that you suspect might be involved.

Here are some caveats:

1. When placing positional markers in combination with hex dump markers, avoid the use of the letters A through F as positional marker letters.
2. Be selective about placing markers within loops, interrupt handlers, or other sections of code with a high frequency of execution. Information overload can occur.
3. Realize that in adding instrumentation code to a program, you may cause the bug to change its behavior.

When you don't yet have a distinct understanding of the relationship between a failure and the execution path of the related section of code, one approach can be to place a marker at each point where a major branching decision is made. If your analysis of the resulting marker stream results in a little better understanding, go back into the program, clean out your initial set of markers, and sprinkle new ones throughout the suspect section.

Designing markers to produce a certain type of visual effect can often be helpful. For example, when dumping a continuous stream of hex words using direct video or a serial terminal, making each unit of information occupy five columns is advantageous, since each new row of words will be positioned directly underneath the previous one. The five columns come from the four hex digits and the blank space written after each word by a macro such as dv_byte (see Section 7.2, "General Instrumentation Macros and Functions"). The key is to make the display width of each item an integer factor of the total display width so that columnar alignment occurs.

Another visual aid can be to use marker characters that represent enclosure at the beginning and end of important sections of code. These characters include (,), [,], {, and }. Note that the < and > characters may be used with special code but cannot be used directly with an assembler macro such as dv_chari, since these characters carry a special meaning to the assembler. The dv_chari macro was introduced in Section 7.2, "General Instrumentation Macros and Functions."

For example, if you need to study the confluence of execution of a certain function and an IRQ handler, embed a dv_chari (at the start of the function, a dv_chari) at the function's end, a dv_chari [at the start of the IRQ handler, and a dv_chari] at the handler's end point.

With this method, upon seeing the pattern ( ) [ ] you can quickly discern that the IRQ occurred while the current point of execution was not within the function. Similarly, the pattern ([ ]) tells you that the IRQ occurred during the function, and [( )] tells you that the function was executed by the IRQ handler or by some other interrupt that occurred during the marked interrupt.

Recursive execution is also made obvious through this method. The pattern (( )) identifies the function as recursive, and the pattern [[[[[[[[tells you that the IRQ's processing time is so long that another IRQ is occurring before the previous one can finish. A crash due to stack runaway is highly likely in such cases.

Markers from Breakpoints

Some debuggers will let you specify the action to be taken when a breakpoint occurs. When one of the choices is to execute a user-specified function, a whole new world of marker possibilities opens up. Providing that an interface is supported whereby a user function can access the state of the program's registers at the time of the breakpoint interrupt, this function can be made to report the location of the breakpoint.

The benefit of this trick is that positional breakpoints are now as simple as setting breakpoints. The drawbacks are that a hex address will result instead of a single marker character, per position and that the number of markers you can place at any one time will be limited by the number of breakpoints the debugger can manage.

The Bug and the Mouse

Once upon a time there was a mouse and a bug.... Seriously now, suppose you are developing a new mouse driver and are experiencing a problem with the interrupt-handling logic. As the mouse is moved horizontally back and forth, the mouse cursor occasionally jumps up to the top of the display for a brief time (see Figure 12.1).

The indication here is that the mouse interrupt is sometimes generated when the system is in a sensitive state—where conditions aren't right. The goal then, is to identify when a mouse interrupt occurs where the failure is evident and what conditions exist at that time which are different from the "normal" conditions.

When dealing with intermittent bugs and interrupt handlers, it is important to design instrumentation that affects the timing of the interrupt logic as little as possible. A good approach is to use direct video markers through an instrumentation driver, where a second display is the destination. Should this

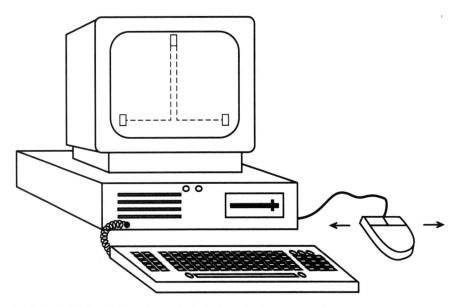

FIGURE 12.1 Spikes in mouse movement.

seem to affect system timing too greatly, try direct inclusion of the marker code (e.g., the `DV.INC` file introduced in Chapter 7).

Now, on to the design of the marker code. What we need to know is when a bad mouse event occurs and what else is going on in the system at the time. One approach would be to place a marker within the mouse interrupt handler that dumps the Y coordinate each time so you can see when a drastic change occurs.

Another approach would be to add a small amount of custom debugging code that would test the value of the Y coordinate. If, when you are exercising the program, you always move the mouse horizontally along the bottom of the screen, Y coordinate values near the upper limit will be generated (e.g., around 639 in a 640 × 480 graphics environment or around 24 in an 80 × 25 text mode environment).

Given this condition, you can make your test code invoke a marker dump only when the Y coordinate value is below a median value, corresponding to a mouse cursor nearer the top of the screen. Not only will this reduce the effect on system timing, since no markers are produced by the interrupt handler until you need one, but it saves you having to scour through the dump output comparing the Y coordinate values—you get a clear indication of when an interrupt occurs where the problem is evident.

Implied in this testing scenario is the existence of instrumentation that will tell you what was going on in the system when the interrupt occurred. This involves placing markers at strategic locations throughout the portion of the program that is running during the times when the bug occurs. Note also that when the Y coordinate range-checking logic within the interrupt handler triggers, it can often be helpful to have additional information dumped from that point as well.

Should the output of these other markers occur on a continuous basis even when the mouse is not being moved, you have a bit more custom coding to add. Once the first piece of custom code detects an out-of-range Y coordinate, one of the actions taken must be to set a flag that will prevent your instrumentation logic from writing any more data to the display. Even though calls will still be made to the central dumping function from the various markers, you must cause them to be ignored, or the information you need to see will soon scroll off of the screen.

Your hope, of course, is that this technique will enable you to discover enough about the state of the machine when the intermittent failure occurs to effect a correction. You will also sometimes learn that even when the mouse cursor is jumping up to the top of the display, the Y coordinates read in by the interrupt handler are always within a range corresponding to the lower region of the screen.

This would indicate that something is happening to the mouse driver's data between when it is initially generated by the interrupt handler and when it is ultimately used to affect the position of the mouse cursor. Sounds like a good time to reposition your custom debugging code a little farther down the chain of processing logic.

12.2 SYSTEM CALL TRACING

Almost all programs make software interrupt calls to the operating system or BIOS. Since these calls are made through known locations (e.g., interrupt vectors), setting a breakpoint or setting up an interrupt intercept driver is a fairly straightforward process. You can begin to gain an understanding about a program's internal operation without having to know where to place breakpoints or instrumentation within the program itself.

Monitoring the system call requests that a program makes not only is easy; it also provides a very concise type of information. Observing when a program accesses certain data files; what methods it uses to open, read, and write those files; and how and when the program uses other system calls to perform such tasks as console I/O gives you a picture that contains a balanced amount of detail. There is not so much detail that you become overloaded with information (as can happen with single-stepping), but there is sufficient detail to be meaningful. Studying these calls will often help you discover a first evidence of the failure in an earlier form.

The following list shows the interrupts that are commonly involved in debugging sessions. This is certainly not a complete list. A number of third-party drivers (either in TSR or device driver form) make services available through different interrupts, such as B-tree file access, graphics functions, or arithmetic functions.

INT21	DOS system services for file, console, and other I/O
INT29	DOS video services (ANSI.SYS)
INT2E	DOS command processor interface
INT2F	DOS system services—miscellaneous
INT10	BIOS video output services
INT13	BIOS disk I/O services
INT15	BIOS miscellaneous services
INT16	BIOS keystroke services
INT17	BIOS printer output services
INT5C	NETBIOS interface
INT67	EMS/VCPI interface

Using an Intercept Driver

An intercept driver could be a device driver such as DDICEPT.SYS (supplied on the Companion Toolset Diskette, see Section 8.13), or it could be in the form of a TSR. It is even possible to make a transient program that establishes one or more interrupt intercepts and then runs the program to be studied as a child process. When the child program terminates back to this analysis tool, the tool backs out all interrupt intercepts and then terminates back to the operating system itself.

Using this type of tool is like placing a telephone tap on the line between a program and the operating system, BIOS, or other service providing entity. Without changing either the program making the interrupt calls or the interrupt service routine, you are able to gain useful information about a program's internal activities.

An important feature of this type of tool is that it can be made to look up and report an English phrase that describes the type of call being made. In addition, it can also be made to identify and display relevant input and output data for each function.

As an example, when an intercept driver is set up to monitor INT21 calls and detects an INT21 function 3Dh call, the tool should display a message like "INT21 function 3D, Open file, handle." On the next line, it should then display the name of the file for which an open operation is being requested (e.g., "ds:dx -> WIDGETS.DAT").

Using a Debugger

A debugger can also be used to spy on the system calls a program makes. But unlike the intercept driver, you have to manually look up the meaning of each call (until you get them memorized). Further, to see any entry and exit parameter strings requires that you enter a data dump command, specifying the appropriate registers for each call.

In other words, you can obtain information about system call activity with a debugger, but you have to work for it. Still, there are many cases where you will already need to be using a debugger for other reasons, so it is important to know how to use it to deal with software interrupt calls.

First and foremost, your debugger must be designed to support a breakpoint on the interrupt calls you need to work with. Were you to use DE-BUG.COM to try to set a breakpoint on DOS's INT21 vector, you would find your machine locked or otherwise crashed. Since this debugger makes INT21 calls from within its breakpoint-handling logic, a breakpoint causes a breakpoint, which then causes another and another until the stack runs out.

When the interrupt service you wish to monitor is handled by code located within a ROM chip, you must either have a hardware-oriented debugger (see Section 6.7, "386/486 Debug Registers," and Section 6.9, "CPU Intercept Pod") or set up an intercept driver in RAM. This type of intercept driver need only be of the simplest design—a device driver or TSR, installed before the debugger, that simply intercepts the interrupt and passes each call on to the previous interrupt service routine.

There is even an advantage to using this simple type of intercept driver when working with interrupt service routines that are already located within RAM (e.g., INT21): It becomes easy to set a breakpoint on the exit of each function call as well as the entry. Although the design of interrupt intercepts is more properly the domain of Section 8.3, "Writing Interrupt Intercepts," we are going to take a look at this special case here:

```
intercept_21:
      pushf
      cli
      call    cs:[previous_21]
      retf    2
```

Given the foregoing interrupt intercept, setting a breakpoint on the pushf instruction would let you observe the entry conditions for each call. Likewise, setting a breakpoint on the retf 2 instruction is an excellent way to track the exit state of each interrupt call. Seeing the exit state of each call allows you to identify which calls result in an error condition.

In the event that you do not have this type of intercept driver available or you only need to see an interrupt call's exit conditions for a small number of calls, you could make use of the following technique. When you break into your debugger at the very start of any software interrupt call, the first doubleword on the stack will always be a far pointer to the return point for that call. By setting a breakpoint at this address, you will arrive at the instruction immediately following the interrupt call and can proceed to examine the exit state of that call.

In Intel style, the first word of this far pointer is the offset within the segment, with the second word being the segment address. In other words, the word at SS:SP is the offset, which we'll refer to as OOOO, and the word at SS:SP+2 is the segment, or SSSS. Armed with this information, you simply issue a go command using the address SSSS:OOOO as the destination. Within a debugger like DEBUG.COM or Periscope, this would simply be G SSSS:OOOO, where the SSSS and OOOO symbols are replaced with the actual values read from the stack.

Within Periscope, there is actually a simpler way to accomplish this same result. The command form G {SS:SP} tells this debugger to read the far pointer at the address within the curly braces and use it as the destination address for a nonsticky breakpoint.

Using Both

An intercept driver excels at providing information on interrupt calls in an easy-to-digest manner, but it is a highly specialized tool, which won't do you a bit of good when it comes time to single-step through an interrupt call, set breakpoints, or examine or modify memory.

A debugger excels at all of these latter tasks but requires you to go through extra tedium to monitor interrupt calls. You have to look up the meaning of each call in your reference books and manually invoke dump commands in order to determine which file is being opened or which subdirectory is being made the current one.

These features do not, however, have to be mutually exclusive. You can have your debugger and your intercept driver too. Simply keep the debugger loaded while using the intercept driver, and break in when you get to an interesting point. A debugger that supports hot key–instigated breakpoints or an NMI breakout switch can easily be used in conjunction with an intercept driver. The control console feature of ROUTER.SYS can also be used, where the dr_ifbrk macro call is placed within the interrupt intercept (see Chapter 7).

This does, incidentally, require that you discern whether you've broken into the program you are testing, the intercept driver, or some other software entity. Section 11.12, "Getting Your Bearings," will tell you more on this subject.

Filtering

Certain software interrupt functions tend to be called a lot more often than others. A program which maintains an on-screen clock display while it is waiting for keystroke input is most likely executing in a loop. First, it makes a call to INT21 function 2Ch to fetch the current system clock value. Then, after updating the clock display, it makes a call to function 0Bh to see if a key has been pressed. Providing no keys are pressed, this loop recycles back around to the time-reading point.

If you are directing the output of an intercept driver to a disk file or similar storage device, you may wish to set up logic within the driver that will let you filter out certain calls. Otherwise, the repeating sequence of calls such as those described above can quickly overfill your storage medium. The `DDICEPT.SYS` intercept driver supports this feature.

When working with a debugger, evaluative breakpoints are usually your best shot. To avoid having to deal with a plethora of calls such as those just described, you would want to have a debugger capable of being told to "break on any `INT21` call except where AH == 2C or AH == 0B." Alternatively, you could study the design of the loop, determine its exit point, and set a breakpoint at that location. Once this breakpoint was hit, you could then resume breaking on each `INT21` call.

Applying Sequence Detection

Sequence detection can be especially helpful when dealing with intermittent types of failures. If, through monitoring the system call activity a program makes, you can determine that a unique sequence of calls is made just before the failure occurs, this method should be considered.

This technique can be implemented in two different ways: through custom code called by a debugger's evaluative breakpoint or through custom code incorporated into an intercept driver. Since the former technique was described in Section 11.9, "Sequence Tracking," the latter will be the focus of this discussion.

When this custom intercept driver code does discover the sequence we have trained it to detect, what action will it take? The best technique is to use a debugger in conjunction with a custom intercept driver. When the driver detects a sequence match, it will execute an `INT03` instruction to pass control over to the debugger. From this point, a more detailed exploration of the system can be done to expose the nature of the failure further.

Explicit logic could be designed, based on the pseudocode model outlined in Section 11.9, or the `dr_seqchk` macro could be used to call upon the sequence detection logic within the `ROUTER.SYS` instrumentation driver. Section 7.4, "Instrumentation Macros and Functions for `ROUTER.SYS`," covers the interface details for this macro.

To put some meat on these conceptual bones, consider the case where, through monitoring and analysis, you have determined that the failure is always preceded by the following sequence of system calls:

```
INT21, entry AX = 4202
INT21, entry AX = 3Fxx
INT10, entry AX = 1301
```

The first call performs an lseek operation on a previously opened file. The second call reads a portion of that file into a buffer, and the third call, an INT10 instead of an INT21, displays some of the buffered information. Note that in some situations, the contents of additional registers may be important in fully qualifying an important sequence.

The term AX = 3Fxx after the second call means that the contents of the AH register are always 3F but the contents of the AL register have been seen to vary. Indeed, the contents of AL are meaningless to an INT21 function 3F call, so this is understandable. To accommodate this, the custom logic in the INT21 interrupt intercept must test for AH = = 3F and, when found, force the internal copy of the AL register to 0 for the sake of consistency.

In designing detection logic that involves more than one interrupt, each element of the sequence list must contain enough information to qualify the event fully. In this case, a pair of words must be used, which means that two calls must be made to dr_seqchk for each event. Here is the data list to be used with the dr_seqchk macro:

```
seqlist dw        6          ; number of elements
        dw        0          ; current element
;==== start of list of dwords
        dw        0021h,4202h
        dw        0021h,3f00h
        dw        0010h,1301h
```

Using dr_seqchk in a multiple-interrupt case requires, of course, that each interrupt intercept formulate a doubleword value that includes an identification of the interrupt. To work with the foregoing sequence list, the INT21 intercept must be made to call dr_seqchk with 0021h as the first word and the AX register value forming the second word (where the low byte is forced to 0 for a 3Fh call). The INT10 intercept must, of course, use 0010h for its first word.

When the call to dr_seqchk made by the INT10 intercept results in a match indication, executing an INT03 will put you into your debugger at a point where you can (you hope) single-step right up to the point of failure.

12.3 DATA AND CONTROL FLOW INTERPRETATION

First and foremost, whenever any analysis is to be done in the pursuit of a bug, presumptions must be seen for what they are and converted into more rationally qualified concepts. While the positional markers you placed in a certain function may not reveal any abnormal behavior about a program's execution flow during a failure, that does not mean that the function is not involved. It is entirely possible that the system is suffering a temporary insanity in between your markers.

Second, make your job as easy as you can. When designing and placing instrumentation markers, ask yourself, "What is this going to tell me?" and "What additional information will I wish I had when it comes time to analyze the resulting output?"

In some situations, you may need to know the elapsed time between certain points within a program, or you may need to know the correspondence between the instrumentation output and the state of the display. Of course, if you are having instrumentation output routed to an alternate display, to a serial terminal, or to another computer where this data can be viewed in real time, perceiving these associations is usually possible.

When the events occur at too high a rate, or when it is not practical for you to sit and watch the marker output while waiting for a failure to occur (e.g., an intermittent failure), it is important to realize that associative data is needed and design it into your instrumentation logic.

Once you have a file full of instrumentation output, you may find it helpful to load it into an editor and use the editor's search and replace function to manipulate the data. If, for example, the marker character a represents entry to a certain function, the letters b, c, and d indicate certain branches made within that function, and e indicates an exit, you could replace these marker letters with short descriptive phrases. A few minutes of editing can sometimes save many more minutes of translation effort.

Converting letters to phrases in this manner often requires a bit of two-stage trickery. Were you to convert all occurrences of the letter a in the file to the phrase `enter define_attrib()`, you would then be in for a surprise when you converted the b markers to the corresponding phrase (the b in `define_attrib` would be converted too). To avoid this problem, you can first convert all a markers to #a, and likewise for the other letter markers.

The next bit of advice concerns the chasing of wild geese. When you've finally managed to capture instrumentation output resulting from the occurrence of an intermittent failure, be careful about making too many determinations based on first appearances. If you compare the marker output of the failing run with the marker output of a run through the same section of the program when the failure didn't occur, the differences you detect may not always be due to the failure.

Were you to compare several good runs with several where the failure has occurred, you may see that certain variances in marker output are normal. Comparing only one good run with one failing one may send you on a wild-goose chase if you can't differentiate a normal variance from an abnormal one. When capturing multiple failing runs is not practical, you should, at least, compare the failing one you have with several good runs.

The final bit of advice concerns the application of "healthy" suspicion. Say that after several hours of preliminary debugging, you have finally discovered that a certain integer variable is being overwritten. Your next task, of course, is to isolate the cause of this data mangling.

Suppose you choose to use instrumentation to monitor the contents of this integer variable through the execution of the program, because using a memory-write type of breakpoint is not practical, there being no easy way to distinguish between a normal write and a bad one. The "healthy" suspicion comes in when you decide to dump not only the memory holding this integer variable but a range of memory before and after as well.

If, from using this wider vision, you notice that memory is being corrupted in a high-to-low order in whole-word amounts, it may be that the program's stack is underflowing. If the entire area is suddenly filled with a repeating value, a likely candidate is a loop that is initializing an array where a bounds error or incorrect-pointer error is occurring. Should you notice the corruption to occur in blocks of 12 bytes, and you happen to know that one of the records in your program is of that size, operations that write those records should be investigated.

12.4 CODE AND DATA CORRUPTION

In a study of bugs, data corruption is a recurring theme. This section explores how instrumentation can be applied to this malady. Refer to Appendix A, the "Tool and Technique Locator Chart," for leads on sections of this book that explore approaches such as the use of hardware or evaluative breakpoints.

The simplest way to use instrumentation to determine when a certain piece of read/write data memory becomes corrupt is to embed positional markers and a data marker that let you monitor the contents of the memory location while the program runs. If you don't yet have a very specific idea of where in the program the corruption might be occurring, place a pair of markers at the entry and exit of each major function. The first marker of this pair would dump a character or number identifying the position within the program, with the second marker dumping the current contents of the memory area being studied.

If you will not be able to sit and constantly monitor the dump output while the program is running, try to add a test function to the program that can be called from each marker location. The purpose of this function would be to disable further dump output as soon as the first evidence of the corruption can be detected. This will prevent the information you need from scrolling off the screen or being pumped completely through a ring buffer.

This automated testing method relies on a determination being made as to when the data is bad. There can be cases, however, when the value overwritten into a memory variable is not intrinsically bad—it's just not the value that is supposed to be there at the time.

In such cases, you might find it helpful to convert each assignment statement to the variable into a call to a function. Before making the assignment, this debugging test function would call another function, which would compare the current contents of the variable with the reference copy. This second function, the one doing the comparing, could also be called from other points in the program to help isolate the point where the variable has been changed through an abnormal memory write.

```
word data_to_watch;
word reference_copy;        /* reference var must be global */

byte data_check()

    if(data_to_watch == reference_copy)
    return(0);
    else
    return(1);


byte assign_data(word new_value)

    if(data_check() == 1)
    return(1);
    else
    data_to_watch = new_value;
```

LISTING 12-2   Pseudocode for an assignment monitor function.

Listing 12-2 shows a pseudocode example of this idea. Note that the reference variable must be initialized to the same value as the variable it is to parallel, so that the first call to the comparison function doesn't falsely trigger.

While monitoring a section of code for corruption, if you can identify a byte of code that is consistently destroyed, simply embed custom logic to report when this byte is changed and halt all further marker dumps. If the corruption doesn't always occur in the same location, try using the dr_dwatch macro within ROUTER.SYS. You can, of course, also build an explicit version of this logic if ROUTER.SYS is unavailable or if its presence in memory is affecting the bug adversely.

Essentially, the logic behind this ROUTER macro makes a copy of the memory to be monitored the first time the macro is called. On successive calls, this macro function will compare the reference copy made on the first call with the current state of the region of memory. A match or no-match result indication is returned and may be used to invoke an INT03 breakpoint instruction or activate other instrumentation code.

12.5   TRACING AND BACKTRACING

OK, so you've finally determined that the program is blowing up because variable A holds an improper value when function E is called. Now it's time for some backtracing. Was variable A ever assigned a correct value in the first place? If so, at what point did it fall from grace?

When you're lucky, you can simply restart the program and begin stepping from point to point with a debugger while monitoring the contents of the variable in question. When the program's execution flow and data manipulations are complex, it will take some extra digging to identify the cause-and-effect relationship behind your bug. In addition, if the bug only shows up once every several hundred trial runs, backtracing is not so simple.

In these more difficult cases, the more history you can have collected while testing a program, the better. Having instrumentation markers dumped to a large ring buffer is one method. Using a debugger with a large backtrace buffer is another.

An analysis of stack data can sometimes be helpful when doing a backtrace analysis, but be careful not to vest too much significance in this method. Stack data is often inconclusive. The program could have traveled along many different paths and still produced the same stack state.

The step-over/step-into method discussed in Section 11.6, "Tracing Into a Crash," can be helpful in backtracing. To further the example proffered at the start of this section, step around functions A, B, C, and so on until you find that, upon return from function D, variable A has been tromped on. From here, restart, but step into function D rather than stepping over it. Then step through this function's code, monitoring variable A as you step over functions D1, D2, and so on.

12.6 DEVELOP A SIMPLE MODEL

When you suspect that a failure stems from the actions of code other than that which you created, it can be beneficial to develop a small test program to seek conclusive proof. Some of the code entities which could be involved are the following:

- The startup code linked into your program
- A standard library function linked into your program
- A third-party library function linked into your program
- A TSR utility
- A device driver
- The operating system
- The operating system's command processor
- BIOS code on an adapter card
- The system ROM BIOS

If you can develop a small-scale model of the section of the program you're having trouble with and get it to evidence the bug, you have greatly reduced the range of possibilities. In addition, this smaller test program will involve far fewer operational steps than the full-sized application after which it was fashioned. Making experimental changes to the code will also be much simpler.

Building a model can also be helpful when you suspect that a stray reference, where some portion of a program is using an improper address to read a piece of data, may be behind your bug.

Should your first attempt not succeed, you've still gained some valuable knowledge: You know that other factors must be involved. You may be able to transfer additional sections of the program over to the model, retesting between each addition, until enough of a similarity exists to evidence the bug. In taking this approach, pay careful attention to order the functions within the model the same as they are in the main application.

To take the next step down this road, you could manipulate the relative positions of the pieces of the program by inserting dummy blocks of code in place of the functions you wish to leave out of the model. In C or assembler, code such as the following could be used. This code assumes that a 100-byte function is to be mirrored by the allocation of 48 bytes of value 0. Filling dummy code space in C:

```
__emit__(0,0,0,0,0,0,0,0,0,0,0,0);
__emit__(0,0,0,0,0,0,0,0,0,0,0,0);
__emit__(0,0,0,0,0,0,0,0,0,0,0,0);
__emit__(0,0,0,0,0,0,0,0,0,0,0,0);
```

Filling dummy code space in assembler:

```
db       48 dup(0)
```

For languages other than C and assembler, if in-line assembler is supported, that method can be used to create a dummy routine of a specific size. Otherwise, include the actual functions in your model and then use DEBUG.COM or some other patching tool to fill the memory occupied by these functions with a constant.

Alas, there will always be cases where there is no way to replicate a problem in any other situation besides having every byte of code and data just as it is within the original application. Other debugging methods will have to be used in this unfortunate event.

12.7   REVERTING TO A TEST BED

In certain cases, it may be helpful to extract a function from the program being analyzed and place it in a test bed program, where it can be exercised and studied. The practicality of this approach depends, of course, on how much work is required to set up the data required.

Where wise development methods were used to initially create a program, each major function was created in a test bed environment in the first place. In such cases, you can simply fetch the original test bed from its archive and begin testing right away.

If it will be necessary to feed a large amount of input data into a function to provide a realistic environment, design instrumentation that will collect this type of data from the actual application. Arrange the routing of this instrumentation output so that the data is placed in a file for use as input by the test bed program.

From here, you can make copies of this file, editing the contents to experiment with the behavior of the isolated function at its boundary conditions. Using and modifying captured data in this way can make it practical to apply the test bed technique where it otherwise would not be.

12.8   SUMMARY

Applying instrumentation to a program makes it report on its execution flow and internal data states in a manner of your choosing.

The simplest way to instrument a program is by adding native-language statements of the form PRINT"at point a".

Instrumentation can also be applied by embedding calls to an instrumentation driver (e.g., ROUTER.SYS) or by using breakpoint markers.

Instrumentation markers can be made to dump single characters; strings; discrete data values such as bytes, integers, and floats; CPU register contents; the contents of the stack; and selected blocks of memory. Information can be displayed in character format, converted to decimal or hexadecimal, or displayed in a debug-style dump (e.g., the format used by the D command of DEBUG.COM).

When a bug behaves in a consistent manner, using a debugger is often the most efficient approach. Instrumentation is most valuable when dealing with intermittent bugs and with programs that must not be interrupted by breakpoints or by single-stepping (e.g., a serial communications program).

Single-stepping provides you with more information than instrumentation. This is certainly good when it happens to help you find a bug more quickly. It can be a drawback in that you must contend with a greater amount of detail.

A marker macro written for assembler must save and restore all registers it affects, including the flags. The amount of in-line code involved in each macro expansion should also be kept to a minimum by making the macro call a common dump function.

Conditional assembly/compilation should be used within instrumentation macros to make it easier to temporarily turn off all macros.

When the use of an instrumentation driver (e.g., ROUTER.SYS) adversely affects a bug; when no such driver is available; or when the instrumentation code must run at the highest possible speed, implanting instrumentation code directly within the application should be considered.

When placing instrumentation markers, consider what information you will wish you had when it's time to analyze output. Avoid placing markers within high-frequency code, such as loops.

If you are unfamiliar with the internal activities of a program, place markers at the entry and exit of each major function and at each major decision point.

When studying the nesting relationships of main-line code and interrupt handlers, the use of brackets and parentheses as marker characters can be helpful.

If your debugger allows a user function to be called as the result of a breakpoint, you can implement breakpoint instrumentation markers.

Monitoring the system call requests a program makes not only is easy; it also provides an overview picture of a program's internal operation that includes a useful amount of detail.

System call activity can be monitored using an intercept driver or a debugger. An intercept driver can be made to annotate each call with a descriptive phrase and a dump of pertinent parameter strings. With a debugger, you must manually look up this type of information.

To trace ROM BIOS calls with a debugger, either the debugger must be capable of hardware breakpoints, or a simple pass-through type of interrupt intercept driver must be used to provide RAM-based locations where breakpoints can be established.

When you first break into an interrupt handler, the top two words on the stack are the return address.

The application of sequence detection to a system call intercept driver can make it possible to break into a program just before an intermittent failure reaches its point of failure.

Once you have collected a file full of instrumentation output, it can be useful to use an editor's search and replace function to convert the marker letters into representative phrases.

Whenever comparing data on a failing run with data from a normal run, be careful not to assume that all differences are associated with the occurrence of the failure. A study of multiple failing and normal runs could show these differences to be normal variances.

When you discover that a certain memory location is being overwritten, set up monitoring on neighboring memory locations as well. This will help you learn more about how the corruption is occurring.

Instrumentation can be combined with custom debugging code to report on the general execution flow of a program and monitor a specific memory location for corruption. When the corruption is detected, the custom code can suspend any further dump output to preserve important information.

When the contents of a memory variable are overwritten with an out-of-range value, the design of detection logic is straightforward. When the overwritten value is one that could be allowed for the variable, it may be necessary to use an assignment function where a reference copy of the last legitimate value of the variable can be maintained.

When a section of code is being overwritten in a consistent manner, a simple comparison test can be used in custom logic. When a variable type of corruption is occurring, the `dr_dwatch` macro, or similar debugging code, should be used.

An important part of backtracing a program is to maintain as much execution history as possible. This may be done through the use of a debugger with a backtrace buffer or through instrumentation that routes the output to a ring buffer or file.

When you suspect that a failure stems from the actions of code other than that which you created, it can be beneficial to develop a small test program to seek conclusive proof.

It is much easier to manipulate and experiment with a situation when a small-scale model can be used.

Moving a suspect function into a test bed environment makes it easier to experiment with the function at its boundary conditions.

CHAPTER 13
Neurosurgery

The techniques presented in this chapter are for the times when you have to crawl around inside and underneath a program, to trace through its plumbing, in search of a mysterious leak or blockage.

13.1 REVERSE ENGINEERING/DISASSEMBLING

Knowing how to reverse-engineer a program can be valuable when you need to do any of the following:

- Debug high-level language code at the assembler level
- Debug library functions for which source is unavailable
- Correct incompatibilities (when your program won't play nicely with the other programs)
- Verify proper compiler action
- Recover lost source code

To reverse-engineer even a small program can involve many hours of analysis and documentation work. Should you need to recover lost source code for a larger program, pace yourself and make sure your chair is comfortable—you'll be sitting for quite a spell.

Much of the work involved in reverse engineering involves chasing down tentacles. This is true for the case where you must analyze an entire program as well as when you only need to understand a specific aspect of a program's operation.

In order to understand the operations of one function, you must understand what happens within each of the functions it calls—its child functions. To understand these child functions, you must study their children; and so on down the calling hierarchy tree.

Then there is the data. Tracing tentacles based on a program's calling hierarchy is a directed process. Each function you encounter is basically a list of other functions you must reckon with. When it comes to analyzing a function's interrelationship with the program's data structures, no such list is provided.

Data analysis requires more of a broad-based inquisition. For each memory variable that is global in scope, you must survey all functions to determine which ones read and write that variable. The use of a disassembler that builds a cross-reference table can make this task a lot easier.

A bottom-to-top approach can be helpful when you must climb around on a program's hierarchy tree. Once you have generated a complete disassembly listing for a program, identify each function that makes no calls to any other functions and then develop the clearest picture you can as to the intent of these childless functions. The use of a utility that will generate a calling hierarchy from an assembler listing is very valuable here.

Armed with this picture of the program's low-level drivers and self-contained transformation functions, you are ready to take on the initialization function. Locate this one by determining the program's entry point. Before attacking the main operational functions, the principal players, it is good to see how the stage is set up at first curtain. This is where you can start building an understanding of a program's global data, as much of it will be initialized in the startup code.

When your goal is to divine the meaning of a specific section of a program, by all means start by analyzing the code involved in that section and hope the tentacles don't spread out too far. Even in this case, it can be very worthwhile to generate an entire disassembly listing and run it through a utility which will generate a calling hierarchy tree.

Monitor System Calls

The use of an intercept driver to study the system calls a program makes will not only help give you an overall view of that program, it will let you see which operations are done in which parts of the program. As you step through system calls, note the CS:IP register values reported for each key operation.

For example, if the failing you must deal with involves the generation of a certain output file, locate the INT21 calls used to create and write this file and note the addresses from which these calls are made. This can be a good clue as to which part of the program contains the code you want to inspect.

The CS:IP values reported will, of course, reflect the current load position of the program. To relate these to the addresses shown in a disassembled listing of that same program may take a little snooping with a debugger, especially when you are working with a program made up of multiple segments. You will need to correlate the reported addresses with the program's initial load position and then apply this as a proportional value to the addresses in the listing.

Be careful, however, not to use disjoint information. If you run a program under an intercept driver, note the CS:IP values for key operations, and then exit the program to determine its load position, you could be in for some confusion. If you load the program in a debugger to see its load position, this won't be the same position as when you loaded the program the first time unless your debugger resides completely within a protected memory board or up in extended memory. The most reliable method is to load the program with a debugger in the first place, noting its load position right at first.

If the program was written in assembler in the first place, it is likely that system calls are made directly from the functions which need them. But when a program is developed in a high-level language, it is more likely that common library functions will be used for many operations involving system calls. When a program makes all of its INT21 calls from the same location, you can know that this is certainly the case.

Should you determine that the system calls relevant to your problem are made from common library functions, all is not lost. The specific function from which these library calls were made, the function you are seeking to locate, is executing at some point in between these calls.

Break in with your debugger at the end of the first system call, just where it is returning to the point of call. From there, trace through the remainder of the common library routine until it returns to its caller. In short order, you should find yourself in the function you need to see. The trick is to be able to identify it for what it is.

Use a Profiler

A profiler can help you identify which sections of a program are the most popular. By intercepting the INT08 timer interrupt and statistically recording what code is executing when each interrupt occurs, a profiler can generate a report of a program's execution hot spots.

When you then start to disassemble and document the program, knowing which sections receive the most execution time can help you direct your efforts. By focusing your analysis efforts on the sections of the program that execute the most often, you're more likely to get a clearer picture.

This technique also requires that you determine the program's initial load position so that you can associate the reported addresses with those in the disassembled listing; see the discussion earlier in this section.

Keep in mind that if the program you are analyzing contains bugs, the introduction of a profiler may be just like placing more bottles on the fence, more targets just inviting a hit.

Use Strings for Clues

In the interest of gaining an overall familiarity with a program, it can be enlightening to use a hex dump utility to examine the message strings contained within the program's binary modules. If the program happens to load its message strings from separate files, your search has just been simplified.

Examining the message strings within a program can help you get an idea of what operations are possible that you haven't yet exercised in your running of the program. Error messages can be particularly interesting. Seeing the failures a program's designer anticipated may give you clues as to the nature of the bug you are chasing. The problem you are experiencing may be an unanticipated derivative of an error condition for which a message does exist.

Your debugger's memory-dumping feature is one tool that can be useful for this type of exploration. Some text file–browsing utilities also have a hex mode capability. You could also construct a filtering program, which would read a binary file and output all sequences of bytes that are comprised of displayable characters and are over a certain minimum length.

To make the prospect of using DEBUG.COM a little more congenial, you could use input and output script files to capture its memory dump of a program in a file. This file could then be loaded into an editor or browsed with a utility that doesn't support a hex mode.

To do this, first load the file into DEBUG and determine the range of addresses necessary to dump the entire file. The initial value of the BX:CX register pair holds the file's size. Then exit DEBUG and use copy con or your editor to create an input script file named x.pat that will make DEBUG dump the file. In the following example, the initial load point for the file was at segment:offset address 334A:100. This was first normalized by adding 10h to the segment and using 0 as the offset, producing the address 335A:0.

Script file x.pat:

```
d 335a:0 ffff
d 435a:0 03e2
q
```

The file being dumped is a little over 64K in size, which results in an entry BX:CX value of 0001:03E2. The first dump command in the script file takes care of the first 64K, and the second takes care of the remaining 3E2 bytes. See Appendix B, "Hex Math," for more details on these types of derivations.

Now, simply use DEBUG.COM as follows to produce an output listing in text file format:

```
debug  yourprog.exe  < x.pat  > output.txt
```

Keying In on a Specific Message String

When a program's failure is marked by the issuance of a specific message, you will want to go into the program and locate the code that emits this message and then determine why it is emitted. A good way to start the location process is to see if a system call is used to display the string. Interrupt INT21, INT10, or INT29 could be used to display text messages to the console.

When the message's display is not a result of one of these system calls, direct video writing is probably being used. If you know the screen location used, and if that part of video memory is not used for anything else at the time, a memory write breakpoint could be set on the video buffer address corresponding to the first character's position. If this won't work, use the step-over/step-around tracing technique while watching for the message to appear.

From a disassembled listing, you could locate the address of the message string and then survey the remainder of the file for any instructions that reference this address. Some disassemblers can be made to generate labels for specific memory locations and then generate a cross-reference table showing where these labeled locations are referenced. Otherwise, load the listing file into your editor and use its search capabilities. Manually searching for such things will make you old before your time.

Patched-In Instrumentation

Should you need precise information on the execution flow of a program for which you do not have source code, patched-in instrumentation markers or markers from breakpoints can be useful. Markers from breakpoints are discussed in Section 12.1, "Instrumentation."

With regards to patched-in instrumentation, there are two basic approaches:

1. Statically patching a copy of the binary module with DEBUG or with a patching tool
2. Dynamically patching the module once it has been loaded into memory

Appendix E, "Patch Techniques," covers each of these topics.

How Disassemblers Work

In simplest terms, the process of disassembly involves nothing more than performing table lookup operations on the binary codes contained within a file or within memory. In fact, the simple disassembly feature of DEBUG.COM does precisely this. While adequate for small, simple programs or small sections of larger ones, this is too limited for serious reverse engineering work.

A more sophisticated tool will not only look up the mnemonics for each instruction, it will also do the following:

- Assign textual labels to the program entry point, function entry points, and branch points
- Assign text labels to memory locations used as data
- Allow you to specify your own label names and comments

- Mark the boundaries of functions
- Determine the boundaries and format of data tables and vector tables
- Determine the program's segmentation structure
- Annotate points in the code where system calls are made or common I/O operations are done

As it processes a module, a disassembler records which addresses are being referenced by various instructions and in what way they are referenced. Disassemblers make several passes through the code, trying to resolve these references and discern what is code and what is data.

A disassembler makes the job of reverse engineering much easier, but it can do very little to interpret the meaning of code. If you don't normally work at the assembler level, don't expect a disassembler to automatically provide you with a good picture of a program. This tool does make digging easier, but you still have to know how to dig and what to do with what you dig up.

Since the disassembly process can take some time for a large program, it can be a good idea to practice using its annotation features on a small file. If you build skill in an environment where you can get fast feedback, then things will go smoother when each run requires more time. As a general rule, derive and assign names for as many functions and branch points as you can and then rerun the disassembly. Often, having more names used after call instructions and for more data within a function will help you understand what that function is doing.

Disassembling with DEBUG.COM

DEBUG.COM can be used with a script of commands to obtain a disassembly of a small program or a portion of a larger one. As a disassembler, this tool is very limited, but it does have enough capabilities to get you through in a pinch. Here are some tricks to make it easier.

Start by manually loading the program with DEBUG and determining the address range. When a file is first loaded, the BX:CX register pair holds the length of the file in bytes. Thus, if the file was loaded at offset CS:0100, a BX:CX value of 0000:032E means that the last memory location occupied by this file is CS:042D (0100 + 032E − 1).

The next step is to browse through the file's contents, jotting down addresses where strings are located. If you can discern the location of any other code or data easily at this point, by all means jot it down.

When you are going to browse through memory after loading a file, you must know how far to go before you must ignore the memory contents. Trying to analyze a file's contents based on the leftover state of memory beyond the bounds of that file is not only a waste of time, it can be very confusing when you don't realize what is occurring. This is why you calculated the ending address of the module, as already described.

Once you've gleaned enough information on this initial pass, exit DEBUG and use your editor to create an input script file based on the address information you jotted down. For strings and data, use DEBUG's D command; use the U command to disassemble code. Even where a group of data or strings are adjacent in memory, it can be helpful to use separate dump commands to help delineate them in the output file.

Always remember to end every DEBUG script with a Q command. When DOS's input redirection feature is used (as it is with a script file), once the end of the file has been reached, the system will be locked unless the script includes a means of making DEBUG terminate.

Once you've created an input script, the basic method is to run DEBUG as follows. In this example, WIDGET.COM is the file to be disassembled, and the file INPUT.SCR contains your input script commands. DEBUG will create a file named OUTPUT.TXT containing disassembly and data dump output based on your input script instructions.

```
debug widget.com <input.scr >output.txt
```

As you analyze the output file, you will probably be tempted to add some descriptive notes. Wait—there's a better way. If you begin adding notes to the output file and then find that you want to refine the input script file and run the process again, you would have to manually transfer your notes from the old output file to the new one.

Since multiple disassembly runs are commonly used, it is better to enter your comments into the script file rather than the output file. What is needed to make this work is a way to enter strings into the input script such that they will appear in the output file but not cause any undesirable side affects. One way to accomplish this is to use the E command to write a string to the read-only ROM BIOS memory. Here is an example script where this annotation method has been used:

```
e f000:0 'main widget-counting array'
d cs:103 113
e f000:0 'the 8 widget status flags'
d cs:114 11b
e f000:0 'message string #1'
d cs:11c 13f
e f000:0 'the calc_widgets function'
u cs:140 442
q
```

To use this disassembly method for a device driver, you must compensate for DEBUG's habit of loading all modules except .EXE modules at a starting offset of 0100. This would also apply for other types of binary modules where the code within the file is intended to be located at a zero offset.

First, manually load DEBUG and use its R command to see what the initial DS value is (the load point). Assuming, for example, that the load point was 1450h and you want to dump a small device driver of 1000h bytes, create an input script such as the following:

```
rds
1460
d ds:0 1000
q
```

Then, issue the command:

```
debug widgets.sys <input.scr >output.txt
```

A major limitation of DEBUG.COM is that it is difficult to work with a multisegment program. To determine where one segment ends and another starts is a very tedious undertaking. Further, when you determine the address of a string, function, or piece of data by browsing, the segment:offset type of address you are using may be very different from the one the program uses when it is actually running. Because of the segment:offset addressing method used by the 80X86 type CPU, it is possible for up to 4096 different segment:offset combinations to all refer to the same physical location within memory.

Document Your Findings

It can often be helpful to sketch a flowchart while analyzing a section of code. The most important thing to remember when doing this is to start in the middle of a large sheet of paper and write small. When starting to work with unfamiliar code, there's no telling which direction and how many directions you will need to go in tracing down the tentacles.

For each piece of data involved, start an entry in a data dictionary text file. Describe the apparent use of the data and list which points in the program read and write the variable. Be careful when recording addresses. If working with a debugger, the segment portion of each address may not be the same at different times that you load the program. If you wish to record addresses, denote the program's initial load address as a base reference at the start of your data dictionary file.

13.2 STRAY BULLETS

A program that writes to memory it does not own, writes over its own code, or corrupts its own read/write memory variables is said to be shooting off *stray bullets*. The most likely cause of a stray bullet–type problem is due to improper pointer operations. This could be through the use of a pointer variable which hasn't been initialized or a mistake in the derivation of a pointer's value. This type of problem is much more common in programs written in C or assembler, where the use of pointers is more natural.

In some cases, a program will always cause the same corruption to the same memory location. In others, the corruption will be totally random in nature, in terms of both the location which gets hit and the frequency of occurrence. When an uninitialized pointer is used in a write operation, the location of the target will change depending on the last use of the memory comprising that pointer.

Note that just because you don't see a regularly occurring evidence of failure doesn't mean there isn't one. With stray bullets where the chosen target varies, you'll only see an evidence of failure when the target happens to be something important. Stray bullets will go undetected when they punch into unused buffers within a program, unused memory above a program, unallocated memory space above the base 640K or into a ROM BIOS address region.

When a program consistently acts normal on its first load but fails on successive invocations, stray bullets are a likely explanation. Further, the target is likely something outside of the memory that belongs to the program. Although it could be that the program is damaging itself each time and the first occurrence just happens to be inconsequential, external damage is more likely providing this pattern is consistent. Suspect damage to the interrupt vector table, the BIOS data area, or some part of the operating system or its drivers.

Another way you may encounter the stray-bullet failure is where program A is run and appears to behave normally. Then, some time later, when program B is used, it exhibits a failure. But when you reboot and load program B under your debugger, you can find no evidence of any problem at all. What actually happened is that program A damaged a portion of the system's common code or data that was not made use of until program B made a certain system call.

Careful observation and an open mind are your best tools in getting a lead into this type of problem. Remember that just because program B is running at the time that a failure occurs doesn't mean program B contains a bug. Presumption will get you if you don't watch out.

Another pitfall of presumption involves the idea that a stray-bullet problem always means good code being damaged by an improper write operation. When you do finally discover a section of code or data that is being overwritten, it could be that the overwrite operation is legitimate and that the underlying code or data was loaded into the wrong position. Be suspicious of this where use is made of code overlays or code relocation. The actual "bug" could be that the overlay's code is loading into what is supposed to be a read/write data area.

A data overwrite that is due to the data being in the wrong place in the first place can happen when data records are dynamically allocated from a memory pool and the allocation logic is buggy. In such cases, the bullets are not the problem; the targets are straying into an otherwise normal line of fire. The techniques presented in this section are based on the more common case, where the "target" is where it should be, but it just shouldn't be a target.

The Need to Reboot

When chasing a stray-bullet type of bug, it is important to reboot after each trial run. The failure may have corrupted the operating system or other vital system components, or your debugger's code may have gotten whacked. Rebooting after each trial brings the best measure of stability that can be had in a situation where demons are having their fun with your system.

You should have already simplified the environment by removing any device drivers from the CONFIG.SYS file, and any TSR's from the AUTOEXEC.BAT file, that aren't necessary. You might also want to add statements to the end of the AUTOEXEC.BAT file to load your debugger and the program being analyzed.

The Need to Rebuild

If a bug involves disk corruption, it can happen that you not only have to reboot on each trial but must also reformat and reload your disk. When this is a possibility, work on a diskette if you can and run diagnostic tools often (e.g., CHKDSK). Keep in mind, though, that it is entirely possible for the data sectors within a file to become subtly altered or completely scrambled without any evidence of the corruption being available to a tool like CHKDSK.

Note also that if you must operate on a hard disk, merely running the program you are debugging in a separate disk partition does nothing to ensure the integrity of other partitions on the disk. If a stray bullet damages any of the code or data the operating system uses to perform disk I/O, any part of any partition on any drive could be affected.

If you don't rebuild after each crash, it could happen that you will see what appear to be new bugs, or new aspects of the existing bug, that are actually due to file corruption caused by the original bug. Since it is difficult to see this type of thing for what it is without going through a full course of debugging, you may wind up spending a lot of time chasing a spinoff type of bug. Although it does take extra time to rebuild a disk after each debugging trial, not doing so carries the risk that you'll spend even more time chasing ghosts.

To be as secure as possible, set up a second machine as a guinea pig (a machine other than your development machine). To reduce the time required for each formatting operation, use the smallest hard disk partition that will accommodate the software you need. Then set up a batch file to automate the rebuild process.

Using Instrumentation

When you determine that a stray-bullet type of memory corruption is occurring, instrumentation can be used to dump the memory region involved to an alternate display, serial terminal, second computer, or other dump device. When only a few bytes of memory are being overwritten and the location is always the same, custom code could be added to test these bytes for a change. The goal, as always, is to discover the incidence of the corruption at the earliest possible point.

If the addition of custom code causes the point being overwritten to change, or if the point under the gun tends to vary within a region of memory, the dr_dwatch macro can be used to monitor a range of addresses. See Section 7.4, "Instrumentation Macros and Functions for ROUTER.SYS," for details on dr_dwatch.

Markers can also be used to show the execution flow and key internal data states of the program, which will help you associate the failure with internal program activity. If the failure occurs on an intermittent basis, you will want to have the instrumentation output routed to a ring buffer or to a file.

When you use a ring buffer, it becomes important to make sure that the information you need will still be within the buffer when you come to fetch it. If the problem occurs too infrequently for you to sit and wait, try to develop custom debugging logic that will gate off the dumping process once the failure occurs.

Using a Debugger

In the ideal case, you load the program being studied with your debugger, set a memory write breakpoint on the location being corrupted and then run the program. Once the break occurs, you are able to see directly how the corruption is occurring.

While things can occur in this ideal fashion, more often it is not so simple and direct. It may be that the corruption you set out to trap on changes its location when the program is loaded with a debugger. It may be that the debugger is hit by a stray bullet itself before the traps you set have a chance to be used. Furthermore, the location of the memory that is being hit may vary wildly due to a stray reference or uninitialized pointer.

When the memory area being damaged is normally used for program data or the stack, setting a simple memory write breakpoint will not be practical. A debugger that supports a state machine or complex evaluative breakpoints may allow you to discover the culprit.

For this approach to work, you must determine which portions of a program are supposed to be writing to the memory area involved and exclude them from breakpoint eligibility. If it isn't easy to determine which sections to exclude, one approach is to cause these sections to make themselves known. Begin by setting the memory write breakpoints and simply running the program.

As each break occurs, if it appears to be caused by an operation that should be allowed write access to the memory involved, modify the breakpoint directives to exclude writes by that code. This approach would not be practical, of course, when the range of memory is large or when the memory is used on a global basis (e.g., as a stack). See Section 13.6, "Stack Bugs," for further techniques.

Should a memory write breakpoint not be practical, consider applying the step-over/step-into technique while monitoring the affected memory area within your debugger's data window.

Effects of Load Position

One factor that often has an effect on a stray-bullet type of problem is the program's load position. Consider for example, the simplistic case of a program that always writes a word of 0 to a point in memory exactly 800 bytes before its initial load point.

When this program is invoked by DOS's COMMAND.COM command processor, some portion of that user interface program will take the hit. When you load this program using a debugger, then the bullet will poke a hole in the debugger (providing it doesn't load into protected memory). If a TSR utility is installed before you run the program, that utility will likely suffer. Finally, if the copy of the environment block loaded before this program is fairly large, containing many SET-type strings, one of these strings would find itself a target.

This is why it is important to stabilize a program's initial load position and use a debugger that loads into a protected memory board or into extended memory. Given the variability inherent in the aiming of stray bullets, a consistent load position won't always make for a consistent type of failure—but it's worth trying for the cases where it will.

When Changes Cause Suppression

If you are trying to use an instrumentation driver but find that it seems to suppress the bug, first determine if just having the driver loaded is causing the problem. Do this by running a copy of the program in which the instrumentation markers have been removed, commented out, or otherwise deactivated.

A consistent suppression whenever the instrumentation driver is loaded, along with consistent activation when this driver is not loaded, would tend indicate some complicity on its part. It could be simply due to the fact that the program is in a different position due to the memory taken by the driver, or it could be due to a stray reference made by the program where some of the driver's code or data is improperly used.

One test that can be helpful in such cases is not to have the driver loaded but force everything in the system to load in the position it would if the driver was loaded. This can be accomplished by using a dummy driver in place of the instrumentation driver, where the dummy has exactly the same resident size as the instrumentation driver did. Note that this size may be configuration-specific, especially if a ring buffer is being used (e.g., the resident size will vary depending on the allocation for the ring buffer). To help stabilize a stray-reference type problem, this dummy driver should contain all 0's (or some other constant) except for the requisite driver header, strategy, and interrupt functions.

If the existence of either the live driver or the dummy does cause suppression, you can try including all instrumentation code directly within the program. On the other hand, if these tests offer no conclusive information, try building a copy of the program containing nullified instrumentation macros. This is where the amount of code memory space parceled out to each marker remains unchanged, but the marker code does not make its call to the instrumentation driver. This will tell you if just having more code within the program is causing the bug to go into hiding.

When just having extra code included within a program adversely affects the bug, first try moving the bulk of the local debugging code to the very end of the code segment or code module. If this doesn't help, try moving it to the very start. If this still doesn't help and markers are important to your diagnosis, you can try loading an instrumentation driver and a dummy TSR containing dynamic patch space. Patched-in instrumentation is tedious but can work as a last resort. See Appendix E, "Patch Techniques."

When using a debugger causes a bug to go into hiding, try using a debugging tool that loads into extended memory or into a protected memory board. Another alternative can be to use a remote-host debugging configuration. While this does still involve the existence of some debugging code within the target machine's base memory, the smaller amount involved may let the bug remain active.

When a debugger can be loaded as a device driver (e.g., Periscope's SYSLOAD feature), sometimes using this memory placement method will prevent suppression of the failure. Of course, if you can set up a remote CPU intercept pod configuration, this will permit you to monitor the target's operation with no change in the program's load position. The debugger is also completely secure from the effects of stray bullets.

Using Load Position Effects to Advantage

It can sometimes be useful to determine which portion of a program is sensitive to the inclusion of instrumentation code. Using binary division, nullify half of the markers and retest. Repeat this until you find which point or points need to move to cause the bug to change. By correlating this behavior with the section of the program that must be moved to see an effect, you can sometimes make inroads toward a solution. See the coverage of program padding in Section 13.4, "Position-Sensitive Bugs."

Tracking Down MCB Corruption

The DOS operating system uses a linked list of memory control blocks (MCBs) to track the allocation of RAM within a system. Each of these blocks starts with a 16-byte header containing information that DOS uses to manage these blocks.

Programs can allocate and deallocate blocks of memory by making system calls through DOS's INT21 service handler. Function 48h is used to allocate a block of memory, function 49h is used to free that block, and function 4A is used to modify the size of an existing block.

The first byte in each block's header must be one of two different letters: M or Z. The Z denotes the last block. All other blocks start with M (or they're supposed to anyway).

The word at offset 3 within each block's header is the size of the block in paragraphs. The segment address of the next block in the chain can be found by adding this paragraph count + 1 to the current block's segment value.

For example, if the first MCB is located at segment:offset address 083C:0000 and its size is 1C02 paragraphs, the next block's address is 243F:0000 (083C + 1C02 + 1 = 243F). When addressing MCB blocks, it is standard practice to derive a segment value that is used with a zero offset value.

If the 16-byte header becomes corrupt in a detectable way, a call to one of the INT21 memory allocation functions will return error number 7, "Memory control blocks destroyed." The resulting action depends on which software module first makes one of these system calls and how it is designed to respond to this error condition.

Each time a program terminates back to DOS's command processor, an INT21 function 48h call is made to check the integrity of the MCB chain. If an error code of 7 is returned, a message such as the following is displayed:

```
Memory allocation error
Cannot load COMMAND, system halted
```

Stray bullets are often the cause of MCB corruption. Boundary errors can also cause this problem. An application that allocates a buffer and then writes beyond the boundaries of that block will overwrite the MCB header that follows the block, which is actually the header for the following block.

If a program you are working with is causing a memory allocation error, you must, of course, pin down exactly when and where this corruption first occurs. While you could periodically trace the chain manually with a debugger, what you really need is a test function that will trace the MCB chain for you and validate each entry.

For either method, we must first find the root of this list. This is done by using function 52h of INT21. Although this system call still isn't officially documented by Microsoft, much has been published about it in other reference works. The following assembler code fragment will result in the AX register holding the segment address of the first MCB block. This first memory block is occupied by the DOS kernel.

```
mov     ah,52h
int     21h
mov     ax,es:[bx-2]
```

The idea is to make a test function that starts with the first MCB and traces the chain through to its end, validating each header record as it goes. By inserting calls to this tracing test function at various points within a program, we can isolate the offending section. Since the first MCB record is not likely to change in position once DOS has booted up, the tracing function will count on its segment address being stored. This, of course, means that the use of this test function must be preceded by a call to an initialization function such as the one shown in Listing 13-1.

Once the starting address of the MCB chain is known, we are ready to call on the validation function. As shown by the pseudocode in Listing 13-2, the job of this function is to trace the chain but be on the watch for any sign of corruption. An assembler implementation is shown in Listing 13-3. Note that rather than reporting an error directly, this function returns a signal to its caller. Further, if an error is found (return AX ≠ 0), the ES register is left pointing to the MCB header where the error was found.

```
mcb_init proc near
        push    ax
        push    bx
        push    es
        mov     ah,52h
        int     21h
        mov     ax,es:[bx-2]
        mov     cs:[mcb_root],ax
        pop     es
        pop     bx
        pop     ax
        ret
mcb_init endp
```

LISTING 13-1   Seeding the MCB-tracing logic.

```
mcb_seg = mcb_root
while(1)
   if(byte at mcb_seg:0 == 'Z')
      if(word at mcb_seg:3 != 0)
      report error

   break out of loop

   if(byte at mcb_seg:0 != 'M')
   report error
   break out of loop

   if(word at mcb_seg:3 == 0)
   report error
   break out of loop

   mcb_seg = mcb_seg + (word at mcb_seg:3) + 1
```

LISTING 13-2 Pseudocode for MCB-tracing logic.

You may wish to modify this logic to report the address of each node and its size and starting letter (the M or Z). It just depends on how much instrumentation output would be helpful and practical to collect.

One good place to incorporate this validation function is within an intercept driver such as DDICEPT.SYS. This will help you narrow the point of corruption down to the nearest system call without requiring any modifications to the program being debugged. You would want to have this function called just before the intercept handler passed the call on to the original service routine and then again upon return.

If the first call indicates an error, you can know that some operation in between this system call and the previous one caused the corruption. If the second call returns an error signal, some action during the execution of the system call is responsible. Note that in this latter case, it would be jumping to conclusions to say that DOS had a bug. Although this is not impossible, other explanations should also be considered:

- The program instructed DOS to self-destruct. This could be done by making a file read request for more bytes than will fit within the specified buffer.
- Another interrupt intercept exists and it caused the failure.
- The system call resulted in a call to a buggy device driver.

```
mcb_trace proc near
        mov     es,cs:[mcb_root]
mct1:
        cmp     byte ptr es:[0],'Z'
        jne     mct2
        xor     ax,ax           ; preset ax for no error
        cmp     word ptr es:[3],0
        je      mctx
        mov     ax,1            ; error, last node size != 0
        jmp     short mctx
mct2:
        cmp     byte ptr es:[0],'M'
        je      mct3
        mov     ax,2            ; error, bad first letter
        jmp     short mctx
mct3:
        cmp     word ptr es:[3],0
        jne     mct4
        mov     ax,3            ; error, node size == 0
        jmp     short mctx
mct4:
        mov     ax,es
        add     ax,es:[3]
        inc     ax
        mov     es,ax
        jmp     short mct1
mctx:
        ret
mcb_trace endp
```

LISTING 13-3 Assembler version of MCB-tracing logic.

- A buggy IRQ handler gained control during the system call. Repeating the test several times to see how consistent the results are can help identify this case.

You could also incorporate this function as custom code within a program. If the program you are debugging was not written in assembler, you might be able to code a version of the validation function in that program's language. Another alternative would be to implement the assembler function shown in Listing 13-3 as an interrupt service routine within a TSR. Select an unused interrupt vector such as INTF0 as the activation vehicle.

With this MCB-tracing function always available in a TSR, you can make calls to it using the interrupt-calling feature of your chosen language, or you could use your debugger to make the call. Many debuggers include the capability to call a user-defined function. When this isn't possible, you can try the following manual method:

1. At one or more key points, break into the program using your debugger's assembler-level interface.
2. Record the current values of the ES, AX, and IP registers.
3. Record the value of the two bytes at CS:IP.
4. Enter the byte CD at CS:IP and the byte F0 at CS:IP+1.
5. Execute the current instruction, which is now the INTF0 call.
6. Note the current AX and ES values returned from the mcb_trace function.
7. Restore the original ES, AX, and IP registers.
8. Restore the original two bytes at CS:IP.

13.3 WORKING WITH COMPILED CODE

When you debug high-level language code with an assembler-level debugger, where you aren't working with the source code directly, it can be difficult to get your bearings. See if the compiler you are using can be made to generate an assembler output. If not, it could be helpful to place markers in the code and note when they appear in conjunction with your tracing of the program.

One thing that can skew the association between high-level logic and the corresponding assembler code is the optimization done by many compilers. A typical example of optimization is the *merging of identical tails*. For example, you might code logic such as that shown in Listing 13-4. An optimizing compiler would recognize that the tail ends of the if clause and the else clause are the same. To produce a final program that will be as lean as possible, the compiler will relocate the call to update_journal() so that it follows the if/else statement. It would be just as if you actually coded this as you should have in the first place (see Listing 13-5).

```
if(day == tuesday)
 print_statements();
 update_journal();
 else
 print_ledger();
 update_journal();
```

LISTING 13-4 A candidate for the merging of identical tails.

```
┌─ if(day == tuesday)
│   print_statements();
├─ else
│   print_ledger();
│
│  update_journal();
└─
```

LISTING 13-5 The effect of merging identical tails.

Other optimizations are certainly done. Some other examples are moving unchanging statements from within a loop and generating in-line code in place of calls to small functions.

When you are working with an optimizing compiler's output and trying to set breakpoints, the optimization can be the source of much confusion if you are not aware of its existence. If you need to break when a certain function is called, and it has been converted to an in-line procedure expansion, you will need to locate the code for each call point.

In the foregoing example, if you set a breakpoint on the first call to update_journal(), thinking it to be the one within the if clause, it could be that when you break on the call, the else clause was the one taken, because it's not Tuesday. If the compiler has moved a statement from within a loop to where it comes before the loop and you set a breakpoint on that statement, you may falsely conclude that the loop counter is incorrect when you only experience one breakpoint.

When bugs arise, you can also try rebuilding the program with optimization disabled and then retest. Hopefully, the bug will still exist in the same form. If it seems to disappear, your choices are to subject the program to a new round of testing in order to try to discover an evidence of the failure in some other form, or to debug with optimization activated. In such cases, it's best to have a debugger that is designed for the compiler.

Mixed Code and Data; Self-Modifying Code

When stepping through compiled code at the assembler level, watch out for interrupt calls that are followed by data. Sometimes you will find an interrupt call, typically within the range of INT34 to INT3F, where several bytes immediately following the interrupt instruction will be data rather than code. If you don't realize that this is the case and try to jump around the interrupt call, you will be causing a breakpoint to be set into the data. This will confuse the interrupt service routine that uses that data, causing it to crash or otherwise misbehave. When you are using the step-over/step-into tracing method to locate the first nonreturning function call, this artificially induced crash can be misleading.

Be especially suspicious of this type of code-and-data mixture when your debugger's disassembly output of the instructions immediately following an interrupt call doesn't make sense. Sometimes you can determine the offset of the next true instruction by inspecting the following code and data. In other cases, you will have to trace through the interrupt call to see how it accesses the data following the interrupt call instruction and how it manipulates the return address on the stack. The reason for writing code like this is that it is simpler in terms of compiler design and it uses fewer interrupt vectors.

13.4   POSITION-SENSITIVE BUGS

Often, when a program's failure is sensitive to changes in its load position or to changes in the relative position of its components, stray bullets are to blame. Much of the information provided within the previous section applies to this discussion, and vice versa. Other situations which can produce position-sensitive bugs are:

- Out-of-bounds array indexing
- An unterminated string
- A stray reference
- Improper stack usage, where a return address is used as data
- Runaway program execution

When changes affect a bug, try to understand what changes have occurred. When a program is loaded with a debugger, the initial load point is higher, certain interrupt vectors may be different, and so on. If adding new code within the program causes a problem, either from instrumentation or from increasing the program's capabilities, carefully consider what portions of the program's code and data are being affected. Positioning the new block of code at different locations within the program can sometimes help identify which area is sensitive.

Varying the position of code and using padding are important to verify that code movement is responsible for the effect you are seeing. It could also be that the new code is buggy or that it is changing the timing of the program's execution to affect another type of bug: timing-sensitive bugs, which are covered in Section 13.5.

Be suspicious when position-sensitive bugs show up in programs made with languages such as BASIC and Pascal. With that type of language, it's much harder to shoot yourself in the foot than it is with languages such as C or assembler. It is somewhat more likely that some other software entity within the system is whacking your program rather than your program being responsible.

Using a Debugger

When you first load a program into a debugger, start by doing a full-speed run to see if the mere fact of loading a debugger first will cause changes in the bug's personality. If the bug does end up being suppressed, you wouldn't want to waste time stepping through the program in slow motion.

If your debugger has two components (as does Periscope), try loading the resident part but don't use the load-and-run utility—just run the program directly. If this doesn't cause the suppression, either use DEBUG.COM to hard-code a breakpoint into the start of the program's binary file, or break into the debugger while still at the command prompt and set a breakpoint on the next call to INT21 function 4B.

If using a debugger affects the failure adversely, try using a debugger that doesn't affect the position of the code being debugged, because it loads itself into a protected memory board or into extended memory. In some cases, using a remote debugging configuration will work since only a small software stub must be loaded into the target machine. Loading the debugger as a device driver (when that's possible) may also help keep the bug from going into dormancy.

Using Instrumentation

When you need to instrument a program with markers, but the inclusion of marker code seems to be causing failure suppression, determine if code size is responsible by substituting an equivalent amount of nop instructions for the dump code and retesting. If maintaining the code size of the markers without actually having active marker code does not cause the suppression, then timing may be the problem. It could also be that the instrumentation is buggy or that a stray reference just happens to read the marker code as data.

If it does look like a position sensitivity exists, try placing just a call at each marker point and move the bulk of the dump code to the very end of the module. The idea is to minimize the shift in position of all the other code and data.

Another alternative is to replace each marker with a unique interrupt call. The set of interrupt vectors normally used for the BASIC interpreter, INT80 through INTF0, are usually a safe choice (unless, of course, you are still using that language system). What is then needed is a device driver or TSR containing an interrupt service routine for each of these vectors you will be using. This will reduce the additional code required for each marker to two bytes.

If this is still too much of an intrusion, you will have to make each marker interrupt call actually replace one or more instructions at the point where each marker is to be placed. Then, of course, replacement instructions must be coded within the corresponding interrupt handler within the driver. Save this approach as a last resort—it is tedious.

Appendix E, "Patch Techniques," discusses dynamic patching. See also the discussion of "Markers from Breakpoints" in Section 12.1, "Instrumentation."

Using Padding

When you add new code to a program and a new bug shows up or an existing one undergoes a distinct personality change, it can be helpful to use a null padding in place of the new code. For assembler language programs, it is a fairly simply matter to determine the size of this new section of code (using a .LST or .MAP file or a debugger) and replace it with an equivalent amount of nop instructions.

When working with a high-level language, introducing this type of padding takes a little more effort. Fortunately, some compilers can be made to generate an assembler listing of the executable binary module they produce. A disassembler could also be used to generate this type of listing, or a debugger could be used to browse the assembler code.

Once you've determined the boundaries of the code you need to nullify, the next trick is to coax the compiler into producing the right amount of nop instructions. Within C, the standard library function __emit__() provides you with a direct link to the code generator section of the compiler. For other languages, where no such support exists, it can be easiest to use a debugger to patch in the nullifying values, modifying a copy of the binary file directly rather than modifying the source and rebuilding.

In cases where it is not immediately clear which specific section of code is the sensitive one, the binary division approach is good. Start by selecting the range you are going to work with and then add the padding block at the end for the first trial. For the second trial, insert the padding at the start of the range. Once you locate a range where an effect is noticed in the second trial but not the first, proceed to move the padding to successive midpoints of subsections of the remainder.

When you find that inserting a pad before a certain function affects the failure, but adding it anywhere after that function doesn't, you can reasonably suspect that something involving the position of that function is involved. It could be that something within that function is getting whacked or that an invalid reference is made to some of its code. Buggy code within that function could also be position-sensitive due to improper stack usage. It could be that the function is emitting stray bullets and that by moving the padding you are changing its aim.

Unfortunately, there is no guarantee that the problem is directly within the function you've isolated. It could be that a stray reference or other coding error is being affected by the operand of a call instruction for this function or some function after it. This could also apply to data values affected by the movement of this function.

13.5   TIMING-SENSITIVE BUGS

This section discusses timing-sensitive bugs in two different aspects: how to deal with a bug that is already acting in a timing-sensitive manner, and how to deal with situations where the introduction of debugging instrumentation seems to suppress a failure due to timing changes.

How can you know when a bug is sensitive to changes in execution timing? In many cases, it just has a certain feel to it. Towards a more concrete determination, if the inclusion of instrumentation affects a bug but substituting nop padding does eliminate this effect, then timing sensitivity is likely. Further, if the effect can be seen to get worse as you insert an increasing amount of dummy time-delay at each instrumentation point, you can feel even more certain about this diagnosis.

There are two basic approaches to dealing with this type of fickleness: to influence the execution of a program so as to make it have a more consistent timing and to use instrumentation that affects a program's execution overhead to the smallest extent possible.

If there is any indication that a consistent keystroke input rate could help, enlist the use of a keystroke macro utility to automate keyboard input. See Section 13.7, "Intermittent Bugs," for more details on the use of this type of utility. Where the execution of a series of individual programs is involved, use a batch file to invoke them with a consistent timing.

Should you suspect that an interaction with an INT08 or INT1C timer interrupt handler is involved, here is a trick that may help bring some stability to the situation. Construct a TSR that contains both an INT08 and an INT21 intercept handler. Before each INT21 call intercepted by this driver is passed on to DOS, a polling loop will wait until the next INT08 interrupt occurs. See Chapter 8 for an example.

This is a simple way to introduce a consistent pacing into the system, and it may just make the failure occur with enough consistency for its cause to be pinned down. You may also find that being selective about which calls are paced in this way will bring the stability you need without slowing the overall program execution down too much.

When dealing with timing-related problems, you will likely want to embed instrumentation markers within the program to study when the failure occurs with respect to the program's internal operations. To prevent the extra execution overhead time required by this instrumentation from distorting the evidence too much, it is important that this debugging code be as fast as possible.

Although limited to the amount of data that will fit within one screen, the use of a direct video display buffer is one of the fastest methods available. To prevent conflicts with the main display screen's output, install a second display adapter and monitor. An EGA or VGA main console with a monochrome debugging display is a good combination.

Using a ring buffer can be good providing the bug doesn't lock the machine, curbing your ability to retrieve the buffer's treasure. If this is a problem, set up a parallel link between two machines and deposit the data in a ring buffer within the second machine. See Section 7.3, "ROUTER.SYS," for more information.

Where the extra overhead involved in going through ROUTER.SYS proves to be detrimental, consider implanting minimal instrumentation code directly within the application. For details on the DV.INC/.H, DP.INC/.H AND DS.INC/.H modules, see Section 7.2, "General Instrumentation Macros and Functions," and Appendixes I through N.

13.6 STACK BUGS

How can you know when a failure is related to a stack problem? The most common way this will become apparent is while you are single-stepping through a program at the assembler level. You may have isolated a crash to a specific function or area of the program using the step-over/step-into technique. Once you step into a function and single-step through the final return instruction, a stack-related failure is indicated if you don't end up back in the code that issued the function call. You may also notice that strange values are loaded into the CPU registers as pop instructions are processed.

When a crash occurs on an intermittent basis, using the step-over/step-into technique is usually not practical. To identify an intermittent failure as stack-related could require that you capture the program's dying moments in a debugger's backtrace buffer. You may also discover this connection by checking out a hunch and applying the custom debugging code and instrumentation described further in this section.

Failures occurring due to stack operations may result from stray bullets mangling the stack's contents, from stack underflow, or because code that performs stack operations is flawed in its design.

In a program written purely in a high-level language, you shouldn't be able to write source code that would generate assembler code bent on blowing up the stack. Stack-related troubles within a high-level language program are most likely going to be due to stack corruption from a stray bullet or stack underflow. Though it shouldn't occur too often, a buggy compiler is another possibility. Code written in C is, of course, an exception to this rule. Using an out-of-range index with an array that is declared as an automatic variable within a function will corrupt a stack in a wink.

Regarding stack underflow, many compilers support an option to include stack verification code at the start of each function. While you probably wouldn't want to include this feature in the released version of a software package, it can be a valuable aid during development. For programming environments where this capability is not built in, techniques are described below to add this type of checking.

It could also happen that memory write operations that result in stack corruption are actually doing what they are supposed to be doing. This would be the case when the wrong region of memory ends up being used for the stack. An improper initial assignment of the SS or SP registers could account for this, as could a program error that changes their value once a program has been initialized.

A peculiar type of failure can occur when the CPU flags register value becomes corrupted while it is stored on the stack. For example, in the following code fragment, let's consider what would happen if the flags data word on the stack were changed by a stray bullet somewhere during the execution of the count_widgets function:

```
pushf
call    count_widgets
popf
```

When this corrupted value is popped into the flags register from the stack, if the trap flag bit happens to be set, INT01 single-stepping will ensue. From here, the behavior of the system depends entirely on what the code pointed to by the INT01 interrupt vector looks like. See Section 13.10, "Performance Bugs," for further coverage of this strange case.

Using Instrumentation and Custom Code

One of the most basic ways to check for stack underflow is to identify the location of the lowest few paragraphs in the stack and set a memory write breakpoint on this range of memory. Alternatively, you could use an evaluative breakpoint that tests for a low value within the SP register. This is represented by the following pseudocode:

```
break if SP < 80
```

Where this type of debugger capability is unavailable, another technique is to add custom code to a program that maintains a copy of the lowest SP register value within a common memory location. The code in Listing 13-6 uses the low word of the INTF0 interrupt vector to maintain this statistic. The use of a common location like this makes this information easy to locate and review using a debugger or interrupt vector–dumping utility.

```
sp_check proc near
        push    ax
        push    es
        xor     ax,ax
        mov     es,ax
        mov     ax,sp
        cmp     ax,es:[0f0h*4]
        jae     spc1
        mov     es:[0f0h*4],ax
spc1:
        pop     es
        pop     ax
        ret
sp_check endp
```

LISTING 13-6 Tracking the lowest SP value in a program.

Note that in order for this technique to function, the tracking word must be seeded with the value FFFFh. Once this function is included within a program, or within a TSR where the SP-checking function is made accessible through another unused interrupt vector, place calls to it at key locations throughout your program. Another good location from which to call this type of checking function is from an interrupt intercept for system calls.

Another way to monitor for stack underflow is to identify the location of the lowest 10 to 15 paragraphs on the stack and use the dr_dwatch macro to call on the memory change–monitoring logic within ROUTER.SYS. If the memory within this bottom-of-stack margin area ever changes, you should enlarge the stack.

Still another technique is to fill the bottom of the stack with a pattern and then break in with a debugger after the program has been run through its paces for a while. By inspecting how far stack usage has encroached on this pattern, you can get an idea of what kind of margin remains. A simple way to initiate the bottom of the stack with a pattern is to break into the program early on and use your debugger's fill command. Within DEBUG.COM, this is the F command. Just make sure you don't clobber the part of the stack currently in use.

Tracking down the origin of a stray bullet that is corrupting data on the stack can be tricky. A stack is a very dynamic data structure. Many languages support automatic memory variables, which are local in scope to a specific function and do not persist between calls. Any time an assignment is made to one of these variables, the contents of the stack are changing in a region of the stack that is above the current stack pointer.

In many cases where stack data is being corrupted, visual monitoring will be the best approach. Instrumentation code would be added to dump the contents of the affected region of the stack to a video display or other device. It would then be up to the operator to determine which changes were legitimate and which were an evidence of the bug.

Using a Debugger

Suppose that you have access to a hardware debugger that includes a state machine. With this, you should be able to qualify exactly when a memory write breakpoint will be active such that normal write activity to the stack within the function you are dealing with will not cause a false breakpoint triggering. What will often still stand in your way is the fact that upon each call to this function, the current depth of the stack will not be the same. It's kind of difficult to set a memory write breakpoint when the location of the stack data involved isn't constant.

All is not lost, however. At the entrance to this function, custom code could be added that modifies the stack pointer's value to always use a specific region of the stack. A corresponding custom code epilogue must also be added at the end of the function to counteract the effects of the prologue.

The first requirement to pull this trick is to determine the lowest SP value that could be in effect when this function is entered. This can be done using one of the techniques described above to monitor for stack underflow. Subtract a suitable margin value from this low SP value to account for the unexpected and then use this new value as an SP modifier. In Listing 13-7, the equated symbol new_sp represents this value.

Note that if the function you would wrap in this custom code accesses entry parameters passed in on the stack, adjustments must be made to account for this stack pointer modification trick. This would also apply for a software interrupt handler that manipulates the copy of the entry flags register located on the stack.

Once this stack depth stabilization logic is in place, check the low word of the INTFO vector to make sure it's zero any time your memory write breakpoint triggers. If not, take note of the SP value record in this vector's high word and use it to modify your new_sp setting. You could also maintain a sticky code breakpoint on the instruction that sets the INTFO vector's low word to make sure you aren't missing valid trigger opportunities.

If you don't mind doing a little gambling, here's another trick that can sometimes pay off. Suppose that you have determined that a random stray bullet is overwriting stack data during the execution of a certain function, but due to the dynamic nature of stack data you are having trouble getting a fix on the source of the corruption. Since the affected region of the stack is constantly being changed by normal memory write activity, using a memory write breakpoint is out.

The gamble you can take is that this stray bullet is actually hitting stack memory a lot more often than is evident through program failures. This

```
new_sp equ 03a4h


; the custom code prologue

        push    ax                          ; save ax, es & bp to gain
        push    es                          ; some working registers
        push    bp
        mov     bp,sp                       ; setup bp to access saved
        add     bp,6                        ; entry registers and to
        push    bp                          ; record the entry sp
        xor     ax,ax
        mov     es,ax                       ; clear intf0 low word to
        mov     word ptr es:[0f0h*4],0      ; indicate success
        mov     ax,sp
        cmp     ax,new_sp                   ; see if sp can be lowered
        jbe     pt1
        mov     word ptr es:[0f0h*4],1      ; signal if not possible
        mov     word ptr es:[0f0h*4+2],sp
        jmp     short pt2
pt1:
        mov     sp,new_sp                   ; make sp consistent
pt2:
        mov     ax,[bp-2]                   ; recover original values
        mov     es,[bp-4]                   ; of the working registers
        mov     bp,[bp-6]


; the function's normal code goes here

        ....
        ....
        ....


; the custom code epilogue

        pop     sp                          ; recover the original sp

; the program's normal return instruction

        ret     (or retf, iret, etc.)
```

LISTING 13-7 Stabilizing a function's stack usage.

can happen when the region of memory that is hit happens to be below the current stack pointer value. Stray bullets that affect an unused portion of the stack could occur very often and not be noticed.

First, use one of the previously described methods to determine the lowest SP value that occurs during the execution of this function; then, set a memory write breakpoint on the portion of the stack below this point. No matter how much normal write activity is going on in the upper part of the stack block, a write to this lower portion should never occur except when stray bullets are flying.

Another approach to stack corruption is to relocate the entire stack to a new location. To do this, you must use your debugger to single-step through the setup code that establishes the stack in the first place. In the case of an .EXE code module, the stack pointer registers are initialized upon entry to the module by the EXEC loader. The values used are derived from entries within the .EXE file header, which were prepared by the linker. While this stack is usually retained, some programs may switch stacks at a later point.

A code module of the .COM type is started with SS equal to the load CS and the SP register is assigned a value of FFFEh. A lower initial SP value would, of course, be used if there is less than 64K of remaining free memory. Again, be aware that this initial stack may be changed by the startup code.

Where can you come up with the memory for a replacement stack? Changing SS:SP to 9000:FFFE would make use of the high end of the base 640K memory region (for a PS/2 with 639K, use 9000:FBFEh). For this to be stable, you must first verify that no part of the program you are debugging will make any other use of this area. During a trial run, where you do not relocate the stack pointer, you could check for use of this area by filling it with a pattern and inspecting it later or by using a memory write breakpoint. A problem with this approach is that the part of the program that you can run before the bug occurs may not use this memory, but some later portion may.

Another location for a new stack can be an unused portion of the video display adapter's memory. If your system has a CGA, EGA, or VGA adapter but the program you're debugging only uses text mode, there is a good chance that the upper 12K of the display memory is sitting idle. For this to work, neither the program under scrutiny nor your debugger can make any use of alternate text pages or any graphics mode. Within the 16K CGA display buffer, the starting stack address point would be B800:3FFE. More memory could be available with an EGA or VGA adapter.

Once the memory normally used for the stack is retired, you can watch for corruption by using memory write breakpoints, by filling that memory with a pattern and inspecting for changes, or by using the dr_dwatch macro and ROUTER.SYS, or custom logic that performs a similar function.

If, however, the corruption occurs within the new stack, at least you have gained some useful knowledge. You know that some type of stack-based addressing is involved. Keep a close eye on the BP register for any abnormal changes. If any calls are made to the INT10 services of the ROM BIOS, the

BP register should be saved and restored around each call. Certain BIOS's have been known to mistreat the BP register.

As a final note on stack-related debugging, there is a certain coding flaw that will cause problems only when a debugger is in use. If you don't see it for what it is, you may be misled into believing that you've found the stack problem you are seeking when you really haven't. The following code fragment illustrates this point:

```
cli
mov     ss,ax
mov     cs:[some_flag],1
mov     sp,offset stack_top
sti
```

Even though this code sequence is surrounded by the cli and sti instructions, the fact that the next operation after the loading of the SS register is something other than the loading of SP will cause problems. The 80X86 family of CPUs will automatically prevent interrupts during the next instruction following any one that changes the SS register. This is intended to guard the loading of the SP register.

In a coding method such as the one just shown, the programmer is presuming that the assignment of SP can safely be deferred, because interrupts are disabled. While this will work correctly during normal program execution, strange things are bound to happen when a debugger is used to single-step through this code. (A system where NMI interrupts occur will also suffer from this type of coding.)

Whenever any instruction is executed in a single-step mode, an INTO1 interrupt is generated even if the interrupt flag is cleared. The one exception to this rule is the next instruction after the one that loads a new SS value, which the CPU automatically guards.

But in code such as the foregoing, this guarding will be wasted on some other instruction besides the one that loads SP. When the next instruction is executed, the resulting INTO1 interrupt will occur, but the SS:SP stack pointer will be in a transitional state. Since stack usage is implicit in the operation of any interrupt call, the memory used as a stack by the INTO1 will be whatever memory SS:SP happens to point to at the time—a debugger-activated stray bullet!

If you do encounter this type of coding weakness, use a go command with a temporary breakpoint to prevent any debugger interrupts from occurring before the new stack is fully defined.

13.7 INTERMITTENT BUGS

As with most of the categories covered in this chapter, intermittence is likely to exist in conjunction with other characteristics of a bug. Stray bullets are often intermittent in nature, as are timing-sensitive bugs and bugs that exhibit a variable type of failure. These adjunct topics are covered in Sections 13.2 ("Stray Bullets"), 13.5 ("Timing-Sensitive Bugs"), and 13.8 ("Variable Types of Failure"), respectively.

The strange thing about intermittent failures is that you can't always know when you've fixed the problem. You can know when something is broken, but cannot always know when it's not. If an intermittent problem disappears when you make a change, it could just be suppressed. It all depends on how clear an understanding of the failure you can develop.

One good way to chop some time off of this kind of bug chase is to set up as many systems as you can to run trials of the program being tested. This will multiply your chances of encountering the bug sooner, and at the same time it helps verify that a hardware failure is not to blame.

Stabilization

When confronted with an intermittent bug, it is important to stabilize the system as much as possible before taking invasive measures. This cad follows a mysterious schedule. The main goal in stabilization is to discover a way to influence that schedule; to make the failure occur as often as possible and in a consistent manner; to strip it of its intermittence.

There are two primary areas through which this influence can be applied: environmental and operational. A prime factor in environmental consistency is the initial state of the system when the program under scrutiny is loaded for execution. The use of a dummy device driver or TSR to ensure a consistent load position was covered in Sections 13.2 ("Stray Bullets") and 13.4 ("Position-Sensitive Bugs"). Some other environmental factors to consider are the following:

- Consistent date and time values in the software clock
- Consistent positioning of data files on the disk
- Consistent initial contents of data files

For example, suppose that you are working with a program that is reported to act up with a strange sort of regularity, where the interval between hiccups is very close to one hour. Does this program read the BIOS timer value at address 0040:006Ch to perform some time delay calculation? Time measurement could be used to determine how long to display a message or how long to wait at a prompt before taking a default action, to play a musical sequence, and so on.

Approximately once each hour, on the hour, the low word of the BIOS timer count will wrap around from FFFFh back to 0000h. It may be that the time delay logic is not designed to handle this wraparound. A good way to test for this is to manipulate the system environment by poking your own count value into 0040:006Ch with a debugger. Using the value FF00 will give you about 14 seconds before the wraparound condition occurs.

Another important factor in environmental consistency is the "cleanness" of the system. If you suspect that a stray reference may be involved, where some addressing error is causing a memory variable's contents to be read from the wrong location, you may find that rebooting between each trial run will make the failure occur in a more regular fashion. Using a debugger to fill all unused memory with a constant value before each trial run may also be helpful. Just in case the flow of execution is branching off into this unused memory, try using the INT03 opcode of 0CCh as the filler byte and keeping a debugger loaded.

Seeking operational consistency involves experimenting with the program in search of the magical sequence of steps that will flush the bug out into the open each and every time. In lieu of full-blown magic, anything you can discover that makes the failure occur more often or with a more consistent behavior is of great value. Some operational factors to consider are the following:

- Consistent pattern of which programs were run since the last reboot
- Consistent order of operations within the program under test
- Consistent timing of keystroke entries

If you observe or suspect that a failure in one program (program B) is related to another program (program A) having been executed previously, an initial qualification can be done by proving that program B will never fail if program A has not been run first. From here, try running program A, then rebooting, and then running program B. If this practice does evidence the failure, program A could be mangling a data file used by program B.

When program A's influence is not able to span across a reboot, it is more likely that this first program is corrupting some part of the interrupt vector table, BIOS data area, or the operating system itself, but that this damage doesn't become apparent until program B is run. When this seems to be the case, treat these two separate programs as if they were merely functions of a one large program, by bonding them together in a batch file.

Write up a batch file that will run the two programs in the same order and with the same command line parameters each time. Within each program, use a consistent sequence of operations, picking the same menu choices, responding with the same value to prompts, terminating the program in the same way, and so on. This effectively makes these two programs to be functions of one larger program, the batch file. Treat this batch file as you would a single program, taking steps to ensure a consistent system environment on each run.

In some cases, it may be helpful to use a keystroke macro utility to automate the operation of the program or programs involved. This would be a type of utility that loads as a TSR and lets you define the sequence of keystrokes that will be received by a program. The consistent timing of responses to menu choices and other prompts might be the magic it takes to flush the bug out into the open.

In the event that you cannot coax an intermittent bug to occur with any regularity, a keystroke macro utility can still be valuable. With instrumentation tooling installed to capture a tracing of a program's internal operations, set up a looping batch file such as the following:

```
:loop
keymac keydata
testprog
goto loop
```

In this example, KEYMAC is the name of the keystroke-stuffing utility, and KEYDATA is the name of a data file containing the sequence of keystroke instructions to be applied. The effect of this macro utility is to automate the operation of the program under test, TESTPROG. Be sure to include the keystrokes required to terminate the program so that the batch file will regain control and cause the entire operation to repeat.

With this robotic keyboard control in place, you can leave the program to run and see what you capture. Of critical importance when applying this technique is that your instrumentation or other custom code be able to detect when the failure occurs and either pause the system or, at least, freeze the contents of your marker capture. If, after a reasonable amount of time, you haven't gotten a nibble, adjust the keystroke script to generate a different sequence of operations and try again.

One thing to be aware of when using a keystroke macro utility to generate keystrokes is that no keyboard interrupts are generated. If the program being debugged establishes an intercept of the INT09 interrupt vector to detect special keyboard scan codes and respond to hot keys, a keystroke-stuffing macro program will not work.

Using Instrumentation

In applying instrumentation to an intermittent bug, the first consideration is the routing method and ultimate destination for the marker output. The tools provided in the Companion Toolset provide for a variety of output methods: direct video, ring buffer, serial (to a dumb terminal), parallel (to a printer), serial link (to a second computer) and parallel link (to a second computer). See Section 7.1, "Use of the Companion Toolset," for a summary of the advantages and trade-offs involved in each of these destinations.

In general, the best method is to set up a high-speed parallel link between two machines. The transmission speed possible with an eight-bit parallel link is high enough to prevent bug suppression in most cases. By using the

CHANNEL.EXE utility at the remote end, the data can be captured in a ring buffer until you press the stop key or a trigger character is detected in the marker output stream. At this point, the ring buffer's contents will be written to a file, where the marker output can be studied and manipulated with an editor.

This method combines high data throughput, high data retention, capture of data in permanent form, and data security. Chapter 7 covers the setup of these tools. Also see Appendix F, "Constructing Parallel and Serial Link Cables." All that is needed for a second computer is a PC with a keyboard, diskette drive, monochrome display/monitor, and, of course, a parallel port.

The second consideration when applying instrumentation is developing a trigger mechanism that will cause marker output to cease when the failure occurs. The need for this becomes more critical when output destinations with shorter data retention times are used, with the most extreme case being where the marker data is being sent to direct video or to a dumb serial terminal. If you can't stop the marker output before key information about the failure scrolls off the screen, all is for naught.

Whenever possible, an automatic method of gating off marker output should be used. This does, however, rely on your having enough understanding about the nature of the bug to design a trap. You may have to resort to a manual gating-off method for some preliminary trials until you can gain enough knowledge to set up custom logic that will stop the dumping at the earliest possible point.

When triggered, custom logic can be made to set a flag that is tested by each marker macro. To prevent a disappointing waste of time, it is a good idea to force a test of any custom trigger code. This would be done with an additional bit of custom debug code, actuated by a hot key, an event counter, or other trigger.

An alternative approach is to establish a special macro or marker character that will cause the central instrumentation code to ignore any further transmission requests. The ROUTER.SYS instrumentation driver supports two different gating methods, and the CHANNEL.EXE capture utility supports a /F option to stop receiving automatically when a certain character is detected.

If you must resort to manual methods to halt the flow of markers, here are some possibilities:

- Reboot or power off the machine under test (for the case where data is captured on a serial terminal or in a second machine).
- Yank out the serial or parallel cable being used to transmit marker data.
- Press a hot key that causes further marker output to be disabled (see the discussion of the Scroll-Lock key in Section 8.6, "Control Interfaces").
- When using CHANNEL.EXE in a remote capture machine, press the stop key.

Using a Debugger

To have much chance for success brandishing a debugger in the face of an intermittent problem requires that you have either a pretty distinct idea of the nature of the beast, or good luck. Whereas instrumentation can be likened more to fishing with a large net, using a debugger is like spear fishing.

In an initial foray, when little is known about the internal details of the failure, the best way to apply a debugger is to make it act like instrumentation. This is done by taking advantage of the debugger's backtrace buffer to maintain an execution history of the program as it suffers through its failure.

The basic technique is to set breakpoints, at key locations within the program, that will log the event in the back-trace buffer but not stop the machine. Whenever possible, one or more additional breakpoints should also be set to stop the machine when the failure occurs. If you can't stop the machine soon after the failure occurs, the information you need to see will be shifted out the far end of the capture buffer, and you won't know much more than you did before you started.

Should the detection of a failure condition require more than your debugger's evaluative breakpoint features can handle, remember that custom code can be added that executes an INT03 hard-coded breakpoint when triggered. Where no form of automatic detection can be managed, you will have to break into the debugger manually using a hot key or NMI breakout switch.

The use of a debugger with a hardware capture buffer offers the advantage of being able to see a complete instruction-by-instruction execution history with little or no reduction in operating speed. Countering this benefit, however, is the fact that this higher resolution of information makes it all the more critical that you be able to freeze the contents of the trace buffer as soon as the failure occurs. You can forget about trying to snap a breakout switch down fast enough when you see the first visual evidence of the failure. A triggering breakpoint will be required.

Once you learn a little more about an intermittent bug, a debugger can be of more use. For example, if you can establish that the failure involves the overwriting of a certain memory area, set a memory write breakpoint on that area and let the program go through its paces.

Analysis

When you finally do manage to capture an execution history showing the failure in action, if it contains a conclusive indication of what's going on, great! In most cases, however, the clues provided will require backtracing efforts in order for the root cause to be uncovered. This is a good time to examine these clues, with an eye for ways to make the failure show up more often so that your future testing trials won't take as long.

Be forewarned that the analysis phase is a place where presumption can rear up and cause trouble. If you compare one execution history where the failure did occur with a similar chronicle where it didn't, you may be tempted to interpret some of the differences as significant when they actually are not. The best way to avoid wild-goose chases is to capture several dump trials of each type before making comparisons.

13.8 VARIABLE TYPES OF FAILURE

When the program you are working with fails in a variety of different ways, there are two possible explanations. There may be one bug at the root of all the mischief, which can take different paths as it propagates through a program. There also may be more than one demon at work—the scourge of multiple bugs.

When the type of failure varies, build a chart while you experiment with the program. Record a description of the failure and the operating conditions that preceded its occurrence. Perform as many of these trial runs as practical, and then review your findings to search for patterns. When no meaningful conclusions can be drawn by using external operating conditions as the criteria, consider using an intercept driver to reveal the system call activity that occurs during each trial.

The idea, as always, is to identify the earliest form of failure you can and seek to correct it first. Most or all of the later evidences of failure may simply be prorogations from this initial point. Should the program exhibit its different failures in different sections of the program, study each and select the one that seems likely to be the easiest to isolate and stabilize.

In your testing, be aware that the position of files on the disk may sometimes have an effect. This would be especially likely if the software you are debugging happens to be a block device driver or a program that interfaces with the operating system's disk I/O logic in a direct manner (e.g., through INT21 function 44h or through calls to INT13, INT25, or INT26).

If this is suspected, you can attempt to stabilize the situation by ensuring consistent positioning of files on the disk. If you are able to operate from a diskette, this will be much simpler. On a hard disk, you would need to work with a separate volume. Just using a separate directory doesn't provide any isolation from file position changes. Any change in any other file on the same volume can affect the position of the files you are working with.

When using a diskette or separate volume, start by copying the files involved directly to the media. As a second trial, try placing a small dummy file on the media first, then copying on the files involved. Through successive trials, note the effects as you either increase the size of the dummy file or increase the count of small dummy files. Use a disk utility to keep lost clusters cleaned up and monitor file fragmentation.

13.9 MULTIPLE BUGS

Multiple bugs can manifest themselves in many ways. One case is that where each of several different bugs all produce the same failure. This is indicated when you locate and correct what you are sure is a cause of the problem, but the failure still exists. More generic types of failures, such as system lock-ups, are usually involved here.

In this type of situation, it is important to verify that your fix is correct to the greatest degree possible and then continue debugging. You can attempt to verify your correction in the midst of other bugs by temporarily removing it and then trying to single-step through the failure when it is caused by the specific problem you have discovered.

Another case where multiple bugs can be at work is where a program exhibits multiple types of failure. Hopefully, these will occur as a result of distinctly different operational sequences within the program. When they don't, apply the statistical survey method described in the previous section.

When descending through the layers of a bug quest, discovering and fixing the root causes of multiple bugs, it's important to look back when you finally get to the bottom of it all and consider if any of the fixes you made for previously found bugs will now be made unnecessary by a fix made for a more recently found bug. For example, to correct the final bug you may have to change the order in which two processes are done. This may totally prevent the conflict that caused an earlier bug. If you added any compensating logic to address this earlier problem, it should now be carefully removed.

When your initial analysis does indicate the presence of multiple bugs, be suspicious and subject the program to a more thorough battery of tests if all bugs disappear when you introduce a fix for one of them. If the other bugs do still exist, but due to the changes made they are no longer evident in the same way as before, you certainly don't want to leave them uncorrected.

13.10 PERFORMANCE BUGS

You've developed a splendid software package that counts and catalogs all types of widgets. But one of your beta test sites reports that once in every 10 to 15 hours of use, your package executes at about one-tenth of its normal speed. The widget processing does appear to continue normally, but it's as if it is being done by a mechanical relay–based computer of the 1950s.

This can happen, for example, if the CPU flags have been pushed onto the stack but become corrupted before being popped off again. If the trap flag just happens to become set due to this corruption, the CPU will enter its single-stepping mode. Note that the `INT01` interrupt vector must point to an `iret` instruction, or a section of code that includes some harmless code followed by an `iret`, for this not to result in a crash.

If you suspect that this may be occurring, try running the program with a debugger loaded. If you suddenly break into the debugger in single-step mode, examine the previous instructions and the contents of the CPU flags register.

Another technique is to make a simple `INT01` interrupt handler within a TSR. Design this tool so that if its `INT01` handler does receive control, it dumps a message to the screen and stalls. This message should include a report of the return address data from the stack. Do not load a debugger after loading this driver. Most debuggers will not bother to restore the `INT01` vector when they are done with it.

If a user of your program complains of slow throughput after certain operations are done, add some custom-time measuring code. It's much more meaningful to have some actual statistics to deal with rather than try to base an analysis on the customer's claims that the system runs slower. You can include instrumentation that will output this timing data to a ring buffer, or you can make the program report its timing statistics to the screen when a special hot key is pressed.

The following are some other problems which can manifest themselves as performance bugs:

1. The diskette drive is included in the list of devices that a program checks when searching for its data files. This could easily go unnoticed when the main computer box is located under a desk.
2. An improper loop count is derived, so that redundant operations are performed.
3. A linked list becomes corrupted, so that the process of tracing it continues for quite a while through "garbage" memory until an end-of-list indicator happens to be encountered.
4. A timer interrupt intercept has been established and its execution time is excessively close to the period between timer ticks.

13.11　DEBUGGING INTERRUPT-RELATED PROBLEMS

Problems related to an interrupt service routine (ISR) can occur in two basic forms: You are trying to develop an ISR and are finding problems with its operation, or you suspect that an existing interrupt handler is involved in a timing-sensitive or intermittent failure.

When source code is available, first scrutinize each ISR to verify that all registers used are saved and restored. Then, does the ISR issue an EOI (end of interrupt) to the interrupt controller at the start, or at the end? Are higher-priority interrupts enabled when they should be? Do all execution paths ensure proper stack balance? Is any stack-relative addressing done that could erroneously write over stack information that it shouldn't? See Appendix D,

"System-Level Knowledge for Debugging," for more information on interrupt handler design.

When an ISR reads or writes data that is also used by the main program flow or by other interrupt handlers, proper protection must be established at all points. For example, when a doubleword field (e.g., a long integer or far pointer in C) is changed, a two-instruction sequence is the shortest sequence possible. One instruction is required to write the low word and a second to write the high word. If an interrupt occurs while the data field is a transitional state and the ISR logic makes use of that variable, confusion and general mayhem will result.

Using a Debugger

Setting a breakpoint within a hardware IRQ handler can be tricky. Your debugger must be designed to support this type of work. When a breakpoint is hit within an IRQ handler, Periscope can detect when an EOI must be issued to the interrupt controller and automatically take care of this detail. With other debuggers, you may have to insert some custom code to issue an EOI at the front of the IRQ handler to provide a safe place for a breakpoint to occur.

Using Instrumentation

To use instrumentation in an interrupt-based section of a program, include marker-generating code directly within the program under test. This debugging code must be fast, and it must not enable interrupts where they were not enabled already. See Section 7.2, "General Instrumentation Macros and Functions," for its discussion of the DP.INC, DS.INC, and DV.INC include files. The use of serial output (DS.INC) may be fast enough if a baud rate of 115,200 is used in a machine-to-machine link. Providing you can freeze the data display when you need to, writing to direct video is the fastest method. Using the parallel binary link is also a fast choice.

Instrumentation can be useful when you must study the confluence of operations between a program's main logic and an IRQ handler. Place one marker at the beginning of the ISR and another at the end. Bracket-type markers can be good for this (i.e., the character pairs: [,], (,), {, }, <, and >). Then place additional markers at key points throughout the program and look for patterns when the failure occurs. Is it always soon after an interrupt happens to occur while a certain section of the main logic is executing?

To check for interrupt-nesting problems, watch for points where a second entry marker is emitted before the corresponding exit marker.

Using Custom Code

Custom code can be helpful when you need to check for nesting. Establish a global counter that is preset to zero, increment this counter upon entry to the ISR, and decrement it upon exit. You could make the custom code execute an INTO3 breakpoint instruction when a nest count above 1 is generated. Alternatively, you could simply have the highest value recorded in a common memory location, where it can be inspected periodically with a debugger.

A portion of an unused interrupt vector can also be a good location for this global counter. In addition, it is wise to make your custom code track the lowest SP value found, using one word of another unused vector. This word would have to be seeded with a value of 0FFFFh so that the custom logic could simply compare the reference word with the current SP value upon each ISR call and update the reference when the SP value is lower. You never know what you will discover.

Of course, if the ISR could gain control when different stacks are in effect (which is usually the case), more complex logic would be needed to track the lowest stack pointer for each possible stack. If you are only interested in the lowest SP value ever encountered for a particular stack, simply make the custom logic pretest for the specific SS register value corresponding to that stack.

Determining Which Vectors a Program Changes

Seeing what interrupt intercepts already exist within a system before a troubled program is run, as well as what interrupt handlers that program establishes, can provide useful clues. For example, if a program establishes an INTO9 intercept just before keyboard problems begin to appear, your range of suspects has just been narrowed significantly.

After a TSR is loaded, a memory/device map–type utility can show which interrupt vectors the TSR has hooked (see Section 9.5, "Memory/Device Map Utilities"). But this approach has its limitations. When multiple TSRs are loaded, if a later one grabs a certain vector, you won't see whether a previously loaded TSR could be intercepting that same one. As a work-around, you could run the vector dump utility after the installation of each TSR.

To study the interrupt vector activities of an application, this type of utility is useless. It can't be run while the application is running. One solution is to run the program under a debugger and watch for system calls to INT21 functions 25h (set interrupt vector) and 35h (get interrupt vector).

In the event that the program reads and writes interrupt vectors directly, this method will not give you a complete picture. Applying a memory write breakpoint to a specific vector or to the entire table is one way to deal with this. Another is to craft custom logic that maintains a reference copy of the vector table and reports any changes. The key thing with this approach is that if this checking logic is not called often, some transitions may be missed when more than one new value is written between comparisons.

Note that if a vector change is detected between system calls, direct vector writing must be occurring. If a vector change is detected during a system call but it isn't function 25h of `INT21`, suspect that an IRQ handler may be effecting the change.

Effect of Interceptions

When a program establishes interrupt intercepts, certain changes in behavior can occur, which you should keep in mind. For example, suppose that you are using a debugger to study the actions of a network interceptor shell. This type of program is typically configured as a TSR or device driver and is responsible for redirecting file and device requests to a network server when appropriate.

If you set a breakpoint on the `INT21` handler and then load the network shell (e.g., when it is configured as a TSR), the only `INT21` calls that will encounter your breakpoint are those that the interceptor shell passes on to the local operating system. Unless you move your breakpoint to the new `INT21` service routine, you will not see any system calls that are directed on to the network server.

13.12 REENTRANCE AND RECURSION

When a function is *reentrant,* or designed to support reentrance, a new thread of execution can enter the function even though another thread is still within the bounds of the function. Reentrance occurs due to the actions of an interrupt handler or due to the existence of multiple threads of execution in a multitasking shell program or a multitasking operating system.

A popular example of a piece of code that does not support re-entrance is the `INT21` interface logic in the DOS kernel. This becomes an issue when writing certain types of TSR utilities and interrupt handlers.

A function designed to reenter itself intentionally is referred to as a *recursive function.* It may be that the function calls itself directly, or it may be that it calls other functions that eventually make a call back to it.

Bugs involving this type of action come in two basic flavors:

1. Reentrance or recursion is supposed to be managed properly but isn't.
2. Reentrance or recursion is not supposed to occur, but it does, or you suspect that it does.

The techniques described in Section 13.11, "Debugging Interrupt-Related Problems," to track interrupt nesting are also applicable to problems involving reentrance and recursion.

13.13 WORKING WITH RESIDENT CODE

Resident code within a computer system comes in a variety of forms, including the following:

- A TSR utility
- A device driver
- The operating system
- The operating system's command processor/user interface shell
- The BIOS in ROM

Problems relating to this type of code entity can occur when you are developing a resident module yourself or when you are experiencing compatibility problems with an existing resident module.

Using a Debugger

First and foremost, your debugger must be designed for use with resident modules. Trying to trace through the DOS kernel, a device driver, or most TSR utilities with the simplistic DEBUG.COM is a sure way to lock a system in short order. Periscope is well suited for this type of work, with Borland's Turbo Debugger providing a degree of support.

The particulars of loading a TSR with a debugger are too debugger-specific for any meaningful coverage to be possible in this type of work. Refer to your debugger's manual for details.

In general, if you only need to debug the nonresident portion of a TSR, you can load it as you would any transient program. Once you step through the initialization logic to the point where the terminate-and-stay resident system call is made (an INT27 or INT21 function 31h), you can either use the debugger's terminate command or reboot the system. In the event that any interrupt intercepts or similar processes have been instigated by the initialization code, rebooting is the safest choice.

If you go ahead and let the TSR load with a debugger in the picture, the TSR will stay resident, but the debugger will terminate. This can leave a strange pocket in memory and can also leave interrupt vectors in an unstable state. The debugger may restore certain interrupt vectors even though the TSR is technically now in the ISR chain.

Sometimes you can temporarily disable a section of a resident module by embedding a temporary branch around the code involved. After system is up and you've loaded your debugger, use it to remove the temporary branch instruction and activate the sleeping code.

When you are developing a new device driver and it won't let the system boot up, you need a debugger that can be loaded as a device driver itself. Periscope includes a `SYSLOAD.SYS` driver, which can be used to load this debugger at `CONFIG.SYS` processing time. To gain control when the driver you are developing is loaded, implant a hard-coded breakpoint at the start of its initialization function.

Another approach is to nullify the driver's initialization logic by changing it to install the driver in the chain only and take no other initialization action. Then make sure the remaining portion of the initialization logic is included as a separate function along with the resident portion of the driver. After the system has booted up, load your debugger and use it to place a call to the now-resident function which comprises the remainder of the initialization logic. For this technique to work, you must, of course, have a clear understanding of what portions of the initialization process can be deferred.

If none of these approaches will work, consider reconfiguring the driver as a TSR for the sake of testing.

13.14   SUMMARY

To reverse-engineer a program involves chasing down numerous tangents and tentacles. While the function-calling hierarchy tends to be more confined and can be mapped by available third-party tools, identifying the operations performed on each unit of data requires a programwide survey.

Monitoring system calls can be an aid in reverse-engineering a program. In addition to providing you with a greater understanding of the program's operation, it enables you to correlate system call activity with the section of the program from which each call originates.

A profiler can also be an aid in reverse-engineering a program, in that it will identify the program's busiest sections. This can help you direct your analysis efforts.

Examining the message strings a program contains, using a hex-browsing utility or debugger, can provide clues as to what error conditions have been anticipated.

A disassembler works by translating binary program code into the corresponding assembler mnemonics; assigning textual labels to branch points, function entry points, and memory locations used for data; determining the program's segment structure; and annotating I/O operations and system calls. A commenting disassembler allows you to assign your own label names and have comment blocks inserted in the listing.

`DEBUG.COM` can be used as a primitive disassembler by using an input script file and capturing the output with output redirection. Comments can be included in the output by including commands in the script such as e f000:0 'this is a comment'.

A program that writes to memory it does not own, writes over its own code, or corrupts its own read/write memory variables is said to be shooting off stray bullets. Improper pointer operations are the most common cause.

Just because evidence of failure is only apparent at certain times doesn't mean that stray bullets are not flying a lot more often. When a stray bullet hits unused memory, the damage is inconsequential.

Stray bullet–induced damage may be caused to common code or data by one program but not be noticed until another program is run. Therefore, when debugging, it is not safe to presume that the program experiencing a failure is always responsible.

When you suspect that stray bullets may be involved in a failure, reboot between testing trials. If disk corruption is a possibility, set up testing on a separate machine and rebuild the disk between trials.

Use instrumentation to identify a program's execution flow and internal data states while monitoring for the earliest evidence of a stray bullet–induced failure.

To use a debugger against a stray-bullet problem requires that you have some idea of the area of memory being corrupted so that breakpoints can be set. If the targeted memory area is normally used for read/write data, state machine logic or an evaluative breakpoint will be required to separate the normal writes from the rogues.

Changes in a program's load position, and in the relative positions of sections in the program, can have a significant effect on a stray-bullet type of bug. The use of stabilization measures is important to make the bug's behavior as consistent as possible.

When you must debug code written in a high-level language at the assembler level, see if the compiler can be made to output an assembler version of the program.

Compiler optimization in the final code generation can skew the correspondence between the high-level source code and the assembler version. Build an executable module with optimization disabled and test again for the bug. Otherwise, select a debugger that is designed to accommodate your compiler's output.

Some compilers generate a mixture of code and data, where one or more words of data are placed immediately after certain software interrupt calls. The interrupt handler locates this data using the interrupt return address from the stack. This return address is then manipulated to prevent execution of the data upon return from the interrupt. Be aware of this possibility when tracing through compiled code.

To prevent wasting time trying to trace a position-sensitive bug when it is in a suppressed state, begin with a full-speed run when you first load a program into a debugger.

If the use of a debugger drives a bug into hiding, try using a debugger that can be loaded into extended memory or into a protected memory board. Configuring a debugger in a remote host mode or loading it as a device driver may help in some cases.

When the inclusion of instrumentation drives a bug into hiding, reduce the code required at each marker point to the bare minimum and move the bulk of the marker code to the very end of the module (or to the very beginning—whatever works). In an extreme case, you may have to resort to the use of breakpoint markers or dynamically patched-in marker calls.

Replacing sections of a program with null padding (e.g., nop instructions) can help stabilize a system when a position sensitivity exists. Varying the position of this padding with a binary division technique can help isolate the sensitive section.

When a bug exhibits a timing sensitivity, apply stabilization methods that will cause the program to execute with a more consistent timing. Add custom code to pace system calls on INT08 timer ticks, or use a keystroke macro utility.

When instrumentation is used to garner a profile of a timing-sensitive bug, use the fastest type available.

When tracing through a function shows it to return to a different point than it was called from, stack corruption or a stack imbalance is likely.

When working with compiled code, take advantage of any compiler-generated stack-checking support. In addition, instrumentation and custom code can be used to monitor for a stack pointer value that is below par. Monitoring a test pattern written into the bottom of the stack area and setting a memory write breakpoint on the bottom area of the stack are other ways to check for underflow.

When a memory write breakpoint must be set on a stack variable, but the stack depth varies between uses of this variable, use custom logic to stabilize the depth.

Using a debugger to relocate a program's stack to unused base memory or an unused portion of video memory can be a helpful trick. This can let you set a memory write breakpoint on the original stack buffer without interference from normal stack activity. If the failure occurs in the new stack, you know at least that it is dependent on the stack pointer's value.

When chasing an intermittent bug, enlist as many computers as possible into the hunt. The more parallel execution trials you establish, the greater your chances of experiencing the failure more often.

Stabilization methods and experimentation are important when working with an intermittent bug. Anything you can do to make the bug show up more often or with more consistency will be worth a lot when you are ready to take more invasive measures.

When applying instrumentation to an intermittent, choose the fastest method with the largest data retention factor. The use of a parallel link to a remote computer in which captured data is stored in a ring buffer is the prime choice. It is also important to devise some method to freeze the contents of the marker dump storage medium once the failure occurs.

Using a debugger to track down an intermittent failure is difficult, especially when you know little about the internal nature of the problem. If, for instance, you can determine that a certain area of memory is being overwritten, then a memory write breakpoint is your best friend.

When analyzing dump output captured when an intermittent failure did occur, be careful not to assume that all differences between the bad trial and a good one are related to the failure. Some variances may be normal. Unless the information is distinct, capture and inspect more than one run of each type before drawing conclusions.

When a failure occurs in different ways at different times, build a chart of program operational activity versus the failure type. Study this chart for trends and tendencies, with an eye for a way to impart some consistency into the situation.

Programs that occasionally begin executing in slow motion are probably suffering from a form of stack corruption that sets the trap flag bit in the CPU flags. Other possibilities are that a linked list has become corrupt or that time is being wasted performing redundant operations due to a mistakenly calculated loop counter.

If an interrupt handler reads or writes any data that is also used by the main-line code or by other interrupt handlers, all sequences must be protected from interrupts if the data operations are divisible (e.g., if an interrupt could occur when the data is in a transitional state). IRQ handlers must also save and restore all CPU registers they make use of.

Instrumentation can be used to reveal when interrupts occur with respect to the execution flow of the main-line code and to check for the existence of interrupt nesting (reentrance).

Use a debugger to monitor changes a program makes to interrupt vectors in order to gather clues about a bug.

To apply a debugger to a problem with a resident code module such as a TSR or device driver, try "neutering" the driver so that it installs itself but defers all other initialization activities until a debugger is used to invoke a completion of the installation process.

Another approach is to let the module install itself but render the resident portion inactive until you are ready with your debugging tools.

APPENDIXES

This Locator Chart is designed to help you get started in a bug hunt. As a result, the types of symptoms and suggested actions this chart deals with tend to be of the more external type: things you can notice about a bug through the user interface or through the use of some of the preliminary types of diagnosis techniques and tools.

To use this chart:

1. Browse through the entries in the Problem List and find the section or sections which fit your problem.
2. Examine the suggested methods, jotting down the numbers for the ones that seem the most appropriate for your situation.
3. Find the "Master List of Methods" at the end of this section and look up the methods you jotted down.
4. For each method in the Master List, a list of the relevant sections within this book is presented. Turn to those sections for help with your problem.

Given the number of variables involved in the operation of a computer system, it is rare when bugs can be classified with clear lines of demarcation. Therefore, you will often find that your bug is partially described by more than one of the following sections.

There are also, of course, many sections of this book that would apply commonly to most types of problems. All of the sections in Chapters 3 and 10 fall into this category.

Further, for each of the specific types of problems listed in the chart, the characteristic of intermittence can be involved as a modifier. When this is the case, consider the following sections in addition to those suggested in the chart:

7.3 `ROUTER.SYS`
7.4 Instrumentation Macros and Functions for `ROUTER.SYS`
7.5 `CHANNEL.EXE`
12.1 Instrumentation
13.2 Stray Bullets
13.7 Intermittent Bugs

As will be obvious, when intermittence is involved, certain of the suggested methods for the following topics will not be practical. One method that is valuable when dealing with a consistent type of bug but impractical in the face of an intermittent is the use of the step-over/step-into debugger technique.

One final note: In the discussions of possible causes for the following problem areas, the possibility that the program has been incorrectly coded applies to all cases, so it isn't mentioned in each one. The possibilities that are mentioned are the more likely of the less obvious.

Problem List

Hard Lock   In a hard lock, the process that was running within the system is stalled and the keyboard is completely nonresponsive. Pressing the toggle-type keys (Caps-Lock, Num-Lock, and Scroll-Lock) produces no change in the corresponding keyboard LEDs. Keying Cntrl–Alt–Del produces no response.

The possible causes are wide-ranging. But the nonresponsiveness of the keyboard indicates that the CPU has shut down from nested exceptions; the `INT09` interrupt vector has been overwritten; the CPU is executing within a loop with interrupts disabled, and so on.

If the process running in the computer is at a point where it is waiting for keyboard input, it can be difficult to tell if the problem is isolated to the keyboard or if a more complete type of system crash has occurred. Keep an open mind for both possibilities.

Sometimes, when you break into a debugger, the debugger will be able to reenliven the keyboard.

Suggested Methods:

02. Load debugger and use NMI switch to break in.
03. Load debugger and use the step-over/step-into technique.
04. Monitor system calls with intercept driver or debugger.
05. Embed markers into source.
08. Use an intercept driver to monitor interrupt activity.

Soft Lock   In a soft lock, the current process is stalled but the keyboard is still responsive to a certain degree. The LEDs for the toggle type keys (Caps-Lock, Num-Lock, and Scroll-Lock) do change when those keys are pressed. You can fill the type-ahead buffer and produce a beep, and keying Cntrl–Alt–Del will cause a reboot.

Suggested Methods:

01. Load debugger and use hot key to break in.
02. Load debugger and use NMI switch to break in.
03. Load debugger and use the step-over/step-into technique.
04. Monitor system calls with intercept driver or debugger.
05. Embed markers into source.

Stuck in an Endless Loop   To fit this category, there must be some evidence that lets you know that the system has become stuck in an endless loop. Typical symptoms are the repeated displaying of a message and repeated disk-writing activity (where the disk LED is pulsing and you can hear the drive stepping).

Be careful not to interpret the case where the diskette LED stays on continuously as necessarily being due to an endless-loop type of problem. Since the INT08 timer interrupt is involved in the deactivation of the diskette motor, any problem that upsets normal INT08 activity could also cause the diskette light to stay on.

Suggested Methods:

01. Load debugger and use hot key to break in.
02. Load debugger and use NMI switch to break in.
03. Load debugger and use the step-over/step-into technique.
04. Monitor system calls with intercept driver or debugger.
05. Embed markers into source.
06. Manipulate source code.

Loss of Keyboard Response   This is where you can tell that the system is still executing the current program with some amount of normalcy—it just won't respond to your keystrokes.

The possible causes that pertain specifically to the keyboard include I/O programming that sets the 8259 mask bit for IRQ01; corruption to the INT09 or INT16 interrupt vectors, corruption of an INT09 or INT16 interrupt intercept; damage to the portion of the operating system that processes console I/O requests; and corruption of keyboard-specific data within the BIOS data area.

The program-specific possibilities include damage to the memory containing the low-level keyboard-handling functions (e.g., getchar()-type functions) and damage to the high-level portion of the program that does console input.

Sometimes, when you break into a debugger, the debugger will be able to reenliven the keyboard.

Suggested Methods:

02. Load debugger and use NMI switch to break in.
03. Load debugger and use the step-over/step-into technique.
04. Monitor system calls with intercept driver or debugger.
05. Embed markers into source.
08. Use an intercept driver to monitor IRQ activity.

Improper Video Display   This could involve the display of messages at the wrong time, the display of garbage, or the instantiation of an improper video mode, color palette, or cursor type.

The possible explanations are numerous: improper stack balance; stack corruption; failure to preserve registers within functions and ISRs; stray bullets hitting the video buffer; I/O programming sequences to the video controller that are not protected from interruption, and so on.

Suggested Methods:

09. Set a memory write breakpoint on select video memory locations.
03. Load debugger and use the step-over/step-into technique.
04. Monitor system calls with intercept driver or debugger.
05. Embed markers into source.
06. Manipulate source code.
07. Check for corruption within the program's code and data files.
08. Use an intercept driver to monitor IRQ activity.
10. Use a stack underflow–monitoring tool.

Abnormally Slow Performance   A certain section of a program executes at an abnormally slow speed, or different points within the program execute slowly at varying times.

Possible causes include stack corruption resulting in the trap flag being set; redundant or unnecessary calculations or disk operations; and excessive operations occurring within a timer intercept handler.

Suggested Methods:

12. Install a tool that traps and reports on INT01 activity.
08. Use an intercept driver to monitor IRQ activity.
01. Load debugger and use hot key to break in.
02. Load debugger and use NMI switch to break in.
04. Monitor system calls with intercept driver or debugger.
05. Embed markers into source.
06. Manipulate source code.

Abnormal Execution Flow Order   When a program terminates unexpectedly, the system reboots by itself, or a process or prompt occurs at the wrong time, the possibilities include improper stack balance; stack, code, or data corruption; and failure to preserve registers within functions and ISRs.

Suggested Methods:

03. Load debugger and use the step-over/step-into technique.
04. Monitor system calls with intercept driver or debugger.
05. Embed markers into source.
07. Check for corruption within the program's code and data files.
10. Use a stack underflow–monitoring tool.

Partial Interrupt Loss   A partial loss of interrupts could be indicated when a serial communication process occasionally drops characters; the movement of a mouse results in jumpy mouse-cursor movement; keystrokes are sometimes missed, excessive disk errors occur; or a time loss is noticed in the software clock.

Regarding a time loss in the software clock, a custom tool could be made that intercepts INT08 and provides a visual indication of timer activity by dumping a marker to direct video. Observe the marker stream for evidence of a rate change as you perform different typical functions in the system. The use of an alternate video display is recommended.

Another approach would be to create a timer intercept driver that outputs a marker to a second machine through the parallel binary link. Then write a second program that will run within the second computer to collect the markers and correlate them with the timer ticks that occur within that machine, reporting on the degree of disparity in the two counts.

Suggested Methods:

05. Embed markers into source.
08. Use an intercept driver to monitor IRQ activity.

Disk or File Corruption is Evident   First, it is important to distinguish between corruption of a disk's structure and corruption of the data within a file. In the latter case, the program that generated the file may have incurred a corruption of the data while it was still within memory. In the former case, where the disk's directory structure or FAT (file allocation table) has become damaged, it could be due to corruption of the operating system or to incorrect operations by a program that interfaces with the disk at a low level (e.g., using system calls such as INT13, INT25, INT26, and the IOCTL subfunctions of INT21 function 44h).

Don't forget that in either case, failure of the disk media could explain the failure. The important questions here are "Does the corruption occur repeatedly?" and "Does it occur on different machines?"

Suggested Methods:

07. Check for corruption within the program's code and data files.
04. Monitor system calls with intercept driver or debugger.
05. Embed markers into source.
06. Manipulate source code.

An Exception Occurs   The most common exceptions are the following:

Divide by zero or divide overflow (INTOO)
Invalid instruction exception (INTO6)

That an exception is occurring may not be apparent without a debugger loaded—it all depends on the default exception handlers installed by the operating system. This could be something you become aware of when a debugger is loaded or when using a device driver designed to trap exception conditions (e.g., DUMPINTO.SYS for INTOO).

Suggested Methods:

11. Install a debugger or custom tool that traps exceptions.
03. Load debugger and use the step-over/step-into technique.
04. Monitor system calls with intercept driver or debugger.
05. Embed markers into source.
07. Check for corruption within the program's code and data files.

Master List of Methods

01. Load debugger and use hot key to break in.

5.1   The Software Debugger
5.3   Breakpoints
11.1   Benefits of Breakpoints Over Single-Stepping
11.2   Consider Your Approach
11.3   Getting an Overview History
11.4   Passive Breakpoints and Backtrace Buffers
11.6   Tracing into a Crash
11.7   Evaluation Breakpoints
11.12 Getting Your Bearings
12.3   Data and Control Flow Interpretation
12.4   Code and Data Corruption
12.5   Tracing and Backtracing

02. Load debugger and use NMI switch to break in.   Same as for Method 01 above, plus:

6.11 NMI Breakout Switch

03. Load debugger and use the step-over/step-into technique.

04. Monitor system calls with intercept driver or debugger.

05. Embed markers into source.

06. Manipulate source code.

07. Check for corruption within the program's code and data files.

08. Use an intercept driver to monitor IRQ activity.

09. Set a memory write breakpoint on select video memory locations.

10. Use a stack underflow–monitoring tool.

11. Install a debugger or custom tool that traps exceptions.

12. Install a tool that traps and reports on `INT01` activity.

APPENDIX B
Hex Math

The intent of this appendix is to guide you through some of the more common types of numerical derivations involving hexadecimal numbers. Although manual conversion methods are covered, obtain or write a calculator program if you must work with hex numbers very often. Programmer's calculator utilities are available within commercial products such as Borland's Sidekick. There are also many such utilities available from bulletin board services and through the pay-by-diskette shareware distribution services.

Manual Conversion

If you really find yourself in a pinch and need to convert hexadecimal numbers to and from decimal, remember that the decimal place value for each hex digit to the left is 16 times the current one and that the letter-type digits represent the following decimal values:

        0Ah = = 10
        0Bh = = 11
        0Ch = = 12
        0Dh = = 13
        0Eh = = 14
        0Fh = = 15

Here are the place values, starting with the rightmost digit position:

Position	Decimal Place Value
1	1 (16 to the 0th power)
2	16 (16 to the 1st power)
3	256 (16 to the 2nd power)
4	4,096 (16 to the 3rd power)
5	65,536 (16 to the 4th power)
6	1,048,576 (16 to the 5th power)
7	16,777,216 (16 to the 6th power)
8	268,435,456 (16 to the 7th power)

To convert the number 3C8Ah to its decimal equivalent, here are the steps:

1. The place value of the rightmost digit, the A, is 1. Thus our tally starts with a seed value of 10 decimal:

        Tally = 10

2. The next digit, the 8, has a place value of 16. Therefore, we add 8×16 to the tally:

$$\text{Tally} = 10 + (8 \times 16)$$

3. The next digit's place value is 256, and the decimal equivalent of the hex digit C is 12. So, here's the new tally:

$$\text{Tally} = 10 + (8 \times 16) + (12 \times 256)$$

4. The leftmost digit follows this same pattern:

$$\text{Tally} = 10 + (8 \times 16) + (12 \times 256) + (3 \times 4096)$$

$$\text{Tally} = 15,498$$

To go the other direction, let's use the decimal number 99,999. Here are the steps:

1. Determine the largest place value that will be used. In this case, it's the 5th place, with a value of 65,535.
2. Divide the number by this first place value, deriving both the quotient and remainder:

$$99,999/65,535 \rightarrow \text{Quotient} = 1, \text{Remainder} = 34,463$$

3. Plug the quotient into a template of the hex number you seek:

$$\text{Template} = 0001\text{xxxx}$$

4. Repeat Step 3 with each successive place value to the right, using the remainder as the new dividend. This would produce the calculations:

$$34,463/4096 \rightarrow \text{Quotient} = 8, \text{Remainder} = 1695$$
$$\text{Template} = 00018\text{xxx}$$
$$1695/256 \rightarrow \text{Quotient} = 6, \text{Remainder} = 159$$
$$\text{Template} = 000186\text{xx}$$
$$159/16 \rightarrow \text{Quotient} = 9, \text{Remainder} = 15$$
$$\text{Template} = 0001869\text{x}$$

5. Finally, the remainder of 15 must be converted to its hexadecimal equivalent F and plugged into the rightmost digit position:

$$\text{Template} = 0001869\text{F}$$
$$99,999 == 1869\text{fh}$$

Determining Interrupt Vector Addresses

As the first example, let's find the address of the INT21 interrupt vector. Since the interrupt vector table starts at address 0000:0000 and there are four bytes per vector, the basic process is to multiply the interrupt number by 4 and use the result as the offset with a segment of zero. This is easier to deal with when approached as a pair of additions:

$$021h + 021h = 042h$$
$$042h + 042h = 084h$$

In this case, the process was simple, since no letters were involved and no carries were required. The INT21 vector is located at address 0000:0084.

When the numbers are a little less accommodating, if you find yourself without a hex calculator, be aware that DEBUG.COM sports an H command, which will add two hexadecimal numbers. Other debuggers support even more. For example, to use DEBUG's H command to derive the address of the INT67 vector, you would enter the following:

```
h 67 67
```

This produces the intermediate tally of 00CEh. Reentering this number produces the final result:

```
h ce ce
```

The INT67 vector is located at 0000:019C.

Converting a File Offset to a DEBUG Address

Most file compare utilities will report the location of a difference between the two target files in terms of a hexadecimal offset from the start of the file. Should you want to load one of these files into DEBUG.COM for further inspection or for binary editing, you will have to reckon with the fact that DEBUG.COM loads the file at an offset of 100h (.EXE files are an exception).

One approach is to convert the zero-based file offset reported by the file compare utility to a 100h-based offset. This is as simple as it sounds—you simply add 100h to the offset reported by the comparison tool.

In the event that you need to investigate several positions within the file, you might prefer to use another alternative. As soon as you load the file into DEBUG.COM, enter the command RDS to change the value within the DS segment register, and then press the Enter key:

```
rds
DS 109A
:
```

Immediately underneath the RDS command in the foregoing example is a line produced by DEBUG. It is a report of the current value within the DS register. The value of 109A is purely hypothetical. The value you receive will depend on how much lower memory is currently allocated within your system.

The colon that appears on the next line is a prompt (DEBUG has lots of different kinds of prompts). What you need to do at this point is add 0010h to the current value of the DS register and enter this new value at the prompt. In this case, 109Ah + 0010h = 10AAh.

The DS register is now set up to be used with the zero-based offsets reported by your file comparison utility. For example, if the compare utility tells you that a problem exists at offset 034Eh, you could use this offset directly as long as you specify the DS register in the dump or unassemble commands:

```
d ds:034e
u ds:034e
```

When the files you are working with are large and difference points are reported beyond the first 64K (where the offset is 10000h or greater), additional steps must be taken. You could either derive a new value for the DS register or simply specify an explicit segment register value. It all depends on how many times you will need to enter these addresses.

Suppose that the file offset you must convert to a DEBUG address is 20CB4h and that you have already added 0010h to the original contents of the DS register to produce a zero-based segment value (going from 109Ah to 10AAh). To form an explicit segment address, form an intermediate value from the file offset by truncating off the rightmost digit and overwriting the remaining three digits on the right with zeros:

$$20CB4h \rightarrow 20CBh \rightarrow 2000h$$

Now add this intermediate value to the current DS register value and you've got the segment portion of the address you need:

$$2000h + 10AAh = 30AAh$$

For the offset portion of your final address, simply use the rightmost four digits of the file offset number:

$$20CB4h \rightarrow 0CB4h$$

To dump memory at the reported file offset would now be done as follows:

```
d 30aa:0cb4
```

To load an .EXE-type file into DEBUG.COM for this type of manipulation, first rename the file temporarily to have a different extension. Any extension will suffice, with .BIN being a common choice.

Address Conversion

After hours of painstaking bug hunting, you've finally determined that a byte of memory at address 3047:699B is being corrupted. But when you isolate the offending instruction, you find that the address it is generating when the corruption occurs is different, being 3107:5D9B instead! How can this be?

An 80X86-type CPU, when running in real or VM86 mode, uses what is known as segment:offset type addressing. One side effect of this addressing method is that one physical address can be equivalent to many different segment:offset type addresses.

To find the physical address for a given segment:offset type address:

1. Convert the segment portion of the segment:offset value to a 1-based number by multiplying it by 16 (decimal) = 10h. This can be accomplished quite easily by simply adding a 0 to the right end of the number.
2. Add this modified version of the segment value to the offset value.

For example, to convert 1234:5678 to a physical address:

$$1234 \rightarrow 12340$$

$$12340 + 5678 = 179B8$$

To convert a physical address to a segment:offset address, first select the new segment value. In this example, we will use a segment value of 150Ch.

Next, multiply this segment value by 16 by adding a 0 to the number's right end:

$$150C \rightarrow 150C0$$

Now subtract this value from the physical address:

$$179B8 - 150C0 = 28F8$$

This final value is now the offset portion. Therefore, the byte at address 1234:5678 can also be addressed through the address 150C:28F8.

Note that it is also possible to convert a physical address to a segment:offset-type address by selecting the offset value first rather than the segment. However, you must be aware that only one out of every 16 offset values will be able to produce a valid address value.

APPENDIX C
Defensive Program Design Tips

Two aspects of program design can result in fewer bugs:

1. Employ a disciplined and structured design methodology in the first place.
2. Design features into your program that make debugging easier.

The first method should be applied to all situations at all times, but an examination of it is, of course, beyond the scope of this appendix.

The second aspect, however, is approachable. Certainly, each different programming environment carries its own unique considerations, but there are some general ideas common to all. While the common ideas covered within this section are by no means all there is, they may be helpful in sparking your imagination.

Allocate Patch Areas

Allocate a small- to moderately-sized patch area within each segment. Within a code segment, this can be done by crafting a dummy function filled with meaningless assignment statements (in C, use __emit__()). Within a data segment, simply allocate a small array that will not actually be used—and document clearly that this is the case so that future programmers will understand its purpose.

Along the lines of allocating extra data, it can be wise to include a small collection of word-sized and pointer-sized variables for possible use by custom debugging code. Should a stray-bullet problem show up, you would then be able to use these variables rather than having to add new ones. The addition of new data could easily cause a change in the behavior of this type of bug.

Catch All Cases

Analyze each decision-making process to ensure that no presumptions are being made. If a variable, when found not to be within a certain set of values, is presumed to hold a certain default value, a warning bell should go off. For example, rather than presume that AL must be 3 if it isn't 0, 1, or 2, include code to verify this condition. An assembler case follows.

Presumption case:

```
cmp     al,0
je      function_zero
```

```
cmp     al,1
je      function_one
cmp     al,2
je      function_two
jmp     function_three
```

Explicit validation case:

```
cmp     al,0
je      function_zero
cmp     al,1
je      function_one
cmp     al,2
je      function_two
cmp     al,3
je      function_three
jmp     invalid_function
```

In C, be sure to include a `default:` handler in all `switch` statement blocks. C programmers should also make liberal use of the `assert()` function.

Similarly, for each calculation performed within a program, an initial verification should be done to all pertinent data on the way in, and exception handling provided for invalid results. Some of the things to watch out for are the following:

- Division by zero
- Division overflow, where a quotient is larger than the data field provided for it
- Multiplication and addition overflow, where a product or sum is larger than the data field being used
- Signed/unsigned conflicts, where a signed number is inadvertently treated as unsigned, and vice versa
- Unacceptable loss of precision

Entry and Exit Functions Parameters

At the entrance to each function, include code to verify all entry parameters for proper range.

Ensure that each function (where appropriate) returns a completion status value and that each call to that function follows up with a test for an error return value.

A Function for Everything

Construct an individual function for all key operations, even if a library function already exists. Such functions make a good place to insert validation tests, breakpoints, or instrumentation.

For example, when working with a serial port, rather than sprinkle I/O statements throughout a program, consolidate them into a function. Make one `serial_process()` function, which is passed the base address, an operation selector number, and any other data, depending on the operation.

This way, if you need to apply instrumentation or set breakpoints to monitor I/O port activities, you have one central section of code to deal with rather than a diffuse sprinkling.

One interesting side note to this method: The use of a central function for I/O activities makes it easier to set up an emulation of the I/O data. You can temporarily replace this I/O management function with one that obtains fake input data from a list in a file rather than from the actual hardware. This can speed and simplify certain testing operations.

Use Typed Constants

Be careful when using constants created through such devices as the `equ` directive in assembler and the `#define` directive in C. This type of symbolic representation carries no type information with it. If you accidentally use an equated symbol for a type of data access different from the original intent, the assembler or compiler will not be able to flag the usage as an error.

For example, you might wish to establish a symbolic name to support access to the keyboard shift-state byte, located at address 0040:0017 within the BIOS data area. Note that in the code sequence below, the instruction `mov al,es:[bdaShiftState1]` is using the symbolic name to access a byte (the intended type of use). But the assembler will also allow a word access, as is shown in the next instruction:

```
bdaShiftState1  equ       17h
        mov     ax,40h
        mov     es,ax
        mov     al,es:[bdaShiftState1]
        mov     ax,es:[bdaShiftState1]
```

A better way is to use either the `segment at` method or a structure. Of these two, the `segment at` construct is preferable, because it allows you to provide the assembler with information about which segment register should be used. With a structure, you would still have to use an explicit segment override. The `segment at` approach works like this:

```
bios_data_area segment at 0040h
        org  0017h
bdaShiftState1 label byte
bios_data_area ends
_TEXT   segment para public 'CODE'
        assume  cs:_TEXT,ds:nothing,es:nothing,ss:nothing
org     100h
        mov     ax,40h
        mov     es,ax
        assume  es:bios_data_area
        mov     al,[bdaShiftState1]
```

In summary, the two benefits this method provides are the following:

1. It tells the assembler that the normal use of the bdaShiftState1 label is for a byte-sized operation. An attempt to access this memory location as a word-sized field would be flagged as an error unless an explicit override declaration was used, such as mov ax,word ptr [bdsShiftState1].
2. It lets you declare which segment register should be used through the assume directive.

APPENDIX D
System-Level Knowledge for Debugging

Obviously, a thorough treatment of systems-level programming would require a book in itself (a *large* book). This section covers topics that tend to come up often when debugging at the assembler level within an IBM PC/XT/AT-class computer.

Basics of Interrupt Service Routines (ISRs)

The 80X86-type CPU supports interrupt calls generated from three different sources:

1. Explicit software instructions (e.g., int 21h)
2. Internally generated events such as INT01 single-stepping and exception processing (e.g., divide by zero or invalid instruction)
3. External hardware (e.g., interrupts from a timer, keyboard, serial port, and disk controller)

When an interrupt call is processed by the CPU, here is a basic outline of what occurs:

- Three words of information are pushed onto the top of the current stack. These are the current value of the CPU flags, the instruction pointer register (IP), and the code segment register (CS).
- The interrupt enable flag is cleared, meaning no hardware interrupts can occur until this flag is again set.
- A far pointer is fetched from the interrupt vector corresponding to the interrupt being processed.
- Execution control is passed to the program code located at this far pointer. This is the Interrupt Service Routine (ISR).
- Once the ISR completes its processing, it executes an `iret` instruction. This retrieves the three words of stack information, which were automatically saved when the interrupt call began, and uses them to restore execution control to the appropriate point.

(Note that the processing of NMI interrupts and of certain types of exceptions on an 80386+ type of CPU can involve additional details and exceptions to this generalized set of steps.)

In the case of an explicit software interrupt call, the restoration process simply involves a return to the next instruction after the interrupt call.

When a hardware-based interrupt, also known as an IRQ (Interrupt ReQuest), occurs, this final restoration process simply causes the flow of execution to resume with the next instruction that would have been executed if the IRQ had not occurred. IRQ-based interrupts are sometimes referred to as asynchronous interrupts, since they can occur at almost any point in time with respect to the execution flow of the main program.

Hardware-based interrupt handlers (IRQ handlers) must also involve themselves with a certain management detail regarding the 8259 interrupt controller chip (actually, within an AT-class machine, there are two of these 8259 interrupt controllers). Once this interrupt management device signals the CPU with an interrupt request, the device must be reset again before any further interrupts will be recognized for that interrupt level or for any lower priority level. The basic way this resetting is done is by writing an EOI (End Of Interrupt) command to the command register of this chip.

While a full discussion of the particulars of interfacing with the 8259, EOI commands, and interrupt priority levels warrant a small book in themselves, one detail that can be of use in a debugging context is the use of the 8259 mask register.

This mask register can be used to temporarily prevent hardware interrupts from occurring, on a selective basis. If the bug you are chasing seems to be involved with a certain IRQ event, or if you believe that you could make a bug more stable by preventing certain interrupts from occurring, the mask register might be the answer. Be careful, though: Disabling the `IRQ01` keyboard interrupt will leave you with a dead keyboard. Likewise, disabling

IRQ06 will disable the diskette drive, and disabling IRQ14 will disable a hard drive (many hard drives use this interrupt anyway).

The IRQ level this technique will be used with most often is the IRQ00 level timer interrupt. Approximately 18.2 times a second, a timer chip within the computer (an 8253) causes an IRQ00 interrupt event to occur. This IRQ level is assigned to the INT08 interrupt vector. The IRQ00 level is controlled by bit 0 of the mask register at address I/O 0021h. When bit 0 within this mask register is set to 1, no further interrupts will be recognized for this IRQ level.

To see how this would work, try the following test:

- At the DOS command prompt, enter the command:

```
prompt $t
```

- Hold the Enter key down for a few seconds and note how your new command prompt lets you see the passing of time based on the computer's software clock.
- Enter DEBUG.COM and use the A command to assemble in the following instructions:

```
in      al,21
or      al,1
out     21,al
ret
```

- Press Return twice to exit the immediate assembler mode, and then enter the G command to run this tiny program. What you have just done is load the current mask register's contents into the AL register, set the mask bit in the bit 0 position (which corresponds to IRQ00), and then write this updated value back to the mask register.
- Now, use Q to quit DEBUG. Then, while back at the command prompt, hold the Enter key down for a few seconds and note that your computer's internal software clock has stopped advancing.
- When you are ready to activate IRQ00 events again, reenter DEBUG, run the following piece of code, and then reset your software clock with the DOS TIME command:

```
in      al,21
and     al,fe
out     21,al
ret
```

Note that while the timer tick interrupt is disabled, certain processes will not operate correctly. Once you access a diskette drive, the motor will continue to run indefinitely afterwards. The BIOS disk logic uses the timer tick interrupt to apply a delay to the motor shutoff.

Stack Addressing with the BP Register

The most basic rule to remember is that any time the SP register is loaded into the BP register, the SS:BP pointer points to what was last pushed onto the stack (the use of the BP register automatically implies the use of the SS segment register unless an explicit segment override is given). From there, an offset of +2 would be used to access each higher word on the stack. See Listing A-1 for examples.

Often, local stack-based storage will be allocated after the BP register is loaded from SP. This results in the use of negative offsets, as shown in Listing A-2.

Given the stack frame laid in place by the code fragment in Listing A-2, here are some examples of byte-level access to stack frame data:

```
; does entry ah == 3c?
        cmp     byte ptr [bp-1],03ch
        je      is_3c
; change stack copy of bl to 2
        mov     byte ptr [bp-4],2
```

Finally, as you'll see if you inspect the assembler code produced by a high-level language compiler such as C, positive-offset BP addressing is used

```
push    ax
push    bx
push    cx
push    bp
mov     bp,sp
mov     ax,[bp]             ; access original bp
mov     ax,[bp+2]           ; access original cx
mov     ax,[bp+4]           ; access original bx
mov     ax,[bp+6]           ; access original ax

push    bp
push    ax
push    bx
sub     sp,4                ; create two words of local storage
mov     bp,sp
mov     word ptr [bp],123   ; write to lower local word
mov     word ptr [bp+2],456 ; write to higher local word
mov     ax,[bp+4]           ; access original bx
mov     ax,[bp+6]           ; access original ax
mov     ax,[bp+8]           ; access original bp
```

LISTING A-1 Using BP to access stack data.

```
        push    bp
        mov     bp,sp
        sub     sp,10       ; create a 5-word local pocket
        mov     [bp-2],ax   ; use highest word
        mov     [bp-4],bx   ; use next word
        mov     [bp-6],cx   ; etc.
        mov     [bp-8],dx
        mov     [bp-10],si  ; use lowest word
```

LISTING A-2   Using BP with a negative offset.

to access stack-based entry parameters, and negative-offset BP addressing is used to access local stack variables. The following code fragment shows two functions within a small-model C program and the corresponding assembler code:

```
---- A pair of C functions
void process_widgets(int parameter_var) {
  int local_var;
  local_var = parameter_var;
  }
void main() {
  process_widgets(44);
  }
---- The equivalent assembler code
_process_widgets proc near
        push    bp
        mov     bp,sp
        dec     sp
        dec     sp
        mov     ax,word ptr [bp+4]
        mov     word ptr [bp-2],ax
        mov     sp,bp
        pop     bp
        ret
_process_widgets endp
_main   proc    near
        push    bp
        mov     bp,sp
        mov     ax,44
        push    ax
        call    near ptr _process_widgets
        pop     cx
        pop     bp
        ret
_main   endp
```

The variable `local_var` is declared within the `process_widgets()` function without the `static` modifier. This makes it a stack-based automatic variable. In the assembler version, the purpose of two `dec sp` instructions is to allocate a word of local stack storage for this variable. So, what a C programmer knows as `local_var` would now be known to an assembler programmer as `word ptr [bp-2]`.

Now let's take a look at how C passes the entry parameter value of 44 into the `process_widgets()` function (the literal value 44 is used when this function is called from within `main()`). In the assembler code version of `main()`, note how the literal value of 44 is loaded into the AX register and then pushed onto the stack. The stack word is the actual entry parameter to the `process_widgets` function. The fact that this data is also within the AX register is purely incidental.

Within `process_widgets()`, this stack-based entry parameter is accessed through the `word ptr [bp+4]` operand. The offset of +4 is used to account for the near return address placed on the stack by the `call` instruction. Here is how the stack is arranged once the stack setup epilogue of `_process_widgets` has been executed (when the current instruction would be the `mov ax,word ptr [bp+4]`):

bp+4	the data passed in for `parameter_var`
bp+2	the near return address
bp+0	the entry BP value
bp−2	storage for the `local_var` variable

Finding a Device Driver's Entry Points

The most common reason you would need to determine the entry points of a device driver is that you need to use a debugger to single-step through the driver's initialization function. To single-step through the initialization of a device driver loaded through `CONFIG.SYS` requires the use of a debugger that can be active during that time. Following are some ways in which this can be accomplished:

- To use a debugger that can be loaded as a device driver itself
- To use a debugger that can be loaded into a protected memory board and survive a warm boot
- To use an ICE or a CPU intercept pod type of debugger

You would need to determine the driver's entry points in order to embed a hard-coded breakpoint.

While it is most typical for a device driver's strategy function to do nothing more than enqueue the pointer to the request header passed to it within the ES:BX register pair, leaving the interrupt function to do the bulk of the processing, this isn't always the case.

Drivers do exist where all function processing is carried out by the strategy function, with the interrupt function being merely a stub (strange but true). Therefore, whenever you are working with a driver you didn't write (and why else would you have to go through a reverse-engineering method to determine the entry points?), you should locate and study both the strategy and interrupt functions. For this example, we will presume a .SYS type of device driver, where the strategy function does only enqueue the request header pointer and the interrupt function performs the bulk of the processing.

First, if you have a disassembler and are familiar with it, using it will be the quickest and simplest way to pinpoint the address of the first instruction within the interrupt function or of the specific function that handles the initialization process. If you don't have a disassembler, dust off your copy of DEBUG.COM and follow these steps:

1. Load the driver into DEBUG.COM:

    ```
    debug widgets.sys
    ```

2. Add 10h to the contents of the DS register. To do this, first enter the RDS command and then press the Enter key:

    ```
    rds
    DS 109A
    :
    ```

    Immediately underneath the RDS command in the foregoing example is a line that is produced by DEBUG. It is a report of the current value within the DS register. The value of 109A is purely hypothetical. The value you receive will depend on how much lower memory is currently allocated within your system.

    The colon that appears on the next line is a prompt. What you need to do at this point is add 0010h to the current value of the DS register and enter this new value at the prompt. In this case:

    $$109Ah + 0010h = 10AAh$$

3. Locate the address of the interrupt function by dumping memory at address DS:0008. You want the word-sized offset at this location, so use the command:

    ```
    d ds:8 12
    ```

    Be aware that the first data byte displayed is the LSB (least significant byte) and the second byte is the MSB. Thus, if the values you see are 4C 01, the offset of the interrupt function is 014C.

4. Use DEBUG's disassembler to inspect the logic at that address. For example:

```
u ds:14c
```

You can either embed a hard-coded breakpoint directly within this function or you can reverse-engineer this function, to determine how it locates and branches to the initialization function.

Memory Control Blocks (MCBs)

MS-DOS uses a structure known as an MCB (memory control block) to manage the allocation of main memory within a computer. The term *main* is used here to differentiate this memory from extended or expanded memory. MCBs are used to manage the base memory within the first 640K.

Each allocated piece of memory is known as a *memory block* and is preceded by a 16-byte header. Memory blocks and their headers are always aligned on a segment boundary and are contiguous.

The memory control blocks form a linked list based on this contiguous relationship. Once the segment address of one block is known, the segment address of the next one may be determined by adding the block's paragraph count + 1 to the current segment. The structure of the MCB data and the operations used on it are described in Table A.1.

The signature field contains the byte 04Dh (an ASCII M) when the block is not the last one in the list. For the last block in the list, the signature byte should hold a value of 05Ah (an ASCII Z).

The return AX value from a successful call to function 48h of INT21 holds the segment address of a newly allocated block of memory. The segment address of the associated MCB record is simply AX − 1. In other words, if this INT21 call results in an AX value of 50CCh, your new memory block begins at address 50CC:0000, and the 16-byte MCB is located at address 50CB:0000.

TABLE A.1   MCB structure

Data Size	Field Name	Description
1 byte	Signature	04D or 05Ah (see text)
1 word	Owner PSP	PSP segment address of owner program
1 word	Block Size	The block size in 16-byte paragraphs
11 bytes	Reserved	

When a program is loaded by the EXEC function (INT21 function 4B), two memory blocks are allocated: one for the program's copy of the environment string block and another for the program's code and data. The PSP is built at the very start of the code and data block, so the corresponding MCB is located at PSP segment − 1. The segment address for a program's environment block can be obtained from the word at offset 002Ch within the PSP.

To locate the segment address of the very first MCB within a system, the root of the linked list, requires the use of the undocumented INT21 function 52h call. The only entry parameter to this call is the function selector of 52h, which must be loaded into the AH register. Upon return from this call, the ES:BX register pair points to an internal DOS data structure which is often referred to as the "list of lists."

The segment address of the first MCB block is located at offset −2 within this list. The following code fragment would result in this value being loaded into the AX register:

```
mov     ah,52h
int     21h
mov     ax,es:[bx-2]
```

As previously mentioned, once the segment address of one MCB block is known, the address of the next block can be derived by adding the block's paragraph size + 1 to the current segment address. An additional detail that must be considered is to check the signature byte of each block to make sure you stop when the list stops. The following assembler fragment outlines this process:

```
        mov     ah,52h
        int     21h
        mov     ax,es:[bx-2]
mcb_loop:
; ax is the segment of the current MCB
        call    MCB_processing_function
; determine the next MCB
        mov     es,ax
        cmp     byte ptr es:[0],05Ah
        je      end_of_list
        cmp     byte ptr es:[0],04Dh
        jne     corrupt_list
        add     ax,es:[3]
        inc     ax
        jmp     short mcb_loop
end_of_list:
```

APPENDIX E
Patch Techniques

Whenever you are able to effect a patch-based fix by overwriting an existing block of code, consider yourself fortunate. As will become clear from the following discussion, locating patch space for the case where a code addition must be made isn't always easy.

Shown below is an excerpt from the program WIDGETS.COM. For the sake of example, say that beginning at offset 0122h, the next three instructions are to be replaced with the two instructions mov bx,cs:[bx+4] and mov es:[3fc],bx. The original three instructions occupy the 13 bytes from offset 0122h through 012Eh, and these two new instructions will require only nine bytes:

```
2709:0115 83EC04          SUB      SP,+04
2709:0118 55              PUSH     BP
2709:0119 8BEC            MOV      BP,SP
2709:011B 53              PUSH     BX
2709:011C 8ADC            MOV      BL,AH
2709:011E 32FF            XOR      BH,BH
2709:0120 03DB            ADD      BX,BX
2709:0122 2E              CS:
2709:0123 8B9F0200        MOV      BX,[BX+0002]
2709:0127 895E02          MOV      [BP+02],BX
2709:012A C746043200      MOV      WORD PTR [BP+04],0032
2709:012F 5B              POP      BX
2709:0130 5D              POP      BP
2709:0131 C3              RET
```

See Section 13.1, "Reverse Engineering/Disassembling," for details on producing this type of disassembly listing using DEBUG.COM.

To effect this patch, you must not only write in the new instructions but also account for the remaining four bytes. If these four bytes are not overwritten with nop instructions, the leftover bytes, 46, 04, 32, and 00, would surely give the CPU a case of indigestion. Here is the final DEBUG script and a disassembly excerpt illustrating the result:

```
---- DEBUG script: widget01.pat
a cs:0122
cs:mov bx,[bx+4]
es:mov [03fc],bx

e cs:12B 90 90 90 90
w
q
```

```
---- Resulting code
2709:0115 83EC04      SUB      SP,+04
2709:0118 55          PUSH     BP
2709:0119 8BEC        MOV      BP,SP
2709:011B 53          PUSH     BX
2709:011C 8ADC        MOV      BL,AH
2709:011E 32FF        XOR      BH,BH
2709:0120 03DB        ADD      BX,BX
2709:0122 2E          CS:
2709:0123 8B5F04      MOV      BX,[BX+04]
2709:0126 26          ES:
2709:0127 891EFC03    MOV      [03FC],BX
2709:012B 90          NOP
2709:012C 90          NOP
2709:012D 90          NOP
2709:012E 90          NOP
2709:012F 5B          POP      BX
2709:0130 5D          POP      BP
2709:0131 C3          RET
```

This type of DEBUG script would be applied using input redirection:

```
debug widgets.com < widget01.pat
```

Note that when using DEBUG's immediate assembler feature, a blank line must follow the last instruction in order to cause an exit from immediate assembly mode and return to the DEBUG command mode. Note also that this type of script must end with a W command to cause the patched memory copy to be written back to the file. An ending Q command is also essential to cause DEBUG to terminate and the input redirection to end.

General points:

1. Whenever the patched-in code is smaller than the original, ensure that none of the old leftover instructions can be executed. If only a few old instructions will remain, they can be overwritten with nop instructions. For a larger remainder, place a jump instruction at the end of your new code to branch around the leftover section.

2. Watch out for branch entry points. If you must move or rewrite code that involves multiple entries, you will have to find all other points in the code that branch to the affected area and adjust the offsets of the jumps. Just to make this more interesting, you'll have to check for any other patches that involve branches to the entry point(s) in question.

3. If you will be freeing up a significant amount of space, document it as available patch memory in your patch log. When you need to

make another patch someday, such pockets can be lifesavers. Design your patch to jump around the unused instructions rather than over-writing the remainder with `nop` instructions. In the event that you are shortening a function, the `ret` instruction at the end of the new section will serve this purpose.

Larger Patches

When the program you are working with was written in assembler, source code is available, and the patch will involve a moderate amount of code, start by generating a `.LST` (assembler listing) file of the program in its original state. Then modify a copy of this source code to implement the bug correction or customization that the patch is to embody, and generate a new `.LST` file.

If at all possible, encode these new instructions in the position within the file they will occupy in the actual patch. When this isn't possible, it is best to position them at the very end of the segment so the addresses of the remaining code within that segment will be the same as in the original version.

When the program you must patch is coded in a high-level language, see if your compiler can be made to produce an assembler listing. If this isn't supported, or if source code is not available at all, disassembly is about your only remaining option.

The Patch Log

If the binary module you are patching has ever been patched before, a *patch log* documentation file should have been started. For each patch, a detailed account of the memory areas affected and the patch space consumed should be given.

Before making any new patch, examine all previous entries to verify that no conflicts will occur. If this type of documentation does not exist, now is the time to review the previous patches and generate a patch-log. If you inadvertently build a new patch on top of an old one, confusion will reign.

Locating Patch Space

There are two cases where some additional memory will have to be found to accommodate your patch:

1. When the block of code being replaced is smaller than the replace-ment code.
2. When no code is being replaced—only new code added.

Of course, if you had the good foresight to allocate a patch space within each segment of your program from the start, you can skip this discussion. If no such area has been allocated, or if there isn't enough room remaining in the patch space, here are some suggestions:

- Locate a function that can be orphaned. Sometimes lesser-used options of a program must be sacrificed to apply critical corrections. One simple way to orphan a function is to patch a `ret` instruction at its entry point. Depending on the function, it may be necessary to insert a few instructions to effect an appropriate return value before this `ret` instruction.
- Make use of memory in the bottom of a stack buffer (where an extra margin should have been allocated in the first place), or in some other data buffer whose size is represented as a constant, so that adjusting that constant can free up a portion of its space.
- Shorten one or more message strings (covered in this section).
- Extend the module (covered in this section).

Allocating a Patch Area

To preallocate a patch buffer within an assembler program is simple. Within each code segment and each data segment, use the `db` directive to allocate a block of bytes:

```
public patch_area
patch_area label byte
        db        80 dup(0)
```

In a high-level language program, allocating a data segment patch space is as simple as declaring an array:

```
byte patch_area1[10];
```

Allocating a code segment patch space with a high-level language program can be accomplished by creating a dummy function filled with instructions that generate code that will never be executed. In the following example, the assignment of one local `dword` variable to another will generate a decent amount of code with only a few source code lines:

```
void patch_func() {
  dword x1, x2;
  x1=x2; x1=x2; x1=x2; x1=x2; x1=x2; x1=x2; x1=x2;
  x1=x2; x1=x2; x1=x2; x1=x2; x1=x2; x1=x2; x1=x2;
  x1=x2; x1=x2; x1=x2; x1=x2; x1=x2; x1=x2; x1=x2;
  x1=x2; x1=x2; x1=x2; x1=x2; x1=x2; x1=x2; x1=x2;
  }
```

Regarding the number of bytes to reserve, patch areas within data segments rarely need to be too large. Most patched-in changes don't involve complex new structure operations. A patch space of 5 to 10 bytes should be adequate for most cases. Should a case arise where this size proves insufficient, you might patch in code that dynamically allocates a block of memory and uses a few of those 5 to 10 bytes to store a pointer to the new block.

In sizing a code segment patch space, it's generally best to be as generous as is practical. Although it's not good to have binary modules inflated by several kilobytes of patch space when that space may never be used, if you need it—you need it.

A typical patch buffer for an assembler program would be in the range of 200 to 800 bytes. For a program written in a high-level language, you'll often find that the extra difficulty in patching these programs in the first place curtails your thirst for patch space, so a few hundred bytes should also be adequate.

To locate your patch area within the binary module, generate a listing file (.LST) or a linker map file (.MAP). In the foregoing example, the public patch_area statement was included to ensure that this variable would be reported within a .MAP file.

Shortening Message Strings

When you must scrounge around for patch space, one approach can be to locate one or more message strings that can be shortened. These strings must, of course, be located within the same segment as the code you are patching.

Once you locate a string, you must determine the termination method used. Some strings will be of the ASCIIZ variety, where a zero indicates the end of the string. Some will use a $ character at the end, where function 09H of INT21 is used to display the string. Still others will use a preceding length byte, as shown by the following assembler source line:

```
msg1    db      27,'Please insert Diskette #3',13,10
```

Next, you must devise a more terse replacement for the string. For example, consider the case of a message produced by the following assembler statement:

```
error1  db   'Index file not found.',13,10
        db   'Make sure Diskette #3 is in A:',13,10
        db   'Press any key to continue',13,10,0
```

Including the terminating zero, this string occupies 83 bytes of memory. To replace it with a more terse version, your DEBUG script could contain a line such as this one:

```
e ds:3099 'Need Disk #3',13,10,0
```

This new version requires only 15 bytes, so there are now 68 bytes available for use as patch space.

To be safe using this method, you must be careful that you don't misjudge the termination method. Just because a string is followed by a zero doesn't mean that it's an ASCIIZ string. To be sure, locate the instructions that display the string.

One final point regarding the modification of message strings: Be aware that one method of producing a foreign-language edition of a program is to use a utility that patches in new message strings.

Extending the Binary Module's Size

If the module you need to patch is configured as a .COM or .SYS file, adding new code onto the end of the application is a possibility. You must, of course, know whether the module contains resident and nonresident sections, and if so, how those sections are arranged within the binary module.

When this type of module is loaded into DEBUG.COM, the BX:CX register pair holds the number of bytes contained within the module. Through the use of the RCX command within a script (and RBX in the large-module case), you can increase its size, making it possible to add patch code at the end of the module.

For example, consider the case of the file WIDGETS.COM, whose directory size is 26,677 bytes. When this file is loaded into DEBUG.COM, the BX:CX registers will hold 0000:6835. Due to the fact that this module is loaded at address CS:0100, the last byte of this module is located at address CS:6934. This is derived by the following calculation:

```
CS:0100 + 6835 - 1
```

The subtraction of 1 is due to the fact that this is a zero-based count.

What this all means is that you can add a new piece of code beginning at address CS:6935, patching in a jump to this new code at the appropriate point within the existing portion of the module. Your DEBUG script would then need to include an RCX instruction such as the following:

```
rcx
6895
```

This value constitutes an increase of 0060h bytes over the original value of 6835.

In the case of a TSR or device driver type of module, this method will only be practical when the code you are patching is contained within the nonresident portion of the program. In a desperate case, you might be able to relocate the first section of nonresident code to the end of the file (increasing the module's size as previously described). Then the freed space could be used for a resident patch. Note that you would need to modify the instructions that determine how much code remains resident to account for this shifting.

The Call to Patch Area Case

In some situations, you will find it possible to effect a patch by changing the address of a call instruction. For example, suppose you discover that a certain register should be preserved around a call to a procedure. Say also that changing the procedure to save and restore this register is not a viable option, since the register is used to hold a return value in certain other places within the code.

```
mov     ax,[t1]
push    bx
call    sort_widgets
pop     bx
jc      sort_error
```

If a push and pop of the ES register needs to be done around the call to sort_widgets, a simple way to fix the omission is to overwrite the line call sort_widgets with a call to the next free address within the patch space.

If the patch space you'll use is located at offset 0410h, the offset of sort_widgets is 1043h, and the original call instruction is located at offset 270C, here is what your DEBUG script could look like:

```
a cs:410
push es
call 1042
pop es
ret

a cs:270c
call 410

w
q
```

The Jump-Away/Jump-Back Case

When you discover that additional instructions must be interjected into a section of code that doesn't lend itself to the calling method just described, you're in need of a *jump-away/jump-back* solution. Following is a small fragment of assembler source code and the corresponding disassembly output from DEBUG.COM:

```
mov     ax,[widget_type]
cmp     ax,w_type1
je      process_type1
```

```
                cmp     ax,w_type2
                je      process_type2
                jmp     bad_type
32DD:2077 A10302         MOV     AX,[0203]
32DD:207A 3D0100         CMP     AX,0001
32DD:207D 741F           JZ      209E
32DD:207F 3D0200         CMP     AX,0002
32DD:2082 743C           JE      20C0
32DD:2074 E9B202         JMP     2339
```

The problem with this code is that the designer forgot to apply a certain manipulation to the [widget_type] variable before testing for w_type1 and w_type2. Assuming that patch space has been located at offset 0294, here's what the patching script could look like:

```
a 2077
jmp 294
a 294
mov ax,[203]
and ax,fff
jmp 207A

w
q
```

In this case, the instruction that is patched into the code fragment is a three-byte jmp instruction. This matches nicely with the three bytes originally occupied by the instruction mov ax,[0203]. Within the patch area, the script implants a replacement for this instruction as well as an and ax,fff, the forgotten manipulation. Then the last instruction written into the patch area brings the flow of execution back to the original section of code, at the address just after the patched-over instruction.

In some cases, the jmp instruction required to branch away to the patch area will be longer than the instruction you want to overwrite. In such a case, you would have to choose a small sequence of instructions that could be patched over, making sure you replicate this entire sequence within the patch area.

When a patched-in jmp instruction does overwrite more than one instruction, you must verify that none of the instructions past the first is the target of another branch instruction. For example, if the assembler code looked like the following and you were to patch a three-byte jmp over the push ax instruction, a crash would occur the first time a branch was made to the entry1 label. In such a case, you must either apply the jump-to-patch-area jmp instruction in another location or find all instructions that branch to the entry1 label and modify them to branch to the patch area.

```
        push    ax
entry1:
        push    bx
        mov     al,4700h
```

Segment Register Adjustment

When working with binary modules designed to load at a zero offset position, you will want to adjust the segment register values that DEBUG establishes, so that patch script offsets match actual program offsets. Device drivers (e.g., a .SYS or .BIN type of file) and certain types of overlay modules fall into this category.

This type of manipulation may also be helpful when patching an .EXE-type module, where multiple code and data segments are common. Since DEBUG.COM will not write an .EXE-type file back to disk, you will have to temporarily rename such files to have another extension, such as .BIN.

The basic idea is to compensate for DEBUG's habit of loading non-EXE type files at offset 0100h with respect to the segment register values it establishes. This is accomplished by adding 0010h to the value within either or both of the DS and ES registers.

The initial value within the segment registers will vary with the current load position at the time DEBUG is run. Therefore, to do this from within a patch script requires that a small piece of assembler code be written into memory and executed. But this piece of code must not interfere with any of the memory occupied by the program to be patched.

The following patch script makes use of a portion of the default DTA (Disk Transfer Address) within the PSP—an area that should never be used for any other purpose during a patching operation.

```
rsp
100
a d0
mov ax,ds
add ax,10
mov ds,ax
jmp 100

g =d0 100
; patching statements go here.
; remember to use ds: prefix.
; for example:    'a ds:1234'
; and:            'e ds:100 01 02 03'

w
q
```

When a patch with this prologue is used, here is what happens:

1. The RSP instruction sets the stack pointer to the safe value of 100. This results in the upper part of the default DTA being used as the stack during the execution of the small section of code that changes the DS register.
2. The A D0 command initiates DEBUG's immediate assembler mode at address 00D0h, another point within the default DTA.
3. Four instructions are assembled into the default DTA area. When executed, these instructions will adjust the DS register upwards by 0010h and then restore the IP register to its initial entry value of 0100h.
4. The G =D0 100 instruction causes DEBUG to execute the instructions placed at address 00D0h, stopping when address 0100h is reached.

Dynamic Patching

To apply a *dynamic patch* to a program is to patch only the live memory image of the program. This is sometimes helpful when debugging a program as a way to test changes without having to break from your testing work, edit, and recompile the program and then restart your testing.

One restriction that doesn't exist in this case, as it does with static patching, is that the patch space memory can be located anywhere within the reach of a far jump instruction. This opens up possibilities of using free memory within the upper portion of the TPA (Transient Program Area), using memory within an unused video page, or using memory within a filler TSR that was loaded for this purpose.

When applying patches to live code, you must consider if the code you are changing could actually be executed while you are running debugger commands. This could happen where IRQ handlers are involved. In this event, you may want to patch a small piece of program code into a free area that will make all of your code modifications with interrupts disabled. You would then use your debugger to execute this piece of code.

Patching Far Jumps and Calls within an .EXE

If you intend to patch over a far jump or call with a near jump to a patch area, you must realize the effects of the relocation table. Within the header portion of an .EXE-type file there is a relocation table, which specifies the location of instructions that need to have the segment portions of their operands modified based on the module's actual load position.

If you must patch over an instruction that will be affected by the processing of this relocation table, you must locate its relocation table entry and modify it. If this patched-over instruction will be replicated within the patch area, you must modify the relocation table entry to point to that instruction in its new location.

If the original instruction will not be replicated, you need a way to nullify its relocation entry. One way to do this is to make the relocation entry be a duplicate of an entry for another instruction within the same segment. Another is to modify the entry to point to memory that you know will not be in use at the time the relocation processing is done (e.g., the lower portion of the program's stack buffer).

APPENDIX F
Constructing Parallel and Serial Link Cables

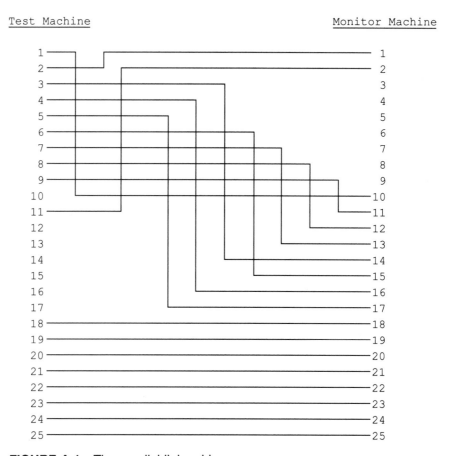

FIGURE A.1 The parallel link cable.

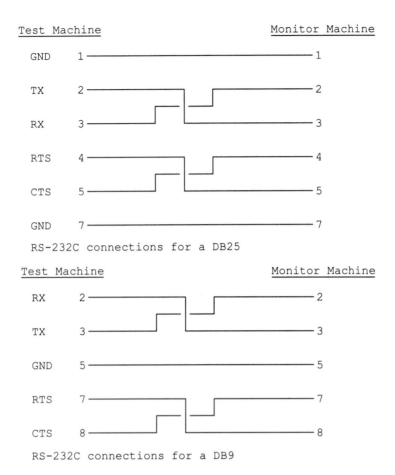

RS-232C connections for a DB25

RS-232C connections for a DB9

FIGURE A.2 The serial link cable.

APPENDIX G
Printf **Macros**

```
/*==== debugging aids ====*/

#ifndef asmtypes
#include "c:\xtools\asmtypes.h"
#endif
```

(continued on next page)

LISTING A-3 The SHMACS.H printf() macros.

```
/* shml - show module and line number */

#ifdef debug
#define shml(x)  printf("%s, m: %s, l: %d\n",x,__FILE__,__LINE__)
#else
#define shml(x)
#endif


/* shsi - show string immediate */

#ifdef debug
#define shsi(x)  printf("%s\n",x)
#else
#define shsi(x)
#endif


/* shc - show character */

#ifdef debug
#define shc(x)   printf(#x " = %c\n",x)
#else
#define shc(x)
#endif


/* shs - show string */

#ifdef debug
#define shs(x)   printf(#x " = %s\n",x)
#else
#define shs(x)
#endif


/* shbh - show byte in hex format */

#ifdef debug
#define shbh(x)  printf(#x " = %02Xh\n",x)
#else
#define shbh(x)
#endif


/* shbd - show byte in decimal format */

#ifdef debug
#define shbd(x)  printf(#x " = %d\n",x)
```

LISTING A-3 *(Continued)*

```
#else
#define shbd(x)
#endif


/* shwh - show word (integer) in hex format */

#ifdef debug
#define shwh(x)  printf(#x " = %04Xh\n",x)
#else
#define shwh(x)
#endif


/* shwd - show word (integer) in decimal format */

#ifdef debug
#define shwd(x)  printf(#x " = %d\n",x)
#else
#define shwd(x)
#endif


/* shdso - show dword in seg:ofs format */

#ifdef debug
#define shdso(x) printf(#x " = %04X:%04X\n",DSEG(x),DOFS(x))
#else
#define shdso(x)
#endif


/* shdul - show dword in longint format */

#ifdef debug
#define shdul(x) printf(#x " = %08lXh\n",x.uli)
#else
#define shdul(x)
#endif


/*==== declare the existence of this module */

#define shmacs 1
```

LISTING A-3 *(Continued)*

APPENDIX H
The ASMTYPES.H Data Structures

```
/*==== assembler equivalent storage types ====*/

typedef unsigned char byte;
typedef unsigned int word;

#define a_ofs 0
#define a_seg 1
typedef union {
  word h[2];                    /* access to each half of the ptr */
  byte far *bptr;               /* ptr for a byte operation */
  word far *wptr;               /* ptr for a word operation */
  unsigned long far *lptr;      /* ptr for a long */
  void far *vptr;               /* for ptr to ptr copies */
  long li;                      /* double word numbers */
  void far (*ffptrv)();         /* ptr to far func returning void */
  int far (*ffptri)();          /* ptr to far func returning int */
  } dword;

#define SETDWORD(x,s,o) (x).h[a_seg]=s; (x).h[a_ofs]=o
#define DSEG(x) (x).h[a_seg]
#define DOFS(x) (x).h[a_ofs]

/*==== declare the existence of this module */

#define asmtypes 1
```

LISTING A-4   The ASMTYPES.H data structures.

APPENDIX I
Dump to Video Assembler Macros (DV_ASM.INC)

```
dv_cols    equ    80                      ; # of cols on display
dv_rows    equ    25                      ; # of rows on display

dv_rowbytes equ dv_cols*2                 ; bytes per row
dv_scrbytes equ dv_rowbytes*dv_rows       ; total bytes in screen
```

LISTING A-5   The DV_ASM.INC video instrumentation macros.

```
dv_vidptr        label dword
dv_vidofs        dw        0

ifdef dv_addr
dv_vidseg        dw        dv_addr
else
dv_vidseg        dw        ?
endif

dv_hxtbl         db        '0123456789ABCDEF'


;===========================================================================
;,fs
; DV_CHARI - dump character immediate
;
; Supply the character to be dumped without quotes:
;
; dp_chari x
;
; If no character is specified, a blank space will be dumped
; Using uppercase letters in the A-F range can be confusing when hex
; dumps are also used.
;
;,fe
;===========================================================================
dv_chari macro char
if dv_active eq 1
        pushf

if dv_cli eq 1
        cli
endif

        push    ax
ifnb <char>
        mov     al,'&char&'
else
        mov     al,' '
endif
        call    char2vid
        pop     ax
        popf
endif
        endm
```

(continued on next page)

LISTING A-5 *(Continued)*

```
;===================================================================
;,fs
; DV_CHARAL - dump the character in al
;
;,fe
;===================================================================
dv_charal macro
if dv_active eq 1
        pushf

if dv_cli eq 1
        cli
endif

        call    char2vid
        popf
endif
        endm


;===================================================================
;,fs
; DV_NL - Dump a newline code.
;
;,fe
;===================================================================
dv_nl macro
if dv_active eq 1
        pushf

if dv_cli eq 1
        cli
endif

        push    ax
        mov     al,0ah
        call    char2vid
        mov     al,0dh
        call    char2vid
        pop     ax
        popf
endif
        endm
```

LISTING A-5 *(Continued)*

```
;=====================================================================
;,fs
; DV_BYTE - dump byte in specified register/memory
;
; Examples:
;
; dv_byte cl
; dv_byte [xyz_flag]
;
;,fe
;=====================================================================
dv_byte macro p1,p2
if dv_active eq 1
.errnb <p2>
        pushf

if dv_cli eq 1
        cli
endif

        push    ax
        mov     al,p1
        call    byte2vid
        pop     ax
        popf
endif
        endm


;=====================================================================
;,fs
; DV_WORD - dump word in specified register/memory
;
; Examples:
;
; dv_word di
; dv_word [xyz_cnt]
;
;,fe
;=====================================================================
dv_word macro p1,p2
if dv_active eq 1
.errnb <p2>
        pushf
```

(continued on next page)

LISTING A-5 *(Continued)*

```
if dv_cli eq 1
        cli
endif

        push    ax
        mov     ax,p1
        call    word2vid
        pop     ax
        popf
endif
        endm


;=========================================================================
;,fs
; dv_init - function to set dv_vidseg based on the mode
;
; in:   none
;
; out:  cs:[dv_vidseg] is defined
;
;,fe
;=========================================================================
dv_init:
        push    ax
        push    es
        mov     cs:[dv_vidseg],0b000h
        mov     ax,40h
        mov     es,ax
        cmp     byte ptr es:[49h],7
        je      vs1
        mov     cs:[dv_vidseg],0b800h
vs1:
        pop     es
        pop     ax
        ret


;=========================================================================
; char2vid - direct video output with scrolling
;
; in:   al = the character to display (or cr or lf)
;       uses cs:[dv_vidptr] globally
;
```

LISTING A-5 *(Continued)*

```
; out:   all registers preserved (except flags)
;        [dv_vidofs] updated
;
;======================================================================
char2vid:
        push    ax
        push    di
        push    es
        cmp     al,13
        jne     chv1                    ; if a carriage return
        mov     ax,cs:[dv_vidofs]       ; calc start of row
        push    bx
        push    dx
        xor     dx,dx
        mov     bx,dv_rowbytes
        div     bx
        mul     bx
        pop     dx
        pop     bx
        mov     cs:[dv_vidofs],ax
        jmp     short chv5
chv1:
        cmp     al,10
        jne     chv2                    ; if a linefeed
        add     cs:[dv_vidofs],dv_rowbytes  ; calc next line
        xor     ax,ax
chv2:
        les     di,cs:[dv_vidptr]       ; if dv_vidofs > lim,
        cmp     di,dv_scrbytes          ; scroll the screen
        jb      chv3                    ; and reset [dv_vidofs]
        push    ax
        push    cx
        push    si
        push    ds
        mov     si,es
        mov     ds,si
        mov     si,dv_rowbytes
        xor     di,di
        mov     cx,(dv_scrbytes-dv_rowbytes)/2
        rep     movsw
        mov     di,(dv_scrbytes-dv_rowbytes)
        mov     cx,dv_cols
```

(continued on next page)

LISTING A-5 *(Continued)*

```
        mov     al,20h
        mov     ah,7
        rep     stosw
        mov     di,(dv_scrbytes-dv_rowbytes)
        pop     ds
        pop     si
        pop     cx
        pop     ax
chv3:
        or      ax,ax                           ; if not linefeed
        jz      chv4                            ; display the char
        mov     ah,7
        stosw
chv4:
        mov     cs:[dv_vidofs],di               ; update offset
chv5:
        pop     es
        pop     di
        pop     ax
        ret


;===============================================================
; al2axhex
;
; in:   al = byte to lookup hex chars for
;
; out:  ah = hex char for high nibble of entry al
;       al = hex char for low nibble of entry al
;
;===============================================================
al2axhex:
        push    bx
        push    cx
        mov     cl,al
        xor     ch,ch
        and     ax,000f0h
        shr     ax,1
        shr     ax,1
        shr     ax,1
        shr     ax,1
        mov     bx,ax
        mov     ah,cs:[dv_hxtbl+bx]
```

LISTING A-5 *(Continued)*

```
        and     cx,0000fh
        mov     bx,cx
        mov     al,cs:[dv_hxtbl+bx]
        pop     cx
        pop     bx
        ret

;================================================================
; bw2v_helper
;
; in:   al = byte to convert and display
;
; out:  none
;
;================================================================
bw2v_helper:
        push    ax
        call    al2axhex
        push    ax
        mov     al,ah
        call    char2vid
        pop     ax
        call    char2vid
        pop     ax
        ret

;================================================================
; byte2vid
;
; in:   al = byte to convert and display
;
; out:  none
;
;================================================================
byte2vid:
        call    bw2v_helper
        push    ax
        mov     al,' '
        call    char2vid
        pop     ax
        ret
```

(continued on next page)

LISTING A-5   *(Continued)*

```
;=================================================================
; word2vid
;
; in:   ax = word to convert and display
;
; out:  none
;
;=================================================================
word2vid:
        xchg    ah,al
        call    bw2v_helper
        xchg    ah,al
        call    byte2vid
        ret
```

LISTING A-5 *(Continued)*

```
;$$$$$$$$$$$$$$$$$$$$$$$$$$$$$$$$$$$$$$$$$$$$$$$$$$ from dv_asm.txt $$$$$
if1
%out !!!!!!!!!!!!!!!!!!!!!!!!!!!!!!!!!!!!!!!!!!!!
%out !!!!!!!!!!!!!! dv_asm.inc included !!!!!!!!!
%out !!!!!!!!!!!!!!!!!!!!!!!!!!!!!!!!!!!!!!!!!!!!
endif

; minimum setup requirements:
; the segment of the display buffer must be initialized either by
; calling the dv_init function or by using the dv_addr variable.

dv_active = 01
dv_cli    = 01
;dv_addr  = 0b800h

include c:\xtools\dv_asm.inc
;$$$$$$$$$$$$$$$$$$$$$$$$$$$$$$$$$$$$$$$$$$$$$$$$$$ from dv_asm.txt $$$$$
```

LISTING A-6 DV_ASM.TXT, to be merged into source file.

APPENDIX J
Dump to Video C Functions (DV_C.H and DV_C.INC)

```
#ifndef asmtypes
#include "c:\xtools\asmtypes.h"
#endif

#define dv_cols  80                        /* # of cols on display */
#define dv_rows  25                        /* # of rows on display */

#define dv_rowbytes dv_cols*2              /* bytes per row */
#define dv_scrbytes dv_rowbytes*dv_rows   /* total bytes in screen */
#define dv_lastrow dv_scrbytes-dv_rowbytes   /* ofs of bottom row */

/*==== function prototypes for debugging functions */

dv_access void dv_chari(byte data);
dv_access void dv_byte(byte data);
dv_access void dv_word(word data);
dv_access void dv_init(word vseg);

/*==== declare the existence of this module */

#define dv_c 1
```

LISTING A-7   The DV_C.H header file.

```
static dword dv_vidptr;
static byte dv_hxtbl[] = "0123456789ABCDEF";

/*===================================================================
; static void vid_scroll()
;
; presumes an 80 X 25 display
;
; in:   none
;
; out:  none
;
===================================================================*/
```

(continued on next page)

LISTING A-8   The DV_C.INC video instrumentation functions.

```
static void vid_scroll() {

   byte fill_cnt;
   dword fill_ptr;

   /* copy rows 1 through max to 0 - (max-1) */

   movedata(DSEG(dv_vidptr),dv_rowbytes,DSEG(dv_vidptr),0,
            dv_scrbytes-dv_rowbytes);

   /* fill the bottom line with blanks */

   SETDWORD(fill_ptr,DSEG(dv_vidptr),dv_lastrow);
   for(fill_cnt=0;fill_cnt<dv_cols;fill_cnt++) {
     *fill_ptr.wptr = 0x0720;
     fill_ptr.wptr++;
     }

   /* update the pointer */

   DOFS(dv_vidptr) = dv_lastrow;
   }

/*==================================================================
; static void char2vid(byte data)
;
; Direct video output with scrolling
;
; in:   data = character to display (or a newline)
;
; out:  none
;
==================================================================*/
static void char2vid(byte data) {

  #if dv_active == 01

  if(data == '\n') {
    DOFS(dv_vidptr) = ((DOFS(dv_vidptr)/dv_rowbytes)+1)*dv_rowbytes;
    if(DOFS(dv_vidptr) > dv_lastrow) vid_scroll();
    return;
    }
```

LISTING A-8 *(Continued)*

```
  if(DOFS(dv_vidptr) == dv_scrbytes) vid_scroll();
  *dv_vidptr.wptr = 0x0700 + data;
  dv_vidptr.wptr++;

  #endif
  }


/*==================================================================
;,fs
; void dv_chari(byte data)
;
; Dump character immediate.  Examples:
;
; dp_chari('x');
; dp_chari(char_variable);
;
; in:   data = the character to dump
;
; out:
;
;,fe
==================================================================*/
dv_access void dv_chari(byte data) {

  #if dv_active == 01

  char2vid(data);

  #endif
  }


/*==================================================================
;,fs
; void dv_nl()
;
; Dump new line
;
; in:
;
; out:
;
;,fe
==================================================================*/
```

(continued on next page)

LISTING A-8   *(Continued)*

```
dv_access void dv_nl() {

  #if dv_active == 01

  char2vid('\n');

  #endif
  }


/*======================================================================
;,fs
; void dv_byte(byte data)
;
; Dump a byte.  Examples:
;
; dv_byte(byte_variable);
;
; in: data = the byte to dump
;
; out:
;
;,fe
======================================================================*/
dv_access void dv_byte(byte data) {

  #if dv_active == 01

  char2vid(dv_hxtbl[(data >> 4)]);
  char2vid(dv_hxtbl[(data & 0xf)]);
  char2vid(' ');

  #endif
  }


/*======================================================================
;,fs
; void dv_word(word data)
;
; Dump a word.  Examples:
;
; dv_word(word_variable);
;
```

LISTING A-8 *(Continued)*

```
; in: data = the word to dump
;
; out:
;
;,fe
=================================================================*/
dv_access void dv_word(word data) {

  #if dv_active == 01

  char2vid(dv_hxtbl[(data >> 12)]);
  char2vid(dv_hxtbl[((data >> 8) & 0xf)]);
  char2vid(dv_hxtbl[((data >> 4) & 0xf)]);
  char2vid(dv_hxtbl[(data & 0xf)]);
  char2vid(' ');

  #endif
  }

/*=================================================================
;,fs
; void dv_init(word vseg)
;
; Define the video buffer segment.
;
; NOTE: this function should only be called once.
;
; in:    vseg = 0 if actual video buffer segment should be determined
;        vseg = 0xb000 or 0xb800 for that specific value
;
; out:
;
;,fe
=================================================================*/
dv_access void dv_init(word vseg) {

  #if dv_active == 01

  dword xptr;

  DOFS(dv_vidptr) = 0;
```

(continued on next page)

LISTING A-8 *(Continued)*

```
if(vseg != 0) {
  DSEG(dv_vidptr) = vseg;
  }   else {
  SETDWORD(xptr,0x40,0x49);
  DSEG(dv_vidptr) = 0xB000;
  if(*xptr.bptr != 7) {
    DSEG(dv_vidptr) = 0xB800;
    }
  }

#endif
}
```

LISTING A-8   *(Continued)*

```
/*$$$$$$$$$$$$$$$$$$$$$$$$$$$$$$$$$$$$$$$$$$$$$$$ from dv_c.txt $$$$$*/

/* NOTE: mem.h must be included here if not already included. */

/* #include <mem.h> */

#define dv_active 01
#define dv_access static
#include "c:\xtools\dv_c.h"

/*$$$$$$$$$$$$$$$$$$$$$$$$$$$$$$$$$$$$$$$$$$$$$$$ from dv_c.txt $$$$$*/


/*$$$$$$$$$$$$$$$$$$$$$$$$$$$$$$$$$$$$$$$$$$$$$$$ from dv_c.txt $$$$$*/

#include "c:\xtools\dv_c.inc"

/*$$$$$$$$$$$$$$$$$$$$$$$$$$$$$$$$$$$$$$$$$$$$$$$ from dv_c.txt $$$$$*/
```

LISTING A-9   DV_C.TXT, to be merged into source file.

APPENDIX K
Dump to Parallel Assembler Macros (`DP_ASM.INC` and `DP_ASM.TXT`)

```
;=====================================================================
;,fs
; DP_CHARI - Dump character immediate
;
; Supply the character to be dumped right after the macro name.
; Do not use quote marks.
;
; dp_chari x
; dp_chari (
;
; If no character is specified, a blank space will be dumped
; Using uppercase letters in the A-F range can be confusing when hex
; dumps are also used.
;
;,fe
;=====================================================================
dp_chari macro char
if dp_active eq 1
        pushf

if dp_cli eq 1
        cli
endif

        push    ax
ifnb <char>
        mov     al,'&char&'
else
        mov     al,' '
endif
        call    char2par
        pop     ax
        popf
endif
        endm
```

(continued on next page)

LISTING A-10 The `DP_ASM.INC` parallel instrumentation macros.

```
;===================================================================
;,fs
; DP_CHARAL - Dump the character in the AL register.
;
;,fe
;===================================================================
dp_charal macro
if dp_active eq 1
        pushf

if dp_cli eq 1
        cli
endif


        push    ax
        call    char2par
        pop     ax
        popf
endif
        endm


;===================================================================
;,fs
; DP_NL - Dump a newline code.
;
;,fe
;===================================================================
dp_nl macro
if dp_active eq 1
        pushf

if dp_cli eq 1
        cli
endif


        push    ax
        mov     al,0ah
        call    char2par
        pop     ax
        popf
endif
        endm
```

LISTING A-10 *(Continued)*

```
;=================================================================
;,fs
; DP_BYTE - Dump byte from specified register or memory location.
;
; Supply any operand to this macro which would be valid as an
; operand to an instruction such as "mov al,?".
; Use <> characters to enclose a multi-term operand.
;
; dp_byte cl
; dp_byte [xyz_flag]
; dp_byte <byte ptr es:[17h]>
;
;,fe
;=================================================================
dp_byte macro p1,p2
if dp_active eq 1
.errnb <p2>
        pushf

if dp_cli eq 1
        cli
endif

        push    ax
        mov     al,p1
        call    byte2par
        pop     ax
        popf
endif
        endm


;=================================================================
;,fs
; DP_WORD - Dump word from specified register or memory location.
;
; Supply any operand to this macro which would be valid as an
; operand to an instruction such as "mov ax,?".
; Use <> characters to enclose a multi-term operand.
;
; dp_word di
; dp_word [xyz_cnt]
; dp_word <word ptr es:[6ch]>
;
```

(continued on next page)

LISTING A-10   *(Continued)*

```
;,fe
;===============================================================
dp_word macro p1,p2
if dp_active eq 1
.errnb <p2>
        pushf

if dp_cli eq 1
        cli
endif

        push    ax
        mov     ax,p1
        call    word2par
        pop     ax
        popf
endif
        endm

if dp_active eq 1


;===============================================================
;,fs
;
; the value of dp_addr must be defined where this module is included
; in a source file.  for example:
;
; dp_addr = 03bch
; include dp.inc
;
;,fe
;===============================================================

paraddr dw      dp_addr


;===============================================================
; char2par - direct parallel output
;
; in:   al = the character to xmit
;       uses cs:[paraddr] globally
;
; out:  all registers preserved (except flags)
;
;===============================================================
```

LISTING A-10 *(Continued)*

```
char2par:
        push    ax
        push    dx
        mov     dx,cs:[paraddr]

if dp_binary eq 0

;=============================== character mode output (to a printer)

; output the data

        out     dx,al

; loop until printer status is good

        inc     dx
c2p1:
        in      al,dx
        jmp    ·$+2
        jmp     $+2
        and     al,0b8h
        xor     al,98h
        jnz     c2p1

; raise the strobe

        inc     dx
        mov     al,0dh
        out     dx,al
        jmp     $+2
        jmp     $+2

; lower the strobe again

        mov     al,0ch
        out     dx,al
        jmp     $+2
        jmp     $+2
else

;======================== binary mode output (to another computer)

        push    ax
        inc     dx
```

(continued on next page)

LISTING A-10   *(Continued)*

```
; loop until busy == 1

cp1:
        in      al,dx
        jmp     $+2
        jmp     $+2
        test    al,80h
        jz      cp1
        pop     ax
        pushf
        cli

; output the data

        dec     dx
        out     dx,al

; toggle the strobe bit

        add     dx,2
        in      al,dx
        jmp     $+2
        jmp     $+2
        xor     al,1
        out     dx,al
        jmp     $+2
        jmp     $+2

; loop until busy == 0

        dec     dx
cp2:
        in      al,dx
        jmp     $+2
        jmp     $+2
        test    al,80h
        jnz     cp2
        popf

endif

        pop     dx
        pop     ax
        ret
```

LISTING A-10 *(Continued)*

```
;==================================================================
; al2axhex
;
; in:   al = byte to lookup hex chars for
;
; out:  ah = hex char for high nibble of entry al
;       al = hex char for low nibble of entry al
;
;==================================================================

hxtbl   db      '0123456789ABCDEF'

al2axhex:
        push    bx
        push    cx
        mov     cl,al
        xor     ch,ch
        and     ax,000f0h
        shr     ax,1
        shr     ax,1
        shr     ax,1
        shr     ax,1
        mov     bx,ax
        mov     ah,cs:[hxtbl+bx]
        and     cx,0000fh
        mov     bx,cx
        mov     al,cs:[hxtbl+bx]
        pop     cx
        pop     bx
        ret

;==================================================================
; bw2v_helper
;
; in:   al = byte to convert and display
;
; out:  none
;
;==================================================================
bw2v_helper:
        push    ax
        call    al2axhex
        push    ax
```

(continued on next page)

LISTING A-10 *(Continued)*

```
        mov     al,ah
        mov     ah,7
        call    char2par
        pop     ax
        mov     ah,7
        call    char2par
        pop     ax
        ret


;================================================================
; byte2par
;
; in:   al = byte to convert and display
;
; out:  none
;
;================================================================
byte2par:
        call    bw2v_helper
        push    ax
        mov     al,' '
        mov     ah,7
        call    char2par
        pop     ax
        ret


;================================================================
; word2par
;
; in:   ax = word to convert and display
;
; out:  none
;
;================================================================
word2par:
        xchg    ah,al
        call    bw2v_helper
        xchg    ah,al
        call    byte2par
        ret


        endif
```

LISTING A-10 *(Continued)*

```
;$$$$$$$$$$$$$$$$$$$$$$$$$$$$$$$$$$$$$$$$$$$$$$$$ from dp_asm.txt $$$$$
if1
%out !!!!!!!!!!!!!!!!!!!!!!!!!!!!!!!!!!!!!!!!!!!!!
%out !!!!!!!!!!!!!! dp_asm.inc included !!!!!!!!!
%out !!!!!!!!!!!!!!!!!!!!!!!!!!!!!!!!!!!!!!!!!!!!!
endif

dp_active = 01
dp_cli    = 01
dp_binary = 01
dp_addr   = 03bch

; if dp_active is set to 0, all instrumentation macros,
; common functions and data will be nullified.
;
; if dp_cli is set to 1, each macro will include code to
; save the current interrupt flag state, disable interrupts
; and then restore interrupts after the dump.
;
; if dp_binary is set to 1, the binary machine to machine
; link protocol will be used, where CHANNEL.EXE is run in
; the remote machine.
; if dp_binary is set to 0, a parallel printer should be
; connected to the port.
;
; dp_addr must be set to the base address of the parallel port.


include c:\xtools\dp_asm.inc
;$$$$$$$$$$$$$$$$$$$$$$$$$$$$$$$$$$$$$$$$$$$$$$$$ from dp_asm.txt $$$$$
```

LISTING A-11 `DP_ASM.TXT`, to be merged into source file.

APPENDIX L
Dump to Parallel C Functions (DP_C.H and DP_C.INC)

```c
#ifndef asmtypes
#include "c:\xtools\asmtypes.h"
#endif

/*==== function prototypes for debugging functions */

dp_access void dp_chari(byte data);
dp_access void dp_byte(byte data);
dp_access void dp_word(word data);
dp_access void dp_init(word paddr);

/*==== declare the existence of this module */

#define dp_c 1
```

LISTING A-12   DP_C.H header file.

```c
static word dp_paraddr;                    /* port address */
static byte dp_hxtbl[] = "0123456789ABCDEF";

/*=====================================================================
; word lc_disablep()
;
; in:   none
;
; out:  retval = previous flags register value
;
;=====================================================================*/
static word dp_disablep() {

    /* embed the machine code for the following instructions:

            pushf
            pop ax
            cli
    */

    __emit__(0x9c,0x58,0xfa);
}
```

LISTING A-13   The DP_C.INC parallel instrumentation macros.

```
/*======================================================================
; void dp_enablep(word old_flgs)
;
; counterbalance for lc_disablp().
;
; in:   flgs = original cpu flags value
;
; out:
;
;====================================================================*/
static void dp_enablep(word old_flgs) {

   /* embed the machine code for the following instructions:

        mov ax,[old_flgs]       ; [bp+4] for small model
        push ax
        popf
   */

   __emit__(0x8b,0x46,&old_flgs,0x50,0x9d);
   }


/*======================================================================
; static void char2par(byte data)
;
; Direct parallel output
;
; in:   data = character to transmit
;
; out:  none
;
=====================================================================*/
static void char2par(byte data) {

  #if dp_active == 01

  #if dp_binary == 0

  /*==== character mode output (to a parallel printer) */

  outportb(dp_paraddr,data);                      /* write char to port */
  while((inportb(dp_paraddr+1) & 0xb8) ^ 0x98);   /* loop til clear */
  outportb(dp_paraddr+2,0xd);                     /* raise the strobe */
  outportb(dp_paraddr+2,0xc);                     /* and lower it again */
```
(continued on next page)

LISTING A-13 *(Continued)*

```
#else

/*==== binary mode output (to another computer) */

word flgs;

while((inportb(dp_paraddr+1) & 0x80) == 0);  /* until busy == 1 */
flgs = dp_disablep();
outportb(dp_paraddr,data);                        /* write char to port */
outportb(dp_paraddr+2,(inportb(dp_paraddr+2) ^ 1)); /* tgl strb */
while(inportb(dp_paraddr+1) & 0x80);     /* loop until busy == 0 */
dp_enablep(flgs);

#endif

#endif
 }


/*======================================================================
;,fs
; void dp_chari(byte data)
;
; Dump character immediate.
;
; For example:
;
; dp_chari('x');
; dp_chari(char_variable);
;
; in:   data = the character to dump
;
; out:
;
;,fe
=======================================================================*/
dp_access void dp_chari(byte data) {

  #if dp_active == 01

  char2par(data);

  #endif
 }
```

LISTING A-13 *(Continued)*

```
/*=================================================================
;,fs
; void dp_nl()
;
; Dump new line
;
; For example:
;
; dp_nl();
;
; in:
;
; out:
;
;,fe
==================================================================*/
dp_access void dp_nl() {

  #if dp_active == 01

  #if dp_binary == 0
  char2par(0x0d);
  #endif

  char2par(0x0a);

  #endif
  }


/*=================================================================
;,fs
; void dp_byte(byte data)
;
; Dump a byte
;
; Examples:
;
; dp_byte(byte_variable);
;
; in:   data = the byte to dump
;
; out:
```

(continued on next page)

LISTING A-13 *(Continued)*

```
;
;,fe
===================================================================*/
dp_access void dp_byte(byte data) {

  #if dp_active == 01

  char2par(dp_hxtbl[(data >> 4)]);
  char2par(dp_hxtbl[(data & 0xf)]);
  char2par(' ');

  #endif
  }


/*===================================================================
;,fs
; void dp_word(word data)
;
; Dump a word
;
; Examples:
;
; dp_word(word_variable);
;
; in:   data = the word to dump
;
; out:
;
;,fe
===================================================================*/
dp_access void dp_word(word data) {

  #if dp_active == 01

  char2par(dp_hxtbl[(data >> 12)]);
  char2par(dp_hxtbl[((data >> 8) & 0xf)]);
  char2par(dp_hxtbl[((data >> 4) & 0xf)]);
  char2par(dp_hxtbl[(data & 0xf)]);
  char2par(' ');

  #endif
  }
```

LISTING A-13   *(Continued)*

```
/*================================================================
;,fs
; void dp_init(word saddr)
;
; init local/private variables to support parallel port output.
;
; in:   paddr = the parallel port's base address
;
; out:
;
;,fe
================================================================*/
dp_access void dp_init(word paddr) {

   #if dp_active == 01

   dp_paraddr = paddr;

   #endif
   }
```

LISTING A-13   *(Continued)*


```
/*$$$$$$$$$$$$$$$$$$$$$$$$$$$$$$$$$$$$$$$$$$$$$$$$ from dp_c.txt $$$$$*/

/* NOTE: dos.h must be included here if not already included. */

/* #include <dos.h> */

#define dp_active 01
#define dp_binary 0
#define dp_access static
#include "c:\xtools\dp_c.h"

/*

if dp_active is set to 0, all instrumentation functions and
data will be nullified.

if dp_binary is set to 1, the binary machine to machine
link protocol will be used, where CHANNEL.EXE is run in
the remote machine.
```

(continued on next page)

LISTING A-14   DP_C.TXT, to be merged into source file.

```
if dp_binary is set to 0, a parallel printer should be connected to
the port.

NOTE!: one call to the dp_init() function must be made before any
serial output is done.  The prototype is:

dp_init(word paddr);

        paddr = the parallel port's base address

*/


/*$$$$$$$$$$$$$$$$$$$$$$$$$$$$$$$$$$$$$$$$$$$$$$$ from dp_c.txt $$$$$*/


/*$$$$$$$$$$$$$$$$$$$$$$$$$$$$$$$$$$$$$$$$$$$$$$$ from dp_c.txt $$$$$*/

#include "c:\xtools\dp_c.inc"

/*$$$$$$$$$$$$$$$$$$$$$$$$$$$$$$$$$$$$$$$$$$$$$$$ from dp_c.txt $$$$$*/
```

LISTING A-14   *(Continued)*

APPENDIX M
Dump to Serial Assembler Macros (DS_ASM.INC and DS_ASM.TXT)

```
; use one of these values for the ax entry
; parameter to the ds_init function.

b12     equ     96      ;    1,200
b24     equ     48      ;    2,400
b48     equ     24      ;    4,800
b96     equ     12      ;    9,600
b19     equ     6       ;   19,200
b38     equ     3       ;   38,400
b57     equ     2       ;   57,600
b11     equ     1       ;  115,200
```

LISTING A-15   The DS_ASM.INC serial instrumentation macros.

```
;=====================================================================
;,fs
; DS_CHARI - Dump character immediate
;
; Supply the character to be dumped right after the macro name.
; Do not use quote marks.
;
; ds_chari x
; ds_chari (
;
; If no character is specified, a blank space will be dumped
; Using uppercase letters in the A-F range can be confusing when hex
; dumps are also used.
;
;,fe
;=====================================================================
ds_chari macro char
if ds_active eq 1
        pushf

if ds_cli eq 1
        cli
endif

        push    ax
ifnb <char>
        mov     al,'&char&'
else
        mov     al,' '
endif
        call    char2ser
        pop     ax
        popf
endif
        endm


;=====================================================================
;,fs
; DS_CHARAL - Dump the character in the AL register.
;
;,fe
;=====================================================================
```

(continued on next page)

LISTING A-15   *(Continued)*

```
ds_charal macro
if ds_active eq 1
        pushf

if ds_cli eq 1
        cli
endif

        call    char2ser
        popf
endif
        endm


;================================================================
;,fs
; DS_NL - Dump newline codes.
;
;,fe
;================================================================
ds_nl macro
if ds_active eq 1
        pushf

if ds_cli eq 1
        cli
endif

        push    ax

if ds_binary eq 0
        mov     al,0dh
        call    char2ser
endif

        mov     al,0ah
        call    char2ser
        pop     ax
        popf
endif
        endm


;================================================================
;,fs
; DS_BYTE - Dump byte from specified register or memory location.
```

LISTING A-15 *(Continued)*

```
;
; Supply any operand to this macro which would be valid as an
; operand to an instruction such as "mov al,?".
; Use <> characters to enclose a multi-term operand.
;
; ds_byte cl
; ds_byte [xyz_flag]
; ds_byte <byte ptr es:[17h]>
;
;,fe
;=====================================================================
ds_byte macro p1,p2
if ds_active eq 1
.errnb <p2>
        pushf

if ds_cli eq 1
        cli
endif

        push    ax
        mov     al,p1
        call    byte2ser
        pop     ax
        popf
endif
        endm


;=====================================================================
;,fs
; DS_WORD - Dump word from specified register or memory location.
;
; Supply any operand to this macro which would be valid as an
; operand to an instruction such as "mov ax,?".
; Use <> characters to enclose a multi-term operand.
;
; ds_word di
; ds_word [xyz_cnt]
; ds_word <word ptr es:[6ch]>
;
;,fe
;=====================================================================
```

(continued on next page)

LISTING A-15 *(Continued)*

```
ds_word macro p1,p2
if ds_active eq 1
.errnb <p2>
        pushf

if ds_cli eq 1
        cli
endif

        push    ax
        mov     ax,p1
        call    word2ser
        pop     ax
        popf
endif
        endm


if ds_active eq 1


;=====================================================================
;,fs
;
; the value of ds_addr must be defined where this module is included
; in a source file.  for example:
;
; ds_addr = 03f8h
; include ds.inc
;
;,fe
;=====================================================================


seraddr dw      ds_addr


;=====================================================================
;,fs
; ds_init - setup the uart
;
; use one of the following for the ax entry value:
;
;  b12    equ     96      ;   1,200
;  b24    equ     48      ;   2,400
;  b48    equ     24      ;   4,800
;  b96    equ     12      ;   9,600
;  b19    equ     6       ;  19,200
```

LISTING A-15 *(Continued)*

```
;   b38    equ      3        ;   38,400
;   b57    equ      2        ;   57,600
;   b11    equ      1        ;  115,200
;
; in:   ax = baud rate divisor value
;
; out
;
;,,fe
;=======================================================================
ds_init:
        pushf                           ; save current int flag
        cli                             ; no interrupts now
        push    ax
        push    cx
        push    dx
        mov     cx,ax
        mov     dx,cs:[seraddr]
        add     dx,3                    ; point to lcr
        mov     al,83h                  ; set dlab=1, 8 data,
        out     dx,al                   ; 1 stop and no parity
        sub     dx,3
        mov     ax,cx
        out     dx,al                   ; set divisor lsb
        xchg    al,ah
        inc     dx
        out     dx,al                   ; set divisor msb
        add     dx,2                    ; point to lcr
        mov     al,03h                  ; set dlab=0, 8 data,
        out     dx,al                   ; 1 stop and no parity
        pop     dx
        pop     cx
        pop     ax
        popf                            ; restore interrupt flag
        ret


;=======================================================================
; char2ser - direct serial output
;
; in:   al = the character to xmit
;
; out:  all registers preserved (except flags)
;
;=======================================================================
```

(continued on next page)

LISTING A-15 *(Continued)*

```
char2ser:
        push    ax
        push    dx
        mov     dx,cs:[seraddr]
        mov     ah,al

if ds_binary eq 0

;======================= character mode output (to a serial terminal)

; if the data-available bit is set, read the input data.
; if the data byte is the xoff character, keep polling the port
; until a non-xoff character is found (presumably an xon).

        add     dx,5
        in      al,dx
        jmp     $+2
        jmp     $+2
        test    al,1
        jz      x2
        sub     dx,5
x1:
        in      al,dx
        jmp     $+2
        jmp     $+2
        and     al,7fh
        cmp     al,13h
        je      x1
        add     dx,5
x2:

; now, check the transmitter-empty bit and keep polling if it is not
; set.  must wait for the previous character to clear the transmit
; register before writing the next character.

        in      al,dx
        jmp     $+2
        jmp     $+2
        test    al,20h
        jz      x2
        sub     dx,5
```

LISTING A-15   *(Continued)*

```
; finally ready to write the data to the transmit buffer.

        mov     al,ah
        out     dx,al

else

;========================= binary mode output (to another computer)

        add     dx,6
        in      al,dx
        jmp     $+2
        jmp     $+2
        xchg    ah,al
        and     ah,10h
        sub     dx,6
        out     dx,al
        jmp     $+2
        jmp     $+2
        add     dx,6
x3:
        in      al,dx
        and     al,10h
        cmp     al,ah
        je      x3
endif

        pop     dx
        pop     ax
        ret


;======================================================================
; al2axhex
;
; in:   al = byte to lookup hex chars for
;
; out:  ah = hex char for high nibble of entry al
;       al = hex char for low nibble of entry al
;
;======================================================================
```

(continued on next page)

LISTING A-15   *(Continued)*

```
hxtbl    db       '0123456789ABCDEF'

al2axhex:
         push    bx
         push    cx
         mov     cl,al
         xor     ch,ch
         and     ax,000f0h
         shr     ax,1
         shr     ax,1
         shr     ax,1
         shr     ax,1
         mov     bx,ax
         mov     ah,cs:[hxtbl+bx]
         and     cx,0000fh
         mov     bx,cx
         mov     al,cs:[hxtbl+bx]
         pop     cx
         pop     bx
         ret


;================================================================
; bw2v_helper
;
; in:   al = byte to convert and display
;
; out:  none
;
;================================================================
bw2v_helper:
         push    ax
         call    al2axhex
         push    ax
         mov     al,ah
         mov     ah,7
         call    char2ser
         pop     ax
         mov     ah,7
         call    char2ser
         pop     ax
         ret
```

LISTING A-15 *(Continued)*

```
;================================================================
; byte2ser
;
; in:   al = byte to convert and display
;
; out:  none
;
;================================================================
byte2ser:
        call    bw2v_helper
        push    ax
        mov     al,' '
        mov     ah,7
        call    char2ser
        pop     ax
        ret


;================================================================
; word2ser
;
; in:   ax = word to convert and display
;
; out:  none
;
;================================================================
word2ser:
        xchg    ah,al
        call    bw2v_helper
        xchg    ah,al
        call    byte2ser
        ret

endif
```

LISTING A-15 *(Continued)*

```
;$$$$$$$$$$$$$$$$$$$$$$$$$$$$$$$$$$$$$$$$$$$$$$$$$ from ds_asm.txt $$$$$
if1
%out !!!!!!!!!!!!!!!!!!!!!!!!!!!!!!!!!!!!!!!!!!!!!!
%out !!!!!!!!!!!!! ds_asm.inc included !!!!!!!!!!
%out !!!!!!!!!!!!!!!!!!!!!!!!!!!!!!!!!!!!!!!!!!!!!!
endif

ds_active = 01
ds_cli    = 01
ds_binary = 0
ds_addr   = 03f8h

; if ds_active is set to 0, all instrumentation macros,
; common functions and data will be nullified.
;
; if ds_cli is set to 1, each macro will include code to
; save the current interrupt flag state, disable interrupts
; and then restore interrupts after the dump.
;
; if ds_binary is set to 1, the binary machine to machine
; link protocol will be used, where CHANNEL.EXE is run in
; the remote machine.
; if ds_binary is set to 0, a serial terminal should be
; connected to the port.
;
; ds_addr must be set to the base address of the serial port.
;
; NOTE!: one call to the ser_init function must be made before
; any serial output is done.
;
; use one of these values for the ax entry
; parameter to the ds_init function.
;
; b12    equ    96    ;    1,200
; b24    equ    48    ;    2,400
; b48    equ    24    ;    4,800
; b96    equ    12    ;    9,600
; b19    equ    6     ;   19,200
; b38    equ    3     ;   38,400
; b57    equ    2     ;   57,600
; b11    equ    1     ;  115,200

include c:\xtools\ds_asm.inc
;$$$$$$$$$$$$$$$$$$$$$$$$$$$$$$$$$$$$$$$$$$$$$$$$$ from ds_asm.txt $$$$$
```

LISTING A-16 DS_ASM.TXT, to be merged into source file.

APPENDIX N
Dump to Serial C Functions (DS_C.H and DS_C.INC)

```
#ifndef asmtypes
#include "c:\xtools\asmtypes.h"
#endif

#define b12      96      /*   1,200 baud */
#define b24      48      /*   2,400 baud */
#define b48      24      /*   4,800 baud */
#define b96      12      /*   9,600 baud */
#define b19       6      /*  19,200 baud */
#define b38       3      /*  38,400 baud */
#define b57       2      /*  57,400 baud */
#define b11       1      /* 115,200 baud */

/*==== function prototypes for debugging functions */

ds_access void ds_chari(byte data);
ds_access void ds_byte(byte data);
ds_access void ds_word(word data);
ds_access void ds_init(word saddr, word sbdiv, byte xoff_code);

/*==== declare the existence of this module */

#define ds_c 1
```

LISTING A-17 The DS_C.H header file.

```
static byte ds_serxoff;                    /* xoff handshaking char */
static word ds_seraddr;                    /* port address */
static byte ds_hxtbl[] = "0123456789ABCDEF";

/*=================================================================
; static void char2ser(byte data)
;
; Direct serial output
;
; in:   data = character to transmit
;
; out:  none
;
=================================================================*/
```

(continued on next page)

LISTING A-18 The DS_C.INC serial instrumentation macros.

```
static void char2ser(byte data) {

  #if ds_active == 01

  byte cts_state;

  #if ds_binary == 0

  /*==== character mode output (to a serial terminal) */

  /* if data is available, loop while the data is the xoff code */

  if(inportb(ds_seraddr+5) & 1) {
    while((inportb(ds_seraddr) & 0x7f) == ds_serxoff);
    }

  /* now, loop until the transmitter empty bit is set.
  then, its time to output the character. */

  while(!(inportb(ds_seraddr+5) & 0x20));
  outportb(ds_seraddr,data);

  #else

  /*==== binary mode output (to another computer) */

  /* read the initial cts state and then output the character */
  cts_state = inportb(ds_seraddr+6) & 0x10;
  outportb(ds_seraddr,data);

  /* wait until the cts line toggles */

  while(cts_state == (inportb(ds_seraddr+6) & 0x10));

  #endif

  #endif
  }

/*=====================================================================
;,fs
; void ds_chari(byte data)
;
; Dump character immediate.
```

LISTING A-18 *(Continued)*

```
;
; For example:
;
; dp_chari('x');
; dp_chari(char_variable);
;
; in:   data = the character to dump
;
; out:
;
;,fe
=================================================================*/
ds_access void ds_chari(byte data) {

  #if ds_active == 01

  char2ser(data);

  #endif
  }


/*================================================================
;,fs
; void ds_nl()
;
; Dump new line
;
; For example:
;
; dp_nl();
;
; in:
;
; out:
;
;,fe
=================================================================*/
ds_access void ds_nl() {

  #if ds_active == 01

  #if ds_binary == 0
  char2ser(0x0d);
  #endif
```

(continued on next page)

LISTING A-18 *(Continued)*

```
  char2ser(0x0a);

  #endif
  }


/*=======================================================================
;,fs
; void ds_byte(byte data)
;
; Dump a byte
;
; Examples:
;
; ds_byte(byte_variable);
;
; in:   data = the byte to dump
;
; out:
;
;,fe
========================================================================*/
ds_access void ds_byte(byte data) {

  #if ds_active == 01

  char2ser(ds_hxtbl[(data >> 4)]);
  char2ser(ds_hxtbl[(data & 0xf)]);
  char2ser(' ');

  #endif
  }


/*=======================================================================
;,fs
; void ds_word(word data)
;
; Dump a word
;
; Examples:
;
; ds_word(word_variable);
;
; in: data = the word to dump
;
```

LISTING A-18 *(Continued)*

```
; out:
;
;,fe
=====================================================================*/
ds_access void ds_word(word data) {

  #if ds_active == 01

  char2ser(ds_hxtbl[(data >> 12)]);
  char2ser(ds_hxtbl[((data >> 8) & 0xf)]);
  char2ser(ds_hxtbl[((data >> 4) & 0xf)]);
  char2ser(ds_hxtbl[(data & 0xf)]);
  char2ser(' ');

  #endif
  }


/*===================================================================
;,fs
; void ds_init(word saddr, word sbdiv, byte xoff_code)
;
; initialize local/private variables to support serial port output.
; the port's baud rate is set and a framing of 8 data bits,
; 1 stop bit and no parity is established.
;
; baud rate divisors are defined within ds_c.h.  They are:
;
; #define b12    96        1,200 baud
; #define b24    48        2,400 baud
; #define b48    24        4,800 baud
; #define b96    12        9,600 baud
; #define b19    6        19,200 baud
; #define b38    3        38,400 baud
; #define b57    2        57,400 baud
; #define b11    1       115,200 baud
;
; in:   saddr = the serial port's base address
;       sbdiv = the baud rate divisor
;       xoff_code = xoff handshaking code (normally 0x13)
;
; out:
;
;,fe
=====================================================================*/
```

(continued on next page)

LISTING A-18   *(Continued)*

```
ds_access void ds_init(word saddr, word sbdiv, byte xoff_code) {

  #if ds_active == 01

  ds_seraddr = saddr;
  ds_serxoff = xoff_code;

  outportb(ds_seraddr+3,0x83);             /* set dlab=1 */
  outportb(ds_seraddr,(sbdiv & 0x00ff));   /* set divisor lsb */
  outportb(ds_seraddr+1,(sbdiv >> 8));     /* set divisor msb */
  outportb(ds_seraddr+3,3);                /* dlab=0, 8 data */
                                           /* 1 stop, no parity */

  #endif
  }
```

LISTING A-18   *(Continued)*


```
/*$$$$$$$$$$$$$$$$$$$$$$$$$$$$$$$$$$$$$$$$$$$$$$$ from ds_c.txt $$$$$*/

/* NOTE: dos.h must be included here if not already included. */

/* #include <dos.h> */

#define ds_active 01
#define ds_binary 0
#define ds_access static
#include "c:\xtools\ds_c.h"

/*

if ds_active is set to 0, all instrumentation functions and data
will be nullified.

if ds_binary is set to 1, the binary machine to machine link
protocol will be used, where CHANNEL.EXE is run in the remote
machine.

if ds_binary is set to 0, a serial terminal should be connected to
the port.

NOTE!: one call to the ds_init() function must be made before any
serial output is done.  The prototype is:
```

LISTING A-19   DS_C.TXT, to be merged into source file.

```
ds_init(word saddr, word sbdiv, byte xoff_code)

        saddr = the serial port's base address
        sbdiv = the baud rate divisor
        xoff_code = xoff handshaking code (normally 0x13)

use one of these values for the sbdiv parameter:

#define b12     96      /*    1,200 baud */
#define b24     48      /*    2,400 baud */
#define b48     24      /*    4,800 baud */
#define b96     12      /*    9,600 baud */
#define b19     6       /*   19,200 baud */
#define b38     3       /*   38,400 baud */
#define b57     2       /*   57,400 baud */
#define b11     1       /*  115,200 baud */

*/

/*$$$$$$$$$$$$$$$$$$$$$$$$$$$$$$$$$$$$$$$$$$$$$$$ from ds_c.txt $$$$$*/

/*$$$$$$$$$$$$$$$$$$$$$$$$$$$$$$$$$$$$$$$$$$$$$$$ from ds_c.txt $$$$$*/

#include "c:\xtools\ds_c.inc"

/*$$$$$$$$$$$$$$$$$$$$$$$$$$$$$$$$$$$$$$$$$$$$$$$ from ds_c.txt $$$$$*/
```

LISTING A-19   *(Continued)*

APPENDIX O
Switch Parameters for ROUTER.SYS

Switch Parameters for Data Output Routing

/VI   The /VI switch will activate dumping to the main video display. The use of this option will cause ROUTER.SYS to determine the address of the video adapter itself.

If the video mode value at BIOS data address 0040:0049 is 7 (for a monochrome system), then dumping will be done to the monochrome display buffer at address B000:0000. Otherwise, the display buffer address B800:0 will be used. This is the base address of the text mode buffer for a CGA, EGA, or VGA card. Graphics modes are not supported.

/VS=hhhh   This switch activates dumping to video display memory using a specific video segment. It would be used when two display adapters and monitors are installed within a system: a monochrome adapter/monitor, and a CGA, EGA, or VGA adapter with appropriate monitor.

If the CGA, EGA, or VGA adapter is used as the main display, specify /VS=B000 to route instrumentation output to the monochrome display. If the monochrome display is the main one, specify /VS=B800 to route dump output to the color display.

/SR=hhhh,dd   The /SR switch specifies serial transmission of dump output in character mode. An ASCII terminal should be connected to the serial port and configured for the XON/XOFF protocol and a baud rate that matches the one specified by this switch. The terminal should also be configured to wrap display output to the next line automatically when the end of one line is reached. A simple three-wire serial cable, where the TX and RX lines are crossed, should suffice.

The first term after the /SR= is the address of the serial port. The second term specifies the baud rate in the following format:

11 for 115,200
57 for 57,600
38 for 38,400
19 for 19,200
96 for   9600
48 for   4800
24 for   2400
12 for   1200

For example, to activate dumping through the 03F8 port at 9600 baud, specify the following:

/SR=03F8,96

/SB=hhhh,dd   The /SB switch directs ROUTER.SYS to output to a serial port in a binary data format. This is designed only for use with the CHANNEL.EXE data capture utility in a two-computer setup. The port address and baud rate value are specified exactly as described for the /SR parameter just described.

A serial crossover cable that supports the proper hardware handshaking connections is required. See Appendix F, "Constructing Parallel and Serial Link Cables," for wiring details.

/PP=hhhh   Use this switch to activate dumping to a standard parallel printer. The term after the /PP= is the address of the parallel port. Use a debugger to dump the BIOS data table at address 0040:0008 to see what ports are installed in your machine. A normal parallel printer cable should be used.

/PB=hhhh The /PB switch directs ROUTER.SYS to output to a parallel port in a binary data format. This is designed only for use with the CHANNEL.EXE data capture utility in a two-computer setup. The port address is specified exactly as just described for the /PP parameter.

A special parallel crossover cable is required. See Appendix F, "Constructing Parallel and Serial Link Cables," for wiring details.

/PR=hhhh This switch tells ROUTER.SYS to allocate a Packetized Ring Buffer (PRB) of the specified size and activate dumping to it. A hex number is used to specify the number of bytes of memory to allocate to the ring buffer. The CHANNEL.EXE utility is used to fetch data from the PRB, convert it to a displayable form, and output it to a file or to a device such as a printer.

Switch Parameters for Gating Control

/G1=0 This switch will set the initial state of the master gate to closed.

/G2 This will activate gate2 (used with the control console feature) and set its initial state to closed.

/G2=1 This will activate gate2 (used with the control console feature) and set its initial state to open.

/SS This will activate the single-stepping portion of the control console feature and set its initial state to free-running mode.

/SS=1 This will activate the single-stepping portion of the control console feature and set its initial state to single-step mode.

/CC=M (Master Control Console) and /CC=S (Serial Control Console) The /CC switch is used to specify that a control console is to be used to control ROUTER.SYS. The /CC=M version selects the master console's keyboard as the control console, and the /CC=S version designates a serial terminal's keyboard as the control console. A control console can be used to control the gating and single-stepping of dump output and the invocation of a breakpoint.

When a serial control console is to be used, either the /SR or /SB switch must be specified to activate the output of debug data to a serial port. The /SR switch would be used when a dumb ASCII terminal is connected to a serial port. The /SB switch would be used when a second computer is being used with a binary serial link and the CHANNEL.EXE data capture utility.

APPENDIX P
Parameters for `CHANNEL.EXE`

Fixed-Parameter Keywords:

SER	Serial port
PAR	Parallel port
PRB	Packetized Ring Buffer
DV	Direct Video
File/Dev	File or Device

Switch Parameters:

/DV	Output to direct video
/W	Wrap text at column 78
/SB=aaaa,bb	Set serial address and baud
	bb = [12,24,48,96,38,57,11]
	(default: /SB=03F8,11)
/C	Character mode
/F=x	Freeze when detect character x
	(where x can be any marker character)
/SK	Activate serial keyboard
/IR=xx	Load one or more ILMRCFxx.BIN modules
	(multiples: /IR=21,15,13)
/PB=aaaa	Set parallel address
	(default: /PB=0378)

Local Usage—to Read from a PRB within `ROUTER.SYS`:

```
CHANNEL PRB, DV              [/IR=xx]
CHANNEL PRB, FIle/Sev        [/IR=xx] [/DV] [/W]
```

Remote Usage—to Gather Data from a Serial or Parallel Link:

```
CHANNEL SER,DV              [/IR=xx] [/SB=hhhh,dd] [/SK] [/C] [/F=x]
CHANNEL SER,Fname           [/IR=xx] [/SB=hhhh,dd] [/SK] [/C] [/DV]
                              [/W] [/F=x]
CHANNEL SER,PRB,DV          [/IR=xx] [/SB=hhhh,dd] [/SK] [/C] [/F=x]
CHANNEL SER,PRB,File/Dev    [/IR=xx] [/SB=hhhh,dd] [/SK] [/C] [/DV]
                              [/W] [/F=x]

CHANNEL PAR, DV             [/IR=xx] [/PB=hhhh]
CHANNEL PAR, Fname          [/IR=xx] [/PB=hhhh] [/W] [/DV]
CHANNEL PAR, PRB,DV         [/IR=xx] [/PB=hhhh]
CHANNEL PAR, PRB,File/Dev   [/IR=xx] [/PB=hhhh] [/W] [/DV]
```

GLOSSARY

.ASM file   The source file of a program written in assembler language.

.BIN file   A file containing binary program code and/or binary data. Some device drivers use this extension, as do some overlay managers.

.C file   The source file of a program written in the C language.

.COM file   A simple type of executable binary file. A maximum of 64K of code and data can be loaded into memory from the file image. This could be either a stand-alone program or a TSR-type program.

.EXE file   A type of executable binary file. Unlike the .COM file, the 64K size restriction does not apply. .EXE files can consist of many segments of code and data. This could be either a stand-alone program or a TSR-type program.

.H file   A header for a C program, containing common data declarations, defined constants, function prototypes, and similar information that would be required to compile a .C source file.

.INC file   A file containing code and/or data that is to be included in a source file by the assembler or compiler.

.LIB file   A file containing a collection of .OBJ modules. This type of file is built by a library management utility for use by the link utility.

.LST file   A file containing an assembler listing, where the address and machine code are shown for each assembler mnemonic. This file is generated by an assembler.

.MAK file   A file containing declarations and instructions for a MAKE utility program, which automates the build process for an application or library by determining which files have changed since the last build.

.MAP file   A file containing the symbol names and their associated addresses for a program. This file is generated by the linker utility. A symbolic debugger uses the information within this file to annotate its disassembly view of a program.

.OBJ file   A file containing an intermediate form of the binary code and data for a program, also referred to as an object module. Both assemblers and compilers generate this form of binary module. Object modules are processed by a linker utility.

.OVL file   An overlay-type binary module containing executable code and binary data. This type of module is designed to be loaded into a shared memory area by the program (typically by an overlay manager library function) once the program is up and running. The shared memory area would typically be used to hold different overlay modules, depending on the processing activities being done by the program.

.SYS file   A file containing the binary program code and data for a device driver. Device drivers are typically loaded into memory by the operating system during boot time, when the **CONFIG.SYS** file is processed. Note that through the use of a special utility program, it is also possible to load device drivers after boot time.

ASCIIZ string   A string of characters (bytes) that is terminated by a byte with a binary zero value. Within the C language, all strings are ASCIIZ strings by default.

Assembler-level single-stepping   To step through the instructions of a program with a debugger at the lowest level possible. Each step results in the execution of a single machine-language opcode (including any associated operands).

Backtrace buffer   A chronicle, maintained by a debugger, that holds an execution history of the program being debugged. The number of execution events that can be recorded depends on the amount of memory allocated for this buffer.

A software backtrace buffer would occupy main system RAM memory, extended memory, or RAM memory provided on a special debugger adapter card. Information is written into this type of buffer by a software debugger as it controls the execution of the target program.

A hardware backtrace buffer would be composed of special high-speed RAM on a hardware debugging adapter card. Information is written into this type of buffer by circuitry on the adapter card from bus signals, signals from a CPU intercept pod, or signals from probe connections.

Binary division   A technique whereby the boundaries of a set of test points are identified and tests are then performed at points within the identified range. The first test would be to confirm that the test point at one end of the range produced a result that is the binary opposite of that produced by the test point at the opposite end. Next, a test point is selected that is approximately halfway between the end points (this could be in terms of execution time or linear code flow). Successive divisions of the test range are made to select the next test point, based on the results of each test.

Binary link   See "Machine-to-machine link."

BIOS   An acronym for Basic Input/Output System. The machine-code firmware, contained within ROM chips, that manages the boot-up process and fulfills requests for low-level I/O operations with peripherals such as the disk controller, keyboard, or video display.

BIOS data area   The memory region from address 0040:0000 through 0040:0100 inclusive. This memory area is used as scratch space by the system ROM BIOS firmware.

Boundary conditions   Data values or operating conditions that cause a system to operate at its extremes.

Breakout switch   See "NMI breakout switch."

Breakpoint   A means of interrupting a program's execution such that a debugger can seize control at a particular point in the program.

Desk-checking   The process of proofreading a piece of software on paper, such as a printed listing.

Device driver   See ".SYS file."

Disassembler   A program that reads the binary executable module for a program (e.g., a .COM, .EXE, .OVL, .BIN, or .SYS file) and produces an assembler listing file (.LST) or an assembler source file (.ASM).

Dynamic patching   To modify a program's binary code after it has been loaded into memory. This is sometimes done in a debugging session as a way to perform tests without having to rebuild the target program.

Evaluative breakpoint   A breakpoint (see "Breakpoint") that stops execution only when the debugger detects a certain set of conditions.

Firmware   Software that is always available and doesn't have to be loaded from disk. The system ROM BIOS, located at address F000:0000 within a PC/XT/AT-class machine, is one example.

Hard-coded breakpoint   The manual implanting of an INT03 instruction within a program.

Hardware trace buffer   See "Backtrace buffer."

ICE   An acronym for In-Circuit Emulator. A complex hardware device that emulates the operations of a CPU through discrete hardware. This approach makes it possible to specify breakpoints within great precision, since all internal CPU states are available.

Instrumentation   The insertion of program code designed to reveal useful information about the execution of a program.

INT00   An interrupt generated automatically by the CPU when an attempt is made to divide by zero or when a divide overflow occurs (when the result of a division will not fit within the register designated for that result).

INT01   An interrupt generated automatically by the CPU at the end of each instruction's execution. The trap flag must be set for this action to occur. The trap flag is one of the bits within the CPU flags word.

INT02   The interrupt assigned to the NMI (Non-Maskable Interrupt) input.

INT03   Unlike any other software interrupt, an INT03 can be generated with a single-byte opcode (all other software interrupt calls require a two-byte instruction). This interrupt was designed to effect software breakpoints.

INT06   An interrupt that is automatically generated by the CPU when an invalid instruction is encountered.

INT08   The timer-tick interrupt. Due to the design of the hardware in a PC/XT/AT-class machine, an IRQ00 hardware interrupt is made to occur approximately 18.2 times per second. The IRQ00 hardware interrupt is vectored to the INT08 software interrupt vector. The INT08 handler in the system ROM BIOS manages the software clock.

INT09   The keyboard interrupt. Due to the design of the hardware within a PC/XT/AT-class machine, an IRQ01 hardware interrupt is made to occur each time a key is pressed or released on the keyboard. The IRQ01 hardware interrupt is vectored to the INT09 software interrupt vector. The INT09 handler within the system ROM BIOS inputs scan-code data from the keyboard to make it available when keyboard request calls are made.

INT10 A system BIOS interrupt service that provides video services such as character display, cursor positioning, mode changing, and color palette definition.

INT13 A system BIOS interrupt service that provides disk services such as resetting the disk or reading, writing, and formatting sectors.

INT15 A system BIOS interrupt service that provides an assortment of services such as intercepting scan codes, switching to or from protected mode, accessing extended memory, and time delays.

INT16 A system BIOS interrupt service that provides keyboard services such as checking for key ready, reading a scan code or key code, or reading the shift state.

INT17 A system BIOS interrupt service that provides printer output services such as resetting a printer, reading printer port status, and outputting characters.

INT1C An auxiliary interrupt which is called by the BIOS **INT08** handler on each timer tick. It is designed to be intercepted.

INT21 The main DOS operating system services interrupt, providing services for high-level disk I/O, console I/O, setting and reading the system date and time, and many other functions.

Interrupt intercept A piece of software that is made to receive control each time a certain interrupt call occurs. This is done by recording the current contents of an interrupt vector before the vector is reassigned the address of the intercept handler's entry point.

Interrupt enable flag A flag bit within the CPU flags word that controls whether hardware interrupts will be recognized. The processing of all hardware interrupts, except for NMI, will be deferred as long as this flag remains set. The assembler instruction cli turns this flag off (disabling interrupts), and the sti instruction sets this flag (enabling interrupts).

Interrupt vector A special memory location within the first 1024 bytes of an 80X86-based computer system's memory. This first 1024-byte area is divided into 256 vectors of 4 bytes each. The first vector contains the address of the **INT00** handler, the second contains the address of the **INT01** handler, and so on up through **INTFF**.

IRQ An acronym for Interrupt ReQuest. An IRQ is a hardware-generated interrupt. An **IRQ00** signal is generated 18.2 times a second by the 8253 clock chip. An **IRQ01** signal is generated by the keyboard controller hardware. Other IRQ hardware interrupt signals are generated by disk controllers, serial ports, and other peripherals.

IRQ00 See "INT08."

IRQ01 See "INT09."

ISR An acronym for Interrupt Service Routine. An interrupt service routine is the piece of code that receives control when its corresponding interrupt call is made. For example, if the **INT00** interrupt vector contains an address such as 1234:5000, then the function at that address, the **INT00** ISR, receives control each time a division by zero is attempted.

Markers See "Instrumentation."

MCB An acronym for Memory Control Block, a 16-byte header used by DOS to track to allocation of blocks of memory.

NMI Breakout Switch   NMI is an acronym for NonMaskable Interrupt. Some debuggers include a momentary contact push-button switch, which can be made to generate an NMI interrupt. This allows a debugger to be entered at any time, even when the keyboard is nonresponsive due to the actions of a bug.

Nonresident section   The portion of a device driver or TSR that does not remain within memory once the driver or TSR is installed. The code within this section typically tends to the details of testing the system environment, processing command line parameters, and preparing for the installation.

Nonsticky breakpoint   A temporary breakpoint, which is not automatically reasserted by a debugger once a breakpoint does occur.

Object module   See ".OBJ file."

Patch   To patch a program is to make changes to its binary code and data directly (usually through the use of a debugger) rather than making changes to the source code and reassembling or recompiling.

PRB   An acronym for Packetized Ring Buffer. A ring buffer is a first-in/first-out (FIFO) type of data construct. When the buffer fills, the oldest information is sacrificed to make room for the new. At any given point, the last X events may be retrieved from the buffer, with the total number X dependent on the size of each item and the total memory allocated to the buffer. A ring buffer which holds records of a fixed size would be a simple ring buffer. One which holds individually-sized packets of data is referred to as a packetized ring buffer.

PSP   An acronym for Program Segment Prefix. This is a standard data structure, consisting of 256 bytes, which DOS builds for each program it executes. It contains such information as the address of the program's environment string block, the address of the program's file handle table, the default file handle table, and the command line tail.

public   This is an assembler directive which causes a symbol to appear in a `.MAP` file or within an `.EXE`-based debugging information block.

RCS   An acronym for Revision Control System. This is a program development tool that acts as a database of different versions of a program's source code modules.

Reentrance   Reentrance occurs when the entry point of a certain section of software is executed once and then again before an exit is made from the first entry to that section.

Recursion   When a certain section of software intentionally causes itself to be re-entered.

Resident section   The portion of a device driver or TSR that does remain within memory after the driver or TSR is installed.

Revision control system   See "RCS."

Ring buffer   See "PRB."

Software trace buffer   See "Backtrace buffer."

State Machine   A way of generalizing a complex decision-making process by associating tests with state levels. A state machine may be implemented either in hardware alone, in software alone, or in a combination of the two.

Static patching   To modify a program's binary code within its executable module. Patch scripts, the means by which a debugger can be made to apply a static patch, can be distributed to an existing user base of a program to make corrections available.

Sticky breakpoint   A breakpoint that is automatically reasserted by a debugger after any breakpoints occur.

Test bed   A program specifically designed to exercise a newly developed function or section of code.

TPA   An acronym for Transient Program Area. In general, this is the memory area between the upper boundary of the resident part of the DOS operating system and the top of the base 640K of memory. This is the memory area into which applications programs are loaded for execution.

Trap flag   See "INTO1."

TSR   An acronym for Terminate and Stay Resident. This is a type of program that installs itself resident in memory. It reserves a portion of the TPA for itself and typically establishes interrupt intercepts or interrupt handlers, through which it communicates with other software processes.

INDEX